environmental ethics for the long term

- Broad in scope, this introduction to environmental ethics considers both contemporary issues and the extent of humanity's responsibility for distant future life. John Nolt, a logician and environmental ethicist, interweaves contemporary science, logical analysis, and ethical theory into the story of the expansion of ethics beyond the human species and into the far future. Informed by contemporary environmental science, the book deduces concrete policy recommendations from carefully justified ethical principles and ends with speculations concerning the deepest problems of environmental ethics. Pedagogical features include chapter outlines, annotated suggestions for further reading, explanations of key terms when first mentioned, and an extensive glossary.

John Nolt is a philosophy professor at the University of Tennessee. He began his career as a logician, but soon took to moonlighting as an environmental activist. The activism eventually drew him into academic work in environmental ethics. He has published many articles and several books in both philosophical logic and environmental studies.

D1614265

JOHN NOLT

environmental ethics for the long term

An Introduction

Routledge
Taylor & Francis Group

LONDON AND NEW YORK

First published 2015 by Routledge
711 Third Avenue, New York, NY 10017

and by Routledge
2 Park Square, Milton Park, Abingdon, Oxon, OX14 4RN

Routledge is an imprint of the Taylor & Francis Group, an informa business

Library of Congress Cataloging in Publication Data
Nolt, John, 1950-
Environmental ethics for the long term: an introduction/John Nolt.
pages cm
Includes bibliographical references and index.
1. Environmental ethics. I. Title.
GE42.N65 2015
179'.1—dc23
2014019801

ISBN: 978–0–415–53583–0 (hbk)
ISBN: 978–0–415–53584–7 (pbk)
ISBN: 978–1–315–75168–9 (ebk)

Typeset in Berling and Arial Rounded
by Swales & Willis, Exeter, Devon

Printed and bound in the United States of America by
Edwards Brothers Malloy on sustainably sourced paper

- To Évora Kreis, Ben Nolt, Jenna Nolt and
  Annette Mendola—and especially to
  my mother, Jane E. Nolt, for inspiring a
  younger edition of me with an abiding love of learning.

CONTENTS

PREFACE

Morality progresses, but slowly. Slavery is now condemned around the world. Virtually every nation has signed the United Nations Universal Declaration of Human Rights. The status of women has improved globally. Prejudice against those whose religious convictions or sexual orientations differ from cultural norms is falling away. Racism is in retreat worldwide. Some of these goals were distant dreams in the minds of the best moral thinkers two centuries ago. Some of them were not yet thinkable.

Yet moral practice lags far behind moral ideals. Still today human rights are regularly violated in many places, and great tragedies are brewing in the destructive power of our technology and rapid growth of our population. Whether and how quickly ethical thinking can alter our behavior remains to be seen.

One measure of moral progress is the enlargement of our conception of the ***moral community***—the set of those whose welfare we hold to be morally considerable. The earliest ethics were tribal. Tribal moral communities were in part non-human, encompassing a host of gods or spirits. Often these were associated with particular natural forces, places, animals and even plants. But as regards human beings, tribal ethics were largely confined to the tribe. If you were a member of the tribe, your welfare mattered; if not, it didn't—and you were therefore a legitimate target of rape, robbery or murder. In the Old Testament book of Joshua, for example, God orders the twelve tribes of Israel to invade the land of Canaan, seize its cities, and put their inhabitants—men, women, children, and livestock—to the sword. This slaughter of innocents who were minding their own business or at worst trying to defend their homes was deemed righteous. The ethic was, after all, tribal, and the victims were not members of the tribes.

As tribes merged into federations, and civilizations grew from city-states to nation-states and empires, the moral community expanded as well. People who formerly belonged to alien groups now were included in one's moral community. Then, occasionally, something remarkable happened: people who had seemed little more than animals gradually became familiar, and the realization dawned that they were not much different from oneself.

During the twentieth century, as civilization globalized, the moral community grew to encompass everyone on the planet. Today it is widely acknowledged that everyone's welfare is equally worthy of moral consideration. We don't, on the whole, live up to this ethic, but some of us try. And that is progress, because for a long time no one tried.

One of this book's themes is that moral progress is far from complete. Even though the moral community now—in theory, at least—includes everyone on the planet, we still usually fail to consider the welfare of the vast majority of human beings: those who are yet to be born. We also tend to exclude animals—even our nearest relatives, the chimps and bonobos—and all other non-human forms of life. Chapter 4 and subsequent chapters consider these omissions.

Environmental ethics, as I understand the term, is the attempt to expand moral thinking and action in two directions: beyond the human species and into the distant future. The word 'environmental' connotes extension beyond the human species. The qualifier 'long term' in the title of this book alludes to concern the time after—sometimes long after—we have died.

Among books on environmental ethics, this one is peculiar in its emphasis on clarity, definition and logic. That is because I was trained as a logician—a vocation that, despite almost 30 years of environmental activism, I still pursue. It is often supposed that objective, cerebral logic and passionate, romantic environmentalism do not mix. But that opinion misconstrues both. The interplay of logic and environmental ethics animates this book.

The book begins, however, with empirical science. Chapter 1 is a compendium of the science presupposed by the later chapters. After a brief introduction to some concepts of evolutionary theory and evolution's connection with value, it traces the history and explains some of the science of six great environmental issues, all of which are concerns of this book. To examine all these problems together is disheartening. There's a lot to worry about. The chapter therefore ends with a note on what *not* to worry about.

Chapter 2 is not directly about environmental ethics either. It is, rather, the methodology chapter. It introduces the logical tools used throughout this book and the ethical theories that comprise its historical and conceptual background. Discussion of environmental ethics *per se* begins in Chapter 3. Chapter 2 explains the central ideas and defines the central concepts necessary for understanding philosophical ethics generally. (Throughout this book, by the way, terms being defined are printed in bold italics—as were the terms "environmental ethics" and "moral community" above. Definitions are also summarized in the Glossary at the end of the book.)

Chapter 3 considers environmental problems through the lens of traditional short-term **anthropocentric** (human-centered) ethics. The most influential of these, at least in policy contexts, is neoclassical economic theory. Though seldom regarded as an ethic, in fact it operates as one. Chapter 3 traces its origins within the western philosophical tradition and explains its moral inadequacies. The chapter then surveys a selection of more plausible anthropocentric ethics and sketches their implications for environmentalism and environmental policy.

But short-term ethics is insufficient. We will be judged posthumously—if only by our descendants. They will praise or blame us for what we did to their world. From their perspective, it will be obvious why we ought now to be guided by a long-term environmental ethic. Chapter 4 takes this perspective seriously. Long-term ethics face an array of surprising conceptual difficulties. These are explained, as are potential solutions.

The remaining chapters concern **non-anthropocentric ethics**—ethics that include some non-humans, as well as humans, in the moral community. Chapter 5 examines the first step beyond the human species. Its central question is, "How should we treat **sentient** animals?" (Sentient animals are those capable of suffering and enjoyment.) Starting with a history of human thinking about and treatment of animals, it then explains what is known about animal consciousness. The rest is devoted to various ethical theories regarding animals. These differ widely, but share many common conclusions. The chapter ends with a catalog of conclusions on which there is consensus, followed by a glance at animal ethics for the long term.

The most radical environmental ethics are discussed in Chapter 6. These are **biocentric** (life-centered) ethics—that is, ethics that include all living beings in the moral community. They are controversial even among environmentalists. The chapter explains and assesses the controversies and attempts to outline a workable biocentric theory.

Together, Chapters 3–6 trace the progressive broadening and deepening of ethics, in response to humanity's escalating power. With each step in that progression, ethics becomes more complex. The question addressed by Chapter 7 is "Given this complexity, how can we manage to act ethically?" There are two ways to answer: practically and theoretically. Accordingly, Chapter 7 is divided into two parts: applications and speculations. The "applications" part illustrates methods for deriving practical ethical conclusions from theory, and the "speculations" part aims to deepen understanding of theory and its relation to action.

Throughout this book you will encounter frequent cross-references. These call attention to important interconnections. I recommend their use. When you encounter one, page backward or forward to the indicated section (or sections) and don't go on until you understand the connection between it (or them) and the section containing the reference. Only in that way can you glean everything that this book has to offer.

ACKNOWLEDGMENTS

Many people helped with the writing of this book. My brother, James H. Nolt, read and critiqued the material on economic theory. Jenna Nolt, my daughter, redoubtable research librarian, found sources that I would never have thought of. Jake LaRivere provided corrections and comments on a draft of the section on environmental economics. John Bohstedt pointed me to appropriate historical sources. With Graham Walford I enjoyed discussions of various elements of nuclear technology. Ralph Hutchison helped with more material on matters nuclear. Eddy Falls read and taught from drafts of early chapters and made a number of helpful suggestions. Robert Nowell also read chapters and assisted with the research. Elena Hamilton suggested corrections to an early draft. Clerk Shaw and Richard Aquila provided aid in matters of philosophical history. A sabbatical from the Philosophy Department at the University of Tennessee gave me time to write. Four members of my summer 2014 environmental ethics class at the Oak Ridge Institute for Continued Learning—Jim Basford, Claudia Lever, Bob Olson and Charles Rutkowski—spotted many errors in the final draft. Finally my thoughts on ethical theory were honed and sharpened, and my style was improved, by conversations with Annette Mendola, my wife, my love, and clinical medical ethicist extraordinaire.

1

scientific background

Environmental ethics demands thinking on expansive scales of space and, especially, time. To understand our current ethical situation, we must know the history of life, which stretches back at least 3.5 billion years, and sometimes peer millions of years forward into the future that we are now shaping. At such scales, common sense and ordinary intuitions falter. We have only empirical data, well-confirmed theory, logical inference, and computer modeling, to project our thought beyond the limits of our senses and imaginations. The technical aspects of the environmental and life sciences are, of course, beyond the scope of this book. But a general understanding of some of their findings is a prerequisite for addressing environmental ethical problems. This chapter presents the necessary basics. Ethical issues, though occasionally alluded to, are not discussed in this chapter. The aim is simply to summarize the science presupposed by later chapters—and, on occasion, to explain what it implies for efforts to change the course of events.

Chapter Outline: Section 1.1 provides a quick review of evolutionary theory, which is necessary for understanding both the life sciences and environmental ethics. The focus is on how evolution creates value. The chapter's central section (1.2) summarizes six great issues, all of which will occupy us later in the book: pollution, human health, climate change, natural resource depletion, biodiversity loss, and human population and consumption. All are considered in long-term global perspective. These problems can be disheartening, but they can also be exaggerated, so the chapter concludes (section 1.3) with a brief reflection on what we *don't* need to worry about.

1.1 FACT, VALUE AND EVOLUTION

In the sciences and philosophy it has been customary to distinguish sharply between fact and value. Value is seen as a matter of subjective opinion, apt to confuse and mislead seekers of fact. But in the life sciences—which include biology, ecology and medicine—that dichotomy must be rejected, for life itself is fundamentally evaluative.

Value arose long before there was any subjective opinion, eons ago in the process of life's evolution. The key to an understanding of evolution is the concept of natural selection. The English naturalist Charles Darwin (1809–1882) was among the first to perceive that natural selection explains the origin of species.

Natural selection is the process by which a population of organisms can, over time, develop into one or more populations of organisms with dissimilar traits. For natural selection to occur, there are two requirements:

1. a varied population of organisms that produce offspring similar to but not always exactly like themselves, and
2. an environment hazardous enough to kill many of the offspring before they reproduce, but not so hazardous as to eliminate the population.

The organisms that succeed in reproducing under these conditions are generally the ones best able to avoid the environmental hazards, and their offspring share most of their traits. But since reproduction is not exact, novel traits arise from time to time. Those that are helpful for exploiting the environment and avoiding hazards tend to be preserved and increased in the population, and those that are not (the majority) tend to be eliminated. Thus, the structure and functions of the organisms that make up the population gradually become better adapted to the environment.

Darwin realized that organisms of a single species placed in different environments would adapt differently—eventually producing, if they survived, wholly distinct species. Extrapolating back over vast spans of time, and consulting the fossil record, he inferred that all earthly species shared common ancestors.

Darwin's conjectures have since been confirmed by a plethora of biological, geological, ecological, paleontological, and genetic studies. A single, largely coherent account of evolutionary history has emerged. Many details, of course, are missing or poorly understood—and, given the limitations of human knowledge, some always will be—but the truth of the fundamentals is beyond reasonable doubt.

Natural selection requires neither a goal nor intelligent guidance. When the two requirements mentioned above are modeled in computer simulations, evolution results automatically. Of course, we might doubt that such simulations reflect reality. But in fast-reproducing organisms, such as bacteria or fruit flies, scientists routinely observe evolution occurring in real time.

Evolution can produce very different results from similar initial conditions (i.e., similar populations in similar environments). Random variations in the environment, in sexual pairings, or in the mutation of genes may divert it into widely differing courses. Thus, though it tends over time to produce organisms that are exquisitely attuned to their environments, evolution has no predefined goal. It is merely a sum of small adaptations to existing and often changing conditions. In no sense does it "plan" or "look ahead."

Yet, remarkably, this accumulation of adaptations results in purposeful function. Into the DNA and RNA of each cell of each living organism is encoded a set of tasks that constitute that organism's biological purposes. In general terms, applicable to all species, these purposes include acquiring nutrients, excreting wastes, and reproduction. The genome peculiar to each species encodes, of course, a host of more specific tasks. If the organism is multicellular, its genome contains the information needed to grow it (given the proper environment) from a single cell. It also contains the organism's operating instructions, telling it, for example, how to synthesize proteins and metabolize nutrients.

Because organisms have biological purposes, some conditions (roughly, those that help them to fulfill their purposes and thus to survive) are good for them and some (roughly, those that interfere with their purposes, such as injury or disease) are bad for them. (A more precise account of goodness and badness for an organism can be found in sections 6.1 and 6.4.2.) Such biological values are independent of us and our opinions—though, of course, the language in which we describe them is not. Indeed, such values existed for several billions of years before humans evolved. During the entire reign of life on Earth, in other words, things happened to organisms that were good or bad for them, and that is a matter of fact.

Notions of what is good or bad for an organism are inescapable in the life sciences, especially those engaged in the practical tasks of healing. Medical doctors, for example, are concerned with conditions or treatments that are good or bad for humans, veterinarians with those that are good or bad for animals, and conservation biologists with those that are good or bad for biological systems. It is in this sense that values in the life sciences are matters of fact.

• 1.2 THE GREAT ISSUES

Section Outline: Section 1.2 introduces some of the scientific basics of six great issues in environmental ethics: pollution (section 1.2.1), threats to human health (section 1.2.2), climate change (section 1.2.3), natural resource depletion (section 1.2.4), biodiversity loss (section 1.2.5) and human population and consumption (section 1.2.6).

There is no attempt at completeness here. This book is about ethics, not environmental science. But to understand what is at stake in environmental ethics, one must be familiar with certain aspects of environmental science. The aim of these sections is to review just as much of the science as is needed for an understanding of the remainder of the book.

Because environmental science advances very quickly, I have tried to cite the best and most recent research. But even that may be superseded by the time you read this. A clear understanding of current science can be obtained only by consulting the scientific literature for yourself. This requires discrimination. The media are rife with financially or ideologically motivated propaganda masquerading as science, or as the debunking of science. Choose sources carefully. The best science is done by people who devote their lives to it; who conduct field observations, do experiments, or construct models informed by data; whose research is painstaking and thoroughly documented; and who publish in expertly reviewed professional journals.

1.2.1 Pollution

Pollution is just about any form of matter or energy that has been introduced into the environment in amounts sufficient to harm humans or other life forms. Contamination of air, water or soil by toxic chemicals of industrial origin is perhaps the most familiar example. Other examples are less familiar. Some pollutants, such as the radioactive radon gas that seeps from the ground in certain places, are of natural origin. Some, such as sewage and the fecal wastes of livestock, are pollutants in part because they harbor disease-causing micro-organisms. And some, such as excessive heat, noise, light or ionizing radiation, are not substances at all, but forms of energy.

Because pollution is by definition harmful, facts about pollution are also facts about disvalue. Yet pollution is not a matter of human subjective opinion. There was natural pollution (from volcanoes, for example) before there were human beings to have any opinion about it. Because we are not responsible for naturally-occurring pollution, however, it falls outside the scope of environmental ethics. Here we are concerned with **anthropogenic** (humanly generated) pollution.

Most pollutants occur naturally, but at concentrations low enough to do little or no harm. We live, for example, with a certain "background" level of ionizing radiation that is mostly emitted by natural sources. Natural selection has adjusted life to this background level. But higher levels are dangerous, and extremely high levels are lethal to all life. Yet ionizing radiation and other forms of matter or energy that are pollutants in high concentrations are not pollutants at background levels. They become pollutants only when they become hazardous. It is sometimes argued that carbon dioxide (CO_2) is not a pollutant because it occurs naturally in the atmosphere. But this is a mistake. In the recent past it was not a pollutant. But since we have made its atmospheric concentration high enough to cause harmful climate change and ocean acidification (both of which are discussed below) it has become one.

Section Outline: Section 1.2.1 begins with a brief review of the history of pollution (section 1.2.1.1), then considers some of the most important contemporary forms and sources of air and water pollution globally (sections 1.2.1.2 and 1.2.1.3).

1.2.1.1 History of Pollution

Anthropogenic pollution had little environmental significance before the development of cities. From very early times, however, the concentration in cities of fires for cooking, heating and industry undoubtedly polluted the air locally, and metal smelting introduced toxic chemicals into soil, air and water. More harmful, however, were human and animal wastes that contaminated soil and water and transmitted infectious diseases. Among the earliest, and most effective, antipollution efforts was the development of sanitary waste-disposal practices. Increases in human life expectancy over the last two centuries have been due more to improvements in sanitation than to anything else.

In the developed nations during the twentieth century, and especially during the economic expansion following World War II, heavy industry, coal-fired power generation, chemical agriculture, above-ground nuclear weapons testing, and petroleum-powered transportation systems became significant sources of pollution. Smog blanketed industrialized cities in Europe and the U.S. In December of 1952 the so-called Great Smog killed thousands in London. The Cuyahoga River in Cleveland, Ohio, was so polluted that in 1969 it caught fire. (It was, of course, an oil slick on the water, not the water, that burned. I lived not far from Cleveland then and will never forget the sickly orange color of the water with its iridescent sheen of oil.) By the early 1960s it was clear that widespread use of pesticides, particularly DDT, was causing many bird populations to decline. Rachel Carson documented these losses in her landmark book *Silent Spring*. Simultaneously, above-ground nuclear testing raised concerns about the spread of radioactive contaminants worldwide—and still greater fears of the cataclysms and apocalyptic pollution that could occur with a full-scale thermonuclear war.

These events precipitated public outrage, which rapidly led to national "command-and-control" antipollution legislation in nearly all of the developed nations. As a result, from the 1970s onward, pollution levels in developed nations dropped dramatically. Skies over big cities turned from grey or orange or white back to blue again. Rivers became cleaner.

The improvement, however, was only regional. As economies globalized, polluting industries moved from the industrialized cities of the developed nations to the rapidly industrializing mega-cities of poorer nations in Asia, Latin America and Africa, where labor was cheap and environmental laws lax. Today, air pollution still kills millions of people each year—the vast majority of them in developing nations (Silva *et al.* 2013).

1.2.1.2 Air Pollution

Among the most important air pollutants are particulate matter, nitrogen oxides, sulfur dioxide, ozone and chlorofluorocarbons. This section briefly describes the causes and effects of pollution by each. Emissions of many toxic industrial substances also have profound effects, generally near the point of release, but are too diverse to be characterized here. The damages done by the air pollutants just mentioned, with the exception of chlorofluorocarbons, are mostly regional rather than global and, once emissions are stopped, relatively short-lived. In the long run, by far the most damaging air pollutants are greenhouse gases, most especially carbon dioxide. But these are dealt with separately, in section 1.2.3.

Atmospheric **particulate matter** is better known as smoke, haze, dust or smog. It is a complex mixture of solid and liquid particles suspended in air. Its components vary but often include sulfates and nitrates, carbon particles (soot), ammonia, mineral dust and water. Particulate matter is concentrated indoors where open fires are used for cooking and heating (predominantly in developing countries) and also where people smoke. Outdoor generators of particulate pollution include traffic, coal-fired power plants, industrial facilities and forest fires. According to the World Health Organization, the health effects of particulate matter (PM) are today greater than those of any other pollutant:

> The effects of PM on health occur at levels of exposure currently being experienced by most urban and rural populations in both developed and developing countries. Chronic exposure to particles contributes to the risk of developing cardiovascular and respiratory diseases, as well as of lung cancer. In developing countries, exposure to pollutants from indoor combustion of solid fuels on open fires or traditional stoves increases the risk of acute lower respiratory infections and associated mortality among young children; indoor air pollution from solid fuel use is also a major risk factor for chronic obstructive pulmonary disease and lung cancer among adults. The mortality in cities with high levels of pollution exceeds that observed in relatively cleaner cities by 15–20%. Even in the EU, average life expectancy is 8.6 months lower due to exposure to PM2.5 [very fine PM] produced by human activities.
>
> (WHO 2011)

In the U.S., long-term exposure to particulate matter (including cigarette smoke) is believed to account for up to 4 percent of all deaths—the equivalent of a one- to three-year drop in life expectancy. Children and the elderly are especially vulnerable.

Two important components or precursors of particulate matter are also pollutants in their own right and are implicated in various other problems. These are **sulfur dioxide** (SO_2) and **nitrogen oxides** (NOx, the x indicating that the numbers of both nitrogen and oxygen atoms in the molecule may vary). Both are products of combustion, chiefly of fossil fuels.

Anthropogenic sulfur dioxide is produced mainly by the burning of coal, which usually contains some sulfur. In addition to being a major component of atmospheric particulate matter, when combined with moisture in the air sulfur dioxide forms dilute sulfuric acid, which precipitates out of the atmosphere in the form of acid rain, acid snow or acid fog. These, together with dry acidic particles that settle directly out of the air are known collectively as **acid deposition**. Acid deposition harms vegetation and aquatic life by acidifying soils and waters. It reduces growth and reproduction in some organisms, and has been correlated with declining fish populations and widespread deaths of forest trees in Europe and North America. Tree deaths unleash a cascade of further ecological losses (Primack 1993: 155–56). Acid deposition also corrodes stonework and unprotected metals.

Like sulfur dioxide, nitrogen oxides contribute to acid deposition. They combine with water vapor to form nitric acid, whose environmental effects are similar to those of sulfuric acid. Again like sulfur dioxide, nitrogen oxides are produced by combustion. Most of the nitrogen, however, comes not from the fuel itself but from the air, so that (in contrast to sulfur dioxide) nitrogen oxides are produced regardless of the fuel burned. Agricultural fertilization and certain industrial processes also emit nitrogen oxides.

In the presence of sunlight, nitrogen oxides combine in the atmosphere with volatile organic vapors (many of which occur naturally, but many of which are also anthropogenic) to produce an entirely new pollutant: ozone. *Ozone* (O_3) is a form of oxygen that has three atoms per molecule instead of the usual two. In chemical reactions it tends to give up the third oxygen atom, oxidizing (in effect, burning) delicate tissues in plants and animals—particularly the respiratory tissues of animals, including humans. Respiratory damage occurs at levels frequently reached in large cities, especially in hot, sunny weather. Health effects include asthma, chronic bronchitis, and other respiratory problems—some of which can be fatal. Some studies also link ozone exposure to cardiovascular disease, strokes, and lung cancer (Desqueroux *et al.* 2002; Hong *et al.* 2002; Kwon *et al.* 2001). Ozone damages many forms of vegetation, too, including agricultural crops.

While ozone is a pollutant in the lower atmosphere (troposphere), it is a critical component of the upper atmosphere (stratosphere). Stratospheric ozone shields the earth from the sun's ultraviolet-B radiation, which can harm many forms of life. In humans it can cause skin cancer and cataracts. When intense, it can also damage plants. Unfortunately, the stratospheric ozone layer has been depleted by yet another class of chemical pollutants: *chlorofluorocarbons* (CFCs). CFCs are compounds of carbon with fluorine and/or chlorine. During the last few decades of the twentieth century, gaseous CFCs, used as refrigerants and spray can propellants, were released in huge quantities. Stable and long-lived, they diffused into the stratosphere and remained there, continually breaking down ozone molecules. After this damage to the ozone layer was discovered in the 1970s, international agreements were negotiated to phase out CFC use, and it has subsequently steeply declined.

One might suppose that the ozone pollution in the troposphere would help to restore the stratospheric ozone layer as atmospheric layers intermix. But ozone is so reactive that it doesn't last long, and the amount of anthropogenic ozone that makes it to the stratosphere is insignificant. Ironically, as emissions of chlorofluorocarbons have declined, anthropogenic nitrous oxide (N_2O), a component of combustion-derived NOx which is more stable than ozone and can react with it, has become the most significant continuing source of stratospheric ozone depletion (NOAA 2009).

1.2.1.3 Water Pollution

Mention of water pollution may call to mind images of industrial effluent pipes disgorging toxic glop into dying waters. This still happens—mostly now in the developing world—and serious problems result, but they are varied and relatively local. The most damaging forms of water pollution are more global and diffuse: sewage, nitrogen compounds from fertilizers and animal wastes, and *ocean acidification* due to carbon dioxide emissions.

Statistically, the most deadly human health effect of water pollution is diarrhea resulting from drinking water contaminated with sewage or animal wastes. According to the World Health Organization, about 1.9 million people died worldwide in 2004 from unsafe water or inadequate sanitation and hygiene (WHO 2009: 50).

Sewage is also implicated in another great water pollution problem. Human and animal waste and agricultural fertilizer are all high in nitrogen. High nitrogen levels in water encourage the growth of algae. Though algae produce oxygen while alive, when they die they sink to the bottoms of lakes, streams, or oceans and decompose. Their decomposition draws so much oxygen from the water that there is a net loss of dissolved oxygen. Without dissolved oxygen, gilled animals cannot live. This process, called **eutrophication**, has become increasingly prevalent in ocean waters at the mouths of rivers that carry heavy nitrogen loads. According to a recent international report,

> The number of observed "dead zones", coastal sea areas where water oxygen levels have dropped too low to support most marine life, has roughly doubled each decade since the 1960s. Many are concentrated near the estuaries of major rivers, and result from the buildup of nutrients, largely carried from inland agricultural areas where fertilizers are washed into watercourses. The nutrients promote the growth of algae that die and decompose on the seabed, depleting the water of oxygen and threatening fisheries, livelihoods and tourism.
> (Convention on Biological Diversity 2010: 60)

Even eutrophication and sewage are, however, merely short-term problems compared with the long-term water pollution that begins with an air pollutant: carbon dioxide.

Carbon dioxide (CO_2), which is emitted into the air chiefly by the burning of fossil fuels, slowly dissolves in the oceans. There it becomes carbonic acid, H_2CO_3, the stuff that makes carbonated drinks acidic. The increased acidity makes it more difficult for shellfish to form shells and for coral and marine phytoplankton to construct their skeletons. The resultant erosion of coral, together with coral "bleaching" due to warming of the oceans, has observably damaged coral reefs at various locations around the world. Because phytoplankton (tiny photosynthetic organisms that live near the sunlit surfaces of oceans) and coral reefs are crucial elements in many marine food webs, acidification threatens many forms of marine life.

Worse, this problem, unlike other forms of water pollution, cannot be readily corrected by elimination of the source. Excess carbon dioxide, once emitted into the atmosphere, stays there for many centuries, slowly dissolving into the oceans. Getting rid of the acid takes much longer than that. A 2009 statement on ocean acidification endorsed by nearly all of the world's academies of science asserts that:

- The rapid increase in CO_2 emissions since the industrial revolution has increased the acidity of the world's oceans with potentially profound consequences for marine plants and animals especially those that require calcium carbonate to grow and survive, and other species that rely on these for food;
- At current emission rates models suggest that all coral reefs and polar ecosystems will be severely affected by 2050 or potentially even earlier;
- Marine food supplies are likely to be reduced with significant implications for food production and security in regions dependent on fish protein, and human health and wellbeing;

- Ocean acidification is irreversible on timescales of at least tens of thousands of years.

(IAP 2009)

1.2.2 Threats to Human Health

Human health is seldom classified as an environmental issue. I include it here for two reasons. First, comparison of environmental hazards with other threats to human health helps to put the former into perspective. And, second, some of the consumption patterns that cause environmental damage also have surprising implications for human health.

Modern life is almost everywhere becoming more urban, and cities almost everywhere are becoming crowded with fossil-fuel-burning vehicles. Thus one might suspect that the worst health effects of modern life come from air pollution. Global statistics, however, reveal a different picture: the chief health threats of modern life come from eating too much of the wrong foods and not getting enough exercise. The top ten leading causes of death are listed in the table below:

Table 1 World's Ten Leading Causes of Death, 2004

Rank	Risk Factor	Deaths (millions)	Percentage of Total
1	High blood pressure	7.5	12.8
2	Tobacco use	5.1	8.7
3	High blood glucose	3.4	5.8
4	Physical inactivity	3.2	5.5
5	Overweight and obesity	2.8	4.8
6	High cholesterol	2.6	4.5
7	Unsafe sex	2.4	4.0
8	Alcohol use	2.3	3.8
9	Childhood underweight	2.2	3.8
10	Indoor smoke from solid fuels	2.0	3.3

Source: WHO 2009: 11.

Five of the top six (tobacco use being the exception) are related to dietary excess and lack of exercise. These five accounted for 19.5 million deaths in 2004, 33.4 percent of the total. The same five account for an even higher percentage of deaths (45.7) in high-income countries (WHO 2009: 11).

These five health threats are interrelated. The causes of high blood pressure are various, but it is known to be exacerbated by overweight and obesity, excessive consumption of salt or alcohol, stress, smoking and inadequate physical activity (NIH 2014b). High blood glucose (or high blood sugar, also known as hyperglycemia) is especially a threat to people with diabetes. Once again the causes are varied, but exacerbating factors include overeating (especially of simple carbohydrates such as cane sugar and corn syrup), inadequate physical activity, and stress (Joslin

Diabetes Center 2006). Cholesterol levels are increased by the consumption of foods containing cholesterol (such as egg yolks, meat, and cheese), saturated fats (fatty meats, dairy products, chocolate, baked goods, and deep-fried and processed foods) or trans fats (found in some fried and processed foods). They are also exacerbated by inadequate physical activity and being overweight (NIH 2014a). The picture that emerges from these statistics is quite clear: many of us are killing ourselves by eating too much of the wrong kinds of fat, sugars and salt, and exercising too little.

These health issues have much to do with the food and energy systems that humans have constructed, which also produce many of our environmental problems. One reason why people get too little exercise, for example, is that we have substituted the convenience of fossil fuel power for the vigor of muscle power in nearly all of our daily tasks. Transportation is a prime example. Many cities are constructed to facilitate automobile traffic in ways that impede or endanger pedestrians and bicyclists. Thus the same fossil fuel uses that pollute the air and water are also obstacles to and temptations against adequate exercise.

Among the remaining top ten causes of death, air pollution shows up at number ten, but primarily in the form of indoor smoke from solid fuels (wood, dung, coal or agricultural residues), not fumes from traffic or power plants. Sixty-four percent of these deaths occurred in low-income countries, especially in Southeast Asia and Africa (WHO 2009: 23). Urban *outdoor* air pollution accounted for about 1.2 million deaths worldwide in 2004.

Malnutrition remains deadly in poor areas, as the ninth item on the list (childhood underweight) indicates. Hunger is, for now, largely a problem of distribution. The world still produces enough food to nourish everyone, but food fails to reach the hungry largely because of political or economic obstacles, corruption, or war. With world population continually increasing, however, and agriculture being disrupted by climate change, the continued adequacy of the global food supply is uncertain.

1.2.3 Climate Change

Humanity's emissions of greenhouse gases are altering the world's weather patterns and climate by increasing the global average temperature—a phenomenon known as **anthropogenic global climate change**. We'll call it **climate change** for short, though it should be kept in mind that on a geological scale climate change has in the past been due to natural causes.

Section Outline: Section 1.2.3 consists of four subsections. Section 1.2.3.1 summarizes the causes and observed effects of climate change. Section 1.2.3.2 describes what we know and don't know about future climate change. Section 1.2.3.3 explains why in the current context, even small greenhouse gas emissions probably over time do significant harm—a point with important ethical ramifications that will be explored in section 7.1.1.1. Finally, section 1.2.3.4 sketches what we know and don't know about controlling climate change.

1.2.3.1 Causes and Observed Effects of Climate Change

Climate change is caused by the buildup of greenhouse gases in the atmosphere. Like a blanket, these gases trap heat radiated from the earth's surface. The heat comes originally from the sun. Without greenhouse gases it would escape into space. But as greenhouse gas concentrations increase, the atmosphere traps more heat, and it in turn heats the land and oceans.

The most important anthropogenic **greenhouse gases** are carbon dioxide (CO_2, mainly from the burning of fossil fuels), methane (CH_4, from various sources), and nitrous oxide (N_2O, a form of NOx, produced by the burning of fossil fuels and the use of nitrogen fertilizers). Another group of greenhouse gases, the halocarbons (gases that contain fluorine, chlorine or bromine), though often extraordinarily effective at trapping heat, are of less concern because they are emitted in much smaller amounts. Water vapor is also an important greenhouse gas, but it does not contribute significantly to climate change, because it readily precipitates out of the atmosphere in the form of rain or snow, so that it does not accumulate there. Climate change is thus due largely to the buildup of the other gases just mentioned, which do not precipitate out. Carbon dioxide is the most important by far, being responsible for about 77 percent of the warming.

Worldwide, the contributions of anthropogenic greenhouse gases to climate change are ranked by the Intergovernmental Panel on Climate Change (IPCC 2007: 36, figure 2.1.) as follows:

Table 2 Sources of Anthropogenic Greenhouse Gases

Source	Percentage Contribution to Climate Change (CO_2 equivalents)
CO_2 from fossil fuel use	56.6
CO_2 from deforestation, decay of biomass, etc.	17.3
CO_2 from other sources	2.8
CH_4	14.3
N_2O	7.9
Halocarbons	1.1

Obviously, the single most important greenhouse gas is CO_2, and its single most important source is the burning of fossil fuels. Fossil fuels are used to power internal combustion engines, most heating and cooling devices, and anything that uses electrical power whenever (as is usual) the grid that supplies the electricity is powered wholly or in part by fossil fuels.

The three main fossil fuels are coal, oil (in the form of gasoline, fuel oil, diesel fuel, jet fuel, etc.) and natural gas (which is mostly methane). Of these, coal is the worst as regards CO_2 emissions. Since coal consists mainly of elemental carbon, burning it (that is, combining it with oxygen) yields mostly CO_2. Oil and natural gas are hydrocarbons, consisting of both carbon and hydrogen. Burning them produces both CO_2

and H_2O—water, which is harmless. Thus they produce less CO_2 per unit of energy than coal does. Natural gas is better than oil, since it has a higher ratio of hydrogen to carbon. Greenhouse gas emissions are increasing globally, primarily because the world burns more coal, oil and natural gas each year (see sections 1.2.4.1 and 1.2.6.2).

Each greenhouse gas molecule can, individually, retain some heat. Therefore, other things being equal, any anthropogenic increase in greenhouse gases raises the global average temperature. Other things, of course, are not equal. Many other variables—including volcanic activity, climatological variations (such as El Niño and La Niña), the sun's energy output, small variations in the earth's orbit, and so on—also affect global temperature. Thus the earth's temperature fluctuates a good bit from year to year, but on larger scales (decades or more) it is closely correlated with greenhouse gas concentrations. If we could somehow hold the other variables constant, we would observe a smooth and steady rise in temperature as greenhouse gases increased.

Greenhouse gases begin absorbing and retaining heat as soon as they enter the atmosphere and continue to do so for as long their concentrations remain elevated. Though many forms of pollution disperse or are broken down in the environment fairly rapidly once their source is removed, this is not true for carbon dioxide. It circulates through the environment, but remains in the atmosphere at elevated level for centuries; and, though it is slowly removed, during all this time it continually adds to global temperatures (Archer *et al.* 2009: 117). (There is a downside to its removal too, which takes place mainly by dissolution into the oceans, for this produces acidification; see section 1.2.1.3.)

So far, our emissions have increased atmospheric carbon dioxide from pre-industrial levels of about 280 parts per million to over 400 parts per million. The resulting global average temperature increase over that period has been about 0.8 degrees Centigrade, or 1.4 degrees Fahrenheit. The warming is greater over land than over water and greatest near the poles. The north polar ice cap has during recent summers shrunk to less than half of its historic extent. Within decades there will likely be open ocean at the North Pole in the summer.

Observed effects of the temperature and carbon dioxide increases include higher ocean temperatures, increased ocean acidity, increased melting of Arctic and Antarctic ice and of glaciers worldwide, rising sea levels, intensified heat waves and droughts, and increases in extreme weather events. These undoubtedly have significant effects on agricultural productivity and human welfare. There is considerable difficulty and hence considerable uncertainty in estimating the number of deaths attributable to climate change. Nevertheless, recent studies put the figure at about 300,000 or 400,000 per year worldwide, nearly all of them in developing nations (Global Humanitarian Forum 2009; DARA 2012).

1.2.3.2 *Climate Change Projections*

Global average temperature, as was noted earlier, has already increased about 0.8°C, or 1.4°F, over pre-industrial levels. We could hold the ultimate temperature increase to little more than that if we ceased all emissions today (Matthews and Solomon

2013; see also Solomon *et al.* 2009). That, of course, isn't going to happen. What actually will happen depends primarily on how much carbon dioxide we emit in total. In 2007 the Intergovernmental Panel on Climate Change (IPCC) projected temperature increases by the year 2100 for six reasonably probable emissions scenarios. In their lowest emission scenario global average temperature in 2100 is likely to be in the range 1.6–3.4°C (2.9–6.1°F) above pre-industrial levels. In the highest emission scenario the likely increase is 2.9–6.9°C (5.2–12.4°F) over pre-industrial levels. Nearly all land areas will warm more than the global average, which means that the temperature rise experienced by land-dwelling humans will be higher (IPCC 2007: 45, table 3.1). So far we are closest to the high emission scenarios.

Global warming will not, however, end in 2100. As emissions are curtailed, carbon dioxide levels will slowly come down; but unless we somehow cool the planet artificially, global temperatures are likely to remain elevated for thousands of years— 23,000 to 165,000 years, according to the most recent projection at the time of this writing (Zeebe 2013; see also Solomon *et al.* 2009). This prolonged heat is expected to result at first from the residual carbon dioxide in the atmosphere and from the slow release of heat stored in the oceans, and, later, from changes in ice sheets, vegetation, ocean circulation, biogeochemical cycling, and other variables.

How hot things ultimately get will depend almost entirely on the cumulative total of our carbon dioxide emissions, and very little on their rate and timing. What matters in the long run, in other words, is how much carbon dioxide we put into the atmosphere (Stocker 2013; Allen *et al.* 2009).

The consequences for humanity, already deleterious, are likely to become much worse. According to the IPCC (2007: 65), "climate change over the next century is *likely* to adversely affect hundreds of millions of people through increased coastal flooding, reductions in water supplies, increased malnutrition and increased health impacts." These adverse effects include forced migration, sickness, injury and death. Even if we assume that death rates do not increase, but remain at several hundred thousand per year, climate change will cause tens of millions of deaths before the end of this century. And given that temperatures will likely continue to increase and remain elevated for thousands of years beyond 2100, the harms of climate change will not cease at the turn of the century.

What will happen even in this century is far from clear. A 2012 report prepared for the World Bank predicts:

> As global warming approaches and exceeds 2°C, the risk of crossing thresholds of nonlinear tipping elements in the Earth system, with abrupt climate change impacts and unprecedented high-temperature climate regimes, increases. Examples include the disintegration of the West Antarctic ice sheet leading to more rapid sea-level rise than projected in this analysis or large-scale Amazon dieback drastically affecting ecosystems, rivers, agriculture, energy production, and livelihoods in an almost continental scale region and potentially adding substantially to 21st-century global warming.
>
> (World Bank 2012: xvii)

It is quite possible, given our current emissions trajectory, that by 2100 the global average temperature will already have increased by 4°C (7.2°F) or more over pre-industrial levels. As regards the institutional effects of such a temperature increase, the World Bank report says:

> With pressures increasing as warming progresses toward 4°C and combining with nonclimate-related social, economic, and population stresses, the risk of crossing critical social system thresholds will grow. At such thresholds existing institutions that would have supported adaptation actions would likely become much less effective or even collapse. . . . stresses on human health, such as heat waves, malnutrition, and decreasing quality of drinking water due to sea-water intrusion, have the potential to overburden health-care systems to a point where adaptation is no longer possible, and dislocation is forced.
>   Thus, given that uncertainty remains about the full nature and scale of impacts, there is also no certainty that adaptation to a 4°C world is possible.
>
> (World Bank 2012: xviii)

Most experts think that we can still avert a 4°C world. But it would require a massive reduction in our use of fossil fuels.

The projected effects of climate change on non-human life are also profound. According to the IPCC:

> The resilience of many ecosystems is *likely* to be exceeded this century by an unprecedented combination of climate change, associated disturbances (e.g. flooding, drought, wildfire, insects, ocean acidification) and other global change drivers (e.g. land-use change, pollution, fragmentation of natural systems, overexploitation of resources).
>
> (IPCC 2007: 48)

The higher the temperature, the worse the problem. "As global average temperature increase exceeds about 3.5°C, model projections suggest significant extinctions (40 to 70% of species assessed) around the globe" (IPCC 2007: 54).

1.2.3.3 Harm as a Function of Emissions

The harms of greenhouse gases continue over such a long time that even small emissions may in the long run cause significant harm. We noted above that despite the plethora of variables affecting the climate system, there is a direct relationship between greenhouse gas concentrations and temperature. Nearly all of the complicating influences that we know of (for example, the increased emission of methane from melting tundra and warming sea floors in Arctic regions or increased absorption of sunlight by water and land as glacial and polar ice melts) amplify, rather than dampen, the temperature increases. Temperature will therefore almost certainly increase continuously with emissions.

Similarly, harm (whether measured in terms of deaths, injuries, disease, economic losses, or biodiversity losses) increases more or less continuously with temperature.

While a death is a discrete event, most of other forms of loss are continuous. (A little more heat in a drought, for example, produces a little more thirst.) Harms probably accelerate as temperature increases, but still the increase is likely to be smooth and, to a close approximation, continuous. In other words, even a tiny increase in temperature produces some increase in harm.

How much harm is not clear. One thing that makes this question especially difficult is that CO_2 emissions produce harm in a way that has few parallels in ordinary human experience. We usually think of harm as a one-time event. A gun is fired and someone gets hurt. A factory releases toxic gas and people get sick. But the harm of a CO_2 emission goes on and on. If I drive my car today, the CO_2 ejected from the tailpipe will contribute to elevated atmospheric levels for centuries, continually absorbing heat. And once we raise the earth's temperature, it will remain elevated for thousands of years. Over this span of time climate change will cause huge numbers of human deaths, illnesses and injuries, produce great suffering and deeply deplete the earth's biotic richness. Because each greenhouse gas emission contributes to these harms in proportion to its relation to the total anthropogenic emissions, and because the total harm will be very great, even the tiny fraction of it contributed by a small emission can still be significant (Nolt 2011 and 2013a).

To summarize: the harms of climate change depend sensitively on emissions, because:

- temperature increases continuously with total emissions and
- harm increases essentially continuously with temperature.

It follows that, other things being equal, any additional emissions of greenhouse gases increases harm. Moreover, the totality of harms is enormous, because

- the effects of even the 0.8°C warming we are now experiencing are already large and predominantly harmful,
- they are increasing rapidly, and
- once global average temperature peaks, it is likely to remain elevated for thousands of years, continually causing new harms.

Thus even small emissions can contribute to great harms.

1.2.3.4 *Mitigating Climate Change*

The most effective thing that can be done to slow climate change is to reduce fossil fuel use as quickly as possible. Every reduction helps. Climatologists H. Damon Matthews and Susan Solomon summarize the basics:

> if emissions were to cease abruptly, global average temperatures would remain roughly constant for many centuries, but they would not increase very much, if at all. Similarly, if emissions were to decrease, temperatures would increase less than they otherwise would have.
>
> (Matthews and Solomon 2013: 438)

Reducing fossil fuel use, which can be accomplished by eliminating unnecessary uses, increasing efficiency of use, or switching to non-fossil energy sources, is the simplest, easiest and ultimately least expensive way to slow climate change. But "simplest," "easiest," and "least expensive" do not mean "simple," "easy," or "inexpensive." Reducing fossil fuel use is an enormous challenge, both for individuals and for nations.

Consequently, people have been devising schemes to protect the planet from the worst effects of climate change if we fail. Two prominent methods are to shade the earth's surface from sunlight or to remove carbon dioxide from the atmosphere.

The two main proposals for shading the earth's surface from sunlight are to put some sort of sun screen, perhaps consisting of a multitude of satellites, into space between the earth and the sun, or to inject reflective gases or vapors into the atmosphere to reduce the amount of sunlight that reaches the earth's surface. For example, water vapor might be injected into the lower atmosphere to whiten clouds, or a global fog of sulfur dioxide might be injected into the upper atmosphere to shade the entire planet. Either method might reduce global average temperatures, but each has the disadvantage that if it ever failed (due, say, to global war or global economic depression), the shield, clouds or fog would disperse, resulting in warming much more rapid and dangerous than we are now experiencing. Moreover, these proposals leave the carbon dioxide in the atmosphere and so do nothing to reduce ocean acidification.

A more comprehensive solution would be to remove carbon dioxide permanently from the atmosphere. Various methods for doing this are under discussion. Reforestation is the simplest. Since trees grow by removing carbon dioxide from the atmosphere, reforestation would help, but it alone would not be enough to solve the problem. Moreover, unless the new forests were permanently protected, the carbon they removed from the atmosphere could be put back (by fires or new deforestation) within decades. Some schemes involve removing CO_2 from the atmosphere and storing it underground. But there are worries that the CO_2 might escape from such storage.

These schemes are all forms of **geoengineering**—which in the context of climate science means using large-scale engineering techniques to transform global climate. All are untested. Most or all probably have unintended side effects. All would be enormously expensive. Some would benefit some regions and harm others, and so would likely generate international tensions. For these reasons, it is imprudent to assume that geoengineering will solve the climate problem. If emissions continue, however, the situation may get desperate enough that some form of it will be attempted. That only reinforces the statement with which this section began: the most effective thing that can be done to slow climate change is to reduce fossil fuel use as quickly as possible.

1.2.4 Natural Resource Depletion

Whereas pollution is harmful excess, resource depletion is harmful insufficiency. The term "resource," as it is typically used by economists and policymakers, denotes a supply of something that can be used to satisfy human preferences. A **natural resource** is one found in the natural environment.

Natural resources are, of course, not *naturally* resources. That is, it is not their nature to be used by humans. We happen to have found ways of using them to satisfy our preferences. But other life forms use them too. We use trees for logs and paper. Birds and squirrels use them for shelter. Water, one of the most important natural resources of all, is a necessity for all life.

Resources are often divided into those that are **renewable** and those that are not. Renewable natural resources are those that capable of being continuously supplied by natural processes. Sunlight and wind, for example, are renewable energy sources. Wood is a renewable resource as well, provided that trees are cut no faster than they grow. But some natural resources are no longer being produced by nature—on Earth, at least. There is, for example, only so much of each metal in the earth's crust. Earth cannot create them; they were formed in the explosions of stars billions of years ago. Thus metals are non-renewable.

Section Outline: As with the other sections in this chapter, the discussion in section 1.2.4 is incomplete, touching only on forms of depletion of direct concern to later chapters. The natural resources to be covered here are fossil fuels (section 1.2.4.1) and fresh water (section 1.2.4.2). Metals—particularly rare earth metals—are also being depleted at a rapid rate, but, though very significant economically, they are less important to environmental ethics and so will not be discussed here. Biodiversity depletion is also harmful insufficiency, but it is loss not merely *to* living things but *of* living things and so has a special character. It is discussed separately in section 1.2.5 and its subsections.

1.2.4.1 Fossil Fuel Depletion

Fossil fuels are extraordinarily concentrated sources of energy. That energy comes ultimately from sunlight gathered over millions of years by prehistoric plants and stored in their tissues as chemical bonds. Those tissues also contained carbon that the plants absorbed from the atmosphere, which was at that time much richer in carbon dioxide and hence much warmer. Over millions more years, this plant material was compressed and heated by geological processes, which transformed it into fossil fuels. Thus when we burn coal, oil and natural gas, we are harnessing the energy of ancient sunlight, putting old carbon back into the atmosphere, and restoring the primeval warmth that prevailed millions of years before humans evolved.

Because it takes nature so long to produce fossil fuels, fossil fuel reserves are finite and, for all practical purposes, non-renewable. BP (the energy corporation) estimates that at 2012 rates of consumption the world's proven reserves of coal would be used up in 109 years, natural gas in 55.7 years, and oil in 59.2 years (BP 2013). These figures mean little in practice, since it is possible that new extraction techniques will be invented, which will make more reserves available, as happened recently with the development of hydraulic fracturing (fracking) for natural gas and of new techniques for shale oil extraction. Such new methods might change consumption significantly, or they might be so costly and energy-intensive as to have little effect.

But more importantly, it is nearly certain that consumption will *not* stay at 2012 levels. Worldwide consumption of all fossil fuels is growing. The U.S. Energy Information Administration projects continued growth at least through 2040 (see section 1.2.6.2). If this is correct, then known reserves will be depleted much sooner than BP estimates.

But even without growth, continuation of emissions at current levels would in the long run yield terrible consequences. Fifty more years of emissions even at current levels would ultimately increase global average temperature by at least 10°C (18°F) (Stocker 2013). There exists, so far as I know, nothing like a comprehensive assessment of what that would mean, but it would be catastrophic.

Anticipating this, the world's nations may act to increase conservation and replace fossil fuels with other energy sources. If such efforts succeed, global fossil fuel consumption could drop sharply before 2040. But nothing guarantees success. Many unknowns are at play. This much, however, is certain: the fossil fuel era is coming to an end. *How* it will end nobody knows.

1.2.4.2 Depletion of Fresh Water Sources

Fresh water is a renewable resource. It falls for free as rain and collects in rivers, lakes, streams and underground aquifers, where it is available in great quantities. But nearly all of the world's rivers, lakes and streams are so polluted that the water cannot be used for human consumption without treatment. And, more importantly, many fresh water sources, both above and beneath the ground, are being drawn down more quickly than they can be replenished. Globally, most of the water is withdrawn for agricultural irrigation, but much of that evaporates before it can be used.

Fresh water use is increasing virtually everywhere, and competition for fresh water is intensifying. A significant portion of the global increase is due to increasing demand for animal feed, as a result of a growing worldwide appetite for meat. In general, meat production requires about eight times more water per calorie than does production of plant-based foods (Fox and Fimeche 2013: 10).

Climate change will bring more rainfall to some regions, less to others. The interiors of continents—places like the American Midwest, the "breadbasket of the world"—will generally become drier. In many areas global warming is temporarily increasing the flow of rivers by increasing melt rates of glaciers. But as the glaciers disappear over decades or centuries, water flow will ultimately diminish (UNESCO 2012: 5).

Because of the uncertainties engendered by increasing water demand and climate change, the UN's *World Water Development Report* (2012) cautions:

> *No water users, anywhere in the world,* can be guaranteed they will have uninterrupted access to the water supplies they need or want or to the water-derived benefits from key developmental sectors such as agriculture, energy

and health. . . . As water demand and availability become more uncertain, all societies become more vulnerable to a wide range of risks associated with inadequate water supply, including hunger and thirst, high rates of disease and death, lost productivity and economic crises, and degraded ecosystems. These impacts elevate water to a crisis of global concern.

(UNESCO 2012: 18)

1.2.5 Biodiversity Loss

Biodiversity is variation among living organisms, species and ecosystems. It can be assessed in various ways, the simplest being *species richness*—the number of species per unit area or volume. Thus, for example, biologists might mark off a hundred square meters of land and count the plant and animal species within it, or sample a liter of ocean water from a specific location and count the number of species of micro-organisms it contains.

But species richness by itself is a relatively poor measure of biodiversity. The number of species in a given plot of forest, for example, may actually increase if the forest is clear-cut, as common fast-growing species of plants, insects and micro-organisms move in. Since such species already exist in great numbers elsewhere, the result may be that rarer and more valuable species are replaced by commoner and "weedier" ones, so that diversity has diminished globally. Local species richness is therefore not the whole story. **Global species *richness***, the number of species of a given type (birds, for example) worldwide, is a more meaningful number.

But even global species numbers can be deceptive. If many species' populations are declining, as is true today, these raw numbers may give a misleadingly optimistic impression. A deeper understanding can be obtained by considering not only global species numbers, but also the abundance of each species, noting especially those populations that are declining, threatened or endangered. These statistics taken together constitute *species diversity*.

There are other measures of biodiversity as well. *Genetic diversity* is variation among genomes, often within the same species. It is crucial for the survival and future evolution of most species, for it is how they adapt to environmental change. (Humans, with their rapid cultural innovations may be an exception.)

The term *biodiversity loss* is used here to refer to losses in any of the above respects, but especially to declining global species diversity. Earth's highest levels of biodiversity by any measure tend to be located on land and in the tropics. It is there that biodiversity loss is greatest.

Section Outline: Section 1.2.5 begins with a quick summary of the 3.5-billion-year-long history of biodiversity (section 1.2.5.1), followed by some remarks on biodiversity's importance to humans (section 1.2.5.2) and an assessment of recent and projected biodiversity losses (section 1.2.5.3).

1.2.5.1 History of Biodiversity Loss

Life, in the form of primitive one-celled organisms, began in the oceans at least 3.5 billion years ago. For more than 2 billion years it evolved in variety and complexity, yet remained single-celled and confined to water. Exactly when multicellular organisms evolved is unclear, since at first they were soft-bodied and left few fossil traces. But by 700 million years ago, the oceans were teeming with multicellular life, much of it weirdly different from life today. Around 400 million years ago plants began to colonize the land, followed within a few tens of millions of years by amphibians and later by reptiles and other land animals. Our species, *Homo sapiens*, evolved only about 200,000 years ago. We are latecomers.

The general tendency of evolution has always been to increase biodiversity. Though all species eventually succumb to extinction, on average more evolve than are lost, so that global species richness increases over time. The increase, however, is not always steady. We know of at least five times in Earth's history when species loss greatly exceeded the evolution of new species. These are the mass extinctions.

A *mass extinction* is defined as an episode in which the planet loses some large proportion (60 or 75 percent, depending on which author you consult) of its species in a geologically short interval. The causes of the earlier mass extinctions are disputed, but seem to involve climate change and/or habitat disruption. The fifth and most recent occurred about 65 million years ago when what was probably an asteroid slammed into the ocean near the Yucatan Peninsula in southeastern Mexico. The impact produced an enormous explosion, huge tidal waves and great forest fires. Dust and smoke from the explosion and fires blocked sunlight worldwide, cooling the earth, disrupting photosynthesis, and driving the dinosaurs to extinction.

Since then, however, biodiversity has not only recovered but steadily increased—until quite recently. By the time *Homo sapiens* evolved, life's diversity was probably at its richest level ever in Earth's history.

Humans began contributing to extinctions when they became proficient at organized hunting with stone tools and at wielding fire. Human hunting probably quickened the extinctions of the large mammals—mastodons, mammoths, ground sloths, and many others—that disappeared at the end of the last ice age (around 10,000 years ago), though climate change and other factors probably also contributed.

Biodiversity loss has accelerated over the last few centuries, as humans increased rapidly in number and spread to the planet's remotest places, hunting with firearms became widespread, fishing techniques grew ever more efficient, and forests were felled for logs, settlement and agriculture worldwide. After World War II, pollution and pesticides added to the toll.

Today biodiversity loss is accelerating at a rate unprecedented in human history. Five causes of today's losses are generally recognized. Two of them have already been discussed: pollution (section 1.2.1) and climate change (section 1.2.3). The other three are overexploitation, habitat disruption, and the spread of invasive species.

Overexploitation is unsustainable taking of wild species. Common forms today are overfishing, overharvesting of wild plants, and overhunting (especially in impoverished rural areas, for bush meat). Populations of overexploited species decline, so that these species become less available, even as exploitation pressure increases. Without regulatory protection, even very populous species may be lost. A classic example is the passenger pigeon, which, though it once darkened North American skies in flocks of billions, was hunted to extinction by the early twentieth century.

On land *habitat disruption* takes such forms as the clearing of forests, draining of wetlands and sprawling growth of cities. Road building, the construction of dams, and other human activities fragment habitats into small areas, blocking migration corridors for land animals and contributing to the decline of many species, including even birds, many of which require large unfragmented forest stands to escape nest predators and reproduce successfully. Strip mining, mountaintop removal, shale oil extraction, and the sprawling growth of cities take their toll. In the oceans, habitat disruption takes other forms. Shoreline development degrades mangroves and salt marshes where ocean species spawn. Absorption of anthropogenic carbon dioxide emissions acidifies seawater, degrading or destroying coral reefs and shellfish reefs. These, together with seagrass beds, are also damaged by trawling. Sea ice habitats, especially in the Arctic, are melting as a result of climate change.

In addition, global transportation has facilitated the spread of *invasive species*—species that are not native to and adversely affect an ecosystem or human habitat. Invasive species are among the toughest, most aggressive species from every region of the globe. The so-called Norway rat, or brown rat, for example—which, despite its name, originated in central Asia—is now a disease threat on all continents except Antarctica. The domestic cat has eliminated many rare and local birds, especially where it has been brought to islands, such as those of Hawaii. But it is not just mammals that are destructively invasive. Everywhere, insects, microbes, fungal diseases and parasites from far-away places are displacing local, delicate, unique, and rare species. As aggressive organisms move in, each ecosystem becomes more like climatologically similar ecosystems everywhere. The trees, along a disturbed stretch of Tennessee River bank near my home, for example, are nearly all invasive species from Asia. Such biological invasions, together with declines in sensitive native species, are thus homogenizing nature.

1.2.5.2 Importance of Biodiversity

Non-human biological life provides much of what is necessary for or conducive to human existence. A very incomplete collection of examples follows. Bacteria, fungi, worms, insects and other decomposers build the soils that are essential to nearly all land-based life, including ours. Insects pollinate crops. Photosynthetic plants and the cyanobacteria of the oceans process carbon dioxide into breathable oxygen and provide much of the basic material for the food chains that feed us both on land and in the sea. Forests provide timber and medicinal plants, build soil and filter pollution from the air. Wetlands remove pollution from water. Mangroves protect coastal regions from hurricane surges. These processes are not only useful but beautiful. Their contemplation nourishes the human spirit. They would be expensive or impossible to provide artificially. Imagine, for example, trying to create them from scratch on Mars. Nature provides them for free. Hence they are called **ecosystem services**.

Ecosystem services are only as resilient as life is, and life's resilience depends on its diversity. When the environment is changing rapidly, as it is today, species must be adaptable in order to survive. Their adaptability depends on a variety of factors, including population size, geographic dispersal and mobility—but especially on the species' reservoir of genetic diversity. Different members of a diverse species respond differently to the same environmental conditions. Thus the more diverse the species, the more likely it is that some of its members will survive and reproduce.

In the long term, moreover, it is diversity that powers evolution. Natural selection cannot operate on a genetically homogeneous population. It must have a variety of genomes to select from. Thus in depleting genetic diversity, we are reducing a prerequisite of the process that creates new forms of life.

1.2.5.3 Current and Projected Biodiversity Losses

In April 2002, 192 nations and the European Union committed themselves to achieve by 2010 a significant reduction of the current rate of biodiversity loss. This target was subsequently endorsed by the United Nations General Assembly. In 2010, the UN-sponsored Convention on Biological Diversity reported the results in its third *Global Biodiversity Outlook*. Its assessment, quoted here from the report's executive summary, is stark:

> The target agreed by the world's Governments in 2002, "to achieve by 2010 a significant reduction of the current rate of biodiversity loss at the global, regional and national level as a contribution to poverty alleviation and to the benefit of all life on Earth", has not been met.

There are multiple indications of continuing decline in biodiversity in all three of its main components—genes, species and ecosystems—including:

- Species which have been assessed for extinction risk are on average moving closer to extinction. Amphibians face the greatest risk and coral species are deteriorating most rapidly in status. Nearly a quarter of plant species are estimated to be threatened with extinction.
- The abundance of vertebrate species, based on assessed populations, fell by nearly a third on average between 1970 and 2006, and continues to fall globally, with especially severe declines in the tropics and among freshwater species.
- Natural habitats in most parts of the world continue to decline in extent and integrity, although there has been significant progress in slowing the rate of loss for tropical forests and mangroves, in some regions. Freshwater wetlands, sea ice habitats, salt marshes, coral reefs, seagrass beds and shellfish reefs are all showing serious declines.

- Extensive fragmentation and degradation of forests, rivers and other ecosystems have also led to loss of biodiversity and ecosystem services.
- Crop and livestock genetic diversity continues to decline in agricultural systems.
- The five principal pressures directly driving biodiversity loss (habitat change, overexploitation, pollution, invasive alien species and climate change) are either constant or increasing in intensity.
- The ecological footprint of humanity exceeds the biological capacity of the Earth by a wider margin than at the time the 2010 target was agreed (Convention on Biological Diversity 2010: 9).

The last point requires explanation. Humanity's **ecological footprint** is an estimate of the area of biologically productive land and water needed to provide the resources we use and to absorb our waste. At the time the *Global Biodiversity Outlook* was written, the most recent (2006) figure indicated that our ecological footprint exceeded Earth's biological capacity by 40 percent (Convention on Biological Diversity 2010: 66), and the excess has been growing since. The result is the increasing degradation described in the report.

As biodiversity continues to decline, conservation biologists are rethinking their fundamental goals. Until recently, it was assumed that we should protect species by protecting their native habitat. But climate change is making that impossible. Because each species does best within a specific temperature range, the geographic ranges of many are shifting. To remain sufficiently cool as the Earth warms, species must migrate either to higher elevations or toward the poles. (Those that are already near the poles—polar bears, for example—and those that are already at the tops of mountains—such as the salamander species endemic to the peaks of the Great Smoky Mountains—may be out of luck.) Because their specific habitat requirements and degrees of mobility differ, species migrate at different rates. Some will need to move hundreds, others thousands, of kilometers closer to the poles (Convention on Biological Diversity 2010: 10). One effect of this is the likely depletion of now-rich tropical areas. Another is that ecosystems will be pulled apart as their current inhabitants move out at different rates and new organisms move in. We must protect habitat, of course, but preserving species in their *native* habitat may be an increasingly unrealistic goal.

Worse may lie ahead. Some biologists now fear that humans have already initiated a new mass extinction. Such an event would have dire long-term consequences. In a recent paper in the journal *Nature*, a group of paleontologists, biologists and ecologists asks "Has the Earth's Sixth Mass Extinction Already Arrived?" Their answer:

> the recent loss of species is dramatic and serious but does not yet qualify as a mass extinction in the palaeontological sense of the Big Five. In historic times we have actually lost only a few per cent of assessed species (though we have no way of knowing how many species we have lost that had never been described).

But, as was noted above, species richness is not the best measure of biodiversity. Many species populations are declining worldwide, and in general these declines are increasing. The authors continue:

> there are clear indications that losing species now in the "critically endangered" category would propel the world to a state of mass extinction that has previously been seen only five times in about 540 million years. Additional losses of species in the "endangered" and "vulnerable" categories could accomplish the sixth mass extinction in just a few centuries.
>
> (Barnosky *et al.* 2011: 56)

They conclude that should that mass extinction occur, recovery of biodiversity "will not occur on any timeframe meaningful to people: evolution of new species typically takes at least hundreds of thousands of years and recovery from mass extinction episodes probably occurs on timescales encompassing millions of years" (Barnosky *et al.* 2011: 51).

1.2.6 Population and Consumption

The severity of all of the harms mentioned so far in this chapter can be understood as a product of two variables, damage per capita and population, and can be written as a simple equation:

total environmental damage = damage per capita × population.

The population in question may be that of a nation or region, or of the planet.

Damage per capita depends, of course, on many factors, but may be roughly equated with the average level of consumption of materials and energy. Generally, the more developed the region, the greater the damage. This may seem paradoxical, since the environmental quality is often best in the developed nations, but we must keep in mind that much of what the developed nations consume is produced elsewhere, so that much of the damage they do is displaced into poorer regions.

This impact equation suggests two broad strategies for reducing environmental damage: reduce consumption and reduce population. Each on its own would help. Doing both would help more.

Section Outline: Section 1.2.6 consists of three subsections. Sections 1.2.6.1–1.2.6.3 cover, respectively, population, consumption, and ethical means for decreasing both.

1.2.6.1 Population

Earth's human population now exceeds 7 billion. It is larger than ever before and still growing. Figure 1's graph tells the story better than words can.

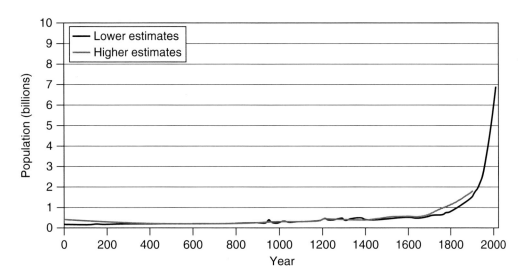

Figure 1 Historical Estimates of World Population

Sources: U.S. Census Bureau:
http://www.census.gov/population/international/data/worldpop/table_history.php
http://www.census.gov/population/international/data/idb/informationGateway.php

This plot covers only the last 2,000 years. If we were to extend it to the left, back to the emergence of *Homo sapiens* about 200,000 years ago, it would have to be a hundred times as wide as this, but we would see no other significant rises. The population curve going left would simply drift downward (with small bumps and dips) for an additional 99 frames, to zero. It is clear that we are living in an extraordinary time.

While world population is still growing rapidly, its growth rate has begun to slow. The curve is, in other words, still rising, but not as steeply as it was in the late twentieth century. UN estimates of world population in 2050 range from 8.3 to 10.8 billion, with the best guess at about 9.6 billion. The variation among these projections is due to differing projections of the values of two variables: *fertility*—the average number of children per woman—and *life expectancy*—the average age of death for a given population. Fertility worldwide has generally been falling, but life expectancy has been rising.

Life expectancy and fertility differ greatly between rich nations and poor. In rich nations life expectancy is high and fertility low, while in poor nations life expectancy is low and fertility high. Thus the populations of rich nations are generally increasing much more slowly than those of poor nations. Populations in much of Europe are actually falling, while those in Africa are growing so rapidly that the African continent is expected to contribute more than half of the world's population growth up to 2050 (United Nations 2013: 1–2).

What will happen beyond 2050 is much less certain, but the UN expects population to continue growing for the remainder of this century. Mid-range 2012 UN estimates put world population at about 10.9 billion by 2100 (United Nations 2013: xv). We seem to be headed for the top of the chart.

1.2.6.2 Consumption

It is not far from the truth to say that consumption of *everything* is increasing. There are, it is true, *temporary* decreases. World oil consumption fell, for example, in the years 2008–9, as the result of a global economic recession, but it is now (2013) rising again and has surpassed its previous high. And there are *local* decreases. Coal consumption in the U.S., for example, has dropped considerably since 2008, as a result both of the recession and of the natural gas boom. World coal consumption, however, has steadily risen. On the whole, with respect to practically all resources, world consumption is increasing. This section focuses only on the consumption of fossil fuels and the land needed to satisfy humanity's rapidly growing demands for food.

Our single most damaging form of consumption is the burning of fossil fuels. Here is a quick review of its effects (all explained earlier in this chapter). Fossil fuel consumption is:

- the largest contributor to anthropogenic climate change—whose effects include: higher temperatures, severe weather events, flooding, droughts, increased melting of glaciers and polar ice, rising sea levels, etc.;
- largely responsible for ocean acidification;
- a major source of atmospheric particulate matter;
- the chief source of anthropogenic sulfur dioxide (mainly from coal);
- the largest contributor to anthropogenic nitrogen oxide pollution and hence to ozone pollution;
- a main contributor to acid deposition;
- a source of nitrous oxide which increases stratospheric ozone depletion;
- a significant contributor to a global decline in human physical activity, which is a chief cause of several of the world's worst health problems;
- one of the most important forms of natural resource depletion;
- directly responsible for habitat destruction in the form of strip mining, mountaintop removal, shale oil extraction, road building, etc.; and
- one of the main causes of biodiversity loss, chiefly through climate change.

Several of the effects of burning fossil fuels—ocean acidification, elevated temperatures and extinctions—are irreversible on timescales shorter than millennia.

Yet the U.S. Energy Information Administration projects continuing global increases in all three forms of fossil fuel consumption (see Table 3). These increases are expected to occur mainly in developing nations (EIA 2013).

Table 3 Projected Global Increases in Fossil Fuel Consumption

Fossil Fuel	Percentage Increase in Consumption Between 2010 and 2040
Oil	32
Natural gas	64
Coal	50

Such projections are based, of course, on extrapolation of current consumption patterns, and events can take unexpected twists. They are forecasts, not inevitabilities. Often in the past similar projections have been wide of the mark. But they are sobering.

Similarly sobering are forecasts for the amount of land needed to feed the growing human population, especially if its appetite for meat continues to grow. (Meat production in general requires much more energy, water and land per calorie or per unit of protein than does production of plant foods.) A recent report by the Institution of Mechanical Engineers notes that

> Forecasts for the amount of land that will be needed to deliver sufficient food to feed the increasing population through the 21st century are highly dependent on assumptions made regarding trends in these dietary preferences. Indeed recent work in this area has attempted to comprehensively and realistically analyse a range of possible scenarios through to 2050, ranging from a high-meat consumption: low production efficiency "worse [sic] case," to one characterised by a "best case" of low-meat consumption: high production efficiency. In the former the total land use area under cultivation would require expansion to 8.83Gha [that is 8.83 gigahectares, which is 88,300,000 square kilometers or about 34 million square miles] by 2050 to meet the food demand, which at about 88% of available productive land is a considerable threat to the world's ecosystems.
>
> (Fox and Fimeche 2013: 10)

(Current land usage is about 4.9Gha.) But the same report suggests that in the best case, with high efficiency and low meat consumption, it may be possible to feed the world in 2050 on 15 percent less land than we use now. (Much of the efficiency in this best-case scenario would, by the way, involve saving and using food that is now wasted—about 30–50 percent.) Obviously, there is a wide range of uncertainty in any such projections. What will happen beyond 2050 if population continues to grow as forecast is still less certain.

1.2.6.3 Decreasing Population and Consumption

Section 1.2.6 began with the observation that there are two ways to reduce environmental damage: decrease population and decrease damage per capita. We can now say something more about how to do this effectively. Population depends on life expectancy and fertility. It is possible, of course, to decrease population by reducing life expectancy, but that is not an ethical option. Hence the only live option for reducing population is to reduce fertility. To reduce damage per capita, of course, we must reduce consumption. Therefore the world can reduce environmental damage by two broad strategies: reducing fertility and reducing consumption.

These strategies are not equally effective everywhere. In poor nations consumption is low—often perilously low—and fertility is high. In rich nations, consumption is high—often excessively high—and fertility is low. Therefore, in general, fertility reduction is the more effective strategy in poor nations and consumption reduction is the more effective strategy in rich nations. These generalizations do not, however, preclude reduction of consumption among the rich in poor nations or reduction in fertility among both the rich and the poor in rich nations—which would also help. Indeed, the impact of a child born to a rich family anywhere is generally far greater than the impact of a child born to a poor family anywhere.

• 1.3 SAVING THE PLANET—OR LIFE, OR US

It is possible to overstate what is at stake in all this. What is at stake is *not* the planet. Earth is a big spherical rock, partly molten in the middle, that has lasted for over 4.5 billion years. It has survived repeated cataclysms (including extraordinarily violent collisions with asteroids) greater than anything we can cause. It doesn't need saving by the likes of us.

Nor does life need saving. We don't have, and are never likely to get, the power to sterilize the planet. Some living things will survive no matter what we do. Life has flourished on this spherical rock for at least 3.5 billion years. It has survived at the deep, hot hydrothermal vents of the oceans and under kilometers of ice. It has survived periods of warming more intense than we are likely to produce and planet-wide deep freezes. It has survived radical alterations of the composition of the atmosphere. It has survived at least five mass extinctions. Its tenacity is mind-boggling. We can, and very well might, precipitate another mass extinction. But that is probably the worst we can do.

Nor do we humans need saving from ourselves—at least not within the next few centuries. Humans are very numerous and diverse. We are intelligent, technologically skilled, and highly motivated to survive. What could we do that would kill us all? Even the worst extremes of climate change probably wouldn't do it. Reduced populations could still find ways to survive. Not even a nuclear holocaust is likely to do it. It might destroy civilization, but some people would survive, if only in underground shelters, and eventually emerge to rebuild.

Probably even a genetically engineered global plague wouldn't do it. Some people would likely be immune or find places of refuge until it passed.

Environmentalism, therefore, is not about saving the planet, or life, or even the human species. It's about protecting some of life's goodness and restoring some of what has been or will be lost.

● SUGGESTIONS FOR FURTHER READING

For an accessible yet philosophically sophisticated account of Darwinian evolutionary theory, *Darwin's Dangerous Idea: Evolution and the Meanings of Life* by Daniel Dennett (Simon and Schuster, 1995) is a good place to start. Much of this book, especially the parts dealing with the evolution of mind and consciousness and the redesign of morality, is speculative, and Dennett views life perhaps too exclusively through a Darwinian lens, but all of it is keenly thought-provoking.

Regarding environmental science, there are many excellent textbooks, but there is really no substitute, if you want to understand the science deeply, for consulting the original sources, many of which are cited in this chapter.

Over the past few decades there have been organized and well funded efforts to discredit environmental science when its discoveries upset financial or ideological interests. For a revealing account of such efforts, see *Merchants of Doubt* by Naomi Oreskes and Erik M. Conway (Bloomsbury Press, 2010).

2

logic, prescriptive reasoning, and ethical theories

This chapter concerns neither environmental science nor environmental ethics *per se*, but the tools and methods of ethics. The concepts and definitions introduced here are used throughout this book. If you are already familiar with this material or would like to go straight to the heart of environmental ethics, you may wish to read ahead, consulting this chapter for reference material, as needed. If you are not, this chapter provides the necessary background.

As in Chapter 1, there is no attempt at completeness here. Many important aspects of logic and ethical theory are not mentioned. My aim has been to explain concepts used later in this book, and nothing more.

We begin with some history. Until the Enlightenment in the seventeenth and eighteenth centuries, ethical belief was in the West, as it always had been throughout the world, shaped largely by tradition and political and religious authority. There had been earlier attempts, particularly in classical Greece, to ground ethics in philosophical reason, but over time these had largely been assimilated into the Jewish, Muslim and Christian religious traditions. These religions, however, were often in conflict. During the century prior to the Enlightenment, for example, millions of Europeans died in inconclusive wars between Catholics and Protestants. Disillusioned, European thinkers began to look to secular reason as a more objective and potentially less divisive moral guide.

Since then, ethical thinking shaped not by anyone's authority but by reason and evidence, has grown in importance globally. It is integral to contemporary, pluralistic societies, which tolerate people of differing faiths, or none. When we converse across divides of religious or political conviction, little but frustration can result unless we offer reasons that appeal, not just to people who share our beliefs, but to those who do not. Effective ethical reasoning aimed at a general audience in a pluralistic society must therefore proceed, not from partisan or parochial premises, but from the common ground of widely accepted principles.

Fortunately, the world's great religions share many such principles. All, for example, advocate justice and compassion for the powerless and poor. All seek to relieve unnecessary suffering. All contain expressions of the Golden Rule. These principles also have strong rational support. Reasoning from such widely shared ethical principles has helped moral reformers to improve whole societies. The nearly worldwide abolition of slavery and significant reductions in racial and gender-based discrimination are cases in point.

Since the Enlightenment, ethical thinking has increasingly, and in some cases successfully, sought to escape narrow and violent prejudice through broader and better informed objectivity. *Objectivity* is a collection of virtues that aim to transcend self-centeredness toward a wider and truer understanding. To be objective is, among other things, to: seek to understand and compensate for your own prejudices; accept the findings of adequately conducted scientific research; strive for consistency; suspend judgment on factual issues when the evidence is inconclusive; cultivate awareness of your own fallibility; and seriously consider the well-informed opinions of others.

Objectivity is not neutrality. To be **neutral** is to refuse to take sides or make ethical judgments, to refrain from action and avoid commitment. Neutrality is tacit acceptance of the *status quo*. Often it is an excuse for moral cowardice. Ethics demands something more difficult: *both* objectivity and engagement.

Objectivity requires logical thinking. Some people distrust logic, regarding it as a tool of oppression, and in some cases they are right. Logic can be misused to rationalize prejudices and bludgeon opponents into agreement, or at least acquiescence. But when employed in an open inquiry whose goal is truth, not power, it can provide fresh insight, unexpected discoveries and illuminating clarity.

Although this book emphasizes the advantages of analytical thought and logical reasoning for ethics, moral progress is never a purely intellectual affair. People are more moved by songs, sermons and stories than by syllogisms. Moral reform involves both the head and the heart. Reason helps us to see through the hard-wired biases of our evolutionary heritage, the delusions of our culture and the deceptive manipulations of opinion-mongers. The impartiality and rigor it demands serve as a check on ignorance and fanaticism, and help us to avoid narrow bigotry and foolish error. But reason accomplishes little without heartfelt commitment.

Chapter Outline: Chapter 2 is divided into four sections. Section 2.1 is a very brief introduction to some fundamental concepts of logic. Section 2.2 explains the application of those concepts to prescriptive—that is, action-guiding—reasoning and, in particular, ethical reasoning. Ethical reasoning starts with ethical premises, and ethical premises are explained and justified by ethical theories. Section 2.3 explains the three most prominent kinds of ethical theories. Section 2.4 addresses the question "Why care?"

• 2.1 FUNDAMENTALS OF LOGIC

Objectivity in ethics requires careful attention to logic. *Logic* is the study and practice of rational thought. Anyone who can think clearly has some logical ability, but rigorous logical thinking is rare. This book uses only elementary logical concepts, but it deploys them with deliberate precision. So it is necessary to define and illustrate them before we begin. That is the purpose of sections 2.1 and 2.2. For those familiar with logic, these sections can be used mainly as reference material, to be consulted later if necessary. Terms being defined are here, as elsewhere in the book, printed in bold italics, in order to make the definitions easy to locate.

Rational thinking is expressed verbally in arguments. An *argument* is a set of declarative statements, one of which is intended as a *conclusion* and the rest of which, the *premises*, provide intended evidence for the conclusion. For example:

> Gibbons are apes.
> All apes share a common ancestor with humans within the last
> 25 million years.
> ∴ Gibbons share a common ancestor with humans within the last
> 25 million years.

The first two statements are premises. The symbol ∴ means "therefore" and is used to mark the conclusion. To analyze arguments, we generally write the premises and then the conclusions, as in this example, but in conversation or writing these components may occur in any order. The premises of this argument provide evidence that the conclusion is true. They in turn have been established by further arguments from paleontological and genomic evidence—arguments requiring specialized knowledge.

There are two main criteria that determine whether or not the intended evidence provided by an argument really does demonstrate the truth of its conclusion:

1. The premises are true
2. The reasoning is valid.

An argument is *valid* if its conclusion is true in every possible situation in which its premises are all true. So, for example, the argument above is valid because, given that gibbons are apes and that all apes share a common ancestor with humans within the last 25 million years, it would have to be true that gibbons share a common ancestor with humans within the last 25 million years.

An argument is *invalid* if it is not valid—that is, if a situation is possible in which its premises are all true and its conclusion is untrue. The following argument is invalid:

> All humans are mammals.
> Some mammals are vegetarian.
> ∴ Some humans are vegetarian.

Each statement in the argument, including the conclusion, is true, and yet, given just the truth of the premises, the conclusion need not be true. That is, given just that all humans are mammals and some mammals are vegetarian, it *might* still be that none of the humans are vegetarian.

A possible situation in which an argument's conclusion is untrue, though its premises are true, is called a **counterexample** to the argument. A situation in which all humans are mammals and some mammals are vegetarian, but none of the humans are vegetarian, is a counterexample to the argument above. This, of course, is not the actual situation (though perhaps it was in the distant past), but its mere possibility is enough to render the argument invalid. The briefest way to define a valid argument is to say that it is one without a counterexample.

An argument that meets criteria 1 and 2 (true premises and valid reasoning) is **sound**. Since the argument about humans and gibbons meets both of these criteria, it is sound. A sound argument proves its conclusion. An argument that fails to meet one or both of the two criteria is **unsound**. The argument for the conclusion that some humans are vegetarian is unsound, because, although its premises are true, its reasoning is invalid.

Here is an argument that is unsound even though it is logically valid and its conclusion is true:

> All metals are toxic, even in small amounts.
> Mercury is a metal.
> ∴   Mercury is toxic, even in small amounts.

What makes it unsound is that it violates criterion 1; the first premise is false. Gold, for instance, is nontoxic, as are many other metals. So even though the conclusion is true, the argument does not demonstrate its truth.

Human knowledge is justified by a rich tissue of argumentation. Often arguments are linked in chains, the conclusion of one serving as a premise for another, and these can be quite complex. The example below is adapted from a line of reasoning developed by Jeffrey T. Kiehl, Senior Scientist at the National Center for Atmospheric Research in Boulder, Colorado (personal communication). It aims to deduce from known principles of physics and premises that can be checked observationally, without appeal to climate models or even to global temperature measurements, the conclusion that our burning of fossil fuels is causing the global average temperature to rise:

1   The level of carbon dioxide in the atmosphere is increasing each year.
2   Increases of such magnitude could only come from either natural organic processes, volcanoes, or our burning of fossil fuels.
3   Carbon dioxide from our burning of fossil fuels has a higher ratio of the carbon-12 to carbon-13 isotopes than does carbon dioxide from natural organic processes or volcanoes.
4   The carbon dioxide that is contributing to the observed increase has this higher carbon-12 to carbon-13 ratio.

∴ 5 Our burning of fossil fuels is increasing the carbon dioxide level of the atmosphere. (1,2,3,4)

6 Carbon dioxide, whether in the laboratory or the atmosphere, is effective at trapping and retaining radiant heat—increasingly so as its concentration increases.

7 The Earth's surface continually radiates heat that it absorbs from the sun back into the atmosphere—and, if it is not trapped there, out into space.

8 By the law of conservation of energy, trapping and retaining additional heat in the atmosphere must cause global average temperature to rise, unless new cooling effects of equal or greater magnitude occur simultaneously.

9 There are no new cooling effects of equal or greater magnitude.

∴ 10 Our burning of fossil fuels is causing global average temperature to rise. (5,6,7,8,9)

The first four statements support the conclusion that our burning of fossil fuels is increasing the carbon dioxide level of the atmosphere. This is indicated by listing the numbers 1, 2, 3 and 4 in parentheses after statement 5. That conclusion, together with the next four statements, then gives the evidence for the final conclusion that our burning of fossil fuels is causing global average temperature to rise. The numbers 5, 6, 7, 8 and 9 in parentheses after statement 10 likewise indicate the premises from which 10 is inferred. This form of annotation is often useful for complex arguments.

The two subarguments and the argument as a whole are valid and the premises are almost certainly true. (Science provides at best near certainty, never absolute certainty.) Some have disputed the premise that there are no new cooling effects that could overcome the warming tendency. But the timely appearance of such countervailing effects would be extraordinary, and none are evident, for global average temperature (as measured by various means) is increasing. Hence the argument stands as a reasonable example of scientific deduction.

• 2.2 PRESCRIPTIVE REASONING

The arguments considered in the previous section consisted entirely of descriptive statements. **Descriptive statements** are assertions about how things are (or were or will be), not about how they should or should not be. (Of course, descriptive statements can also *mis*describe things, in which case they are false.) Ethics, law, prudential advice, and other action-guiding endeavors, however, often employ **prescriptive statements**. These assert, for example, that an action is right or wrong, that we ought or ought not (or may or may not) do it, or the like. Many prescriptive statements can be formulated as **imperatives**, suggestions or commands that tell us to do X or not to do Y. Thus, instead of "You shouldn't drive so much," we could use the imperative "Don't drive so much." The imperative form emphasizes the action-guiding role of prescriptive statements. Descriptive statements cannot be formulated as imperatives.

Prescriptive reasoning is reasoning whose conclusion is a prescriptive statement. If, for example, you give or consider reasons why a hydroelectric facility should or should not be built, then you are engaging in prescriptive reasoning. Likewise, if you argue for a certain economic policy, or try to convince a friend not to litter, or think through various lifestyles you might adopt, you are also reasoning prescriptively. Prescriptive reasoning is the sub-discipline of logic that is most relevant to ethics. Hence it deserves special attention here.

Section Outline: Section 2.2.1 introduces what is perhaps the most fundamental principle of prescriptive reasoning: that to prove an "ought" statement you need to assume an "ought" statement. Sections 2.2.2 and 2.2.3 describe its two most important forms: rule-based and consequentialist reasoning.

2.2.1 The Fallacy of Inferring "Ought" from "Is"

One very useful principle of prescriptive reasoning is: *there is no valid way to deduce a nontrivial prescriptive statement from non-prescriptive premises.* (There are some technical but trivial and empty exceptions; these need not concern us here.) Philosophers often express this by saying that you can't derive "ought" from "is," meaning that if your premises are purely descriptive (asserting only what "is"), you can't validly infer a nontrivial prescriptive conclusion (an "ought"). The facts alone don't tell us what we ought to do.

A notable historical instance of the fallacy of inferring "ought" from "is" involves evolutionary theory. Near the end of the nineteenth century, certain theorists called Social Darwinists held that because evolution operates by "survival of the fittest" (natural selection), it is morally right that the weak perish and the strong survive. Social Darwinism influenced Nazi ideology. Some Nazis, imagining themselves members of a "superior race," assumed that this gave moral justification to their aspirations for world dominance. Darwin himself, of course, never drew any such conclusions—and rightly so, for nothing like them follows from his theory. For one thing, those who happen to be in power are seldom in any relevant sense the fittest (the Nazis were a case in point). But, more importantly for our purposes, the inference from "the fittest survive" to "we ought to promote the survival of the fittest," is a textbook instance of the fallacy of inferring "ought" from "is." There are many counterexamples; we can easily image that the fittest survive, and yet that what we ought to promote is mutual care, or human diversity, or survival of the smartest (who may not be the fittest)—or something else entirely. From what *is*, nothing follows about what we *ought* to do.

To validly deduce a prescriptive conclusion (an "ought") we must assume one or more prescriptive ("ought") premises. These can take various forms.

2.2.2 Rule-Based Prescriptive Reasoning

Prescriptive premises are often expressed as rules that state what is to be done under certain specific conditions. To decide what to do, we look for justifiable rules that fit our situation and follow them. I call this ***rule-based reasoning***. A rule-based argument assumes one or more prescriptive rules, usually together with some additional premises stating that the conditions of the rules are fulfilled, to derive a prescriptive conclusion. Since this book is about ethics, the rules considered here are predominantly ethical ones. But a quick comparison of ethical rules with legal rules, which have similar action-guiding roles, may help to delimit our subject matter.

Law differs from ethics in at least two ways. First, it is in some respects less comprehensive. Many actions that are legal are nevertheless morally wrong. Unjustifiably breaking a promise that is not legally binding, convincing someone to buy what they don't really need or want, or repeating true but hurtful gossip are examples. Law exists to discourage behavior that society deems dangerous or disruptive enough to warrant governmental intervention. But it does not and should not encompass all ethical standards. In part this is because people reasonably disagree about which standards should be legally enforced, and attempts to enforce unpopular standards may spark social unrest. But also it is because for some sorts of misconduct, government is not the best arbiter. Conduct in the professions, for example, is often best overseen by professional organizations, which can enforce ethical standards by censuring violators or revoking their credentials. More personal forms of ethics govern friendships or familial relations, and sometimes even a person's responsibilities to herself. Law is too clumsy an instrument for such specialized or intimate affairs.

Though not all ethical principles should be laws, all laws should be ethical. Not all are. Laws mandating apartheid or segregation are historic examples. Many laws worldwide give unjust advantages to the interests of powerful groups or individuals. When law and ethics clash, ethics provides a higher court of appeal. It may justify overturning such laws, or disobeying them, if necessary.

Ethics not only opposes ill-considered or outmoded laws, but spurs the development of new ones. Today's laws (including many environmental laws) originated in the activism, and sometimes the sacrifice, of yesterday's moral reformers. This transformative process continues.

Rule-based legal reasoning is basically a matter of ascertaining the relevant facts, locating the laws which govern such facts, and drawing the conclusions specified by the laws. Suppose, for example, that a Tennessee resident attends local dog fights, but does not train or own fighting dogs herself. Has she done anything legally wrong? The law provides a clear answer. The relevant Tennessee statute (TCA §39-14-203) reads in part as follows:

(a) It is unlawful for any person to:

    (1) Own, possess, keep, use or train any bull, bear, dog, cock, swine or other animal, for the purpose of fighting, baiting or injuring another such animal, for amusement, sport or gain;

(2) Cause, for amusement, sport or gain, any animal referenced in subdivision (a)(1) to fight, bait or injure another animal, or each other;

(3) Permit any acts stated in subdivisions (a)(1) and (2) to be done on any premises

(4) Be knowingly present, as a spectator, at any place or building where preparations are being made for an exhibition for the fighting, baiting or injuring of any animal, with the intent to be present at the exhibition, fighting, baiting or injuring.

The legal reasoning needed to answer the question is straightforward. The statute, taken as a prescriptive premise establishes, together with the facts of the case, the prescriptive conclusion that the woman's behavior is legally wrong. (Other statutes stipulate applicable punishments.)

Statutes are enacted by legislatures. But there are also large bodies of case law, comprised of precedents established in the courts, and regulatory law, which is established by administrative bodies, such as the Environmental Protection Agency. This plurality of sources introduces conflict and complexity, so that, although rule-based legal reasoning is simple in principle, its use and interpretation in practice often requires specialized knowledge and training.

Rule-based reasoning in ethics is like legal reasoning, except it appeals to ethical instead of legal rules. Sometimes these ethical rules are explicitly formulated as codes of ethics that prescribe behavior standards for particular professions. Here the resemblance to legal reasoning is especially close. Suppose, for example, that an American logging company intends to clear-cut a forest by methods that will cause significant soil loss. One way to argue against this plan would be to cite the Society of American Foresters' code of ethics. The first item of this code's Principles and Pledges reads:

> Foresters have a responsibility to manage land for both current and future generations. We pledge to practice and advocate management that will maintain the long-term capacity of the land to provide the variety of materials, uses, and values desired by landowners and society
>
> (SAF 2000)

This is an ethical prescription. To cause significant soil loss would violate it by reducing "the capacity of the land to provide the variety of materials, uses, and values desired by landowners and society." Thus there is a sound argument, based on a professional code of ethics, to the prescriptive conclusion that the logging should not be carried out as planned. Of course that argument would probably not by itself settle the matter. One could expect wrangling over the factual premise that the proposed methods of logging would produce significant soil erosion, and the debate might shift to the evidence for this premise.

Still, arguments from professional ethics carry some practical weight. The Society of American Foresters' bylaws provide

processes through which a member's violation of the code may lead to repri-
mand, censure, expulsion from the Society, or other disciplinary action. Any
two persons, whether or not SAF members, may charge a member with violation of the code. Such a charge must be made in writing to the SAF President
and must refer to the specific Pledges alleged to have been violated.

(SAF 2000)

By such means, professional codes of ethics generate pressure for better behavior.

Ethical principles are not always formally codified. But if an ethical argument is to
have wide appeal, then the principles it assumes as premises should at least express
widely held beliefs. Consider this example:

> Climate change is causing and will continue to cause a large number of
> human casualties, mainly in the developing nations of Southeast Asia and sub-
> Saharan Africa.
> Climate change is caused primarily by the burning of fossil fuels in the highly
> developed nations of the northern hemisphere, for their own benefit.
> When some nations perform actions which for their own benefit inflict casu-
> alties upon other nations, the nations causing these casualties owe compensa-
> tion to the nations suffering them.
> ∴ The highly developed nations of the northern hemisphere owe compensation
> for the large number of present and future casualties they are inflicting on the
> developing nations of Southeast Asia and sub-Saharan Africa by their burning
> of fossil fuels.

The first two premises of this argument are true factual descriptions. The third is an
ethical rule. Together the premises validly imply the prescriptive conclusion. The
third premise expresses a principle of international justice that is widely endorsed,
though not so widely practiced. This principle, and principles closely akin to it, have
been invoked since the early 1990s in so far largely unsuccessful efforts to include
such compensation in international treaties on climate change. The fact that this
argument has not yet appreciably affected behavior does not mean it is unsound. We
may know what is right without doing what is right.

Of course, not all rule-based reasoning is valid. The following argument employs
rule-based reasoning fallaciously:

> A ban on driving during the summer months would reduce ozone pollution
> in populated areas.
> We should reduce ozone pollution in populated areas.
> ∴ We should ban driving during the summer months.

The first premise is factual, the second a prescriptive rule. The conclusion may
seem to follow, yet reflection reveals that it does not. Here is a counterexample:
assume that the premises are true; still, there are many ways to reduce ozone pollution without banning driving (one might, for example, strategically limit driving, or

adopt stricter emissions limits), and one or more of these alternatives might better accomplish that goal. More generally, given that we ought to accomplish A, the fact that policy B would accomplish A does not by itself show that we ought to adopt policy B. There may be better ways of accomplishing A.

If, however, policy B is the *only* feasible way to accomplish A, then we might have a solid argument. Here is an argument the likes of which convinced the nations of the world to agree in the late 1980s to the Montreal Protocol on Substances that Deplete the Ozone Layer:

> We ought to stop stratospheric ozone depletion.
> Because the current stratospheric ozone depletion is caused by our use of certain CFCs, the only feasible way to stop it is to ban use of these CFCs.
> ∴   We ought to ban use of these CFCs.

The first premise is a plausible prescriptive statement. Stratospheric ozone depletion, as was noted in section 1.2.1.2, puts everyone on the planet at greater risk of skin cancer and cataracts, and is harmful many other ways. So, once the threat was convincingly demonstrated, there was a wide consensus on the first premise. The second premise is factual. The reasoning, properly interpreted, is valid. Thus the argument is sound, and it proved convincing.

But this pattern of reasoning (that we ought to accomplish A and policy B is the *only* feasible way to do it) is not always sound. Consider this example:

> We ought to eliminate suffering.
> The only feasible way to eliminate suffering is to eliminate all sentient beings.
> ∴   We ought to eliminate all sentient beings.

The first premise is a prescriptive rule. It recommends what appears at first glance to be a laudable goal. The second premise seems true enough. (Sentient beings are those animals, including humans, that can enjoy or suffer.) Sentient life seems inescapably to involve some suffering. If so, then in order to completely eliminate suffering in actual practice we would have to eliminate all sentient beings. The reasoning is valid. Yet the conclusion is plainly false (not to mention horrific), for it requires the elimination of all sensate animals, including humans.

What has gone wrong? Given the argument's validity, the only possible source of error is a premise; and if the second premise is true, the error must lie in the first. The prescriptive claim of this premise is in fact far too strong. We should avoid causing needless suffering and sometimes help alleviate suffering that already exists. But we are not morally obligated *eliminate* suffering altogether—especially not if that requires eliminating all sentient life.

How can we tell when an ethical premise is acceptable and when, like the first premise of this last argument, it must be rejected? The task can be easy when we have a good professional code of ethics to work with; we simply take the required premises from the code, if they are there. But codes of ethics may themselves be flawed. Sometimes they need modification. And if so, then the modifications must themselves be justified. Ultimately, to justify ethical premises, we must appeal to ethical theories. Ethical theories are the subject of the second half of this chapter. But before turning to them, we need to consider another important form of prescriptive reasoning.

2.2.3 Consequentialist Reasoning

Rule-based ethical reasoning is a lot like legal reasoning. Once one has an applicable rule ("law"), one simply judges an action right or wrong by whether or not it conforms to that rule. But there is a different kind of ethical reasoning, *consequentialist reasoning*, according to which the rightness of an action is determined, not by its conformity with ethical law, but by the goodness of its known or probable results. Consequentialist reasoning is the sort of prescriptive reasoning typically used in planning a course of action—a vacation, a political campaign, or an engineering project, for example. In such endeavors, we try to avoid what we regard as bad outcomes and aim for what we consider to be good ones.

Consequentialist *ethical* reasoning does this as well, but it employs more impartial conceptions of good and bad. Consequentialist ethical reasoning surveys various options for action, evaluates the likely consequences of each, and selects one with the aim of creating the most benefit, not just for us or our group, but for all those affected. It is this impartiality that gives the reasoning its moral character.

Section Outline: Section 2.2.3 considers two main kinds of consequentialist reasoning: simple consequentialist reasoning (section 2.2.3.1) and decision tables (section 2.2.3.2). Simple consequentialist reasoning is used when the consequences of our actions are known with practical certainty. Decision tables are used when we're not certain of the consequences of our actions but can estimate their probabilities and are willing to do a little math.

2.2.3.1 Simple Consequentialist Reasoning

Consequentialist reasoning is simplest when the important consequences of each option we are considering are known with practical certainty. Here is an example from public health policy:

1   We have two reasonable options: either to add a small quantity of chlorine to public drinking water or add none.
2   The major consequences of adding a small amount of chlorine are that there will be a slightly higher rate of cancers and cancer deaths, due to the chlorinated compounds in the water, but many fewer deaths by infectious disease; the major consequences of not adding chlorine are that we will have a slightly lower rate of cancers and cancer deaths but a much higher rate of death by infectious disease.

      3   There is greater total benefit in having a slightly higher cancer rate and a much lower fatality rate from infectious disease than in a slightly lower cancer rate and a much higher rate of death by infectious disease.

      4   When faced with a choice of actions, we should choose the one with the greatest total benefit for those affected.

So 5   We should add chlorine to our public drinking water.

Such reasoning has made the addition of chlorine to drinking water a standard public health practice. We are here concerned, however, not with health policy but with the form of the argument. This argument, like every completely articulated consequentialist argument, has five parts, corresponding to the five numbered statements above:

1. **A listing of all the feasible options (courses of action):** It is important to consider all feasible options; if you ignore one, it might be the one that should have been chosen. In our example there are essentially only two options: add the chlorine or not.

2. **A listing of all the important consequences of each option:** In our example, this listing is provided by the second premise. If important consequences are ignored, then the argument can be refuted by pointing them out. I have tried to include the important consequences in this argument, but, not being an expert on the subject, I could be wrong. If the consequences of a given option may vary depending on factors we do not control, then we need to factor in the probabilities of the various possible outcomes. The next section explains how to do that. The basic sort of reasoning discussed in this section works only when we know the consequences of an option with reasonable certainty.

3. **An overall evaluation of the consequences of each option:** In the argument above, this evaluation is expressed in the third premise. The evaluation here seems obvious and hardly in need of further support, but in other arguments it may need to be justified by additional premises. A given option may have various consequences, some positive (e.g., much lower death rate from infectious disease) and some negative (e.g., slightly higher cancer rate). The evaluation of a given option must take all of these into account and arrive at a general assessment. If the values can be expressed numerically on a single scale (with negative values represented by negative numbers), then the value of the option is just the sum of the values of its consequences. But where numerical assessments are not available, we must proceed more informally, as in the example above.

4. **A choice principle:** This is the prescriptive premise needed for deriving the prescriptive conclusion. It is what takes us, in other words, from "is" to "ought." In our sample argument it is the fourth premise. The classical choice principle is: choose the option with the greatest total benefit—or, in case there are no good options, least total loss—for all those affected. However, as is explained in section 2.3.2.3, choice principles may take other forms as well. The choice principle is the fundamental ethical assumption of consequentialist reasoning—so fundamental that it is generally taken for granted and seldom explicitly stated. Yet logically it is essential to the argument. It is a kind of ethical rule, but one

that is much more abstract and general than those typically used in "rule-based" reasoning.

5. **The conclusion:** The conclusion is that we should take the action recommended by the choice principle in conjunction with the other premises. Here it is statement 5. Consequentialist reasoning that takes this form is valid. To criticize it, you must raise doubts about the truth of one or more of the premises.

The premises of the sample argument are all pretty solid, but with regard to the first premise we might question whether something other than chlorine could be added to the water that would not be carcinogenic and yet would prevent infectious disease. If so, then that premise is false and the argument is unsound. To make the argument sound, we would need to consider that third possibility, and things would get more complicated.

2.2.3.2 Decision Tables

Often we do not know the consequences of potential actions with certainty. If we choose a particular option, then, so far as we know, any of several outcomes might occur. In this case consequentialist reasoning takes a more complex form known as a *decision table*, which determines which option is most *likely* to produce the best result. Decision tables are often used by policymakers and economists in cost–benefit analysis (see section 3.2.3.3), but their application is not limited to such contexts.

Construction of a decision table begins—as does simple consequentialist reasoning—with a listing of the feasible options for action. Suppose, for example, that we are designing a storage tank for some hazardous substance and must decide whether to make the tank double-walled or single-walled. These two choices constitute our options. (In a real engineering situation, there would probably be other options, such as varying the thickness of the walls or other design features of the tank, but we are simplifying.)

In the simple consequentialist reasoning of the previous section, each option is assumed to lead with certainty to a given outcome, which may in turn have various consequences—e.g., in that example, a higher cancer rate and lower disease rate. Each option listed in a decision table may, by contrast, have several possible outcomes, each likewise having various consequences. We aren't certain which outcome will occur if we choose that option. In our current example, suppose we consider three possible outcomes for each option:

> Tank never leaks
> Tank develops only a small leak
> Tank develops a major leak.

These outcomes must be *mutually exclusive*; that is, each must rule out the others (for example, if the tank develops only a small leak, that means that it doesn't not leak and it doesn't develop a major leak). And they must also be *exhaustive*; that is, they must cover all the reasonable possibilities (in our example, one of the three outcomes must occur; there is no fourth possibility). The requirements of mutual exclusivity and exhaustiveness are necessary for the analysis to be valid.

Having defined the feasible options and possible outcomes, we must next determine the probability of each outcome, given each option. This step has no parallel in the simple consequentialist reasoning of the previous section, where it was assumed the outcome of each option was already known. Probabilities are usually expressed on a numerical scale from 0 (impossible) to 1 (inevitable). It is helpful to set them out in a decision table, as shown in Table 4. According to this table, the probability of a single walled tank never leaking is 0.9, the probability that a single-walled tank will develop a minor leak is 0.09 and so on. The probabilities of leakage are smaller for a double-walled tank, since it is safer. In practice, these probabilities would be derived from field studies on similar tanks, from engineering considerations, or from computer models. Their accuracy is crucial to a good decision.

Table 4 Probability Table for Design of a Hazardous Materials Storage Tank

Options	Possible Outcomes		
	Never leaks	Minor leak	Major leak
Single wall	0.9	0.09	0.01
Double wall	0.99	0.009	0.001

Notice that the sum of the three outcome probabilities for each option (horizontal row) is 1. This is a result of the fact that the outcomes are mutually exclusive and exhaustive. One and only one of them can happen, so that, given a particular choice of option, the probability of one or another of them happening is 1. That is, one of the three will surely happen.

We must add one more element to the table before it can yield a decision: an estimate of the value (or disvalue) of each possible outcome for each option. To keep things simple, let's suppose we can put a dollar value on the consequences of each outcome for each option: namely the profit or loss to our company resulting from the outcome, given the option. (This makes our decision amoral, since the only interests considered are those of the company, but it will do as an illustration.)

The profit or loss figures for our company are calculated from the total set of consequences for each option and outcome. In our example, these consequences would probably include: the cost of installing and maintaining the tank, the profit gained from using the tank over a specified time period, and the repair and cleanup costs, if any, that we would incur if the tank should leak. If the tank never leaks, we expect to make a profit. But if it leaks, the cost of repairs and cleanup will cut into our profit and may result in a net loss. The loss will be greater the more serious the leak. In Table 5, I have made up some dollar figures that represent the value of the overall consequences for each option and outcome. These profit or loss numbers are placed next to their respective probabilities on the decision table (losses being indicated by negative numbers). The table indicates that if we build the single-walled tank, we will (over some specified period of time) realize a profit of $20,000 if it never leaks, break even if it develops a minor leak and lose $90,000 if it develops a major leak.

Table 5 Decision Table for Design of a Hazardous Materials Storage Tank

Options	Possible Outcomes					
	Never leaks		Minor leak		Major leak	
Single wall	0.9	$20,000	0.09	$0	0.01	–$90,000
Double wall	0.99	$10,000	0.009	–$1,000	0.001	–$100,000

If we built many such tanks, we would expect to realize the $20,000 profit 90 percent of the time, break even 9 percent of the time and lose $90,000 1 percent of the time. Thus, on average, we would expect to realize a profit of (0.9 × $20,000) + (0.09 × $0) + (0.01 × –$90,000) = $17,100 per single-walled tank. This "average profit" is called the expected value of the option (in this case, the option of building the single-walled tank). More generally, the **expected value** for an option is the sum of the probabilities times the values for each possible outcome of that option. Turning to the second option, if we built many double-walled tanks, we'd expect to make an average profit of (0.99 × $10,000) + (0.009 × –$1,000) + (0.001 × –$100,000) = $9,791. This is the expected value of the double-walled option.

Since, on average, we'd expect to make more money with the single-walled option, our best choice is to build the single-walled tank. That is the decision which the table yields. The choice principle here is to maximize expected value—that is, choose the option that on average produces the greatest positive value or (if loss is unavoidable) the least loss for our company.

In general, decision problems may consider any number of options and any number of outcomes. For each option–outcome pair, we must, as in our example, supply a probability and a value (cost or benefit). In our example, costs and benefits were measured in dollars, but in theory the procedure would work with non-monetary measures of value too.

To summarize: A decision table is constructed in five steps (which, incidentally, do *not* correspond point-for-point with the five parts of an elementary consequentialist argument that were discussed in the previous section):

1. List the possible *options* for action. These must be mutually exclusive; that is, it must be impossible for more than one to occur.
2. List all the possible *outcomes* (i.e., sets of consequences) for each option. These must be mutually exclusive and exhaustive. They are exhaustive if, once that option is chosen, at least one of them must occur.
3. Determine the probability of each possible outcome for each option.
4. Assign a value (positive, negative or zero) to each possible outcome of each option.
5. Select the option (or, in case of a tie, any one of the options) with the greatest expected value.

Step 5 is the application of the *choice principle* for the decision table—that is, the prescriptive premise that is needed to derive the prescriptive conclusion that tells us which option we should choose.

The only costs and benefits considered in the previous example were for a firm whose sole concern was profit. We ignored the environmental and human costs of a leaky tank, except as these might result in costs to the firm. Hence our decision was, at best, prudential (with respect to the firm's interests), not ethical.

It is possible to include environmental and human costs and benefits in a decision table and hence use it for ethical, rather than merely financial, purposes. Indeed, the decisions made by policymakers often include these things. Let's see how this might alter our example. Suppose, for example, that the storage tank was to be located near a sensitive wetland and also that a serious leak might result in human injury or death. Then, from an ethical point of view, we would need to include harm to humans or the environment in evaluating losses. We might therefore regard the $90,000 and $100,000 figures or losses in the case of a major leak as gross underestimates.

Human or environmental losses, however, are not readily quantifiable in monetary terms. If a dangerous leak occurs and someone is killed, how could we quantify the losses to that person and those who care about her? Is a human life worth $1,000,000? $10,000,000? Sometimes amounts such as these are assigned arbitrarily. Sometimes other considerations are used. It has been argued, for example, that the worth of a human life is equal to that person's earning power over a lifetime—or that the worth of a life can be calculated from the amount of risk a person is willing to accept in order to earn a given salary. Both suggestions, and others like them, are problematic. Is the life of a retired person who will henceforth earn no money therefore worth nothing? Is the life of a rich person who is willing to accept little risk to earn more money thereby worth more than a poor person who must accept a high risk job to support a family?

And how do we quantify potential injury done to a wetland? Is it simply the loss of dollars due to decreased hunting and fishing in the area? Or should we include the "scenic" value of the wetland as well? Should we count dollar loss just to people now alive, or dollar loss to future people affected by the damage? What about injury to the plants and animals in the wetland themselves? Should their losses be part of the equation, or don't they count? What about the wetland ecosystem? Is it an entity capable suffering loss over and above the losses of the individual organisms that comprise it? If so, should its losses count in the decision?

The practice of assigning monetary figures to things whose value is not normally understood monetarily is called *shadow pricing*. Though water quality or human life have no standard monetary values, we may attempt to assign them shadow prices. Environmental economists have developed methods for doing this. (These methods are discussed in more detail in section 3.2.3 and its subsections.) The effect of including such shadow prices on the outcome of a decision table analysis can be significant.

To illustrate how different values can produce a different decision, suppose we include shadow prices for the threat to both humans and the environment from a serious leak.

We assume that a minor leak will not significantly harm humans or the environment, but a major leak would on average do damage in the range of $1,500,000 to humans and the ecosystem. Then, adding this loss to the previous figures for a major leak, the decision table would look like Table 6. The expected value of the single-walled option is now $(0.9 \times \$20,000) + (0.09 \times \$0) + (0.01 \times -\$1,590,000) = \$2,100$ and the expected value of the double-walled option is $(0.99 \times \$10,000) + (0.009 \times -\$1,000) + (0.001 \times -\$1,600,000) = \$8,291$. When we thus consider human health and the environment, the double-walled tank is the better option.

Table 6 Revised Decision Table for Design of a Hazardous Materials Storage Tank

Options	Possible Outcomes					
	Never leaks		Minor leak		Major leak	
Single wall	0.9	$20,000	0.09	$0	0.01	-$1,590,000
Double wall	0.99	$10,000	0.009	-$1,000	0.001	-$1,600,000

There are four questions to ask in evaluating the reasoning of a decision table. The first two concern the options for action and the possible outcomes (the categories listed to the left and at the top of the decision table); the second two concern the probabilities and values that are listed in the table, respectively:

1. Have all the options been considered and are they categorized in a way that makes them mutually exclusive? If the analysis neglects an option which might be better than any of those considered, the decision can easily be suboptimal. Perhaps, for example, the best option in the storage tank case is one we never even considered: not building the tank at all and changing the manufacturing process so that the chemical it was to contain is no longer needed. If the options are not mutually exclusive, then the best decision might be to choose more than one of them, but the analysis will be insensitive to that.
2. Have the outcomes been categorized in a way that makes them mutually exclusive, exhaustive and also perspicuous? If they are not mutually exclusive, then more than one of them can occur simultaneously, which may cause us to misrepresent their probabilities. If they are not exhaustive, then the analysis will ignore possible consequences that might affect the decision. The categorization of the outcomes should also be perspicuous, so that they illuminate, rather than obscure, important aspects of the decision. It should not lump disparate results into the same category. The outcomes we considered in the storage tank case all had to do with leakage of the tank. This way of conceptualizing the problem may lead us to overlook other distinctive outcomes, such as a tank explosion. Presumably, this would fall under the category "Major Leak". But if we had considered it as a separate category, our decision table might have been quite different. Explicit consideration of this possibility may have led us to revise values or probabilities and, ultimately, to make a different decision.
3. Are the probabilities listed in the decision table accurate? The best probabilities are extrapolated from a track record of solid data. Unfortunately, good data are

not always available, and we may have to guess. In such cases, it is wise to calculate expected values using a range of probabilities, to get some sense of whether and, if so, how the decision would change if the probabilities were wrong.

4. Are the values listed in the decision table appropriate and accurate?

The fourth question is the most difficult of all. The systematic effort to answer such questions is called **axiology** (the theory of values). Axiology is traditionally bound up with ethical theory, and the effort to disentangle and understand the two occupies much of the remainder of this book.

• 2.3 ETHICAL THEORIES

Section 2.2.1 explained this fundamental logical principle: *there is no valid way to deduce a nontrivial prescriptive statement from non-prescriptive premises*; you can't get an "ought" from an "is." To prove an action-guiding conclusion, in other words, we must assume one or more action-guiding premises—one or more "ought" premises. In rule-based reasoning, those "ought" premises are the prescriptive rules. In consequentialist reasoning, the "ought" premise is the choice principle.

How can we tell whether such "ought" premises are correct? In many cases we can't. But where we can, the best way to do it is by appeal to ethical (or moral—I use these two terms interchangeably) theories. Ethical theories are broad philosophical accounts of what moral action is and how it is justified. Originated by the world's great moral visionaries, they are, over time, sharpened by logical analysis, tempered by the lessons of history, adjusted to the discoveries of science, and corrected by the critiques of those whom they have marginalized. Thus they undergo constant—and lately quite rapid—development. Well-developed ethical theories embody more careful thought and wider experience than any of us could attain alone. Though not the final ethical truth (if there even is such a thing), they are the best that human reason has to offer at present.

One of the functions of an ethical theory is to define the scope of ethics. It was noted in the Preface that over time this scope (there called the "moral community") tends to broaden. Within the moral community it is useful to make additional distinctions. Those entities for whom ethical action can occur and who themselves, or whose welfare or interests, matter ethically are said to be **morally considerable**. Morally considerable beings comprise the moral community. They are sometimes also called **moral patients**. For a long time the only moral patients widely recognized by mainstream ethical theories were people; but, as Chapters 5 and 6 explain, some recent theories of animal and environmental ethics include other living beings as well.

Among moral patients, there are certain special individuals, known as **moral agents**, who are competent to perform ethical actions and whose actions ought to be governed by ethics. Moral agency requires both an understanding of ethics itself—at least to the extent of being able to distinguish right action from wrong—and the self-control necessary for choosing the right action. Normal human adults, including you and I, are moral agents, but not all humans are. Infants, for example, or certain mentally impaired adults, though they are morally considerable, do not understand ethics or are incapable of acting on it, and hence are not moral agents. A patient who is not an agent—a baby, for example—is called a **mere patient**. But anyone who is a moral agent is a moral patient as well. A complete ethical theory explains who the moral agents and patients are and why they or their interests matter ethically.

Section Outline: The three most widely used kinds of ethical theory are deontology, consequentialism and virtue theories. Broadly speaking, deontology (section 2.3.1) justifies the sorts of ethical rules used in rule-based reasoning, consequentialism (section 2.3.2) justifies the choice principles and value assessments used in consequentialist reasoning, and virtue theory (section 2.3.3) provides means of assessing actions by their contributions to and expressions of human character.

These are not the only kinds of ethical theories (others are introduced in later chapters), nor is this section a complete introduction to any of them. Only the basics needed for an understanding of later chapters are presented here.

2.3.1 Deontology

The rules assumed in rule-based ethical reasoning prescribe a particular action under certain specific conditions. Such rules (which are sometimes regarded as ethical "laws") are most often justified by deontological theories. **Deontological theories** are ethical theories that provide procedures for determining what the ethical "laws" are and that evaluate actions as right if they conform to these "laws" and wrong if they violate them.

Because deontological theories evaluate actions by their accord with the rules, they regard the *consequences* of actions with detachment. Whether the results of a particular action are good or bad is irrelevant—or, at best, secondary—for them. One does what is right on principle, because it is right, not because of anticipated benefits, either for self or others. Assuming, for example, that ethical "law" prohibits harming innocent people and that future people are innocent, it follows that we should not harm future people—not even if doing so produces more good than harm. Duty trumps benefit. Proper treatment of individuals is more important than the welfare of the whole.

Section Outline: Section 2.3.1 begins with an account of history's most influential deontological theory, that of Immanuel Kant (section 2.3.1.1), then moves on to more contemporary deontologies (section 2.3.1.2), and finally to a brief discussion of the most important criticisms of deontological theories (section 2.3.1.3).

2.3.1.1 Kant's Deontology

A deontological theory must, of course, say what the ethical rules are. But a moral theory is more than just a list of rules. It also explains how to tell correct rules from incorrect ones. Sometimes, as in the seminal deontological theory of Immanuel Kant (1724–1804), the rules are all supposed to be derived from a single fundamental principle. Kant called this fundamental principle the ***categorical imperative***. "Categorical" in this context means "without conditions"—that is, applicable regardless of one's aims. Kant, a leader of the European Enlightenment, thought that any rational being could see the legitimacy of the categorical imperative, independently both of her personal aims and of religious dogmas. That is why it is "without conditions."

Kant formulated the categorical imperative in several ways, which he regarded as different expressions of the same idea. But scholars today treat them as distinct. I'll mention two of them here, since these two have had the most influence on the environmental ethics.

One is known as the ***formula of humanity***: "Always treat humanity, whether in yourself or another, as an end and never merely as a means." To treat a person as an end is to treat her as an autonomous individual, whose purposes are legitimately her own, not as a mere instrument for furthering one's own purposes, or as a mere object. Such treatment is called ***respect***.

The formula of humanity limits the class of moral patients to "humanity." "Humanity," as Kant uses the term, does not mean the species *Homo sapiens*, which is what it ordinarily means and what it means elsewhere in this book. Rather, it signifies the "human" nature embodied in the capacities for **autonomy** (free choice and self-control) and rationality. These are among the capacities that make us moral agents. Angels or aliens from other planets might have them as well, though they are not *biologically* human. Morality can exist, according to Kant, only because there are such free and rational agents. This gives them an unconditional and superlative moral value that he calls **dignity**. Kant's esteem for free, rational beings reflects the optimistic humanism of the Enlightenment era. It is of a piece with newly emerging conceptions of political freedom, enlightened progress, democracy, and human rights.

Yet the imperative to treat persons as ends is hardly sufficient to determine in any detail what the ethical rules ought to be. For this purpose, another formulation of the categorical imperative, known as the ***formula of universal law***, offers more guidance. Kant states it as follows: "act only according to that maxim by which you can at the same time will that it should become a universal law." A ***maxim*** is a prescriptive rule. The formula of universal law provides a test for determining which maxims are correct. The test works like this: given a proposed maxim, consider whether you can consistently and rationally will it to be law that everyone should obey. If so, then that maxim is legitimate. If not, then it isn't.

Suppose, for example, that you are wondering whether humans ought to stop reproducing, in order to prevent further damage to non-human life. The proposed maxim in this case might be: when human destructiveness to non-human life reaches a certain level, none of us should have children. Could we consistently and rationally will this maxim to be a universal law, knowing that if it were, and if we had reached the specified level of destructiveness, humanity would within a century or so cease to exist? Not on Kant's view, for that would be rationally to will the elimination of rational will—a kind of self-contradiction. Moreover, it would treat humanity as a mere means, to be sacrificed for sake of other forms of life. So, according to Kant's procedure, the maxim must be rejected; to obey it is morally wrong.

The beauty of the categorical imperative, in either formulation, lies in its impartiality. It requires consistency and fairness. In this and other respects it resembles the Golden Rule: "do unto others as you would have others do unto you." The formula of universal law says, in effect, "do as you could rationally and consistently will everyone (including yourself) to do." But there are differences. The Golden Rule tells us only how to treat others, but not how to treat ourselves. Moreover, as traditionally formulated, it relies too heavily on the preferences of the person applying it. A recluse, for example, who wanted only solitude, might by the Golden Rule conclude (incorrectly) that he should leave others alone—even if they need him. The formula of universal law does better in both these respects. Each, however, evokes the same spirit of impartiality and fairness.

For Kant that spirit was not a dogma, to be accepted on the basis of external authority, but a deliverance of pure reason, lucidly evident, or capable of being made so, to the conscientious, autonomous and rational self. Right actions, says Kant:

> need no recommendation from any subjective disposition or taste, so as to be looked upon with immediate favor and delight; nor do they need any immediate propensity or feeling for them; they present the will that practices them as the object of an immediate respect, and nothing but reason is required to *impose* them upon the will.
>
> (Kant 1785, 4:435)

In concluding *Critique of Practical Reason* Kant wrote "Two things fill the mind with ever new and increasing admiration and reverence, the more often and more steadily one reflects on them: *the starry heavens above me and the moral law within me*" (Kant 1788: 5:161). So highly did the Enlightenment esteem rational morality.

2.3.1.2 Contemporary Deontologies

Kant's ethics is classic deontology. But Kant's formulations of the categorical imperative are subject to many interpretive difficulties, and their use in deriving ethical rules is controversial. Contemporary deontologists are more pragmatic and less inclined to posit an awe-inspiring and absolute "moral law within." Their aim is typically more modest: to construct workable ethical rules that can be understood and accepted by reasonable people in a social context. They may hold that the correct ethical rules are simply those that no informed, reasonable person could from an objective point of view reasonably reject as a framework for social order. A deontological theory that tests its rules by such a criterion is, accordingly, called a **social contract theory**.

In social contract theory much depends, of course, on what counts as a reasonable person. Purely selfish people can be in a narrowly instrumental sense rational, but they are not "reasonable," in the relevant sense. Genuinely reasonable people understand the differing views of others and are willing to cooperate honestly with them by obeying mutually acceptable rules, even at some cost to themselves. They must, in their behavior at least, transcend narrow and immediate selfishness.

One way to achieve that transcendence in thought is deliberately to ignore individuating features of one's own identity: gender, race, income, talents, etc. In the metaphor of philosopher John Rawls, one places oneself behind a "veil of ignorance" with regard to such features, imagining that upon emergence from the veil one could be anyone in any position of society. Only behind the veil does one decide (in negotiation with others behind the veil) what the rules should be. The aim of this exercise is to strip away bias so that the resulting rights and rules are fair to all. Such a thought process is not easy; nor does it always produce agreement. But it does point us in the right direction.

Often the rules of social contract theories are formulated as rights. A *right* is a claim to respectful treatment that engenders correlative duties for moral agents. One ethical rule justified by nearly all deontological theories is the right that everyone has not to be harmed without good reason. Correlatively, this right imposes a duty on moral agents not to harm anyone without good reason. This rule is justifiable on a social contract view because reasonable people cannot will, or agree to, letting others harm them without good reason. As with all deontological rules, this one holds regardless of benefit. I may not harm you even to provide a much greater benefit to myself—or even to someone else—or even to you.

There are, of course, exceptions. A person may be harmed if she gives her consent. So, for example, if I need surgery, I may consent to have a surgeon cut me open (a kind of harm), for the benefits that may result. But a surgeon may make no incision without consent. There are exceptions also for self-defense; I may harm an attacker to prevent harm to myself. And there are other sorts of exceptions; the details vary from theory to theory.

2.3.1.3 Weaknesses of Deontological Theories

One of the weaknesses of deontological theories lies in such exceptions. Once all the exceptions are stated, the rules become very complicated—and many alleged exceptions are controversial, so that no formulation ever seems to make the rules quite right.

Moreover, all deontological theories face the problem of what to do when ethical rules make conflicting demands. As the human world becomes increasingly complex, so do the demands made by deontological rules. Conflicts are especially acute in times of environmental, political or economic crisis, when to save one thing we must forego another. In such situations it may be impossible to obey all the rules or respect all the rights that deontology posits, so that we seem forced to resort to the weighing of alternatives that is characteristic of consequentialist reasoning. Some deontologists hope to resolve conflicts by prioritizing ethical rules, so that some take precedence over others. But it is difficult to get rational consensus on any such prioritization, and prioritization itself adds to the complexity.

Deontology has difficulty, too, in defining the class of moral patients. Traditional deontologists (including Kant) overlooked this problem. But, as was noted above, not all human beings (in the biological sense)—that is, members of the species *Homo sapiens*—are moral agents. Infants, small children, and the severely mentally disabled, lack the rationality necessary for moral agency, yet obviously they matter morally. They are therefore moral patients. This raises the question of whether there are other non-rational moral patients as well—which is the topic of Chapters 5 and 6.

Another problem with deontology is that strict adherence to its rules (and corresponding neglect of consequences) can be very costly—and not just in terms of wealth. Kant himself endorsed the slogan, *fiat iustitia, pereat mundus* (do justice though the world perish)—though, shrinking perhaps from its horrific implications, he softened it to "Let justice reign, even if all the rogues in the world perish because of it" (Kant 1795: 8:378–79). Still, the potential for abuse of such an idea is obvious.

Yet precisely because of this insistence on principle regardless of consequences, deontology has promoted moral steadfastness, even in the face of chaos and violence. Deontological ethical theories lend intellectual integrity to such landmark documents as the American Bill of Rights and the United Nations Universal Declaration of Human Rights (1948). And they have figured large in the struggles for women's rights, civil rights and gay rights worldwide.

2.3.2 Consequentialism

Yet deontology is not the best theoretical framework in all circumstances, for often consequences *are* what matters most. Consequentialist reasoning takes this for granted. The aim of such reasoning is *not* (as in deontology) to determine what is right according to some prescribed set of ethical rules, but to evaluate potential actions by the good or bad effects they would produce. In general, a consequentialist theory is any theory according to which the rightness or wrongness of an action depends on the goodness or badness of its consequences.

Consequentialist *ethical* theories understand "goodness" and "badness" not just as goodness or badness for ourselves, but for all moral patients affected by the action, considered impartially and collectively. Thus a **consequentialist ethic** holds that the rightness or wrongness of an action is determined by the likely overall goodness or badness of its outcome for all affected moral patients. Any consequentialist ethic can be divided into two parts:

1. An **axiology**—that is, a theory of moral value—which determines the class of moral patients, defines what counts as good or bad for them, and explains how to aggregate (that is, add up) and compare degrees of goodness or badness for groups of them; and
2. A **choice principle**, which stipulates how the rightness or wrongness of actions depends upon their good and bad consequences for these individuals. The choice principle provides the "ought" premises in consequentialist reasoning.

This book considers several different consequentialist ethics. In all cases, it is important to distinguish and define the axiology and the choice principle.

This section introduces the main ideas of consequentialism by considering its most prominent form: utilitarianism. *Utilitarianism* is a kind of consequentialist ethic that defines goodness as happiness or welfare and badness as unhappiness or lack of welfare and that regards right action as action that promotes aggregate goodness.

Section Outline: Section 2.3.2 begins with a general characterization (section 2.3.2.1) of utilitarianism and then considers various utilitarian axiologies (2.3.2.2) and choice principles (2.3.2.3). Section 2.3.2.4 explains the important distinction between act and rule consequentialism. Section 2.3.2.5 provides a general critique of consequentialist theories.

Once again, discussion here is restricted to ideas that turn up in later chapters.

2.3.2.1 Utilitarianism

The term "utilitarianism" is often misunderstood. It has nothing to do with usefulness, as in the term "utility knife," which denotes a knife with many uses. *Utility*, as the term is used in utilitarian theory, is the degree to which the good results of an action exceed its bad results. *Classical utilitarians*—most especially Jeremy Bentham (1748–1832) and John Stuart Mill (1806–1873)—who identify goodness with happiness and badness with unhappiness take the utility of an action to be the degree to which the happiness it produces exceeds the unhappiness it produces, for all moral patients affected by it. Utility in the classical sense can be positive (when happiness predominates over unhappiness), negative (when the opposite is true) or zero (when happiness and unhappiness are either absent or precisely balanced).

A moral patient is, according to classical utilitarianism, any being capable of happiness or unhappiness. This implies that many non-human animals, as well as humans, are moral patients. However, the classical utilitarians, while admitting the ethical importance of animals, ignored them in the bulk of their writings, as did nearly all utilitarians through most of the twentieth century. This section does too, but section 5.4 and its subsections and section 5.6 consider utilitarian animal ethics in detail.

The choice principle for Mill's and Bentham's classical versions of utilitarianism is: maximize utility. That is, we ought to perform whatever action produces the greatest total utility—i.e., the greatest possible excess of happiness over unhappiness—not just for the one performing it, but for all moral patients who are affected by it. If two actions each maximize utility, then they are equally acceptable. Where outcomes are uncertain, so that decision-making requires a decision table, the classical utilitarian choice principle is: maximize *expected* utility—that is, expected value, value being understood as utility (see section 2.2.3.2).

Ideally, the values used in a utilitarian decision table would be measured not in dollars, as in the examples in section 2.2.3.2, but in units of goodness—utility units. But because utility is notoriously difficult to measure, there is no standard way to do this. Economic value is therefore often used as a kind of proxy for utility, in ways that will be explained in section 3.2 and its subsections.

Utilitarianism has a number of variants that play important roles in later chapters. One source of variation is that there are three different concepts of utility. These yield three different utilitarian axiologies.

2.3.2.2 Axiologies

The first and oldest of the utilitarian axiologies is **hedonism**—the idea that goodness is pleasure and badness is pain. Mill and Bentham sometimes also equate *happiness* with pleasure and the absence of pain. More precisely, **hedonistic utilitarianism** defines utility as the sum of the values of pleasure, which count positively, and of pain, which counts negatively. Situations in which there is much pleasure and little pain therefore have positive utility. Those in which there is much pain and little pleasure have negative utility. Those in which pleasure and pain are precisely balanced have a utility of zero. Hedonistic utilitarians think that the aim of ethics is to create a more pleasurable and less painful world. The best actions are therefore those that bring about the greatest pleasure with the least pain, not just for those who perform the action, but for all affected.

But pleasure and the absence of pain are a crude and incomplete measure of goodness. Pleasure, after all, can be induced by drugs or even by direct electrical stimulation of the pleasure centers of the brain. When unconnected with the rest of our lives, such pleasures, however intense, have little meaning and can hardly be said to be good. Many people prefer other things of value—accomplishment, meaning, knowledge, fame, power or moral duty—to pleasure, and might still want these things even if they produced no pleasure.

Thus many utilitarians conclude that goodness should be defined, not as pleasure and the absence of pain, but as fulfillment of desire (preference satisfaction). This view, which is called **preference utilitarianism**, is the second of the utilitarian axiologies. It defines utility as the degree to which preference satisfaction exceeds preference frustration. When preference frustration is greater than preference satisfaction, utility is negative. Whereas hedonistic utilitarianism simply stipulates that the good is pleasurable experience (and nothing else), according to preference utilitarianism what counts as good varies, depending on a person's preferences. Often preference utilitarians assume that we can each autonomously determine what is good for us by choosing our life projects.

Preference utilitarianism is highly influential. It provides a justification for democracy, for (in theory, at least) people's preferences regarding how they are governed are in aggregate maximally satisfied if each has an equal vote. It also underlies neoclassical economics, as will be explained in section 3.2.1.

But preference utilitarianism, too, has problems, for preference satisfaction is not the same thing as goodness—or as happiness. Many preferences are frivolous or arbitrary; satisfying them may leave us empty and disappointed. The satisfaction of other preferences (e.g., for addictive substances, junk food, or child pornography) is degrading or harmful. Sometimes a thing for which we had no preference at all turns out to be good for us. Sometimes, too, we do better by just not wanting so much—that is, by eliminating preferences rather than satisfying them. Preference satisfaction, then, differs significantly from both goodness and happiness. (This point is further elaborated in section 3.2.5.)

Faced with such objections to the equation of goodness with preference satisfaction, preference utilitarians often qualify their view. Rather than defining goodness as satisfaction of preferences in general, they define it as satisfaction of **considered preferences**—preferences that a fully informed person has carefully examined and rationally endorsed. But even considered preferences, though less susceptible to the problems just mentioned, are not immune from them. There seem, for example, to be rational people, as fully informed and cognizant as anyone, who still prefer to play video games all day, eat too much, smoke, do drugs, oppress others, or commit suicide. One can object that these people are not *fully* rational or *fully* informed. But who among us is?

We might, of course, idealize, defining considered preferences as those which a *perfectly* rational and *perfectly* well informed person would endorse, on the assumption that such a person would prefer only what is good. But the problem with this strategy is there are no such people. If we have an idea of what they would prefer, we certainly did not get it from them. Probably it is just our best guess as to what is genuinely good for people.

Preferences, then, seem to have been a distraction. We set out to define goodness or happiness in terms of preferences. But definitions in terms of the preferences of real people proved to be inaccurate. Then we idealized, trying to consider only the preferences of perfect people. But that requires a prior conception of goodness. Why not, then, just forget preferences and ask directly, "What really is good for people?" This brings us to the third utilitarian axiology.

Objective welfare utilitarianism (sometimes called objective-list utilitarianism) holds that goodness does not depend on what we prefer but on certain objective aspects of our lives. These may include health, adequate wealth, longevity, security, freedom from oppression, knowledge, meaningful work, rich interpersonal relationships, or the like. Sometimes objective welfare theories also count enjoyment and the absence of suffering as objectively good, thus subsuming hedonistic welfare under objective welfare.

Of course, people do not entirely agree on which objective features to include in this list. Not everyone values all of these things. Someone who does not value security—preferring, for example, a life of danger and adventure—might object that security is not good for him. It seems patronizing to respond that security is good for him, regardless of what he thinks. So there is tension between preference-based and objective-welfare-based conceptions of goodness. Utilitarian ethical reasoning may employ either, but each, as we have seen, has disadvantages. To evaluate such reasoning intelligently, then, one must understand the relative merits of these axiologies.

2.3.2.3 Choice Principles

The second major component of any consequentialist theory is its choice principle, which determines how, according to the theory, the rightness or wrongness of actions depends upon their good and bad consequences. The choice principle is what makes the theory prescriptive. It transforms axiology into ethics, carrying us from "is" to "ought."

The choice principle of the classical utilitarianism of Bentham and Mill is: *maximize* utility. It urges us in moral matters always to do what is absolutely best. But there is something frenzied about such an ideal. If strictly interpreted, it implies that courses of action whose results would be good, but not maximally good, are forbidden; our duty is always to produce the highest level of utility possible. This seems excessive.

A more plausible variant of the classical view allows for degrees of rightness and wrongness, considering an action right to the degree to which its consequences approximate utility maximization. We may then relax the choice principle a bit to allow actions that do not maximize utility but are nevertheless "good enough." (Of course, we then need an account of what "good enough" means in a given context.) Appealing to such a relaxed choice principle is called **satisficing**. Satisficing agrees with maximizing in rejecting all options at the lower end of the utility scale. But it is comfortable with a wider range of options at the higher end.

Section 4.6.2 will briefly consider yet a third choice principle: maximizing average utility—that is, utility per capita. But it is best to postpone discussion of that principle until the stage is properly set.

Every consequentialist argument must assume, either implicitly or explicitly, a choice principle. Maximizing total utility, satisficing and maximizing average utility are three common choice principles, but not the only ones. In evaluating consequentialist reasoning, it is important to identify the choice principle that is used and to ask whether it is appropriate.

2.3.2.4 Act vs. Rule Consequentialism

One problem with most choice principles is that they require us to keep a careful tally of the likely consequences of each of our ethically significant actions. Consequentialist theories that require this sort of action-by-action calculation are instances of **act consequentialism**. Act consequentialism may be impractical. For one thing, we often don't have enough information to be able to predict consequences accurately—especially when we are dealing on long time scales. For another, the effort required to gather information and make the relevant evaluations can be so time-consuming as not to be worth the bother. Thus it seems absurd to require that we perform a utilitarian calculation for each of our ethically significant actions.

But maybe we don't need to. Many consequentialists have pointed out that the usual rules of everyday ethics—maxims, like "don't steal," and even abstract principles like the Golden Rule—usually produce better consequences when followed than when ignored. Like deontologists, these so-called **rule consequentialists** accept ethical rules as a basis for action, but unlike deontologists they justify the rules by the good consequences they produce. To act ethically, they say, we need not evaluate the consequences of each action; we just follow the rules, using rule-based reasoning as discussed above. Some rule consequentialists regard such rules as definitive of ethics and hence always to be obeyed. Others regard them as approximations that may be disobeyed in special cases when following them would obviously not produce the best consequences. In these exceptional cases, they say, we do need to do our best to tally the utilities of consequences for a given action or construct a decision table to arrive at a correct decision.

In deciding what to do, rule consequentialists generally use rule-based reasoning, just as deontologists do. They may even use the same rules. But when a rule is in question, they will not appeal, like Kant, to pure reason or, like many contemporary deontologists, to an idealized social contract. Rather, they will reason consequentially, from some axiology and choice principle, to that rule.

2.3.2.5 *Weaknesses of Consequentialism*

The classic objection to consequentialism is that it permits underserved harm to achieve greater good—in other words, that it allows injustice. Suppose, for example, that it benefits a populous community to dump their sewage in a river that provides the water supply of a much smaller community downstream. To build a sewage plant or dispose of the sewage in any other way would cost them great trouble. They are, of course, causing trouble for the people downstream. But since the number of people downstream is small and the number in the upstream community is great, the dumping (let's suppose) produces more happiness upstream than unhappiness downstream. Suppose also that all other options produce less utility overall. Then, by consequentialist reasoning, the dumping should continue!

No deontological theory would permit this conclusion, for the dumping disrespects the people downstream, causing them undeserved harm. They could not reasonably consent to being treated this way. Both the Golden Rule and the categorical imperative would forbid such dumping.

So why does consequentialism not forbid it—or even require it? The problem is that consequentialism considers only the totality of harms and benefits, not their distribution among individuals. It thus permits a majority to benefit at the expense of a minority, if that maximizes goodness. This is unjust. Deontology, which posits individual rights, sees things from the individual's point of view, and so condemns such injustice.

Consequentialism also faces complex and often technical problems concerning which axiologies and choice principles to use. But since these matters will occupy us much in later chapters, they need not be discussed further here.

2.3.3 Deontology and Consequentialism Contrasted and Conjoined

The most prominent objection to consequentialism, as was noted in the previous section, is that it permits injustice for the sake of the common good. But deontology suffers from the opposite problem: it sometimes insists on justice to the detriment of the common good. (Recall Kant's endorsement of the slogan "Do justice though the world perish.") This tension between justice for the individual and the collective welfare of the group haunts ethical decision-making. To decide well, we need to consider both—that is, think deontologically *and* consequentially.

The wisdom of considering both is instructively illustrated by the structure of the United States Constitution. Valuing overall welfare, the framers of the Constitution saw the advantages of democracy, a government designed to maximize preference satisfaction in the political realm. That was applied preference utilitarianism, a form of consequentialism. But they realized, too, that democracies are subject to "the tyranny of the majority," when a majority satisfies its preferences by using its voting power to suppress or exploit a minority. Hence the framers also crafted inviolable rules, in the form of a Constitutional Bill of Rights that limits the powers of the majority by guaranteeing fundamental rights (freedom of speech, freedom of religion, etc.) even if these frustrate the preferences of the majority. This is applied deontology. The practicality and resilience of the resulting political institutions lies in a somewhat uneasy balance between these two kinds of thinking.

We have considered deontological and consequentialist ethical theories in their pure forms. Even so, the discussion has been oversimplified. More sophisticated ethical theories often have hybrid features, allowing them to support both consequentialist and deontological reasoning. But to go any deeper into these matters would take us too far afield.

2.3.4 Virtue Theories

Deontology and consequentialism are the two most influential kinds of ethical theory. But they are not the only kinds. This section considers their chief rival: virtue ethics. Virtue ethics are distinguished by a fundamental difference in aim. If the deontologist's characteristic question is "Which actions are right, according to the moral law?" and the consequentialist's is "Which actions produce the best consequences?" the virtue theorist's is "What sort of person should I be?" Whereas deontology and consequentialism focus on proper action, virtue theory considers the whole person. To be virtuous is not merely to act morally; it is to have attained a disciplined integrity of thought, habit, feeling and action. A *virtue ethic*, in other words, is an ethic that aims for excellence of character.

Virtue ethics has its own form of prescriptive reasoning. Consider this example from philosopher Tom Hill:

> A wealthy eccentric bought a house in a neighborhood I know. The house was surrounded by a beautiful display of grass, plants and flowers, and it was shaded by a huge old avocado tree. But the grass required cutting, the flowers needed tending, and the man wanted more sun. So he cut the whole lot down and covered the yard with asphalt. After all it was his property, and he was not fond of plants.
>
> It was a small operation, but it reminded me of the strip-mining of large sections of the Appalachians. In both cases, of course, there were reasons for the destruction, and property rights could be cited as justification. But I could not help but wonder, "What sort of person would do a thing like that?"
>
> (Hill 1983: 47)

Hill evaluates the neighbor's actions neither by their accord with ethical rules nor by the value or disvalue of their consequences, but by their contribution to or expression of his moral character. Implicit in this passage is the thought that only a person of poorly developed character could so fail to appreciate natural beauty as to destroy it wantonly, merely for his own convenience.

Virtue ethicists usually analyze character into virtues and vices, and they use consistency with virtue as a criterion of moral rightness. So, for example, later in the same paper Hill says that what is wrong with covering one's lawn with asphalt is that it violates the virtue of humility. More generally, to obtain a prescriptive conclusion, virtue ethicists often:

- Consider how performing or not performing a given action will exemplify this or that virtue or vice, thus enhancing or detracting from the agent's moral character;
- Assume (this is the requisite prescriptive premise) that one ought or ought not perform an action insofar as one becomes more virtuous or more vicious in doing so; and
- Draw their conclusion accordingly.

But reasoning in virtue theory is quite varied, and this is only an example. Virtue-ethical reasoning, however, generally requires an understanding of what the virtues are. Thus it presupposes an ethical theory.

Aristotle (384–322 BCE) is often regarded as the founder of virtue theory. He and other classical Greeks recognized four great virtues: wisdom, justice, temperance and courage. On Aristotle's theory, each virtue is a mean between two extremes, both of which are vices. Thus, for example, courage is a mean between the vices of cowardice and recklessness. But later theorists pointed out that this scheme works well only for certain kinds of virtues. To the Greek virtues, later Christian thinkers added faith, hope and love. (The last of these, which is in Greek *agape* and in Latin *caritas*, is sometimes also translated as "charity.")

Environmental virtue theorists sometimes propose new virtues, on the ground that the environmental crisis demands novel forms of moral excellence. According to

Ronald Sandler, for example, the environmentally virtuous person has a "capacity to appreciate, respect and love nature," and this capacity not only promotes ethical behavior but enriches her life (Sandler and Cafaro 2005: 3). Lisa Newton holds that the cardinal environmental virtue is simplicity, which is "marked by the strict pruning of material desires and intellectual conceits until the least possible demand is made upon the natural environment" (Newton 2003: 40). Dale Jamieson proposes the new environmental virtue of mindfulness, which involves attending to and taking responsibility for the environmental consequences of the production and disposal of the items one consumes (Jamieson 2007: 325). Some virtue theorists, however, maintain that the old virtues, properly understood and practiced, suffice for environmental responsibility.

But how are lists of virtues and vices chosen? It is common among virtue ethicists to seek them in the lives of exemplary people. Environmental virtue theorist Ronald Sandler lists Rachel Carson (the naturalist and author of *Silent Spring*), Aldo Leopold (ecologist and author of *A Sand County Almanac*), John Muir (naturalist and founder of the Sierra Club) and Julia Butterfly Hill (who lived in a redwood tree for two years to prevent loggers from cutting it down) as exemplars of environmental virtue (Sandler and Cafaro 2005: Introduction). To understand their moral characters, he thinks, it is not enough to know merely what they thought and did. We must also appreciate what they saw and felt—and most especially how they integrated love for wild creatures and wild places into their lives and actions. Sandler thinks that by doing so we can learn more virtuous ways to live.

One problem, of course, with trying to identify virtuous actions in the lives of exemplary people, is that we must first decide who the exemplary people are. If we try to pick out these people by the virtues they exhibit, then the whole process becomes pointlessly circular. We infer from the characters of our chosen exemplars the very virtues by which we chose them in the first place.

One way to avoid this problem is to justify the categorization of virtues and vices by either deontological or consequentialist arguments. Thus Jamieson, for example, uses a utilitarian argument to justify his claim that mindfulness is a virtue. Cultivating mindfulness, he thinks, will help us act in ways that produce the best consequences for all. Similarly, Sandler holds that a virtue is a character trait that promotes goodness, thus giving his environmental virtue theory a consequentialist backdrop (Sandler 2007: ch. 1).

Some strict virtue theorists, however, oppose their approach to consequentialism and deontology, which they see as too abstract to deal with the bewildering complexity of ethical choices. Ethical decision-making, on this particularist view, is not a technique of abstract reason, but a skill acquired by practice in the cultivation of virtue. Such virtue theorists are often skeptical of the techniques of logical analysis used throughout this book. Right action, they hold, is neither action in accord with ethical law, nor action that promotes goodness, but simply and purely action in accord with virtue. But then, once again, we may wonder how the virtues are chosen.

But we need not regard virtue theory as opposed to either consequentialism or deontology. Some philosophers think that the best way to understand all three is as tools for different ethical tasks. Consequentialist theories are right tool for guiding us toward a better world. For making sure that individuals are not treated disrespectfully or unjustly, deontology works best. For developing moral character, we need virtue ethics. None of the three excels in all these roles.

Virtue theories are sometimes criticized for focusing attention selfishly on the agent's own character, to the exclusion of genuine concern for moral patients. *Environmental* virtue ethicists, in particular, may be accused of esteeming their own "green" virtues more highly than the natural creatures and systems that those virtues are supposed to protect. Perhaps in some cases the accusation is true. Still, that does not amount to a general indictment of virtue theory. It merely points to a pitfall that virtue ethicists ought to avoid.

• 2.4 WHY CARE?

This chapter has sketched in very broad outlines the nature of contemporary ethical reasoning and ethical theory. But why care about ethics? The question is especially pressing now, given the increasing likelihood of environmental tragedies. I sometimes hear this sort of objection from students: "It's all going to hell no matter what I do. So why should I bother?"

The objection makes several assumptions and so requires several answers. The first answer is that it is not *all* going to hell. Much that is valuable and beautiful is being and will be lost. But life on Earth is unimaginably old and astonishingly resilient. Much will survive. We are not likely even to eradicate ourselves (section 1.3).

Second, the student's question assumes that if one's actions make no difference, then there is no point in acting. It thus presupposes consequentialism as the sole ethic. For the idea is *not* that there is never any point in doing anything (that would be nihilism—a deeper problem and one that cannot adequately be addressed in this book), but merely that there is no reason to act if one's actions are inconsequential. But why assume that? Deontologists find ethical worth in doing what is right, regardless of consequences. Great deeds sometimes spring from this conviction. (It is, however, a two-edged sword; when based on false ethical or factual beliefs, it can produce horrors.) Similarly, virtue theorists find ethical worth not in what we make of the world but in what we make of ourselves. Indifference to the plight of life on Earth is no virtue. Often it springs from intentional ignorance or cowardly despair—vices that diminish a person's character. So there can be reasons for acting even if one's actions are inconsequential.

Third, one's actions, even if they don't change the world at large, may have good consequences for oneself or one's relationships. I'll illustrate with a personal story. After the birth of my daughter in 1985, I found myself depressed. Superficially I had nothing to be depressed about. I was strong and healthy, my marriage was happy, my life was going well, and now I had this wonderful, healthy baby girl. What was wrong? Had I succumbed to a male variant of the postpartum blues? Gradually I realized what was wrong. I wasn't *depressed*; I was angry. What was bothering me was that the world into which my daughter would grow up would be neither as wild, nor as green, nor as beautiful as the world that I had known as a child. I imagined a time 20 or 30 years later when she and her generation might ask of me and my generation, "How could you have let this happen?" I wanted an answer. At least I wanted to be able to say, "Some of us tried to stop it." That realization launched my extracurricular career as an environmental activist. I channeled my anger into action. What had felt like depression lifted and did not return. Almost 30 years have passed. I have seen some successes and many defeats. I have tried to live sustainably, and succeeded only in doing a little better. But I can look my children in the eye and say "some of us tried."

There is a fourth answer, too. It is that your actions are *not* entirely inconsequential for the world at large. You *can* make a difference, if only a small one. Not *everything* is going to hell. Some of what is good and beautiful and hopeful can be restored; some of it still need not be lost. People are working to defend and heal Earth's life in every nation of the world. They need help. There is still good work to do.

• SUGGESTIONS FOR FURTHER READING

For a more detailed and practical introduction to logic, I am partial to my own book, *Informal Logic: Possible Worlds and Imagination* (McGraw-Hill, 1984), but many other fine introductions to logic are available.

Decision tables are a small part of the large field of decision theory. *Choices* by Michael Resnik (Minnesota, 1987) is a good introduction.

One of the best contemporary surveys of ethical theory is Russ Shafer-Landau's *The Fundamentals of Ethics*, 2nd ed. (Oxford, 2011).

For environmental virtue ethics, I recommend *Environmental Virtue Ethics*, edited by Ronald Sandler and Philip Cafaro (Rowman & Littlefield, 2005).

3

near-term anthropocentrism

In ancient times, both legal and ethical rules evolved by custom, and there was little distinction between them. Occasionally new rules were decreed by chieftains, kings, priests, or other authorities. Sometimes these human authorities claimed for their rules the higher authority of gods. Rules extended only as far as the authority of the ruler did. Different tribes, nations or cultures had, accordingly, different rules, often endorsed by different regional deities.

As culture became more cosmopolitan, a wider view developed: the diverse deities were increasingly seen as subjects of a supreme ruler or high god. Eventually, advanced thinkers rejected the regional gods (who had begun to appear unreliable, irrelevant, or immoral—and for whom there was, after all, no good evidence) in favor of one supreme, wise and benevolent God, the creator and law-giver of the universe.

The consequences of this **monotheism** (belief in one supreme God) for ethical thinking were momentous. God, as the just ruler, not merely of some particular nation or people, but of the universe, would surely regard all people similarly, perhaps even equally. Morality as instituted by God must therefore be the same for all. Thus monotheism fostered—among progressive thinkers, at least—belief in an ethic that values all human beings impartially.

That belief, however, took hold only gradually, and often against violent opposition. Impartiality threatens anyone whose power depends on tribal, national, ethnic, sectarian, racial, gender-based or class loyalties. Yet it also appeals ineluctably to humanity's perennial longing for justice. Once the vision of an impartial ethic took hold, it could not be eradicated. Eventually it gave rise to the great ethical theories of Kant, Bentham and Mill, which in turn shaped the global ethics of the modern world. Today it flourishes in such aspirational documents as the United Nations Universal Declaration of Human Rights. It still arouses opposition, of course, and is violated regularly, often gruesomely, but its influence is pervasive. I assume that readers of this book do not need to be persuaded that in some morally important sense all human beings—regardless of nationality, religion, place of origin, race, class, gender, sexual orientation, and all other irrelevancies—are equally morally considerable. There have been times and places when and where that assumption would have been naïve. The moral progress since then reflects, in part, the influence of monotheism.

As it transformed ethics, monotheism also transformed axiology—that is, human conceptions of value. Early humans experienced the world as a chaos of opposing forces (animals, humans, nature spirits, gods, demons), each with its own inscrutable will, purposes, and values. But with the rise of monotheism in late antiquity, Western philosophy came to see the world as an exquisitely designed hierarchical structure in which all things had God-given values and purposes. Inanimate substances, like water and air, existed to serve the needs of plants, animals and humans. Plants served as food for animals and as food and clothing for humans. Animals served as food for other animals and, again, as food and clothing for humans. Thus everything had its place, purpose, and value within God's creation. Philosopher Arthur Lovejoy (1961) dubbed this arrangement the Great Chain of Being. Medieval thinkers projected the Great Chain upward beyond humans, to supernatural beings—angels, archangels, and so on and, at the highest level of all, to God, from whom the whole system was assumed to emanate. As section 3.1 explains, however, this tidy cosmology and its attendant axiology did *not* survive unscathed into the modern world.

Chapter Outline: Chapter 3 consists of six sections. Section 3.1 introduces the central idea of this chapter and the next: anthropocentrism (i.e., human-centeredness) in both its axiological and ethical forms. Section 3.2 explains and critiques the ethic that is now most pervasive in global public discourse and policy-making: preference utilitarianism, specifically in the form of neoclassical economics. Objective welfare utilitarianism is discussed in section 3.3 as an alternative to it. Section 3.4 considers the roles played by deontological theories in near-term anthropocentric environmental ethics. But near-term anthropocentric ethics are shaped by other tendencies as well, four of which—feminism, relational ethics, pluralism and pragmatism—are discussed in section 3.5. Section 3.6 provides a general critique of near-term anthropocentric ethics.

3.1 ANTHROPOCENTRISM

During the Renaissance, and increasingly thereafter, skeptics, emboldened by the successes of secular power, and later of science, gradually rejected belief in the supernatural. Conceptually this truncated the Great Chain of Being, leaving man at the top. (The sexist language is appropriate, for at the time, women were usually overlooked, excluded, or assigned secondary roles.) All things "below" man were thus reinterpreted as resources, existing exclusively for man's use.

The West's understanding value thus became more **anthropocentric** (from the Greek word *anthropos*, meaning man—or, if we drop the sexism, human being). Values, formerly believed to be assigned to things by and for God's purposes were now assumed to be assigned to things only by and for human purposes. This assumption is called **axiological anthropocentrism**.

If all values are values for humans, then it is natural (though not necessary) to infer that only humans matter morally. Hence axiological anthropocentrism was typically conjoined (or confused) with ethical anthropocentrism. In its purest form, **ethical anthropocentrism** is the view that *only* humans (i.e., members of the species *Homo sapiens*) are morally considerable. In more dilute forms, it allows that some non-humans too are morally considerable, but not very significantly so. Pure ethical anthropocentrism implies that all moral concerns about non-humans (whether pets, porpoises or prairie ecosystems) is ultimately concern for human beings. A pure ethical anthropocentrist might, for example, oppose cruelty to animals because it degrades human character, or because it can lead to callousness or cruelty toward other humans, but not because it wrongs the animals themselves.

Ethical anthropocentrism has both long-term and **near-term** forms. Near-term ethical anthropocentrism, the topic of this chapter, is focused entirely, or almost entirely, on humans whose life spans overlap ours. It is the kind of thinking that is limited by the quarterly report, the next election, the five-year plan, the rest of our lives, or at best the next few generations. What happens after that is presumed to matter much less, or not at all.

Long-term ethical anthropocentrism, the topic of Chapter 4, considers not only our contemporaries but also people who will be born after we have died—some decades, centuries or even millennia later.

Near-term anthropocentrism is the dominant ethical perspective of contemporary public life. Even environmentalists whose ethical convictions are long-term or non-anthropocentric rely mostly on near-term anthropocentric reasoning in the political arena, since it is much more likely to persuade policy-makers and the public. This need not be hypocritical, since they, like everyone else, assume the ethical importance of contemporary humans. But for them it is not the whole story.

● 3.2 PREFERENCE UTILITARIANISM

Near-term ethical anthropocentrism can take consequentialist, deontological and virtue- theoretic forms—and, as will be explained in section 3.5, other forms as well. Its most influential form today, however, is a version of preference consequentialism: neoclassical economic theory.

Section Outline: Section 3.2.1 sketches the fundamentals of neoclassical economics and explores its preference utilitarian roots. Section 3.2.2 presents the main environmental challenge to it—a problem that Garrett Hardin dubbed "the tragedy of the commons." Neoclassical economics attempts to meet this challenge with a variety of strategies that together comprise the discipline of environmental economics. These are discussed in section 3.2.3. But, as is argued in section 3.2.4, neoclassical economics is biased in ways that invalidate its preference utilitarian credentials.

Section 3.2.5 presents an even more fundamental criticism: preference itself is not an adequate criterion of value. Given the failure of the ethical justification for neo-classical economics, many thinkers reject economics-based environmental policy-making, arguing instead for policies shaped by democratic process. But democratic process, too, relies on preferences, and so, as is shown in section 3.2.6, is subject to some of the same ethical difficulties.

The upshot is not that democracy or the market should be abandoned, but that neither reliably advances the common good without an informed, empowered and ethical citizenry.

3.2.1 Neoclassical Economics

"Let the market decide" is an imperative often heard in environmental policy debates. Yet the market is an impersonal economic or social arrangement, not a moral agent. Why should *it* decide? The standard answer lies in **neoclassical economics**—the widely held theory of how supply, demand and various constraints shape markets, determining prices, production, labor costs and so on. Neoclassical economics arose in the late nineteenth century, replacing the classical economic conception of value as cost of production with a more sophisticated preference utilitarian conception. An explanation and critique of its ethical assumptions is crucial here, because its influence on environmental policy is profound. Many economists like to think of their discipline as a social science, not an ethic. But to the extent that it issues pre-scriptive recommendations, which it does regularly, it is drawing ethical conclusions and hence making ethical assumptions. (You can't get an "ought" from an "is.")

The heart of neoclassical economics is the idea of the market. A market is a social mechanism for adjusting supply to demand. Demand consists of human preferences for marketable goods and services. To meet demand is to satisfy those preferences. That is the market's aim. But why satisfy human preferences? The neoclassical economic answer has its roots in preference utilitarianism (section 2.3.2.2).

Like any form of consequentialism, preference utilitarianism can be analyzed into an axiology and a choice principle. Preference utilitarian *axiology* defines positive value (goodness) as preference satisfaction and negative value (badness) as preference frustration. Neoclassical economics accepts this definition. It assumes, moreover, that the only preferences that matter are those of human beings. It is therefore steadfastly anthropocentric.

Classical *non*-economic preference utilitarianism's *choice principle* is: maximize total preference satisfaction. Contemporary economists, however, often reject the idea of maximizing the *total*, because they doubt that interpersonal comparisons of preference satisfaction are possible, and if they are not possible, then no total can be defined. Instead, the usual choice principle is: satisfy preferences *efficiently*. Economic definitions of efficiency need not concern us here, but the general idea is to satisfy preferences as well as we can, given that interpersonal comparisons are impossible. The notion that the market actually does this is the ethical justification for the imperative, "Let the market decide." The market is a social mechanism for implementing this modified preference utilitarian choice principle. If it works, it is in theory an efficient preference-satisfaction machine.

Real markets, however, are *not* efficient in this way. They are routinely influenced by political power and off-the-market financial deals. In "letting the market decide," then, we cede power to whomever is manipulating the market and advance whatever their agenda is. But to pursue that objection would take us well beyond environmental ethics. We will instead focus on objections more relevant to our topic.

Another problem is that human preferences rarely extend very far into the future. This means that, considered as an ethical theory, neoclassical economics is near-term in scope. But we need long-term ethics, as is explained in Chapter 4.

The market, moreover, is subject to a peculiar limitation: it can satisfy only preferences for *marketable goods and services*. But often we want what money can't buy.

3.2.2 The Tragedy of the Commons

Among the things that money can't buy are environmental goods: fresh air, oceans, wild lands, fishable rivers—and so on. These things can't be bought because they are not marketed. In some cases, they are not market*able*. This point was made with great force in Garrett Hardin's seminal essay "The Tragedy of the Commons." There Hardin (1968) argued that unrestrained exploitation of environmental goods by many individuals inevitably leads to collective ruin.

The paper's central trope is the idea of the commons—literally, grazing land held in common by an agricultural village. "Picture," writes Hardin,

> a pasture open to all. It is to be expected that each herdsman will try to keep as many cattle as possible on the commons. Such an arrangement may work reasonably satisfactorily for centuries because tribal wars, poaching, and disease keep the numbers of both man and beast well below the carrying capacity of the land. Finally, however, comes the day of reckoning, that is, the day when the long-desired goal of social stability becomes a reality. At this point, the inherent logic of the commons remorselessly generates tragedy.
>
> (Hardin 1968: 1244)

The commons, according to Hardin, can be sustainably grazed so long as the numbers of cattle and herders remain low. But if peace prevails and the number of herders increases or some become rich enough to acquire more cattle, overgrazing occurs, the cattle become less well nourished, and productivity per animal drops.

Hardin's central insight was that if the herders are blindly self-interested profit maximizers, then as their wealth or population increases, this degradation *must* occur. For each herder realizes a certain profit in meat or milk for each cow. But, since the commons is finite, the herder also incurs a cost in adding a cow, since the commons, the food supply on which his cattle depend, is further degraded. The cost, however, is not borne just by that one herder but shared by them all. For each individual, it is small relative to the profit to be gained from adding a new cow. Thus, for each herder individually, the benefit of adding a cow outweighs the cost. And since each herder is, by hypothesis, a blind profit maximizer, each will, given the opportunity, add one cow, then another and another . . . In the end, the pursuit of self-interest by each undermines the self-interest of all. That is the tragedy of the commons.

The metaphor caught on. Ocean fisheries, the pollution-absorbing capacity of rivers or air, old growth forests, wild game, and many other unowned resources have subsequently come to be understood as "commons." Given unbridled profit maximization and increasing wealth or population, the same pattern tends to recur with them all.

Hardin's intent was not to prophesy doom. He sought, rather, to characterize the problem and explain how to avoid it. Anticipating the tragedy, the herders might realize that in the long run everyone, themselves included, will suffer unless each does what is not in his or her *individual* interest: limit grazing. But, since each is selfishly motivated, none can do this unilaterally. The best way to do it, says Hardin is by coordination, in the form of democratic self-government. The herders must negotiate and enforce limits on use of the commons; "mutual coercion, mutually agreed upon," was his memorable phrase. In that way use can be moderated and kept within the bounds of sustainability, for the benefit of all.

The reasoning by which Hardin sets up the problem may be summarized as follows:

1   It is in the individual interest of each person to use as much of the commons as possible.
2   If all use as much of the commons as possible, the commons will be degraded or destroyed.
3   If the commons is degraded or destroyed, then all the herders are harmed.
∴   4   If each herder does what is in his/her individual interest, then all the herders are harmed. (1,2,3)
5   People are fated to do what is in their individual interest, unless coerced to do otherwise.
∴   6   All the herders will be harmed unless they are coerced to do what is not in their individual interest. (4,5)

The final conclusion, 6, states the dilemma facing the herders: suffer coercion or suffer tragedy.

Premise 1 is true if it is in people's interests to maximize profits, for that is what using as much of the commons as possible accomplishes. Each herder reasons as follows: if the others limit their use of the commons, then any cow I add has little effect on the degradation, and so I might as well add more; if they do not, then the commons is going to be destroyed anyway, so I might as well get as much of the action as I can now. Either way, it is in my self-interest to add as many cattle as I can.

Premise 2 is also true if (as Hardin assumes) the herders are rich enough to keep adding cattle, or their population is increasing. For in either case the number of cattle on the common land will eventually exceed the land's *carrying capacity*—the number it can support indefinitely without degradation. Thus degradation will occur—and perhaps, in the long run, destruction.

We may doubt premise 3. Some herders might maintain their livelihoods, despite the degradation, by muscling the others out. But if we presume (as Hardin apparently does in this idealized case) that all the herders keep herding, then 3 is true and degradation or destruction of the commons will reduce or eliminate the livelihood of each.

The intermediate conclusion 4 follows logically from 1, 2 and 3.

Premise 5 is the most controversial of the assumptions. Hardin here takes a dim view of human nature, assuming that in the absence of external coercion we are more or less condemned to act selfishly—that is, to maximize our own profits, even at the cost of ultimate self-destruction. Neoclassical economics assumes more or less the same thing—that producers, such as the herders, always act to maximize profits. This is not always true. Sometimes people decline to maximize profits, sometimes even for ethical reasons. So there is hope of escaping the tragedy by ethical action. But for the moment, let's assume for the sake of argument that premise 5 is true. Then we must accept conclusion 6.

Hardin summarizes: "Ruin is the destination toward which all men rush, each pursuing his own best interest in a society that believes in the freedom of the commons. Freedom in a commons brings ruin to all" (Hardin 1968: 1244). Ruin can be avoided, therefore, only if the commons is not free; that is, if each individual is constrained from using too much of it. Such constraint, though irksome, avoids the much greater limitation of freedom that would result from the destruction of the commons. Constraint is least irksome, Hardin thinks, when imposed by democratic self-government.

Hardin's solution to the tragedy of the commons—"mutual coercion, mutually agreed upon"—suggests a democratically negotiated deal. But, given Hardin's assumption of self-interestedness (premise 5), such a deal is likely to emerge only if the individuals or groups of them have roughly equal power. If some are powerful enough to exclude others from the commons at small cost to themselves, then, being purely self-interested, they will do so. Thus they will magnify their own profits and perhaps even prevent the tragedy. That, of course, would be unjust. But so long as there are significant disparities of power and (as the example assumes) self-interest is the only motivation, nothing prevents such injustice.

From this we may conclude that mutual coercion among purely self-interested agents is feasible only so long as power is fairly evenly distributed among them. But in reality there are often significant power disparities within societies. If injustice is to be avoided in such power-diverse societies, then, people must be motivated by something other than pure self-interest.

Hardin considers another possible solution to the tragedy: privatization. This solution too is predicated on human self-interest. If what once was the commons becomes owned, whether by an individual or a corporation, its fate is determined not by the self-interests of many individual users, but by the interests of the owner. The owner, whom we likewise assume to be self-interested, will likely turn the land to profit by, for example, charging a fee for its use. Use of the land thus becomes a marketable commodity and acquires a price. In order to sustain profit in the long run, the owner must limit grazing so that productivity is preserved. Thus he will set the user fee high enough so that only a modest number of herders can afford it, averting the tragedy.

Or maybe not. The new owner might have self-interested reasons to permit rapid overgrazing so as to cash in quickly. Then the tragedy would occur anyway—and the other herders would in the meantime have been forced to pay for what was originally free.

Privatization, whether or not it helps to preserve the land, may have other nasty effects. In the historical case of the British commons, a series of laws called "Inclosure Acts," promulgated mostly in the eighteenth and nineteenth centuries, privatized common lands, largely to the benefit of already wealthy landholders. Deprived of the use of common lands, many small farmers were forced into the Dickensian slums of industrializing cities.

Another reason why privatization might not be a good solution is that for some kinds of "commons," such as the atmosphere, private ownership is hardly possible. For others, such as aquifers or ocean fisheries, claims of ownership could spark political tension, perhaps even war.

It is sometimes argued that privatization has at least the advantage of avoiding governmental coercion. But that is a mistake; privatization too requires coercion. Private property can be maintained only under a power structure that secures property ownership—in the best case, by a governmental police force; if not, by the ministries of hired thugs.

Though most of the vast literature on Hardin's essay focuses on resource depletion, Hardin's primary concern was overpopulation. The commons *can* be used freely and sustainably, he thinks, but only so long as wealth and population remain modest. The trigger for the tragedy is the increasing wealth or population of the herders, for this is what enables them to add more cattle. A commons, he concludes, can remain free only so long as population and wealth remain low. If population grows, we face either repeated iterations of the tragedy across many different commons or a continual loss of freedom through privatization or government regulation. If we wish to avoid these dismal prospects, then we must, he says, relinquish yet another kind of freedom: "the freedom to breed." We'll return to the population problem in sections 4.6.2 and 7.1.5.

3.2.3 Environmental Economics

One of the lessons of Hardin's paper is that many things that people value—clean air, wilderness, or biodiversity, for example—cannot be marketed; hence the market can take no account of their value. Markets take account of the value of things by giving them prices. But these "non-market" goods have no price—and hence, so far as the market is concerned, no value; they are worthless, and therefore negligible.

But that is only so far as the market is concerned. In fact, they do satisfy human preferences—and thus should, according to neoclassical economics, have value. There is, accordingly, a mismatch between the way in which neoclassical economics defines value (as preference satisfaction) and the way in which it takes account of value (market price). If, for example, a polluter degrades the air, then the preferences of those who must breathe the degraded air are frustrated, which is a cost to them. Yet, assuming that the polluter pays no price for the pollution, this cost is not noticed by the market. Costs or benefits that remain in this way unaccounted for by the market are called *externalities*.

Externalities are common with environmental values. Market price is therefore not an adequate measure of value for environmental policy-making. A special sub-discipline of neoclassical economics called *environmental economics* has developed to address this problem. Since policy must consider monetary costs, environmental economics retains the neoclassical concept of value (price), but it finds ways of assigning prices to non-market goods as well.

Environmental economics should not be confused with *ecological economics*, which considers economies primarily as subsystems of ecosystems and hence as subject to ecosystemic constraints (Daly and Farley 2004: 431, 432). Ecological economics is discussed in section 7.1.4.

Section Outline: The next three sections present topics in environmental economics. Section 3.2.3.1 explains several methods for dealing with environmental externalities; section 3.2.3.2 concerns the delicate matter of pricing human life; and section 3.2.3.3 discusses the uses and abuses of cost–benefit analysis.

3.2.3.1 Internalizing Externalities

Like neoclassical economics generally, environmental economics seeks to satisfy human preferences. It is therefore ethically anthropocentric. But it aims to account for people's preferences for non-market environmental goods either by creating a market for them or by assigning them monetary values that are then used to guide policy. In either case, once human preferences for these goods have been taken into account, economists say that these externalities have been *internalized*. Environmental economics thus aims to internalize environmental externalities.

One way to internalize externalities is to create markets for previously non-market goods, so that they acquire genuine market prices. The best example of this is *cap-and-trade* policies for reducing pollution. In a cap-and-trade scheme the good being priced is the right to pollute. This may sound appalling, but in fact cap-and-trade schemes are efficient means to reduce pollution to some specified safe level and to keep it there. A cap-and-trade program starts by defining a limit (the *cap*) on allowable emissions of a given pollutant. The cap is typically lower than historic pollution levels and is justified primarily by safety and environmental considerations. The government then assigns each polluter an allowance giving that polluter the right to emit a certain quantity of the pollutant. The sum of emissions permitted by all such allowances is no greater than the cap. If a company can reduce emissions below its allowance, it is entitled to sell the unused portion of the allowance to another polluter that needs to emit more. Emissions are monitored to ensure that all emitters comply with the allowances they own, but how they comply is up to them. The ability to buy and sell allowances (the *trade* part of cap-and-trade) gives polluters flexibility as regards the timing and means of pollution reductions. The price of allowances fluctuates according to market conditions. If demand for the right to pollute is high, the price rises. If demand is low, it falls. The total quantity of allowances, however, remains constant, or perhaps is gradually lowered, so that overall emissions always remain at or below the cap.

Cap-and-trade schemes have proved effective in practice. They have, for example, been used successfully in the U.S. to reduce emissions responsible for acid precipitation. They can also be used to reduce greenhouse gas emissions, but for that use they have met with greater political opposition.

Cap-and-trade schemes internalize externalities by converting a non-market good, the right to pollute, into a good that is priced on a market. Another way to internalize externalities is to assign monetary values, called **shadow prices**, to non-market environmental goods. Nothing, of course, can be accomplished, for example, by an environmental economist sitting in her office and declaring that the value of the continued existence of the mountain gorilla for ten more years is $X million. To be meaningful in preference utilitarian terms, shadow prices must reflect aggregate human preferences. The economist cannot, therefore, simply stipulate prices; she must somehow base them on actual preferences. We'll consider how this is done shortly, but suppose that she can assign prices in ways that accurately reflect people's preferences. Still, that by itself won't change anything either. Shadow prices are not market prices. The continued existence of the mountain gorilla is not going to be bought or sold. To effect change, shadow prices must be employed by governments to set policy priorities, establish fees or tax rates, or otherwise regulate environmental behavior. Thus employed, shadow prices become tools for implementing "mutual coercion, mutually agreed upon" and can henceforth affect both the market and the environment.

There are two general methods for assigning shadow prices to non-market goods: **revealed preference** methods, which use market data to infer a price, and **stated preference** methods, which base the price on preference surveys.

Revealed preferences are inferred from people's actual buying behavior. One might, to take a simplified example, determine how much money people are willing to pay for clean air by noting the difference in housing prices between two neighborhoods, one of which has clean air and one of which doesn't but is otherwise similar.

A typical stated preference technique, called **contingent valuation**, is to survey people regarding their willingness to pay for a particular non-market good. Suppose, for example, that someone, when asked, honestly says he is willing to pay $10, but no more, for a conservation program that would insure the survival of the mountain gorilla for ten more years. Then $10 is assumed to be the value of the survival of the mountain gorilla over that time for that person. If economists were to survey everyone interested in the gorilla's survival, then the sum of all such values would constitute a kind of "demand" that could then be taken as the value of preserving the gorilla. Of course, in practice, not everyone can be surveyed. So a real survey selects a representative sample and uses it to estimate the shadow price. This shadow price may then guide policy-makers in deciding how much money to spend on preserving the gorilla, or how reasonably to regulate or tax activities that are threatening it.

3.2.3.2 Pricing Lives

Some environmental issues, however, are matters of life and death. For these issues, environmental economists may need to assess the value lost when someone is killed. Consider, for example, a decision table for the construction and operation of a nuclear power plant. Construction by itself is inherently dangerous. On large projects, worker deaths are not unusual. Moreover, with an operating nuclear plant, there is a small, but non-negligible, risk of an accident that costs many lives.

To account for these risks, environmental economists assign each human life a monetary value. One way to do this is to value lives based on the estimated number of years that remain in them, assuming a standard lifetime of, say, 80 years. Thus the death of a 20-year-old, who would lose 60 years, would be a loss six times greater than the death of a 70-year-old, who would lose 10. To turn this into a monetary value now requires some prior estimate of what a year of life is worth—a figure that might be obtained, for example by surveying people to find out how much they would be willing to pay for an extra year of life. Suppose, for illustration, that the figure is $200,000. Then the death of a 20-year-old is a loss valued at $12,000,000, while the death of a 70-year-old is a loss valued at $2,000,000.

The values for years might also be adjusted for quality. The 20-year-old typically has some of the best years of his life ahead of him, while the last decade of the 70-year-old may be spent in declining health. Hence we might want to value some of the 20-year-old's years at more than $200,000 and some of the 70-year-old's at less. But even with such adjustments, this sort of valuation is problematic. A respondent with no money and no hope of an income could not honestly be willing to pay anything for an extra year of life. A rich person might be willing to pay all that she has. Are the lives of the rich, then, more valuable than the lives of the poor? Should there be an additional adjustment for wealth?

There are other ways of estimating the monetary value of a life (sometimes just a single lump sum, equal for all lives is used), but nobody thinks that the values obtained by any such method are the "real" monetary values of human lives— whatever that might mean. Their chief justification is pragmatic: decision tables yield better results when we take some account of the value of human life than when we take none.

Such pragmatic justifications are not to be dismissed lightly. Shadow pricing the value of human lives is better than taking no account of their value at all, which is what may happen without the shadow prices. Despite its theoretical problems, environmental economics has brought an orderly form of accounting for environmental values and the value of human life into public policy.

3.2.3.3 Cost–Benefit Analysis

The numerical values supplied by environmental economists are often combined with economic cost and benefit estimates to produce **cost–benefit analyses** that assess policy options. The reasoning involved is that of a decision table. The example of the chemical storage tank in section 2.2.3.2 illustrates a simple cost–benefit analysis.

In the proper context, cost–benefit analyses are useful decision-making tools. They are often appropriately used, for example, in corporate decision-making. But for environmental decision-making they have serious deficiencies and should be used, if at all, only with critical awareness of these deficiencies.

Some of them are broad and theoretical. The next section explains why prices (including the prices calculated by environmental economics) are not accurate measures of value conceived as preference satisfaction. Section 3.2.5 explains, further, why preference satisfaction itself is not an adequate conception of value, not even near-term anthropocentric value.

But even if we dismiss these broad theoretical concerns (not that they should be dismissed), there are specific practical problems that can invalidate cost–benefit analyses used in policy-making. Decision-making agencies may determine prior to the analysis which options and outcomes they will consider, and how these options and outcomes are to be categorized, thus prejudicing the analysis. Both the probability estimates and the numerical estimates of value used in decision tables may embody misjudgments or errors.

To make matters worse, the technicality of cost–benefit analyses is intimidating, making public scrutiny difficult. If the process is not deliberately made wholly transparent, it practically invites manipulation. Sometimes politicians call for costly and lengthy cost–benefit analyses to simply entangle and delay environmental regulation. Decision-makers may use them to depersonalize responsibility for judgments that are ultimately theirs.

Finally, long-term cost–benefit analyses frequently discount future costs and benefits. When the costs and benefits are genuinely monetary, there are good reasons for this. When they are not, these reasons typically fail. This, however, is primarily a long-term issue, so I'll defer it to section 4.1.3.

To summarize: the market is—in theory, at least—a socially organized system of incentives designed to direct the behavior of individuals so that together they satisfy human preferences for marketable goods and services. Its traditional ethical justification is classical preference utilitarianism. Environmental economics aims to bring neoclassical economics closer to the preference utilitarian ideal. Recognizing that there are preferences for non-market goods, environmental economists develop techniques for satisfying those preferences as well. They do this either by estimating shadow prices for non-market goods and using these shadow prices to guide governmental regulation, or by assigning property rights and creating markets for previously non-market goods, as in cap-and-trade schemes. The shadow prices provided by environmental economists may serve as input to consequentialist decision-making techniques. If employed openly and democratically, these techniques can facilitate the kind of "mutual coercion, mutually agreed upon" that Hardin saw as the solution to the tragedy of the commons. If not, they are likely to conceal abuses of political power.

3.2.4 Ethical Critique of Neoclassical Economics

The conceptual foundation of neoclassical economics—and hence of environmental economics, which is a development of it—lies in preference utilitarianism. Preference utilitarianism aims to make people better off by satisfying their preferences. This is the alleged justification for the market. The argument goes something like this:

1 The market distributes goods and services according to people's willingness to pay.
2 People's willingness to pay accurately expresses the strength of their preferences.
∴ 3 The market distributes goods and services according to the strength of people's preferences. (1,2)
4 Satisfaction of preferences in accord with their strength is good for people.
∴ 5 The market distributes goods and services in ways that are good for people. (3,4)

Let's grant for the sake of argument that the market does distribute goods and services according to people's willingness to pay (premise 1). Still, the other assumptions (2 and 4) are both false: willingness to pay, as this section explains, does not adequately measure preference strength, and preference satisfaction, as section 3.2.5 explains, is not an adequate conception of goodness or welfare for people. Moreover, both assumptions are false in ways that do not depend on the fact that neoclassical economics counts only preferences for *marketable* goods and services. Hence their falsehood tells against the ethical adequacy of environmental economics as well as of neoclassical economics generally.

We turn first to the critique of premise 2. Willingness to pay does not accurately represent preference strength, even for marketable goods and services, because people with little disposable wealth have, overall, little willingness to pay. If you can barely afford groceries and rent, then your willingness to pay for anything else may be zero. This has nothing to do with your preferences or desires. You may have many desires for things other than food and shelter, but these other desires will not show up in your buying behavior. In your case, unwillingness to pay stems, not from lack of desire, but from poverty.

Conversely, if you are rich, you are probably willing to pay for many things. Your buying behavior will reflect many more of your desires, and many more of your preferences will register on the market. Economic value (price) is in this way determined more by the preferences of the rich than by the preferences of the poor.

There is, however, no defensible reason to suppose that satisfaction of the preferences of the rich is more valuable than satisfaction of the preferences of the poor. Preference utilitarianism, as originally conceived, ignored a person's wealth. It sought to satisfy preferences *impartially*, for the rich and poor alike. If two people, one rich and one poor, had preferences of equal strength, then it counted satisfaction of those preferences equally. Wealth didn't matter. The market, however, counts the satisfaction of the rich person as more valuable, because the rich person is willing to pay more.

In the extreme case of individuals who do not participate in the market at all (isolated tribespeople, the destitute, prisoners, future people, or sentient animals, for example) willingness to pay reveals nothing at all about preferences. Such individuals have no current willingness to pay, though, obviously, they have (or will have) preferences. For them, willingness to pay has no relation at all to preference strength.

In sum, premise 2 is false; people's willingness to pay is not an accurate measure of the strength of their preferences. By taking it as the measure of preference strength, both neoclassical economics and environmental economics treat the rich as having greater preferences the poor—and the penniless as having no preferences at all. If we let the market decide, we tacitly endorse this inequality. But there is no ethically justifiable reason for it. Hence neither neoclassical economics nor environmental economics (both of which measure preferences by willingness to pay) is ethically justified by preference utilitarianism.

3.2.5 Why Preference Satisfaction Is Not an Adequate Conception of Value

Premise 4 of the justification for neoclassical and environmental economics (section 3.2.4) asserts that satisfaction of preferences according to their strength is good for people. But, like premise 2, this premise is in general false. Its falsehood is a problem not only for neoclassical and environmental economics, but (as was noted in section 2.3.2.2) for preference-based theories generally. In this section, however, we focus specifically on why it undercuts the presumed ethical justification of neoclassical and environmental economics. We are no longer worried about wealth-based differences. Here the issue is whether preference satisfaction itself is good for us.

Note first that not all preferences are equally good indicators of value. People who are knowledgeable, reflective, and ethically decent usually want what is good. But people who are ignorant, stupid, or vicious also have preferences, and they often want what is bad, even for themselves. Preference utilitarians know this. So, as was explained in section 2.3.2.2, they often retrench, defining goodness in terms of considered preferences—preferences based on complete and accurate information and adequately reasoned judgment.

But that response, whether or not it is appropriate for ethical theory, is irrelevant in actual markets, since it is not in general *considered* preferences that determine market behavior. Philosopher Mark Sagoff provides a nice illustration. Sagoff once described for his environmental ethics class a plan by Walt Disney Enterprises to build an enormous ski resort in Mineral King Valley, an undeveloped area in the midst of Sequoia National Park. (The U.S. Forest Service approved the development in the 1960s.) Sagoff asked who among the students would use the ski resort if it were built. Many hands went up. Then he asked whether the students thought the U.S. Forest Service was right to approve the development:

> The response was nearly unanimous. The students believed that the Disney plan was loathsome and despicable, that the Forest Service had violated a public trust by approving it, and that the values for which we stand as a nation compel us to preserve the little wilderness we have for its own sake and as a heritage for future generations. On these ethical and cultural grounds, and in spite of their consumer preferences, the students opposed the Disney Plan to develop Mineral King.
>
> (Sagoff 1988: 51)

The students' consumer preferences apparently differed significantly from their values. In just this way, our consumer preferences may have little to do with our considered preferences, which reflect more fundamental values. Our consumption patterns don't always reflect our best judgments.

Actual markets, of course, distribute goods and services according to whatever preferences influence buying behavior. Considered preferences play some role, but so do arbitrary urges, addictive cravings and thoughtless whims. In fact, marketers deliberately create *un*considered preferences. Advertising exists chiefly to induce in people preferences for things that they would not have preferred on their own. It often bypasses rational judgment altogether, appealing instead to unreflective lust, envy, greed, or fear. Many ads foster misconceptions or false beliefs. Certain brands of cigarettes, for example, were once advertised as healthful. Today we are inundated with ads touting "clean coal."

It is unsurprising, then, that much of what we prefer is not good for us. Consider, for example, the junk food so heavily advertised and massively consumed around the world. Though junk food is a major cause of global health problems (section 1.2.2), buying behavior indicates that vast numbers of people prefer it anyway. But there is little reason to think that satisfying this preference makes them, on the whole, happier, or is in general good for them.

There is another reason why many people prefer junk food, even though it is not good for them: some desires are genetically based and, though they were appropriate for the conditions under which humans evolved, they are appropriate no longer. Humans evolved on the African savanna, where foods high in fats and sugars were valuable but rare. Individuals with strong appetites for such foods were more likely to survive. We have therefore inherited their desires. Now, however, when sugars, fats and salt are abundant, frequent satisfaction of these desires does more harm than good.

Preference satisfaction is not always good for us, too, because getting what we want sometimes leaves us empty, bored or more miserable than we were before, and getting what we didn't want sometimes makes us happier.

It follows from all this that welfare, happiness, and goodness are all quite distinct from preference satisfaction and that satisfaction of preferences in accord with their strength is not in general good for people. Premise 4 of the argument of the previous section is therefore false.

Let's summarize. What an ideal market—if such a thing existed—would satisfy is wealth-weighted consumer preferences for marketable goods and services. With the addition of regulatory policies recommended by environmental economists, it could also satisfy some wealth-weighted human preferences for environmental amenities. But it would still assign greater value to satisfaction of the preferences of the rich, and it would still function, mindlessly and indiscriminately, to satisfy uninformed, irrational, manufactured, or manipulated preferences. Even the numerical values carefully calculated by environmental economists incorporate these deficiencies. Therefore, once again, the alleged preference utilitarian justification of neoclassical economics (including environmental economics, cost–benefit analysis, and the like) is unsound. It follows, too, that where matters of moral importance are at stake, it makes no sense at all to let the market decide.

3.2.6 Democracy, Considered Preferences and the Environment

Sagoff argues that instead of ceding environmental policy decisions to the market or to economists and policy wonks, we ought to make them democratically. This has several potential advantages. In a democracy, decision-making power is in theory distributed equally, according to the principle *one person, one vote*. This comes closer to the utilitarian ethical ideal than does the principle that *de facto* governs neoclassical and environmental economics: *one dollar, one vote*. (The term 'vote' is, of course, metaphorical; instead of registering preferences in the form of votes, the market registers them in the form of purchases. The more you buy, the more "votes" you cast.)

Another advantage of democratic process, Sagoff thinks, is that in the give-and-take of public debate, citizens become more educated and so develop better informed preferences or values. Their votes are therefore more likely to express considered values than consumer whims. Sagoff notes as an illustration that, despite its consumer appeal, the plan to build the ski resort in Mineral King Valley (section 3.2.5) was eventually abandoned in the face of principled public opposition.

Democratic government can, moreover, accomplish things that markets can't. It can, for example, enact enforceable "command-and-control" legislation that strictly prohibits certain harmful actions. In the U.S. by the early 1970s, for example, air and water quality were deteriorating rapidly (section 1.2.1.1). Congress responded by passing the Clean Air and Clean Water Acts with strong bipartisan support. These command-and-control laws banned or limited many types of air and water pollution, and in the ensuing years air and water quality greatly improved. Such a solution could not have been achieved by a market unregulated by democratic process.

Democracy, of course, is not opposed to markets. It is compatible with many different economic arrangements—including markets of many designs. Sagoff's point is simply that letting people determine environmental policy in an open democratic process more reliably advances human values than letting economists or the market decide.

But, we may reasonably ask, are real democracies any more virtuous than real markets? Political systems can be gamed or corrupted just as markets are. Voter behavior can be manipulated by propaganda or advertising just as consumer behavior is. A case in point is the concerted effort, extremely successful in the English-speaking world, to discredit climate science. Funded by fossil-fuel interests and free-market ideologues, it has impeded political action on climate change for decades.

Even when not so manipulated, citizens' values and beliefs may still incorporate a heavy dross of instinctive prejudice, blind custom, or narrow self-interest. Even a well-informed populace operating democratically can therefore produce policies that are on the whole harmful to humanity or disrespectful to individual humans.

All of this is true. None of it, however, amounts to a blanket indictment of either markets or democracies. It merely points to means for their improvement. Both markets and democracies work best when their consumers or citizens are well informed, rational, and concerned not just with making money or satisfying preferences, but with the objective good of humanity.

3.3 OBJECTIVE WELFARE UTILITARIANISM

Let's take stock. In this chapter we are assuming near-term ethical anthropocentrism. We are supposing, in other words, that the aim of ethics is the good of contemporary humanity. This aim cannot be achieved merely by social schemes for satisfying preferences, since many preferences are, for the reasons indicated in section 3.2.5, foolish, and their satisfaction does more harm than good. Satisfaction of people's *considered* preferences would be closer to the mark, because these are informed preferences that have survived careful rational examination. But the point of such rational examination is, pretty obviously, to attune our preferences more closely to what really is good for us. If so, why base our axiology on preferences at all, since these are mere subjective indicators, and (as was noted in section 2.3.2.2) unreliable ones at that, of goodness? Why not base it instead directly on the objective good of humanity?

Section Outline: Section 3.3 concerns near-term objective welfare utilitarian environmental ethics. These employ objective welfare axiologies of the sort introduced in section 2.3.2.2. Section 3.3.1 takes a close look at the concept of objective welfare and considers the difficulties of measuring and aggregating it. Section 3.3.2 sketches some of the implications of an environmental ethic based on it. Section 3.3.3 critiques that ethic.

3.3.1 Objective Welfare Axiology and Choice Principles

Can anything be *objectively* good for human beings? Don't all human values spring from subjective human preferences? Many people regard that as obvious, but its apparent obviousness is historically a recent development (see section 3.1). It seems obvious in part because it is built into the neoclassical economic ideology (more popularly called consumerism) that many of us have imbibed since childhood. But that is no evidence for its truth.

With a little reflection, the apparent obviousness dissolves. If it were true that all values spring from human preferences, then something could be good for us only if we (on the whole and upon adequate consideration) preferred it. But in many cases it makes much more sense to say that we prefer a thing because it is good for us. Take health, for example. Nearly all of us prefer health to injury or illness, but our preferring it is not what makes it good for us. We prefer it, rather, because it really is good for us.

That, at least, is the way objective welfare utilitarians see it. Someone who believes in the subjectivity of all value might reply that a person's health is valuable to her only so long as she prefers to be healthy; if she doesn't care about her health, it loses its value for her.

But what would it mean to have no preference at all for one's own health? It's not easy to think of actual cases. A mother, for example, might take a job that ruins her health because she needs to support her children, but that doesn't mean she wouldn't prefer to be healthy. Some people wreck their health by smoking, but usually that's not because they don't want to be healthy; it's just that for them smoking has a stronger and more immediate appeal.

People who have no preference at all for their own health are in fact extremely rare. Some may not care because they think that health for them is somehow impossible. If so, and if they are right—if they are incurably ill, for example—then what makes health pointless and valueless for them is its objective impossibility, not their lack of preference. But if they are wrong—that is, if they could be healthy, both physically and mentally—then they *would* be better off actually being healthy, despite their lack of preference. Hence the goodness of health does not depend on our preference for health.

It is rooted, rather, in our biological nature. Living beings—those that can maintain or restore their own integral functioning—are most likely to survive to reproductive age and hence pass their genes to the next generation if they are healthy. Evolution therefore selects for organisms that by various means (from cell walls to immune systems to behavioral avoidance of noxious stimuli) maintain their own health. In this way the goal of health is built into all living beings, as a natural and objective good. Since it was good (for our non-human ancestors and other prehuman creatures) to be healthy even long before humans evolved, it is implausible that the goodness of health for us today is merely a product of human subjective preferences.

But although we are biological creatures, we are not merely that. Some objective goods arise from our social nature. Examples include: freedom from oppression, engagement in useful work, intimacy, friendship, wisdom, education, self-expression, and the respect of others. Humans are, of course, diverse, and such goods benefit some of us more than others. But they are good for us even if we spurn them—and people who spurn them would be better off if they didn't.

Objective welfare utilitarianism holds that we ethically ought to promote what is objectively good for ourselves and others. Rather than guiding our behavior by subjective preferences, in other words, we ought to guide it by (and cultivate preferences for) goods that objectively improve human life.

Juggling such a plurality of goods poses practical challenges. Many objective goods are not quantitatively measureable. (What is the measure, for example, of the value of friendship?) Some, while measurable, are not measurable on the same scales as others. (Education, for example, can perhaps be assessed by academic degrees earned, and overall health by longevity, but there is no common scale on which to measure both.) Thus there is no obvious way to express the welfare of even a single person as a single quantity. Things get worse if we try to determine the total welfare for a group of people that results from a given action, and worse yet when we try to compare this total with the totals for other possible actions. But that is what objective welfare utilitarianism requires us to do.

In certain special cases comparison of totals is possible, even without quantitative measures. If action A makes everyone's welfare in all relevant dimensions less than it would be on action B (A, for example, might be nuclear war), then the total welfare resulting from A is clearly less than the total resulting from B. Clearly, too, a policy that increases some people's welfare in some ways, while leaving the welfare of the others unchanged, increases total welfare. But such principles cover only special cases, and do not amount to a general theory of welfare aggregation and comparison. Utilitarian choice principles, however, require a general theory.

There have been efforts to combine quantifiable measures of different kinds of objective welfare into a single numerical measurement. The average longevity, level of education, and wealth, for example, of people in a given society, are measurable. These three quantities are combined somewhat arbitrarily into a single number called the Human Development Index (HDI), which provides a rough measure of the general objective welfare of a society. Some policy-makers regard the HDI as a better indicator of overall welfare than, for example, the Gross Domestic Product (GDP), or any other purely economic measurement.

But all agree that it is far from perfect. It does not account for many of the other conditions of human welfare mentioned above, which are themselves mere examples. The problem here is quite general: concepts of objective human welfare that include many such conditions must either be numerical but somewhat arbitrary, or else nonnumerical and perhaps merely qualitative. How, then, are we to make decisions?

If we have a single numerical scale, such as the HDI, then we can use the classical choice principle: maximize utility (which, in this case, is understood as objective welfare). But then our choices will be to some degree arbitrary. If, on the other hand, we insist on a plurality of conditions that are not combined into a single numerical scale—conditions, for example, as diverse as health and education—then in cases where one person is healthier and another more educated (other things being equal), the welfare of the two may be *incomparable*. To say that two values are incomparable is not merely to say that we don't know how to compare them. It is to say, rather, that neither is in fact greater than, equal to, or less than the other. But if not all values are comparable, then there may be no way to maximize value. What choice principle should we use then? There are difficulties either way. I will not attempt to address these difficulties here. But we will meet them again in sections 6.4.3, 6.4.4 and 7.3.2.

3.3.2 Environmental Policy Implications of Objective Welfare Utilitarianism

Regardless of the procedures by which welfares are measured and choices are made, objective human welfare utilitarianism aims for policies that promote all the components of objective welfare: health, adequate wealth, education, etc.

Since health is a necessary condition for full enjoyment of nearly all other human goods, it is noteworthy here that five of the six leading causes of death worldwide are related to poor diet and inadequate exercise (section 1.2.2). In part this is a reflection of the mismatch between our genetically based desires and the contemporary urban environment (section 3.2.5). But it also reflects the fact that there are corporate profits to be made in manipulating people to prefer highly processed foods and labor-saving devices that substitute fossil fuels for muscle power.

An objectively healthy human environment would provide wholesome food, clean water, fresh air, adequate sanitation, freedom from undue stress, and so on. It would be unpolluted, physically safe, and not excessively crowded. It would provide for vigorous physical activity—not merely as something one must "find time for," but as an integral part of human work and play. Instead of encouraging or requiring long hours in chairs or in cars, it would be arranged for movement: walking, biking, the frequent use of muscle power to accomplish daily tasks.

From the need for wholesome food, further implications follow. Since, for example, nearly all food originates with photosynthetic plants, it follows that an environment good for humans has a rich green flora. (Green plants are, of course, also good for other purposes, such as keeping the air breathable and the climate moderate.) Food production also requires rich soils or productive waters. All of these things are maintained by ecosystem services (section 1.2.5.2). Ecosystem services are another of the kinds of things that are objectively good for us, because without them—unless we provide inordinately costly substitutes—we cannot in the long run survive. Objective utilitarian environmental policy would therefore seek to maintain or restore them.

Natural environments may have objective benefits for *psychological* health as well. Many of us feel happier and less stressed in the woods, among mountains, or by the ocean, than in purely artificial surroundings. Outdoor experiences may raise our spirits and help to build character. We find nature beautiful, and its beauty fills us with joy.

Education, as was noted above, is another cultural good, but nature itself is a source of learning. The entire biosphere is a vast library, whose books are the genomes of organisms, alive or long dead, formulated in molecular languages that we have just begun to read. If learning is objectively valuable to us, then the potential contribution of these information sources to human welfare is great. An objective utilitarian environmental ethic provides reason to preserve them.

Nature offers more mundane goods as well. Social welfare requires artifacts, and artifacts are made from raw materials, which ultimately must be taken from the environment. Minerals, metals, chemicals, fuels, medicines, stone, leather, lumber, fiber, and the like all have their uses. Objective utilitarian policy would aim to use them not merely for maximizing preference satisfaction, but for objective human good.

These examples suggest that near-term objective welfare utilitarianism can support a fairly robust environmental ethic.

3.3.3 Critique of Objective Welfare Utilitarianism

Proponents of objective values do not always agree, of course, as to which values those are. The case for objectivity is probably strongest with the value of health, for it is rooted in evolutionary biology, as indicated above. For conditions said to be objectively good for us in terms of our social nature (especially intimacy and friendship), the argument may appeal similarly to an objective evolutionary origin, since these conditions are valued not only by people of all cultures, but also by many animals. But none of this is entirely uncontroversial.

The controversy is motivated in part by a legitimate fear: what if some political authority gets to decide what the objective values are and bases policy upon them, and we value something else? Objective value theories thus seem open to serious political abuse.

Obviously, that sort of dictatorial scenario is to be avoided. This can be demonstrated on purely consequentialist grounds, since oppression leads to social and political unrest. Clearly, the best way to enact objective welfare utilitarian policies is democratically, through the efforts of an educated citizenry, who value not just what they instinctively want or what is being marketed to them, but what is actually good for them.

Finally, objective welfare utilitarianism also faces the problem that plagues all, or nearly all, utilitarian ethics: though it promotes the general good, it may not adequately consider how goodness is to be distributed. It values overall goodness, but (unlike most deontological theories) it does not directly value individuals themselves. Hence it may too readily sacrifice the goods of individuals to the good of the majority. Utilitarian policies have, for example, approved the creation of national parks for the benefit of millions of people. But in doing so, they have displaced local inhabitants from their homes, tragically disrupting their lives. Typically these people have been compensated, on the grounds that that would decrease the unavoidable harm. But still utilitarianism is in principle willing to override strong interests of the few in favor of weaker interests of the many, so long as the interests of the many are greater in total.

In public policy decisions such trade-offs may be unavoidable. But it is widely held that there are ethical limits—that certain actions, because they violate the rights of individuals or are otherwise unjust, are unethical even if necessary to maximize total goodness. People who advocate such limits are not strict utilitarians.

3.4 DEONTOLOGY

Deontology requires justice. Thus when issues of justice and environment intersect, the appropriate ethic is likely to be deontological. But deontology is appropriate, too, when the issue is fairness among nations.

Section Outline: Section 3.4 begins (section 3.4.1) with an examination of the fact that some people are forced to endure environmental hazards that benefit others, who do not have to endure them, and the role of deontology in addressing that injustice. Section 3.4.2 turns to issues of international environmental justice.

3.4.1 Environmental Justice

The worst environmental problems have often been inflicted upon the poor and members of racial or cultural minorities, frequently in the form of toxic pollution from industries located near their homes. Some health-threatening industries (occasionally with the collusion of governments) have intentionally located in communities where people are poor, disempowered or desperate for jobs, assuming that local opposition will be less effective there than elsewhere. In the U.S., beginning in the early 1980s, and in other nations, at various times, local resistance arose against such facilities at various places. Organizers met and exchanged ideas, and the environmental justice movement was born.

Modeling itself on the civil rights movement, the environmental justice movement frames the issue of pollution in terms of class, ethnicity and race. It holds that disempowered people are disproportionately subject to injury, illness and unjust discrimination by industries that mainly benefit wealthy white people who live far from the smokestacks and the effluent pipes.

But what is wrong with such an arrangement? Those who suffer from it are a minority. Hence, conceivably, consequentialist reasoning (which favors the collective over the individual and tends to neglect just distribution of burdens and benefits) could support it. Unsurprisingly, then, polluting industries tend to reason consequentially. The health effects of the pollution, they argue, are overestimated, while the benefits to society as a whole (in terms of wealth and employment) are great.

Environmental justice advocates may try to respond point-by-point to such consequentialist arguments. But often the available information fails to settle the matter. Health effects studies are frequently inconclusive. And other effects, such as loss of neighborhood integrity or decline of property values near toxic sites, may be controversial.

More typically, however, in the tradition of the civil rights movement, environmental justice advocates make their case on deontological grounds. The crux of the matter, as they see it, is not costs and benefits, but justice. Thus they often pursue legal enactment and enforcement of deontological rules in the form of statutes, court decisions, or administrative rulings.

In the U.S., one of the most important sources of administrative rulings is the Environmental Protection Agency (EPA). For issues of environmental justice, such rulings are often justified by deontological ethical theories. The U.S. EPA characterizes environmental justice as follows:

> Environmental Justice is the fair treatment and meaningful involvement of all people regardless of race, color, national origin, or income with respect to the development, implementation, and enforcement of environmental laws, regulations, and policies. EPA has this goal for all communities and persons across this Nation. It will be achieved when everyone enjoys the same degree of protection from environmental and health hazards and equal access to the decision-making process to have a healthy environment in which to live, learn, and work.
>
> (EPA 2013)

Implicit in this statement are two general ethical rules:

1. All people, regardless of race, color, national origin, or income, should enjoy the same degree of protection from environmental and health hazards.
2. All people, regardless of race, color, national origin, or income, should have equal access to the environmental decision-making process (the development, implementation, and enforcement of environmental laws, regulations, and policies).

Such principles might be justified by the Golden Rule (since to treat others as you would have them treat you is to treat all equally), some version of the categorical imperative, or any of various contractarian conceptions of ethics. They are also explicitly anthropocentric. Each states a right applicable to "all people." Though they are *not* explicitly near-term (concerned just with people whose lives overlap with ours), often they are interpreted that way.

The environmental justice movement began as a grassroots effort by neighborhoods or communities to protect themselves from pollution-generated health hazards. But it quickly took on a transnational dimension. Heavily polluting industries have largely fled wealthy nations, which have enacted strong environmental regulations, and relocated where people are more desperate and labor is cheaper. Typical of such places is the region of Mexico just south of the Rio Grande, where *maquiladoras* (manufacturing or export assembly plants, attracted by cheap labor, low taxes and lax environmental regulation) have contaminated water, air and land. Because the *maquiladoras* do business internationally, they can evade some of the legal and moral restrictions that prevail in nations with more resources. Thus the concerns of the environmental justice movement today are increasingly international.

Many people enjoy the low prices of products manufactured under such degraded conditions. But buying these products in effect amounts to "voting" for the conditions of their production. This raises vexing questions of consumer ethics.

Near-term anthropocentric deontological theories may have other implications for environmental ethics as well. Some thinkers have, for example, argued for a human right to a safe and healthy environment (Nickel 1993). Such a right would require government action to restore environmental health and safety where it has been lost.

3.4.2 Climate Change and International Justice

Deontological thinking has played an important role in the troubled international negotiations over climate change. Here the chief issue is *international* justice. Since the start of the Industrial Revolution, the now-industrialized nations have enjoyed the economic benefits of burning fossil fuels. Given the human and environmental costs of climate change and the finitude of fossil fuels, those benefits must end in the foreseeable future. Unfortunately, the coal, oil and natural gas consumption of developing nations (most notably China and India) is rapidly accelerating. Moreover, the worst impacts of climate change over the next century will fall largely upon the poor in Southeast Asia and sub-Saharan Africa—regions that have so far contributed virtually nothing to the problem (IPCC 2007: 48–50, 52 and 65). Thus the industrialized nations that have mainly caused the problem have acquired great wealth from doing so, the developing nations may be prevented from benefitting as much, and some of the nations least responsible for the problem will suffer most. Widely held deontological principles of justice imply that, as a result, the industrialized nations owe the others some sort of compensation (Caney 2005; Shue 1999). Whether and how they might be brought to fulfill this obligation is a central issue of current international climate negotiations.

● 3.5 OTHER APPROACHES

Deontology and consequentialism are, of course, not the only forms of ethics. There are near-term anthropocentric versions of other forms as well. Nothing needs to be added here to the discussion of virtue ethics in section 2.3.4, since that section has already dealt with their near-term anthropocentric environmental form.

Section Outline: Section 3.5 considers several other approaches—feminism and ecofeminism (section 3.5.1), care ethics and other relational ethics (section 3.5.2), and pluralism and pragmatism (section 3.5.3)—to near-term anthropocentric environmental ethics. These are not wholly distinct. They often blend and hybridize, both with one another, and with the more established ethical theories.

3.5.1 Feminism and Ecofeminism

Until the late twentieth century, women had little opportunity to shape ethical theory, having been largely excluded from professional philosophy. But today women are producing philosophy in significant numbers. They shine an often critical light on the philosophical tradition, which had until recently been formulated almost entirely by men.

Feminist ethics have developed rapidly over the last few decades. *Feminism* is the idea that women are systematically subject to certain forms of oppression and that this is wrong. Feminist ethics, then, is mainly concerned with issues that affect women, often in the near term. That is why I have placed this section in a chapter on near-term anthropocentric ethics. But feminism is by no means as narrow as this placement may suggest. Many feminists are non-anthropocentrists as well, and many are concerned about the long-term future.

Ecofeminism is a synthesis of feminism with environmentalism. The environmentalism may be near-term or long-term, anthropocentric or not. What forges the synthesis is the idea that the domination of women reflects the same patterns of thought and behavior as the domination of nature. Ecofeminist Karen Warren describes these thought patterns as oppressive conceptual frameworks (Warren 1990). Oppressive conceptual frameworks can be racist, nationalist, homophobic, and so on, as well as sexist or exploitative of nature. They have, says Warren, two important features.

The first is that they tend to interpret the world by means of *value dualisms*—opposed pairs of concepts, one of which is traditionally valued as superior and the other as inferior. Here are some examples, with the allegedly superior concept on the left and the allegedly inferior one on the right:

culture	nature
reason	emotion
male	female
mind	body
human	nature
normal	deviant

Thinking that relies uncritically on such dualisms, says Warren, fosters prejudice and obscures the uniqueness of the things to which these dualisms are ascribed.

The second feature of oppressive conceptual frameworks is what Warren calls a logic of domination. This is embodied in the assumption, usually tacit, that what is superior is justified in dominating what is inferior. Combining these two features, we arrive, for example, at the idea that culture in general is justified in dominating nature in general or that men in general are justified in dominating women in general. This crude thought pattern sounds silly, of course, when stated so baldly. But that is Warren's point. It *is* silly. Making it explicit exposes its silliness and so helps to dispel its power.

Ecofeminism has not (yet) developed into a complete environmental ethic, on a par with deontological, consequentialist or virtue theoretic environmental ethics. Some ecofeminists, in fact, oppose such abstract theorizing, maintaining that it reinforces the oppressive conceptual frameworks that Warren decries. They argue, among other things, that the impartiality and objectivity advocated by the established ethical theories is illusory and that because these theories are predominantly created by men, the illusions they foster may be used to conceal and rationalize male privilege.

Critics of impartial ethics, not all of whom are feminists, also offer objections such as the following. A house is on fire. Trapped in one room is a person you love dearly. Trapped in another are three strangers. You have time to save only those in one of the rooms. What should you do? On impartial ethics, including standard versions of deontology and utilitarianism, all four people, or their interests, are morally equal. Therefore the correct choice is allegedly "rescue the three," for in that case one better respects persons or maximizes total utility. Many people find this answer abhorrent.

3.5.2 Care Ethics and Other Relational Ethics

The reason for its abhorrence, according to **relational ethics**, is that our moral responsibilities depend upon our relationships. Because you have a strong relationship with the person you love and no relationship with the three strangers, you have a greater responsibility to her, and she is the one you should save. In good relationships the parties trust one another, and their mutual trust engenders mutual responsibilities of loyalty. Each has a special responsibility, for example, to help the other in times of need—perhaps even if it means ignoring strangers to save her from a fire. Relational ethics need not deny that we have responsibilities to strangers. But they maintain that our first responsibilities are to those with whom we have relationships.

One important form of relational ethics, often associated with feminism, is **care ethics**. The central aim of a care ethic is neither justice, nor aggregate good, nor virtuous character, but the fostering of meaningful relationships. Care ethics were proposed by psychologist Carol Gilligan, to explain differences in ethical reasoning between boys and girls that she observed in studies of childhood moral development. According to Gilligan, feminine ethical thinking typically attends to relationships rather than rights, interdependence rather than autonomy, and care rather than justice. It proceeds less by the logical application of abstract ethical rules, than by the sharing of the stories of the people involved and by the nurturance of their relationships. Of course, not all women think this way, and Gilligan knew it. This, she thought, is only the usual pattern; some women think in characteristically masculine ways and some men think in characteristically feminine ways.

Care ethicists regard people not as completely autonomous individuals but as **relational selves** whose identity is at least partly constituted by their relationships with others. I am not just me. I am the son of my parents, the husband of my wife, the father of my children, a friend of my friends, and so on. To lose any of these relationships would be to lose a part of myself. Care ethicists emphasize how dependent we are on others, and how integral our relationships with them are to our identities. They note that each of us for some part of our lives (always at the beginning, as infants and children, and often at the end) requires care. Even in our prime, when we regard ourselves as fully autonomous moral agents, our lives are maintained, often to a much greater extent than we appreciate, by the care of others. Typically those others are women. Hence, care (in the form of what traditionally was regarded as "women's work") is far more central to human life than is usually assumed—and healthy relationships are far more central to moral value. It is on the basis of and for the sake of these special relationships, according to care ethics, that we have special obligations to the people with whom we have them.

Nearly everyone agrees that significant relationships do engender special responsibilities. Most advocates of impartial ethics find some way to justify these special responsibilities within their theories. They would allow us to rescue the one we love from the fire, rather than the three strangers. Whether they do so consistently is a difficult issue that need not concern us here. But in any case, environmental ethical theories need to account for responsibilities based on special relationships, for they frequently figure into practical attempts to live an environmentally responsible life.

Suppose, for example, that you have an aging parent who lives far away. Your parent would like you to visit often. Your relationship is close, and you would like to oblige. But getting there requires that you burn lots of fossil fuel. Burning fossil fuel harms others well into the future. Is it worthwhile to harm others (strangers, presumably) to visit your parent? Impartial theories pull us toward a negative answer—unless we can show that the harm to strangers is outweighed by the benefit of visiting your parent, or is overridden by a stronger obligation to do so. Care ethics pull us toward a positive answer.

We have relationships to communities to as well as to individual people. Relational ethics that focus on relations to community are called **communitarian ethics**. Communitarian ethics sometimes enter into local environmental politics. If a community is threatened by gas-drilling, strip-mining, logging, the construction of a landfill, or some other form of environmental degradation, community loyalties may unite opponents. Thus arises the so-called NIMBY ("Not In My Back Yard") phenomenon, which pits community groups against corporate or governmental initiatives. The communitarianism is often conjoined with concerns about environmental justice.

An important objection to relational ethics is that they may underestimate responsibilities to those with whom we have no special relationship: people living in distant places or future times, for example, whom we will never meet or know and who do not affect our identities. Those responsibilities will be discussed in Chapter 4. Too exclusive a focus on community responsibilities can, moreover, foster strife among rival communities. Much of the moral progress of recent times (the doctrine of universal human rights, for example) has been achieved by aspiring toward greater impartiality.

Gilligan herself did not advocate exclusive use of the care ethic. Rather, she thought it should be practiced along with the more "masculine" and impartial forms of ethical theory as equally valid and important. That combination, she believed, would result in a richer and better balanced moral life.

3.5.3 Pluralism and Pragmatism

In advocating the use of two different forms of ethics, Gilligan embraced ethical pluralism. In practice most of us do. It is usually only philosophers who consistently advocate a single theory—though some philosophers are pluralists, too. An *ethical pluralist* is a person who uses more than one ethical theory as a moral guide.

The problem, of course, is that different theories sometimes yield conflicting recommendations. What should we do then? If we don't like the advice of some strict imperative of deontology, for example, we might jump to a theory that yields more congenial advice. And in this way we might cleverly rationalize corrupt behavior.

Pluralists often reply that the standard ethical theories actually agree more often than not, so that this is not as big a problem as philosophers (who are always looking for inconsistencies) make it seem. When the various ethics are employed sensitively, not merely mechanically, by people of integrity, they argue, genuine conflicts are rare. When they arise and cannot be resolved, we may simply be faced with a range of alternatives, any of which is ethically acceptable.

A more radical approach is to shun theory and rely on proper procedure instead: set up democratic political institutions, educate people to be responsive to empirical evidence, give them freedom to experiment, open the doors wide to rigorous public debate, and good results will follow. This is the essence of *pragmatism*, a characteristically American philosophy that advocates empiricism, experimentalism and democratic process. It is just such a pragmatic approach that Mark Sagoff advocates as an alternative to environmental economics (section 3.2.6).

Ethical theories, say pragmatists, are too abstract, too one-size-fits-all, for the intricate work of either ethics or public policy. Like some feminists, they prefer to approach ethical decisions, not via deontological rules or consequentialist calculations, but by considering the stories of stakeholders and debating the values that emerge from their narratives, and relying on good public process. Such an approach is, of course, likely to produce different solutions to the same problem among different communities, and the solutions are likely to change over time. Thus pragmatists tend to shun universal ethical principles.

Because pragmatic values emerge from democratic debate, pragmatists tend to be axiological anthropocentrists, regarding all value as assigned to things by and for humans. Moreover, because those humans are contemporaries, pragmatists tend to think predominantly, though not exclusively, for the near-term.

Despite their axiological anthropocentrism, environmental pragmatists generally oppose neoclassical economics—and, indeed, all systematically consequentialist approaches—often for the reasons mentioned in sections 3.2.4, 3.2.5 and 3.3.3. Pragmatists are skeptical of deontological theories as well, primarily because they doubt both that it is possible adequately to encapsulate ethics in any set of rules and that there is one correct action for each decision. Ethical principles can, they say, at best narrow our choice to an unranked range of reasonable options. In the end, the final choice must rest on open public process.

A persistent worry with pragmatism is that its faith in the results of open inquiry may be naïve. Reliance on democratic procedure may inadvertently legitimize ill informed and much manipulated popular ideas as well as better informed views. We need standards to sort out helpful narrative from irrelevant narrative, good prescriptive argumentation from bad, narrow group-centered interests from broader ethical concerns. Without informed and empowered citizens committed to such standards, democratic process may go badly awry. But the search for standards brings us back to ethical theory.

3.6 BEYOND NEAR-TERM ANTHROPOCENTRISM

At the end of section 3.1 it was noted that decision-makers are sometimes influenced by near-term anthropocentric environmental arguments, but seldom by long-term or non-anthropocentric ones. Thus many environmentalists choose for pragmatic reasons to stick with near-term anthropocentric reasoning, in public at least. This may be politically shrewd. Even so, it does not follow that near-term anthropocentric thinking is best for all contexts. Public policy is not the only arena in which ethics matters. Environmental ethics finds roles in film, music, the visual arts and literature. It is taught in universities and preached from pulpits. It may influence our private lives: what we hope for, the careers we choose, the sorts of energy we depend on, what we buy, what we eat. It is doubtful that for all these purposes near-term anthropocentric thinking is best.

All near-term anthropocentric ethics have two limitations: (1) they are near-term, and (2) they are anthropocentric. Both limitations restrict their objectivity. The near-term limitation restricts ethical consideration to those whose life spans overlap with ours. The anthropocentric limitation restricts ethical consideration to human beings. Like the tribal, national, racial, religious, or gender-based prejudices of the past, these limitations seem to have arisen largely through the workings of uncritical tradition. The following chapters examine them critically and evaluate attempts to transcend them.

• SUGGESTIONS FOR FURTHER READING

For a more detailed philosophical critique of neoclassical economics than is presented in this chapter, see Alan Buchanan's *Ethics, Efficiency and the Market* (Rowman and Allenheld, 1985).

Environmental Economics: A Very Short Introduction by Stephen Smith (Oxford, 2011) is just what the title says it is and is a fine place to start if you want to learn more.

Mark Sagoff's *Economy of the Earth: Philosophy, Law and the Environment* (Cambridge, 1988) provides the classic philosophical critique of the use of cost–benefit analysis in environmental policy and an argument for a more democratic approach.

An important, but difficult, work in ecofeminist ethics is Val Plumwood's *Feminism and the Mastery of Nature* (Routledge, 1993).

The best account of environmental ethics from a politically pragmatic point of view is John O'Neill, Allan Holland and Andrew Light's *Environmental Values* (Routledge, 2008).

4

long-term anthropocentrism

Humans have a tendency to divide one another into the good (themselves and their friends), the inferior (those whom they dominate, or can at least ignore) and the evil (those who threaten them). In terms of presumed moral responsibilities, this means, roughly: those who matter morally, those who matter less, and those who matter not at all. Occasionally, however, even in ancient times, and, as we have seen, increasingly since the Enlightenment, some exceptional thinkers have sought to free themselves from the customary prejudices of their tribe, race, class, gender, religion or nationality, and helped us all to progress toward an ideal of human moral equality.

Yet in practice we still do not count most human beings as our equals, for we routinely overlook the great majority of them: *future people*—those who will live but have not yet been born. This chapter is about remedying that oversight. Its focus is not on the generations of our children and grandchildren—people whom we are likely to know and for whom our existing moral ideas work fairly well—but rather on *distant future people*—those who will be born after we die—for they pose the most revealing ethical problems. More specifically, our topic is *long-term anthropocentric ethics*—the theory of our responsibilities to distant future people.

Chapter Outline: Chapter 4 begins with a careful examination of the moral status of future people (section 4.1). We then investigate a long-term version of Hardin's tragedy of the commons: Stephen Gardiner's pure intergenerational problem (section 4.2). There are various ways of solving this problem. Sections 4.3 and 4.4 explain and criticize communitarian and deontological approaches, respectively. Section 4.5 introduces a new conceptual difficulty that seems especially to threaten deontological principles of non-harm: the non-identity problem. Long-term utilitarian ethics are explained in section 4.6, which considers several problems specific to them. Section 4.7 explains the concept of sustainability and some ethical justifications for it. Finally, section 4.8 traces the limits of our responsibilities to future people.

● 4.1 THE MORAL STATUS OF FUTURE PEOPLE

Traditional ethics said almost nothing about distant future people. It didn't need to. When the great ethical traditions were developed, there could hardly have been any question of moral consideration for distant future anything; for in those days people couldn't affect their distant future much—and, where they could, they couldn't do it predictably. Our ancestors had, in other words, two legitimate excuses for ignoring their distant posterity: they couldn't harm them, and even in the rare cases when they could (by, say, deforesting or desertifying land) they didn't know that they could. We no longer have those excuses. We know, for example, that by disrupting Earth's climate we are causing large-scale suffering and death over the coming centuries; hence we need an ethic that includes even distant future people in the moral community.

Section Outline: Though this chapter as a whole focuses on *distant* future people, section 4.1 considers future people generally. It argues for three conclusions about the moral status of future people: that future people matter morally (section 4.1.1), that they matter no less than we do (section 4.1.2), and that the economic practice of discounting future non-monetary harms and benefits is morally unjustified (section 4.1.3).

4.1.1 Why Future People Matter

The adjective "future" in the term "future person" does not describe the person herself. It only indicates the temporal perspective from which she is being described. In that respect it is analogous to the term "foreign." Just as a foreigner is anyone whose home is not here, in our nation, so a future person is anyone whose time is not yet, with respect to our time. People of another nation are not foreigners from the perspective of their nation. Likewise people of future times are not future people from the perspective of their time. From the perspective of their own time, they are present people and we are past people. Likewise, from the perspective of our time, we are present people and our predecessors are past people.

Since futurity is in this way merely a matter of perspective, future people are not, simply in virtue of being "future," inherently different from us. Knowing that a person is "future," like knowing that she is "foreign," tells us nothing about her moral status. Discrimination against people merely because they live in the future is, therefore, like discrimination against foreigners, an arbitrary prejudice.

Of course, if certain foreigners were unknown to us or so distant that we could not affect them in any way, then it would be pointless, if not impossible, for us to have ethical concern for them. But if we could affect them, and we knew it, then we would have at least the negative responsibility of not harming them. Likewise, since we can knowingly affect many future people, we have that sort of ethical responsibility toward them.

Yet there is this difference between us and future people: we exist now but they don't. How could we have responsibilities to non-existing people?

Easily. Consider this example: a dying person who is anticipating having grandchildren may in her will set up trust funds for them, even though they do not yet exist. This places the executor of her will under both a legal and an ethical obligation to the currently nonexistent grandchildren to manage and preserve the funds for them. That is one simple way in which we can have responsibilities to non-existing people.

The grandchildren, of course, will presumably exist within decades. But we also already recognize some responsibilities to distant future people. For decades, the U.S. government has been planning to open an underground storage facility for high-level radioactive waste at Yucca Mountain, Nevada. Because the waste remains dangerously radioactive for tens of thousands of years, its release could pose significant risks to distant future people. Thus the government has gone to great expense to study the long-term geological stability of the site and to incorporate safety and security features designed to protect people and the environment far into the future. Whether these measures are adequate remains controversial, as does the entire project. But there has been little or no dispute concerning the need for long-term safety and security measures. If we had no responsibilities to future people, such *long-term* measures would not be necessary, though we would still need to ensure the safety of currently living people. But both those who favor the project and those who oppose it seem to agree that if we bequeath to people living centuries or millennia from now a leaky or insecure high-level nuclear waste repository, then we will have wronged them. If this is right, then we do have responsibilities to people who not only do not exist now, but who will not exist for a very long time.

Not existing *yet* is, like being a future person or a foreigner, a matter of the perspective from which the description is made. To us, future people do not exist now. But there will be a time when they exist that they will call "now." Similarly, though we exist at a time that we call "now," from the perspective of our predecessors we do not exist yet. If our predecessors had had a way of knowingly harming us, it would have been wrong of them to do so, even though we did not exist yet. Just so, since we have ways of knowingly harming future people, it is wrong of us to do so, even though they do not exist yet.

It is sometimes claimed that future people differ from us in another ethically relevant way: they are nameless and faceless—an undifferentiated collective ("future generations" or "posterity") rather than specific individuals. But in fact they don't differ from us in this way. It is true, of course, that we can't *know* future people as individuals—at least distant future people. But neither can we know as individuals people who live now in places we will never even hear of—though in fact they are individuals. Similarly, future people will in fact be individuals, even if we can't know them as such. Once again, a shift of perspective makes this obvious. For we ourselves are individuals, and we are future people to our predecessors in the same way that others will be future people to us.

There is yet another objection to treating distant future people as our equals: there may not be any distant future people. If we look far enough into the future, this is quite certain. But the distant future, as defined above, starts within the next hundred years. It is not likely (as was noted in section 1.3) that anything we will do before then will eliminate the human race. Of course nature could do the job herself. Earth might, for example, collide with an asteroid, as it did 65 million years ago. That might eliminate *Homo sapiens*. But we are a tenacious and intelligent species. There is no guarantee that it would. Besides, since an impact of that magnitude hasn't happened in the last 65 million years, the chances of it happening over the next few centuries or even millennia are quite small.

If we knew that there would be no distant future people, and that this was inevitable, we would not need a long-term ethic—at least not an anthropocentric one. If we knew that the near-term extinction of humanity was highly *probable* no matter what we did, we might have rational grounds for reducing long-term ethical concern. But we do not know these things. The probability of near-term human extinction is extremely low. But the probability of human extinction *by a given date* increases as that date moves further into the future. We do not know how far into the future we have to advance the date before human extinction becomes likely. But, whatever the probability of extinction by any given date is now, it can be altered by the policies we pursue between now and then. It would therefore be foolish simply to assume that beyond a given date there will be no people.

4.1.2 Do Future People Matter Less?

Distant future people matter ethically. But they seem to matter less the more distant they are. We normally worry less about the distant future than about the near future. Is this, too, a mere prejudice?

In part, yes. But there are complications. Let's begin with a simple analogy. Once, my son, then about three years old, was with me in my office, on the eighth floor of a campus building. He had climbed onto a chair and was looking out the window at the ground below. Suddenly he giggled. "What's funny?" I asked. "The people are teensy, like ants," he replied.

Adults are familiar with this visual illusion. We're not fooled by it. We know how to compensate for the effect. But an analogous and more bewildering illusion occurs in ethics: people seem "morally smaller"—that is, diminished in moral significance—the farther they are away from us in space, or in time.

This is not *mere* appearance. There are obvious ways in which we do typically have greater responsibilities to people closer to us in space and time. Care ethicists emphasize the importance of ethical responsibilities that stem from our relationships with family, friends and co-workers. To these people we have special obligations, in part because they are the people to whom our actions matter most. They are, moreover, usually close to us in space and time. Thus it is natural to think of responsibility as varying with spatiotemporal distance. Our responsibilities to these people are determined, however, not by spatiotemporal distance, but by the nature of our relationships with them. Responsibilities to a family member, for example, may change but do not necessarily diminish if she or he goes (or is sent) somewhere far away.

To approach the same idea from a different angle, consider a stranger—someone with whom we have no special relationship at all. Despite this lack of relationship, we still have ethical responsibilities to that person—pre-eminently the responsibility of non-harm. Whether she lives in our home town or on the other side of the world, our responsibility not to harm her is the same. It would be just as wrong, for example, to send her a letter bomb if she lived halfway around the world as it would be if she lived a few blocks away. Distance alone makes no moral difference. The same is true for separation in time. It would be just as wrong to rig a bomb that we could be sure would kill someone in the far future as to rig a bomb that we could be sure would kill someone today. Temporal separation alone also makes no moral difference.

But there is something other than relationship that does make a difference in determining reasonable degrees of ethical concern: probability. If we couldn't be sure that the letter bomb to the future would kill someone, then sending it, though still heinous, might be less wrong. It is reasonable to concern ourselves less with distant future harms than with near future harms if those more distant are less probable. But, again, this is not a function of temporal separation. We rightly ignore improbable consequences in the *near* future too, even if they are dire. We know, for example, that it is possible to kill someone in an automobile accident any time we drive a car. But we don't worry much about it, because we think that a fatal accident is unlikely. Rational ethical concern regarding an outcome does depend—as was noted in the discussion of expected value in section 2.2.3.2—on both its value and its probability. Killing someone is a very bad outcome. But if its probability is low enough (if, for example, we are sober, alert and careful), it may be reasonable to take the risk and drive. The point, once again, is that our responsibility may vary with the probabilities of outcomes, but that is not the same thing as varying with temporal distance.

A big problem with many distant future events is that we have no clear idea of their probability. This is not just because we can't accurately predict the effects of our own actions on the distant future, but also because we don't know how things will be affected by people who live in the meantime. In one way, these intermediate people make our ethical burden lighter, since they too bear some of the responsibility for what happens in the distant future. It's not all up to us. But they also make predicting the outcomes of our actions and understanding our contribution to future effects more difficult.

Our ignorance of the probabilities of distant future events contributes to another powerful illusion. Many people confuse ignorance of probability with low probability. So, if they are ignorant of the probability of a future outcome, they may automatically infer that that outcome is unworthy of much consideration, as if it were improbable. Since ignorance increases toward the distant future, it can thus seem as if moral significance diminishes with temporal distance: distant future people may thus appear morally "teensy." This, however, is a serious error.

The illusion is exacerbated if known probabilities are ignored. In the case of global climate change, for example, it is known that on business-as-usual carbon emissions scenarios over the next few decades the probability of reaching catastrophic global average temperatures (say, 4° C or more above pre-industrial levels) becomes significant and continually *increases* with the passage of time over the next few centuries. People who are ignorant of this and who confuse their own ignorance with low probability may infer we can relax about climate change.

To summarize: the moral significance of an event does not diminish merely with its separation from us in space or in time. We do have special responsibilities to those with whom we have special relationships, and these people are usually close to us in space and time, but it is the closeness of the relationship, or the degree to which our actions affect these people, not the spatiotemporal closeness, that determines the degree of responsibility. Ethical concern regarding an event may, moreover, legitimately decrease as the probability of the event decreases. But we must be careful not to confuse ignorance of probability with low probability. Our ignorance of events tends to increase with their spatiotemporal distance from us. But probabilities of events do not in any regular way decrease with temporal distance. Some decline (e.g., the probability that humans will still exist). Some increase (e.g., the probability of our having achieved interstellar travel). Some stay the same (e.g., the probability that a random coin toss will yield heads). Others vary in just about every imaginable way.

4.1.3 Social Discount Rates

Given that the ethical significance of future events does not decline merely with their distance from us in time, it is remarkable that contemporary policy-makers assume just the opposite. They assume, in fact, that the values of future events decline toward zero with their distance from us in time, in accord with a quantity known as the *social discount rate*. A social discount rate is an annual percentage rate by which future outcomes, regardless of whether they are gains or losses, are counted less than present ones. The more distant they are in the future, the less they count—that is, the more closely their value approaches zero.

A social discount rate is akin to a rate of return on an investment. Its justification is economic, so an economic example makes the best illustration. If we compare, for example, $1,000 received today with $1,000 received a year from now, it is easy to see the greater value of the former. Assuming that we can invest money at a 5 percent annual rate of return, the amount we would have to invest today to have $1,000 in a year is $952.38. (Five percent of $952.38 is, rounding to the nearest cent, $47.62, which when added to $952.38, gives $1,000.) So if we had the $1,000 today, we could spend $47.62, invest the rest, and still have $1,000 in a year. Economists infer that at a 5 percent rate $1,000 a year from now is worth only $952.38 today. In these purely economic terms, taking the money today is clearly the better choice. Similarly, to get $1,000 in two years at a 5 percent rate, we would have to invest only $907.03, and so on.

This example assumes that the only relevant factor in determining the difference in value between $1,000 today and $1,000 a year from now is the rate of return on investment. Given that assumption, the discount rate equals the rate of return: 5 percent annually. Social discount rates used in environmental policy-making are a bit more complicated. They typically incorporate other factors, including a **pure time discount rate**—a rate of reduction in value based not on return on investment, but purely on how far in the future that value occurs. For the reasons explained in section 4.1.2, this sort of discount rate has no sound ethical justification.

There is a general formula for calculating how discount rates affect future values. If x is a cost or benefit y years from now, and the social discount rate is n percent, then the value of that cost or benefit today is:

$$\frac{x}{\left(1 + {}^n/_{100}\right)^y}$$

Discount rates of 3 percent, 5 percent, or more, are not unusual in policy-making. Over the time spans considered in long-term ethics, these produce severe devaluation, as Figure 2 illustrates.

The value of an outcome that is worth $1,000 now is reduced, if it occurs 200 years from now, to a value of $2.70 at a 3 percent rate, and to less than $0.06 at a 5 percent rate. If we count a human life as worth $10 million today, a human life is worth $350.53 in 200 years—and 0.7¢ in 500 years.

Social discount rates are regularly used to discount the values used in cost–benefit analyses (section 3.2.3.3). They figure significantly, for example, in the current

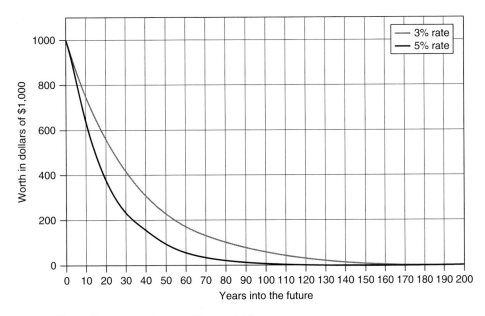

Figure 2 Effect of Discount Rate on Future Values

debates over economic investment in the mitigation of climate change. The substantive issue is simple: how much money should we spend now to avoid inflicting a given level of damage on future people? The answer, according to economists, depends largely on which discount rate we assume: the higher the rate, the less we should spend.

Various reasons have been given for discounting. Prominent among them are these four:

1. Future gains are worth less now than present benefits because money spent now on future gains can be invested to accrue interest, so that it would be a much greater amount by the time the future gain occurs. (This justification was illustrated in the example above.)
2. Future events are less probable than present events.
3. Our preferences for obtaining benefits or avoiding losses become weaker the further in the future those benefits or losses occur.
4. Future people will be better off than we are; hence the same level of loss or benefit will matter less to them than it does to us.

We'll consider each in turn.

Reason 1 makes good sense—and in fact is almost mandatory—in economic contexts, given the assumption of a growing economy in which investments reliably pay off. But it has little relevance to long-term policy-making. In policy-making, the social discount rate is applied to all values, including the value of a human life, not just to the values of marketable goods and services. The ethically most significant worry with climate change (assuming anthropocentrism) is vast numbers of future human casualties. Unlike the benefits of money or marketable goods and services, the harms of suffering and death are not subject to interest rates, and they do not decrease with temporal distance from us. It is sometimes argued that if we invest money now instead of spending it on preventing climate change, then that will enable us to compensate future generations for their losses by providing them with the fruits of increased economic growth. But it is doubtful that future people, faced with the mortal dangers of an inhospitable climate, would find any such compensation adequate.

Reason 2 is simply false. Though our ignorance increases the further we look into the future, probabilities of different kinds of events vary, as was noted at the end of section 4.1.2, in all sorts of ways. Probability considerations do not, therefore, justify any single uniform discount rate. Moreover, even if the probability of all events did decline in lock step with temporal distance from us, that would not be a reason to discount values. The probability of an outcome is not a component of the value of that outcome. It is a separate variable. It affects whether and how we ought to act to prevent or promote that outcome, but not how beneficial or harmful that outcome would be if it occurred. The latter is, for ethical purposes, its value.

Reason 3, that our preferences tend to weaken with distance from us into the future, is true. But it is a reason for discounting only if we assume that the values of future events should be determined by the preferences of present people. The preferences of present people are, however, as we saw in section 3.2.5, not accurate indicators of goodness even in the present. More to the point for the purposes of this chapter, if only the preferences of present people, and not those of future people, determine value, then we are counting the preferences of future people as important only insofar as they matter to us. That is unjust discrimination. (Imagine, by way of analogy, an axiology that takes the preferences of one race or gender into account only insofar as they matter to members of another race or gender.)

A common rejoinder is that we *can't* take the preferences of future people into account because we have no way of knowing their preferences. But that is false. Human preferences for life and health remain relatively constant over time. At least in matters of life and health, then, we know the preferences of future people and can, if we decide to, count them equally with ours. We'll return to this idea in section 4.6.1.

Reason 4, that future people will be better off than we are, extrapolates the last few centuries of human progress. But in a long-term ethic the assumption that the future will generally be better than the past cannot be taken for granted. Historically, civilizations have risen and fallen. The probability of a new dark age over the next few centuries or millennia, though unknown, is not negligible. Even if civilization survives largely intact over that period, it is likely to have ups and downs. Progress reliable enough to justify a steady numerical discount rate is unlikely.

In sum, the use of a single social discount rate in long-term anthropocentric ethics is not justified by the arguments commonly offered in its favor. Discount rates are .often appropriate for near-term costs and benefits that can be expressed in monetary terms. They may even have specific, focused uses in long-term policy-making. But their purposes must be clarified and justified adequately in each application. Applied indiscriminately over the long term, they trivialize future tragedies. Philosopher Derek Parfit, summarizing a more thorough critique of the arguments for a social discount rate than is possible here, concluded: "All these reasons need to be stated and judged separately, on their merits. If we bundle them together in a Social Discount Rate, we make ourselves morally blind" (Parfit 1984: 486).

• 4.2 THE PURE INTERGENERATIONAL PROBLEM

We have ethical responsibilities to distant future people, yet we are not fulfilling them. We understand, for example, the long-term consequences of increasing the carbon content of the atmosphere, yet we continue to increase it. Short-term self-interest repeatedly triumphs over long-term responsibility. Why?

Stephen Gardiner (2003) sheds some light on this question. Gardiner compares the current impasse in climate policy to Hardin's tragedy of the commons and finds that the long-term case has special features that make its solution much more difficult. These special features, considered abstractly, constitute the ***pure intergenerational problem***.

Gardiner calls the problem "pure" because it is an idealization, designed to make the essential features of our predicament as clear as possible. Like frictionless planes in physics or infinitely tiny points in geometry, some of these features are not realistic. But once we grasp the essential idea, we can see how it applies to messier "real-life" situations.

The pure intergenerational problem is a souped-up version of Hardin's tragedy of the commons. What makes it a more difficult challenge is that the succession of generations rules out Hardin's solution: mutual coercion, mutually agreed upon. The problem, in pure form, can be boiled down to four assumptions (Gardiner has five; the version here is somewhat simplified):

1.   Generations can be numbered, starting with generation 1 (which we may think of as the present generation), so that those with higher numbers exist later in time than those with lower numbers.
2.   All the people in one generation die before anyone in the next generation is born, so that although earlier generations can benefit or harm later ones, later generations can do nothing that makes any difference to earlier ones.
3.   People can only act in the interests of members of their own generation; they don't care about, and cannot act in the interests of, later generations.
4.   There is a certain kind of action, call it A, that each generation could perform, which benefits that generation itself but harms later generations. However, the benefit that each later generation could gain by performing A is less than the harm imposed on it if earlier generations perform A.

We'll assume for the sake of illustration that A is large-scale burning of fossil fuels, and that the harms are those of climate change, but the idea is more general than that. Given these assumptions, tragedy follows.

According to assumption 4, each generation except the first would fare best if all generations refrained from using fossil fuels. But this will not happen. The sticking point lies at generation 1. By assumption 4, generation 1 benefits from burning fossil fuels. By assumption 3 it must therefore burn them, since it always acts for its own benefit, regardless of the consequences to later generations. Moreover, given assumption 2, later generations can do nothing to prevent this. Thus generation 1 will burn fossil fuels.

Now consider generation 2. It might at least have had a moral motive (though not a self-interested motive) to refrain from polluting if generation 1 had done so. For that would have set a precedent and saved it from harm. Thus it might reasonably have felt ethically obligated to do the same for its posterity. But generation 1 burns fossil fuels and no such precedent is set. And since, in any case, generation 2 acts from the same self-interested motives as generation 1, it must likewise burn fossil fuels, as must every succeeding generation, while the fossil fuels last.

The result is an escalating tragedy that harms every generation, apart from generation 1. For, starting with the second generation, each loses substantially more by the fossil fuel use of previous generations than it gains from its own fossil fuel use.

The total loss thus increases with each generation, becoming much greater than the benefit to generation 1 and getting worse without end.

The people in this hypothetical scenario are behaving this way because Gardiner's assumption 3 expresses a negative assessment of human nature, akin to Hardin's. Hardin supposed that each person is fated to maximize his own profit, unless coerced to do otherwise. According to assumption 3, although individuals need not act in this purely self-interested way, generations must. Each person is fated to act only on behalf of members of his own generation, unless coerced to do otherwise. The members of each generation are, in other words, near-term anthropocentrists of a fairly narrow sort.

Besides assumption 3, what makes the pure intergenerational problem so hard to solve is that later generations cannot affect earlier ones (assumption 2). This rules out Hardin's solution: mutual coercion mutually agreed upon. You cannot coerce those whom you cannot affect. If a herder wants to put too many sheep on the commons, the other herders can stop him. If our generation wants to put too much carbon into the atmosphere, future generations can do nothing.

Fortunately, this is an idealization, and neither assumption 2 nor assumption 3 is true. We may therefore hope that making the assumptions more accurate reveals ways to avoid the tragedy.

It does, but these ways are not easy.

Assumption 2—that all the people in one generation die before anyone in the next generation is born—is blatantly false. In reality, of course, there is a continual overlap of generations. The role of assumption 2 in the idealization is to ensure that later generations cannot coerce earlier ones—that is, to rule out Hardin's solution. In actuality, young people, who belong to later generations, can exert some pressure on older people, who belong to earlier ones. We see this, for example, when young climate activists accuse older people, particularly those with power, of ruining their future.

But this sort of moral pressure can be applied only when generations overlap. People alive in 2150, who will probably suffer more from climate change than those who are young today, are voiceless and powerless, so far as anyone living today is concerned. They might exert a kind of indirect pressure; we may worry that if we cause them enough grief they will dishonour our memory, abandon our unfinished projects, or write histories in which we figure as selfish louts. Yet few people today are much discomfited by such worries. So, apart from the influence that young people have on the old, members of later generations cannot exert effective pressure on members of earlier ones.

Moreover, the pressure that the young can put on the old is small in comparison to the allure of self-interest. And young people who are willing to exert such pressure are relatively few. Thus, although assumption 2 is false, something not too different is true: the influence that later generations have on earlier ones, while not negligible, is relatively small. Later generations can therefore do little to pressure earlier ones into reducing their fossil fuel use. The falsehood of assumption 2 is no big help.

Assumption 3 is also false. People do sometimes care about and act in the interests of future generations or their members. Parents, especially, care about what happens to their children. Grandparents care about what happens to their children and grandchildren. Great-grandparents care about what happens to their children and grandchildren and great-grandchildren, even if they don't live to see those great-grandchildren—sometimes. But familial caring typically doesn't extend much beyond that. There are, however, other kinds of long-term caring. Philanthropists found institutions that carry on good work for many generations. Cities and nations look to their futures. Religious concerns span millennia. These examples point to the possibility of solving the now-not-so-pure intergenerational problem by generation-transcendent ethical concern. The next few sections consider various forms that such an ethic might take.

• 4.3 COMMUNITARIANISM

Several of the examples cited in the previous paragraph were based our ability to care about intergenerational communities of various sorts: professions, religious groups, political parties and nations, for example. Such intergenerational communities typically last many generations. They thus have a kind of community self-interest that can extend far into the future. Community self-interest is not, of course, anything mystical; at bottom it is just the concern of the community's members, or of its leaders at least, for the long-term welfare of the community. Such concern is the basis of communitarian ethics, which were considered briefly in section 3.5.2.

The idea of a communitarian intergenerational ethic was first articulated by Avner De-Shalit (1995). According to De-Shalit, the communities to which we belong (there may be many for each of us) help to constitute our identities—that is, to make us what we are. In particular, as community members we are part of something greater and longer-lasting than ourselves, something in whose benefits and privileges we share. But with those benefits and privileges come responsibilities to both the community itself and its members. And for intergenerational communities, these responsibilities extend not only to their present members, but to their future members as well, and to the future community as a whole.

Intergenerational communitarianism avoids the pure intergenerational problem (in theory, at least) by rejecting the assumption that people can act only in the interests of members of their own generation (assumption 3). Instead it insists that they can act for the long-term benefit of their communities.

One specialized version of long-term communitarianism offers a solution to the pure intergenerational problem that is remarkably analogous to Hardin's solution to the tragedy of the commons. The relevant communities in this version are nations. Nations are like Hardin's herders in two important ways. First, like the herders, they are concerned about their own future welfare—but nations usually have a much longer future than individual herders do. Second, like the herders, and unlike distant future generations, nations are capable in the present of coercion. Consider once again the issue of climate change. Able to see climate disaster coming and wanting to avoid it, nations might, like the herders, recognize the advantage of mutual coercion mutually agreed upon, and seek to negotiate international agreements to limit greenhouse gas emissions. Their reasoning would parallel that of the herders, but it would assume long-term community self-interest instead of individual self-interest. As a result of their negotiations, they would each trade their present ability to burn fossil fuels for the long-term stability of the global climate, just as the herders trade their present ability to graze additional livestock for the long-term viability of the commons. The result would be, ultimately, in the interest of each nation.

To their credit, the world's nations understand this. To their discredit, their negotiations have so far failed to produce effective agreement. Perhaps they will yet succeed. If not, there is another, less desirable, communitarian solution. Some especially powerful nation or confederation of nations might, out of concern for its future, force the rest of the world to stop burning fossil fuels by coercion that is not mutual: war, or credible threat of war.

Though communitarianism provides a solution to the pure intergenerational problem, it is not a complete solution. According to De-Shalit, we have more responsibility for the near future of our communities than for their distant future, since our identities are tied to our communities through the set of values they embody during our lifetimes, but over time these communities may evolve other values that we would never have endorsed. Hence our responsibilities to our communities fade into the distant future. Moreover, the lives of communities themselves are finite, and strict communitarian ethics do not tell us how to treat people born after the community itself has ceased to exist. In these ways communitarian ethics are not *very* long-term.

Furthermore, as with communitarianism generally, communitarian intergenerational ethics, taken by themselves, provide no impartial perspective from which to adjudicate clashes among communities. Suppose that our nation tries unjustly to seize resources from another nation. An ethic that ties our obligations strictly to our communities might blind us to the injustice and even lead us to support it.

A long-term ethic demands a more impartial transnational perspective. So we turn next to deontological and consequentialist ethical theories, whose hallmark is their impartiality.

4.4 DEONTOLOGY

Like communitarianism, deontology addresses the pure intergenerational problem by rejecting the assumption that people can act only in the interests of members of their own generation (assumption 3). But it amends the main shortcomings of pure communitarianism by taking a more impartial view.

Section Outline: Section 4.4 begins by considering first the extension of Kantian deontology to long-term ethics (section 4.4.1) and then the contractualist deontology of John Rawls (section 4.4.2). Both are critiqued in section 4.4.3.

4.4.1 Kantian Deontology

Can we take a purely impartial moral viewpoint? Kant thought we could, on the basis of reason alone. The most fundamental principle that we arrive at by pure reason, according to Kant, is the categorical imperative (section 2.3.1.1). In the version known as the formula of humanity, it is the imperative to treat each person as an *end*—that is, as an individual with purposes that are legitimately her own—and not as a mere instrument for furthering our purposes or as a mere object. This implies a principle of non-harm—that we should not without good reason harm innocent others in pursuit of purposes of our own—for that would be to treat them not as ends, but as mere things.

There is, moreover, no reason why this principle of non-harm should not apply to future, as well as present, people. We might therefore use it as the foundation of a long-term deontological ethic. Political theorist Steve Vanderheiden does just that. He bases his ethic on two simple deontological principles: "the moral duty to avoid causing predictable harm to others" and "a basic principle of equality that refuses to discount harm simply because it accrues in the future." Both of these can be justified straightforwardly by a temporally impartial version of the categorical imperative. Vanderheiden goes on to infer subsidiary deontological principles, including the right of future people to "climatic stability" and an "imperative to sustainably manage the atmosphere" (Vanderheiden 2008: 137).

4.4.2 Rawlsian Contractualist Deontology

The best known deontological intergenerational ethic is that of John Rawls. Rawls' ethic changed over the years from its initial statement in *A Theory of Justice* (1973) to the more mature view of *Political Liberalism* (1993) and *Justice as Fairness* (2001). It is the more mature view that is described here. Rawls develops a version of **contractualism**—a kind of ethical theory that regards morality as an idealized social contract to which all reasonable people can rationally assent. His ethic also a form of **liberalism**, the view that people should within reasonable limits be free to conduct their lives in accord with values and goals that they choose. It therefore does not assume any particular conception of the good.

Rawls aims to develop principles of justice that self-interested but reasonable people (even those with conflicting values) could all accept under certain ideal conditions. To simulate such ideal conditions, he imagines deontological rules (which together constitute a kind of social contract) being negotiated behind a **veil of ignorance**, whose purpose is to ensure a rigorous impartiality. Those behind the veil lose all sense of their identity—age, gender, class, race, disability status, talents, ideology, and so on. They retain, however, a comprehensive and general knowledge of science and human nature, of the fact that people have different interests and values, and of the fact that since resources are finite, not everyone can have all that she wants. Once the rules are established, the negotiators must come out from behind the veil and live by them. The negotiators are, Rawls assumes, self-interested but they are also ignorant of their identities. This motivates them to create rules that treat everyone justly and decently, since they have no idea of who they will be when they emerge from behind the veil.

Over the years, Rawls wrestled with the problem of how to set up this thought experiment so that it would generate adequate rules for intergenerational justice. Since he saw justice as embodied in a contract resulting from reasoned cooperation, and cooperation between widely separated generations is impossible, he rejected the idea of imagining people of different generations behind the veil. He therefore assumed that the negotiators all belong to the same generation—though behind the veil they don't know which generation that is. Moreover, in his later work, he made it a condition of the negotiators' acceptance of any contract that they would want, not only their own generation, but all generations, to live by it.

Rawls' main concern was the just distribution of goods. Writing initially in the 1970s, he did not envision the calamitous futures that we now contemplate. He sought, rather, to ensure the perpetuation of those primary goods, including "rights and liberties, opportunities and powers, income and wealth," that are necessary for a just society.

The negotiators behind the veil of ignorance would want, Rawls assumes, to be treated fairly by past generations and so, given his requirement that they would want all generations to live by the same rules, they would agree to treat their successors fairly. Not knowing who they were or which generation they belonged to, they would want to ensure a decent life for all members of all generations—or, if that were not immediately possible, at least progress toward a decent life. If there were people too poor to have a decent life in their generation, they would thus see the need for the well-off in that generation both to transfer some of that wealth to their contemporary poor and to save some of it to pass on to the next generation. When, however, the just society was finally achieved, each generation would need to pass on to its successors only as much as it received from the previous generation. This, presumably, would ensure sustainability with respect to primary goods. The just society could thus endure.

The primary rule that emerges from Rawls' thought experiment, therefore, is the ***just savings principle***, which requires each generation to pass on to its immediate successors, insofar as is within its power, means sufficient for a just society. Rawls does not presume that this requires economic growth. It is compatible, he thinks, with an economic "steady state," which in turn would require a stable population.

The just savings principle is the result, not of an actual contract, but of a hypothetical one. Yet because this principle applies to overlapping generations, there is some possibility of enforcing it by mutual coercion. Rawls' view does not, however, entail any responsibilities to distant future people. The responsibilities of each generation are fulfilled by passing the means for a just society on to its immediate successors. By thus keeping the future time horizon for any given generation short, Rawls fails to come to grips with the pure intergenerational problem. In following his just savings principle, we might succeed in passing the wherewithal for a just society on to our immediate successors while bequeathing to the distant future a planet that is unlivably hot.

4.4.3 Critique of Deontology

It is not clear that Kantian deontology yields a *practical* solution to the pure intergenerational problem either. In theory its solution is straightforward: our understanding of the harm we are doing to future people should convince us by impartial reason that we ought to desist.

But post-Kantian deontologists tend to be skeptical of impartial reason. Often they view ethics as a hypothetical social contract, which reasonable people endorse out of a broad sense of cooperative self-interest. We know that if we all obey the rules, we will all be better off; so we are willing to act in accord with this arrangement in the expectation, reinforced by social sanction and law, that others will do the same. So we monitor one another and take steps to ensure broad compliance. We are motivated to obey the rules, in other words, not merely by impartial reason, but by fear that others will create difficulties for us if we cheat. But, as Gardiner reminds us, we have little fear that future people will create difficulties for us, or that present people will do so on their behalf. Hence this contractualist solution, too, appears to be impractical.

In fact the original Kantian approach is probably superior. Some people do want to do what is right simply because it is right, and not for any selfish reason. Of course human motives are complex and seldom pure, but I know of no sound reason why such selfless conscientiousness cannot be part of the mix.

Kantian reasons for refraining from harm to future people can, moreover, synergize with other reasons. The impartiality required by a deontological ethic might promote a sense of community with all of humanity and thus provide a very broad communitarian justification for not harming future people. Religions that encourage us to view the world impartially, as God might, can also motivate a long-term view.

For some people, moreover, long-term ethics may be reinforced by self-interest. Many have already suffered from extreme weather events that were probably exacerbated by climate change. Many more are threatened. Even if they don't care specifically about future people, they may for their own benefit favor policies that reduce future harm. Others, too, have a self-interested stake in the future. Insurance companies, which face escalating claims for damages resulting from climate change, have a profit interest in reducing fossil fuel use. So do investors and businesspeople involved in sustainable energy enterprises. But profit may not be their only aim; they may have chosen such businesses or investments at least in part for ethical reasons.

In sum, despite the fact that distant future people are unable to coerce us in any way, we still have some motives for acting consistently with long-term deontological rules.

Yet long-term deontological ethics faces other problems as well. All deontological theories face difficulties in formulating the rules, dealing with exceptions, and establishing procedures for when (not if) the rules conflict (see section 2.3.1.3).

Deontological theories that rely heavily on principles of non-harm bear an especially heavy burden, for virtually any action with long-term effects will harm some people and benefit others. If, for example, we cut carbon emissions today, that may harm many people in the near term and benefit many people in the long term. If we don't, we will avoid some harm to people in the near term, but inflict harm on many people in the long term. When no choice is harmless, a rule of non-harm is unhelpful. Even principles of fair distribution may be unsatisfiable. We need to weigh the harms and compare them with potential benefits. But deontological rules provide little or no guidance in weighing harms and benefits.

And there is yet another problem which purports to deliver a fatal blow to long-term principles of non-harm . . .

• 4.5 THE NON-IDENTITY PROBLEM

Most long-term deontological theories assert principles of non-harm. But some people worry that such principles have no application to the *distant* future, because of a remarkable line of reasoning that purports to show that it is impossible to harm *distant* future people. This alleged impossibility has nothing to do with limits on our knowledge or power. Rather, it has to do with the identities of future people.

The idea is subtle, so it is best introduced by example. Once again we consider climate change. If we continue producing greenhouse gases as usual, say the climatologists, climate change may become catastrophic within a century or so and continue for many centuries thereafter. Suppose this does happen, so that people two or three centuries from now live in a sweltering post-apocalyptic world. Let's call them the post-apocalyptic people. Their lives will be hard and often short, though (let us assume) still worth living.

This is a bad result, and so we may be moved to prevent it. This would require a quick and deep global reduction in the use of fossil fuels. That would produce wide-ranging economic shifts, occurring first in energy-related industries. The economic changes would alter where and how people live, who they meet, and hence eventually with whom they or their children reproduce. These effects would ramify, so that after a century or two nobody would be alive who would have been alive had we continued business as usual. The population of the world would consist entirely of different people. Hence if we change climate policy now to save the post-apocalyptic people from harm, we will not be doing them a favor. Rather, the result will be that they will never be born.

Now here's the kicker: to harm someone you have to make them worse off than they would have been otherwise. But in this case "otherwise" means never being born.

The post-apocalyptic people are not worse off than that. Hence our business-as-usual pollution isn't harming them. In sum:

1.   Under business-as-usual the post-apocalyptic people will exist, and their lives, though hard and short, will still be worth living.
2.   Under any other policy they will never exist; an entirely different population will exist instead.
3.   People whose lives are worth living are not worse off than if they had never existed.

∴   4.   The post-apocalyptic people will be no worse off under business-as-usual than under any other policy. (1,2,3)

5.   People are harmed by a policy only if it makes them worse off than they would have been under some other policy.

∴   6.   Our policy of business-as-usual does not harm the post-apocalyptic people. (3,4,5)

Because this reasoning concerns a choice that results in two distinct populations—populations consisting of different (i.e., non-identical) people—it is called the **non-identity problem**. It was made famous in the 1980s by the British philosopher Derek Parfit, though he was not the first to notice it.

The upshot of the argument, once again, is that it is impossible to harm the post-apocalyptic people no matter what we do. Therefore it seems that in their case we cannot violate the deontological principle of non-harm. Even if our emissions kill them, we have done them no wrong!

Of course, if we choose to curtail emissions, other people will exist instead of the post-apocalyptic people, and they will presumably be better off. Aggregate welfare (that is, the sum of the welfares of individuals) will be greater in that case, and so curtailing emissions would have better consequences. But deontologists are concerned with proper treatment of individuals, not with consequences. And, either way, no individuals have been badly treated—or so it would seem.

Can this argument be sound?

Premise 1 seems reasonably probable, though some may doubt that the post-apocalyptic people would have lives worth living. But life is precious, even when it is hard. Though a life of unmitigated suffering may not be worth living, probably even post-apocalyptic people would have their hopes, loves and pleasures. It seems reasonable, then, to grant premise 1, at least for the sake of argument.

Premise 2 might be doubted, for there are infinitely many possible policies other than business as usual, and it's not clear that under all of them an entirely different population would be produced. But for our purposes this objection, too, is superficial. We may grant premise 2 as an idealization that helps us to focus on an extraordinary conceptual problem.

Premise 3 seems obviously true, and the intermediate conclusion 4 follows validly from 1, 2 and 3.

Premise 5 also seems obvious, for it merely states a widely accepted criterion of harm. But that criterion is false when applied to non-identity cases. To see why and how, consider a particular post-apocalyptic person. She is, let's say, born in 2200 into the greenhouse world. Her life is hard, but she is generally healthy and unharmed. Then one day a huge storm brought on by climate instability causes her house to collapse on her and cripples her for life. Since our greenhouse gas emissions caused the climate instability that resulted in the storm, our emissions caused her to be crippled. To cripple her is to harm her. Thus she is harmed, but not worse off than she would have been otherwise. Hence premise 5 is false.

What is wrong with premise 5 is that it lumps all of the consequences of our business-as-usual policy together. But consequences can be considered separately. If in giving you a million dollars I happen to break your arm, you might on the whole be no worse off than you were before. But it doesn't follow that in breaking your arm I haven't harmed you. The two consequences are separable. Likewise, if in polluting in a way that results both in the birth of this woman and also in her being crippled by the storm, we may not make her worse off than if we hadn't polluted. But that doesn't mean we haven't harmed her by causing her to be crippled. That is why premise 5 is false (Nolt 2013a).

The non-identity problem does not, therefore, render deontological principles of non-harm inapplicable. There is, nevertheless, something revealing in the non-identity argument, for the reasoning up to statement 4 is valid. The post-apocalyptic people really wouldn't be worse off under business as usual than otherwise. Yet curtailing emissions is obviously the right choice, because it provides better-than-post-apocalyptic lives for the people who would be born if we chose it. It is a mistake, therefore, to focus, as the non-identity argument does, solely on how our choice affects the post-apocalyptic people. When our choices affect who will exist, we must decide by considering for each option only the consequences for the people who would exist if that option were chosen. The obvious way to do this is to adopt a long-term utilitarian ethic.

• 4.6 UTILITARIANISM

For long-term utilitarianism, the choice between continued emissions resulting in a hot post-apocalyptic future or an immediate emissions reduction followed by a moderately warmer future is a no-brainer; there is greater total welfare in the second option, so it is correct.

For long-term applications, utilitarian ethics also have another advantage over deontological ethics—especially those that rely on principles of non-harm. Because long-term policies always harm someone, principles of non-harm by themselves are unhelpful. We need some way of dealing with trade-offs among harms and benefits. But that is just what consequentialist theories are designed for. Trade-offs are their trademark.

Section Outline: A long-term utilitarian ethic, like any consequentialist ethic, has two parts: an axiology and a choice principle. The axiology defines utility for the long term. Section 4.6.1 surveys the options and concludes that an objective welfare conception is most appropriate. Consideration of the choice principle leads into the puzzling conundrums of population ethics. That happens in section 4.6.2. Sections 4.6.3 and 4.6.4 examine important criticisms of long-term utilitarianism.

4.6.1 Axiology

Sections 2.3.2.1–2.3.2.2 noted that utilitarians typically define utility in one of three ways:

- The degree to which pleasure exceeds pain (hedonistic utility);
- The degree to which preference satisfaction exceeds preference frustration (preference utility); and
- Objective welfare, as defined by some list of objective characteristics.

The hedonistic conception of utility, taken by itself, is dubious for reasons explained in that section. Though pleasure and absence of pain are sometimes regarded as elements of objective welfare, pure hedonism has no advocates that I know of in long-term ethics and so will not be further discussed here.

The preference conception of utility, however, needs to be reckoned with, primarily because of its foundational role in neoclassical economics. It is sometimes used to argue *against* long-term ethics. We know little or nothing, so this argument claims, about the preferences of future people. Maybe they would appreciate vast nature preserves, but maybe they would prefer a world of fast roads and planet-wide shopping malls. Not knowing what they would prefer, we can have no responsibilities toward them. For obvious reasons, this argument has come to be known as the ***argument from ignorance***.

It is, however, unsound, for the claim that we know nothing of the preferences of future people is false. We can't know all of their preferences, of course, but we can know a good many of them. We can reliably predict that future people will want and need sources of food, clothing, shelter, clean water and clean air. They will prefer to live into maturity in an environment that is not dangerously contaminated with toxic or radioactive substances and with a climate that is not wildly unstable.

The point can perhaps best be appreciated by shifting to the perspective of our predecessors. Some of them knew very well what many of us would prefer. The founders of the American nation, for example, designed its Constitution with future people explicitly in mind. Its Preamble states:

> We, the people of the United States, in Order to form a more perfect Union, establish Justice, ensure domestic Tranquility, provide for the common defence, promote the general Welfare, and secure the Blessings of Liberty to ourselves

and *our Posterity*, do ordain and establish this Constitution of the United States of America.

(Italics added)

Americans today belong to that posterity and still benefit from the founders' foresight in understanding our wants and needs.

Similarly, the U.S. National Park Service Act of 1916 specified that the parks are to "conserve the scenery and the natural and historic objects and the wild life therein and to provide for the enjoyment of the same in such manner as will leave them unimpaired for the enjoyment *of future generations*" (Peirce 2000: 47–48, italics added). We are those future generations—American or not—since they benefit non-Americans too. Clearly those who drafted that Act knew something of our preferences. Decades, centuries, probably even millennia from now there will likewise live people of whose preferences we are not wholly ignorant.

We not only know something about what future people will want, but we can to some extent influence what they will want. In part we do this by creating their intellectual heritage. But we can also affect their wants directly by the alterations we make in the physical world. If we obliterate all traces of wilderness, for example, then we ensure that future people will never develop a taste for wilderness; for how could they learn to love what they will never experience? (Sagoff 1988: ch. 3). If, by contrast, we preserve some relatively wild places, then we will bequeath to them the possibility of that love.

For all these reasons, it is foolish to think that we can know nothing of the preferences of future people. We know a lot. But we know it, not by knowing their preferences directly, but by having a general idea of the objective requirements for a decent human life.

Those requirements are more relevant than preferences anyway. Section 3.2.5 explained why preference satisfaction is not an adequate conception of value. Similar reasons apply here: preferences may be uninformed, irrational or manipulated; getting what we want may be bad for us; not getting what we want may be good for us; and sometimes it is better to eliminate preferences than to satisfy them.

The preference theorist's standard response to such criticisms is to restrict attention to *considered* preferences. But what makes preferences considered is that they are responsive to knowledge and reasons. The more carefully our preferences are considered, the more many of them approximate criteria of objective human welfare. The rest, those considered preferences that are specific to individual tastes, are irrelevant to long-term ethics anyway, for they are genuinely unknowable from a temporal distance.

An objective conception of human welfare is therefore most appropriate for long-term utilitarian ethics. Such a conception defines welfare for present and future human individuals by various objective criteria, such as health, absence of suffering, adequate wealth, longevity, security, learning, and freedom from oppression. Such criteria constitute our best long-term conception of utility.

4.6.2 Choice Principles and Population Policies

Classical utilitarianism seeks to maximize total utility. But in the long term maximization may produce unacceptable results. To see why, recall that total utility is the
sum of the individual utilities for all the individuals in the population. Individual
utility is simply a measure, ideally a numerical measure, of the welfare of the individual. On an objective welfare conception, such a number would represent the
individual's overall "score" relative to the various objective criteria. In traditional
ethics, the usual way to increase total utility (i.e., total welfare) is to improve the
welfare of many individuals, while lowering the welfare of few or none. But in the
long term, there is, at least in theory, a second way: increase the population. If we
think of welfare roughly as happiness, then the first way is to make people happier;
the second is to make more happy people.

Increasing the population can increase total welfare, because the more people there
are the more numbers get added to the sum that comprises total welfare. This
increase, of course, is likely to come with a cost. If the population is already large
and we add more people, we will make some of the existing people less happy.
There may be crowding, unemployment, increased competition for resources. So
we have to be careful not to add too many. Still, there seems to be great value in a
new life, and one additional person would have very little effect on the welfare of
each of the others.

Suppose, then, that we add one person whose welfare level is w, and that this results
in a slight decline in the welfare of others. Still, if the total loss for the others is less
than w, we have increased total welfare. Since our aim is to *maximize* total welfare,
we can keep adding people, so long as the gain in welfare resulting from adding each
one is even a little higher than the loss in welfare to the people already there. We
must stop only when adding one more person would produce a total decrease for the
others that balanced or outweighed the gain of adding that person.

But this seems crazy, since in the process the welfare of already existing individuals
would have been declining all the while. Thus pursuit of maximization may lead us
to increase total welfare by increasing the population, while lowering the welfare
of already existing individuals. Derek Parfit dubbed this bizarre consequence the
repugnant conclusion (Parfit 1984: ch. 17).

The repugnant conclusion emerges starkly in long-term ethics because generations
can vary in population. Traditional ethics tended to ignore problems of population
size because, given its short time horizon (a few generations at most), it assumed
that the population was fixed, or nearly so. Problems like the repugnant conclusion,
which depend on varying the population, generally escaped its notice.

One way to avoid the repugnant conclusion is to modify the choice principle. Instead
of maximizing *total* welfare, we might introduce a new choice principle: maximize
average welfare. Average welfare is total welfare divided by the population. We
can think of it as welfare per person. In the case of the repugnant conclusion, as we
increase the population, average welfare declines, though total welfare increases.
Maybe we should have been attending to average welfare all along.

But the averaging choice principle has problems too. Here is one that is a kind of reverse repugnant conclusion: suppose the population is not very high, there are plenty of resources, and everyone is happy (their welfare is high). Since there are plenty of resources, adding a new person would not detract from anyone's welfare. Now suppose that a couple wanted to have a child but (perhaps through genetic testing) they knew that that child would be born with a slight disability as a result of which his welfare would be slightly less than average, though still quite high. Then it follows, using the averaging choice principle, that they may not have the child, even though he would enjoy life and not detract from anyone else's welfare. That seems wrong in a way opposite to the repugnant conclusion. Having the child would actually be better overall (it would increase total welfare) but the averaging choice principle prohibits it.

Because both the maximizing and the averaging choice principles seem sometimes to yield inappropriate results, Parfit embarked on a search for new choice principles that would yield more reasonable long-term population policies. He called it the search for Theory X (Parfit 1984: § 122 ff.). He examined many candidates and found problems with them all.

It is possible, though, that some of these problems are not fatal. This may be true even of the repugnant conclusion—which, however repugnant, is not absurd. We recoil from it because it increases population at the expense of individual welfare. We would prefer to live in a world in which our individual welfare is high. But this doesn't prove that the maximizing principle is wrong. Ethics, after all, is not just about our preferences. Consequentialism often requires some people to make sacrifices for the welfare of others. As Michael Huemer (2008) has noted, there is nothing absurd in that.

The most substantive worry with utility maximization is that it might force us to accept a very high human population. No doubt that would be so in hypothetical worlds with limitless, or nearly limitless, land and resources. But it is almost certainly false today in the actual world—for three reasons, two having to do with current human suffering and the other having to do with future human suffering.

Consider current suffering first. Since suffering has a negative value, more happiness can in principle be produced by making a being that was suffering happy than by creating a new equally happy being. For the latter only adds a positive quantity of happiness to the total, while the former adds the same quantity and also removes a negative quantity. Thus in a world beset by suffering, one can in principle produce more happiness per person by making existing people happy than by creating new happy people.

Second, given Earth's enormous population, we may already be past the point at which adding one more person increases total happiness. The added person may (or may not) be happy, but her presence increases environmental degradation, which also increases human suffering. This is especially true in the world's most crowded places, which are also among the most degraded and most miserable.

We must also consider the suffering of distant future humans. Per capita global carbon emissions are still growing, so until we power human civilization with something other than fossil fuels, each new person adds to atmospheric carbon dioxide levels. The consequences for distant future people will, as we saw in Chapter 1, be long-lasting and dire. Therefore increasing population now will almost certainly reduce total long-term human welfare.

It follows, by the traditional utilitarian maximizing choice principle, that we should not increase population. The repugnant conclusion is thus irrelevant to our world. In fact we have good reasons to limit (and even reduce—see section 7.1.5) human population.

Even if we can keep the classical maximizing choice principle for population ethics, that doesn't mean it is the right choice principle for all occasions. A wide variety of choice principles, including many that Parfit did not examine, are possible. We might sometimes have good reason, for example, to adopt a satisficing principle (section 2.3.2.3) that allows many different courses of action, so long as the resulting total welfare is "good enough." It may be that there is no overall best choice principle, and the various plausible alternatives are simply competing strategies for protecting and improving human welfare.

Whatever choice principle we use, it is unrealistic to expect that actual calculations will determine the distant future costs and benefits of our actions. Such calculations, even if our axiology could provide a numerical scale of value (and there is little prospect of that; see section 3.3.1), would demand far more information than we could hope to acquire. We can do some rough qualitative consequentialist reasoning about the distant future, as I did above in concluding that population increase in the near future would almost certainly reduce the total long-term welfare of humanity. But sometimes we may need to base our decisions on rules that *tend* to produce consequences satisfying some reasonable choice principle. In other words, we may need to use a form of rule consequentialism (section 2.3.2.4). Much of our ethical reasoning will then be rule-based, even if ultimately justified by consequentialist ethical theory.

Long-term consequentialism deals with the pure intergenerational problem in the same general way that Kantian deontology does—by adopting an impartial, generation-transcendent ethical view. Admittedly, such an impartial view is not by itself highly motivating for most people. It can, however, as was noted in section 4.4.3, work in synergy with communitarian or religious motives, and with certain kinds of self-interest. And we might hope (or, better, work) for continued moral progress.

4.6.3 The Demandingness Objection

One clear imperative of contemporary long-term ethics is, as we have seen, the need to limit population. Another is to minimize the use of fossil fuels. Since many people rely on fossil-fuel-generated energy for transportation, heating, cooling, lighting, and a plethora of other needs (not to mention satisfaction of desires), and since alternatives, even when available, tend to be expensive or inconvenient, the demands of long-term ethics on the present generation may seem invasive, excessive, or economically prohibitive.

One might then object that, given human nature, an ethic that requires us to make substantial sacrifices for others who are very distant in space or in time is too demanding for us to take seriously. Such an ethic, it might be argued, leaves us too little time, resources and energy for our own projects or interests. Perhaps we simply cannot accept it. Who, for example, is actually willing to forego buying their child the latest electronic gadget for Christmas in order to feed the hungry in Africa, or pay a carbon tax to help stave off climate change? That sort of worry is called the *demandingness objection* (Mulgan 2008: § 1.7).

Some theorists have sought to soften the responsibilities of long-term ethics by supposing that we may assign greater weight to our own interests than to the interests of other people. On this view, each of us may appropriate to ourselves what we need for a fulfilling life before worrying about spatially or temporally distant others. Such a principle is called an *agent-centered prerogative* (Mulgan 2008: § 4.1).

Agent-centered prerogatives are supposed not to be discriminatory, since they are granted equally to all agents. But in fact they are. As a wealthy American, I may use my agent-centered prerogative to comfortably pursue my own interests, and perhaps those of my family, but someone who is reduced to destitution may have few opportunities to pursue hers. Allowing her to give greater weight to her interests will not increase her opportunities and hence will do her no good. Agent-centered prerogatives are useful, then, roughly in proportion to the wealth and power of the agent. In practice, they are unjust to the poor and powerless, including all those future people who have no power in relation to us.

4.6.4 Collective Action Problems

Collective actions (those involving many agents) often pose special problems for consequentialist ethics, for sometimes they seem to make action futile. It is often held, for example, that an individual's greenhouse gas emissions can have no effect on the global climate. I disagree (Nolt 2011 and 2013a), but let's grant that claim for the sake of argument. Then, so the argument goes, only if others agree to reduce greenhouse gas emissions is there any reason for me to bother; for what makes an action worthwhile on a consequentialist theory is its consequences, and there will be no appreciable consequences if I act alone. This sets up a vicious circle: I'll cut my emissions only if you cut yours, and you will cut yours only if I cut mine. The result is that each of us waits for others to act, and nothing happens. This is what is called a *collective action problem*.

The core of this particular problem is expressed in the following argument:

　　1　The effect of an individual's reducing carbon emission is negligible.
　　2　The effect of many people's reducing carbon emission is beneficial.
　　3　The only reason to act is to produce good consequences.
∴　4　A single individual has no reason to reduce carbon emissions unless many others do as well.

We have granted premise 1 for the sake of argument, but we may still question premise 3, which expresses a narrow consequentialist view. Deontologists would reject this premise. A deontological rule—say, that we should not needlessly contribute to harm—applies regardless of consequences. We should do what is right, simply because it is right, even if that doesn't change anything. Similarly, virtue theorists would reject premise 3; they hold that the right action is the virtuous action, even if nothing good results from it.

For utilitarians, however, collective action problems pose a serious challenge. Dale Jamieson, who is a utilitarian, meets this challenge by proposing that where collective action problems threaten to become paralyzing, we ought to stop calculating and second-guessing ourselves, and simply act in accord with what he calls "green" virtues. These may be traditional virtues, such as humility or temperance, that have environmental applications, or new virtues developed specifically for our current situation. Jamieson mentions in particular the novel virtue of mindfulness, which involves appreciating and assuming responsibility for the spatially and temporally remote consequences of our actions. Though Jamieson's thinking sounds virtue-theoretic, its justification is utilitarian: given a collective action problem, acting in accord with virtue, rather than considering consequences, is what maximizes utility (Jamieson 2007). So, in cases such as this, Jamieson concludes, utilitarians should act as virtue theorists—though for utilitarian reasons. This conclusion nicely illustrates the pluralist point that different ethical theories may act in concert.

A tougher sort of collective action problem has been posed by Benjamin Hale (2011). Hale argues on psychological and economic grounds that (absent certain unlikely conditions) market incentives will inevitably cause all fossil fuels to be consumed. This prediction is uncertain, but suppose that it is right. Then, given that the harm of climate change is dependent largely on the total emissions, not on their timing (see section 1.2.3.2), it doesn't matter whether we as individuals or organizations burn fossil fuels or not. If we do not, others will burn them anyway. The total harm will be precisely the same regardless of our choice. There seems, therefore, to be no consequentialist reason to favor one choice over the other.

This follows, however, only on the assumption that the burning of all fossil fuels is inevitable. This assumption may yet prove false. Humanity might stop short of burning all fossil fuels. We have overwhelming moral reasons to do so (see section 7.1.1 and its subsections).

Even if, however, the consumption of all fossil fuels were certain, there might still be a consequentialist reason to conserve now. For in that case people living at the end of the fossil fuel era would have a climate hot enough to imperil civilization. Some of them might need fossil fuels just to survive. If so, then long-term consequentialism would advise us to slow down and save a little fuel for them.

Finally, even if the burning of all fossil fuels were certain, and no one needed them after they were used up, we would still have moral reasons for conserving now. In that case, of course, we could not affect the overall outcome. Others would burn whatever fuel we saved. Future people would suffer the agonies of apocalyptic climate change no matter what we did. Yet, as Hale reminds us, both the consequences and the behavior of others are irrelevant in deontological theories. They are also irrelevant in virtue theories and in those forms of rule consequentialism according to which we ought to follow the rules whose universal acceptance would produce the most good even if others are not following them. We still, in other words, have moral reasons to refrain from contributing to an apocalypse—even if it is inevitable.

• 4.7 SUSTAINABILITY

One thing on which all long-term ethics agree is that we ought to act sustainably. But sustainability means different things to different people. Historically, the idea has two sources. The first is the notion of sustainable harvest or maximum sustainable yield that emerged in the disciplines of ecology and wildlife management during the middle of the twentieth century. The second is the economic notion of sustainable development, which dates from the United Nations' Stockholm Declaration of 1972. From this second root has sprung lively controversy in international policy circles, with various factions, representing corporate, political, social justice, and environmental interests, each interpreting the idea differently and putting it to its own uses. Because the term offered something for everyone, its proliferation was rapid. Nowadays it is used to describe just about anything that someone wants to wrap in a "green" mantle. But sustainability is not the easy thing that popular imagination takes it to be.

The most widely cited definition of sustainability is that of the 1987 report by the World Commission on Environment and Development entitled *Our Common Future*. It is often called the Brundtland report, after the commission's chair, Gro Harlem Brundtland, an extraordinarily accomplished woman, who was three times prime minister of Norway and also led the World Health Organization. The definition is as follows:

> *Sustainable development is development that meets the needs of the present without compromising the ability of future generations to meet their own needs.*

This is, strictly speaking, a definition of sustainable development, not of sustainability. But it provides a helpful template for other concepts of sustainability as well. The Brundtland definition sets out two requirements:

1. We meet the needs of the present generation; and
2. We do not compromise the ability of future generations to meet their needs.

To meet needs is to ensure that people have the basics of life. Globally we are still far from doing this. Hence we have not even satisfied the first requirement of the Brundtland definition. Moreover, since global development efforts are still based largely on the burning of fossil fuels, we are also not satisfying the second.

Sustainability, even with respect to the basics of human life, is thus an enormous challenge.

Though the Brundtland commission was concerned with the meeting of human needs, other theorists have focused on sustaining other values, some quite specific (e.g., grain yields in Ghana). A more generally applicable definition may be formulated as follows: we are acting **sustainably** *with respect to a particular value* if:

1. We adequately realize that value for our generation; and
2. Our actions do not compromise the ability of future generations to realize it adequately (Nolt 2010b).

Many things that we value might be sustained: the productivity of ocean fisheries, fresh water supplies, and biodiversity, to mention just a few. But three particular notions of value have played the largest roles in long-term anthropocentric ethics: economic capital, a combination of economic and natural capital, and objective human welfare.

A neoclassical economic conception holds that the value to be sustained is *capital*—that is, wealth in all of its forms, which is the means of satisfying human preferences. Capital includes not only money, but such forms of wealth as property, natural resources, technological infrastructure, and "human capital" (i.e., a work force). It may be defined more generally as the means for satisfying preferences for goods and services. It is assumed that capital is *fungible*—i.e., interchangeable—that, in other words, markets provide means to replace one form with others that satisfy the same preferences (Solow 1993). Do we lack steel for construction? Then use some of our capital to develop or buy other building materials. Are we running out of oil? Then charge the batteries of electric cars with power from nuclear reactors. Given fungibility, it makes little difference what form the capital takes.

One problem with this economic conception is that not all the things we value are fungible. Breathable air, the stratospheric ozone layer, the cyanobacteria that form the base of oceanic food webs, and many other forms of so-called "natural capital" are traditionally unrecognized forms of wealth on which all economies depend. *Natural capital* includes the sorts of things that Garrett Hardin called "commons" (section 3.2.2) as well as ecosystem services (section 1.2.5.2). Unregulated markets tend to use up or destroy natural capital and thus undermine important sources of their wealth. A sustainable economy must therefore sustain natural, as well as economic, capital.

But even sustainability of both natural and economic capital is too narrow a conception ethically. Both forms of capital could in theory be maintained under powerful rulers (either governmental or corporate) who protected natural capital, kept most of the wealth to themselves, and maintained dominance over a cowed and impoverished populace. Capital would thus be sustained, but freedom from oppression and provision for everyone's needs would not. Obviously, then, we ought to sustain more than capital, even if this includes natural capital.

What we morally ought to sustain, given an anthropocentric ethic, is objective human welfare. Objective human welfare requires some degree of wealth or capital, of course, but it requires much more than that. It requires freedom from oppression, as was just noted. But more fundamentally, it requires health, and all the necessary conditions for health: wholesome food, clean water, fresh air, uncrowded living conditions, places for exercise and recreation, and so on. These in turn require the full array of environmental values discussed in section 3.3.2.

These values, of course, are all anthropocentric, as befits the subject of this chapter. If we extend moral consideration beyond people, then we may need to consider other non-anthropocentric values. We will do so in subsequent chapters.

Arguments for sustainability generally take either deontological or consequentialist forms. Deontologists, assuming the equality of all people, present and future, regard sustainability as a matter of justice. Rawls, as we saw (section 4.4.2) derives an imperative of sustainability (his just savings principle) from a prior conception of the just distribution of goods. Others, more impressed by the harm that we are doing to future people, invoke rights derived from non-harm principles. Vanderheiden, for example, infers an "imperative to sustainably manage the atmosphere" from the right to climatic stability (see section 4.4.1), which in turn follows from his principle of non-harm (Vanderheiden 2008: 137).

Consequentialist arguments for sustainability are more straightforward. Classical consequentialism assumes that we ought to maximize some particular value (e.g., objective human welfare). This is more or less a matter of keeping that value as high as possible indefinitely—that is, sustaining it. Satisficing forms of consequentialism do not require maximization of that value, but merely its *adequate* realization, as in the general definition of sustainability given above. In either case, an imperative of sustainability is a fairly direct implication of consequentialist moral theory, assuming that the value in question does not diminish with distance from us in time.

A standard weakness of consequentialism is that it need not distribute welfare fairly. But that problem is diminished in the case of intergenerational distribution. Except under very unrealistic conditions, it is impossible to maximize welfare indefinitely while allowing it consistently to drop. Hence in practice consequentialism seems to require at least a rough equality, if not increase, in welfare over time. It thus recommends a fairly just and equitable *inter*generational distribution—though it may still have problems with *intra*generational distribution.

• 4.8 THE LIMITS OF RESPONSIBILITY

Section 4.6.3 considered the demandingness objection, which is often raised against consequentialist theories in particular. But any version of long-term ethics can be demanding, and all are more demanding than the corresponding near-term versions, since they entail responsibilities for events that happen far in the future. Are our responsibilities, then, limitless?

Of course not. This section explores their limits. More specifically, it considers three common-sense principles that keep our responsibilities within reasonable bounds. In order to be fully ethically responsible for harming others we must be able to:

1. Cause that harm;
2. Recognize which of our actions cause it; and
3. Act in less harmful ways.

Failure to meet any of these three conditions reduces or negates our ethical responsibility for the harm. But as we gain knowledge and power, the conditions become easier to meet, and our responsibilities grow.

Condition 1 is perhaps too obvious to be worth mentioning, but I include it here for completeness: we are not responsible for harm we can't cause. Only since the Industrial Revolution, for example, have humans been powerful enough to disrupt the Earth's climate. Hence (obviously) nobody was ethically responsible for climate change originating before that.

Condition 2 is the ability to recognize which of our actions cause the harm. If we cannot know this, then our inescapable ignorance may excuse us from moral blame. But the excuse is solid only so long as the ignorance is total and genuinely unavoidable. It is more difficult to excuse willful ignorance, or failure to take reasonable precautions. The basics of climate change were not understood until the late nineteenth century. Before that, no one could have had any good reason to suspect that humans could cause harm by emitting greenhouse gases. Hence condition 2 could not have been met. People at that time had an ethically relevant excuse. By the late 1980s, however, the potential for harmful climate change was well known, and since then it has become obvious that we not dealing with mere potential. Moreover, we know which of our actions are causing the harm. Condition 2 is clearly met.

The third condition of ethical responsibility is the ability to act in less harmful ways. We are responsible for harm only if we could reasonably have acted otherwise. With respect to greenhouse gas emissions, we evidently can act less harmfully. Even though climate change is already occurring and more is inevitable, we know how to mitigate it and we have the technologies to do so. Condition 3 is therefore satisfied as well.

In sum, for the harms of climate change, all three conditions are met. We have lost the excuses that our ignorance and lack of power once provided. Our responsibilities have expanded accordingly.

Still, these responsibilities are not limitless. Much still lies beyond our ethical purview. Catastrophic climate change might, for example, after thousands or millions of years produce great and utterly unforeseeable *benefits*. (Weirder things have happened. The catastrophic asteroid impact that ended the reign of the dinosaurs led to the evolution of large mammals, and ultimately of us—an astonishing and unforeseeable benefit.) Or our actions today might produce vast and utterly unforeseeable harms. But since we have no way of knowing which of our actions might cause such distant consequences, by condition 2, all such events lie beyond the current limits of our ethical responsibility.

• SUGGESTIONS FOR FURTHER READING

Much contemporary philosophical thinking has been stimulated by part IV of Derek Parfit's brilliant but difficult masterpiece, *Reasons and Persons* (Oxford, 1984). Appendix F of this work is an outstanding critique of the moral use of social discount rates.

Stephen M. Gardiner's article "The Pure Intergenerational Problem," *Monist* 86, 3 (2003) raises one of the fundamental challenges for intergenerational ethics. Gardiner has also written an important book on climate change: *A Perfect Moral Storm: The Ethical Tragedy of Climate Change* (Oxford, 2011).

A useful collection of recent thinking on intergenerational ethics is *Intergenerational Justice*, edited by Axel Gosseries and Lukas H. Meyer (Oxford, 2009).

On communitarian intergenerational ethics, the best source is Avner De-Shalit's *Why Posterity Matters: Environmental Policies and Future Generations* (Routledge, 1995).

Lisa Newton's *Ethics and Sustainability: Sustainable Development and the Moral Life* (Prentice Hall) is a brief introduction to the ideas of sustainability and sustainable living.

Sustainability Ethics: 5 Questions, edited by Evan Selinger, Ryan Raffelle and Wade Robison (Automatic/VIP Press, 2010) is a survey of contemporary philosophical conceptions of sustainability.

5

animal ethics

Prior to Darwin, nearly the entire Western world thought that species were immutable categories established in an act of intelligent creation. It was also widely believed that the creator gave each species a fixed form and purpose, thus establishing a permanent hierarchy of value (the Great Chain of Being) in which "lower" beings served the "higher." Thus the natural purpose of plants, which are "lower" than animals, was to serve both human and non-human animals as a source of food and other resources. Similarly, the natural purpose of non-human animals was to serve humans as sources of food, clothing, locomotive energy, and so on.

The most influential proponent of this view was Aristotle. The divisions of this hierarchy of natural purpose extended, Aristotle thought, even into the human species. Thus barbarians (being, in Aristotle's view, less rational than, and hence inferior to, Greeks) had naturally the purpose of serving Greeks as slaves—though not, like the lesser animals, as lunch.

Medieval Western philosophers, largely under Aristotle's influence, also posited a natural hierarchy of purpose among living beings. But, in line with their Jewish, Christian or Muslim theologies, they assumed that the hierarchy was legislated by God. Thus many held, in particular, that God had created animals for human use.

Darwinian evolutionary biology refuted most of this. Species are not immutable. They change slowly. New ones evolve; others succumb to extinction. It is not true that some are designed for the use of others. Rather, some organisms have evolved ways of exploiting others, and the exploited ones have evolved elaborate ways to survive and reproduce nevertheless. Non-human animals, in particular, did not come into existence for the use of humans. They have lives of their own, and many of them flourished for hundreds of millions of years before there were any humans.

More fundamentally still, instead of a natural hierarchy, evolutionary theory reveals universal kinship—the descent of all living things from common ancestors. Other animals are, by biological standards, our relatively close kin.

Evolutionary theory thus transformed our understanding of the relations between humans and other animals. It is still transforming ethics. Of course, since "is" does not imply "ought", evolutionary theory alone implies nothing about how we ought to treat animals. But, emboldened in part by a Darwinian understanding of natural history, animal advocates have been developing ethical theories that do have substantial implications for our treatment of animals.

Chapter Outline: Chapter 5 surveys and evaluates some of those theories. Section 5.1 sketches the history of human thought about animals and the treatment of animals in science and agriculture. This leads in section 5.2 to a discussion of the nature and extent of animal consciousness. Section 5.3 considers reasons for and against extending moral considerability to animals. Peter Singer's utilitarian animal ethic is discussed in section 5.4. Section 5.5 presents and critiques the contrasting deontological animal ethic of Tom Regan. Gary Varner's rule utilitarian theory, which has affinities with the theories of both Singer and Regan, is explained in section 5.6. Section 5.7 briefly considers Peter Carruthers' contractualist view. Section 5.8 is devoted to care ethics. The next two sections concern ethics developed specifically for application to wild animals. Section 5.9 considers the animal ethic of one of the founding fathers of environmental ethics, Holmes Rolston III. Section 5.10 explains and criticizes the more recent relational view of environmental ethicist Clare Palmer. Section 5.11 provides a summary of the chapter and draws some conclusions. Section 5.12 takes a long-term perspective.

5.1 HUMAN TREATMENT OF NON-HUMAN ANIMALS

Humans evolved as hunter-gatherers and hence as omnivores. They used animal flesh and eggs for food and animal skins for clothing and sometimes shelter, and they fashioned animal sinews, bones, teeth and horns into tools, ornaments and weapons. We know nothing directly about the ethics of these early hunter-gatherers, of course, but their practices, like those of tribal people who persisted into historical times, were no doubt intertwined with magical and animistic beliefs. Tribal people often regard animals as fellow beings, with thoughts, feelings and sometimes languages of their own. Some believe that animals offer themselves as food for the hunter or that they are gifts of the gods or spirits. Some think that certain animals have magical powers that might be acquired by killing and eating them.

The earliest hunting methods probably differed little from predation by non-humans and did little damage to ecosystems. Non-human predators seldom drive their prey to extinction. In part this is because they usually rely on a limited number of prey species. If the population of an important prey species drops precariously, the predators tend to decrease in numbers as well, until the prey species recovers.

But since humans are omnivores, if one of their prey species becomes rare, they can switch to other foods, including vegetable foods, to maintain their population. Moreover, as humans acquired stone-tipped weapons, learned how to wield fire, and developed language and social organization, their hunting became increasingly effective. Stone-age hunters, though tiny and weak in relation to a mammoth or mastodon, could by strategy and weaponry slay and butcher it, acquiring a bountiful supply of meat. By such primitive means, they may have contributed to the extinction of many large animals. Particularly striking are the rapid extinctions of many large mammals, including mammoths and mastodons, in North America around 10,000 years ago—probably shortly after humans from Asia spread across the continent. Disease, however, and a warming climate following the recently ended ice age probably also contributed to these extinctions. Whatever the role of hunting was in these early extinctions, it is certain that it has produced many extinctions and near-extinctions in more recent times.

Section Outline: Our treatment of animals both affects and is affected by our understanding of them. Sections 5.1.1–5.1.4 consider, respectively, how animals have been understood in religion, philosophy, science and agriculture.

5.1.1 Animals in Religion

From earliest times, animals have also played important roles in religion. Humans have long offered animals (including, occasionally, other humans) in religious sacrifice. Sacrifice was prominent, for example, in traditional African religions (where it still persists) and among the ancient civilizations of the Mediterranean. Though spurned by most Christians, it was, and still is, practiced by some Jews and Muslims. Like all the major world religions, however, Judaism, Christianity and Islam discourage or prohibit wanton cruelty to animals

Nearly all religions have permitted the consumption of some kinds of animal flesh, milk and eggs, and the use of animal skins for shoes and clothing. But in each religion saints or sects have practiced stricter ethics. Among Hindus, for example (who believe that the souls of dead humans may be reincarnated as animals) vegetarianism has been common, though far from universal, since ancient times. Many Buddhists believe that since the Buddha's fundamental precept of compassion applies to all sentient beings, they ought to refrain from eating meat. Early Christians discussed the propriety of eating meat (Romans 14), and among modern Christians, Seventh-Day Adventists are noteworthy for their vegetarianism. The Jain religion of India is unique in requiring strict vegetarianism of all its practitioners. Jains espouse a doctrine of non-violence (*ahimsa*) that prohibits not only the consumption of animal flesh, but also unnecessary harm to insects, and even plants.

5.1.2 Animals in Philosophy

Initially, religious and philosophical conceptions of animals were closely allied. Aristotle taught that animals are composites of body and soul. Their souls, however, are not (as is typically thought in many religious traditions) immaterial entities capable of existing on their own. Rather, they are integral to bodies, providing their form and purpose. Even plants have "vegetative" souls, which explain their powers of growth, metabolism and reproduction. Animals have vegetative souls too—since they, like plants, can grow, metabolize and reproduce—but they also have animate souls that account for their powers of sensation, desire and movement. Humans have both vegetative and animate souls, and also a third kind: rational souls, which explain our special powers of reason.

It was this rational soul, according to many philosophers from the Greeks onward, that distinguished humans from all other animals. Socrates and Plato thought that it was separable from the body and immortal, and this view strongly influenced later Christian and Islamic thought.

René Descartes (1596–1650) offered, at the beginning of the modern period, a startling new view of animal minds. Much of the tradition had assumed, with Aristotle, that the sensations of animals and humans are fundamentally similar. But Descartes disagreed. Animals, he thought, do not have minds or souls as humans do. Rather, like today's robots, they respond behaviorally, but without conscious awareness, to the inputs registered by their eyes, ears and other sense organs. And although animals exhibit behavior similar to ours when injured, they feel no actual emotion or pain.

Descartes had no empirical evidence for this strange idea. His reasons were metaphysical and theological. Steeped in the Catholic tradition, he had convinced himself by arguments now widely regarded as fallacious that the conscious human mind is an immaterial thinking substance, among whose functions were the production of reason and language. Since he thought that reason and language do not occur in animals, he concluded that animals lack conscious minds.

Descartes conjectured that the human soul interacts with the nervous system through the pineal body, a small pituitary gland. (The location of this gland near the center of the brain seemed to indicate that it played some special role.) But neither he nor anyone else, then or since, could say how immaterial soul stuff could interact with a material human body, let alone with a specific organ of it. Moreover, this conjecture was open to a second objection: non-human vertebrates have pineal glands too. If ours is a sort of relay station for signals between the body and an immortal soul, why isn't theirs?

But we need not ponder this question further, for Descartes was simply on the wrong track. Today we know that the pineal gland functions mainly to regulate sexual development and circadian rhythms (sleeping and waking). Surgical excision of the gland (usually for treatment of tumors) does not impair our ability to perceive, talk or reason. It clearly is not the relay point that Descartes thought it was.

Perhaps Descartes had an ulterior motive for thinking that animals are unconscious and feel no pain, for in addition to being a philosopher, he was an anatomist. Vivisection—in the form of fastening an animal to a board or table and dissecting it alive—was an accepted practice among the anatomists of his day. The thought that the animals' cries were unconscious responses to unfelt physical stimuli was, no doubt, consoling to those who watched or performed such procedures.

5.1.3 Animals in Science

Given such beginnings, it is perhaps not surprising that a hard-boiled attitude toward animal suffering "for the sake of science" persisted for centuries thereafter. Generations of scientists were taught that objectivity requires not only the suppression of one's own emotions but also skepticism toward emotions generally, and toward the suffering and emotions of non-human animals in particular.

To a certain extent this skepticism is justified, for our spontaneous attributions of emotions, desires or beliefs to other animals are often imaginative projections of our own experiences. This makes it difficult to appreciate how utterly different some animals are from us. *Anthropomorphism*—the tendency, evident even in very young children, to attribute human thoughts and feelings to non-human animals—is thus a common source of error.

But extreme skepticism leads to other sorts of errors. Through most of the twentieth century, a prominent school of psychologists, the *behaviorists*, hoping to transform their discipline into a rigorous empirical science, rejected talk of emotion, suffering or consciousness as "unscientific." Behaviorists seldom seriously denied the existence of pain, emotion or consciousness—at least in the case of humans. Most insisted that their purge of mental vocabulary was merely a requirement of scientific method. But perhaps their studied indifference toward suffering, especially the suffering of non-humans, lent an aura of scientific legitimacy to like indifference elsewhere in Western culture. By the second half of the twentieth century, this hard-boiled attitude had become institutionalized in the laboratories where animals were increasingly being used as research subjects and in large-scale mechanized meat production. The latter was excused as an economic necessity backed by the authority of animal science.

The treatment of laboratory animals is a major issue in animal ethics; but since it has less to do with environmental matters than does animal agriculture, we will bypass it here. The practice of greatest concern to environmental ethics, in terms of energy use, water use, air and water pollution, greenhouse gas emissions, and the sheer amount of animal suffering, is factory farming. So we turn next to the treatment of animals in contemporary agriculture.

5.1.4 Animals in Agriculture

Traditional farmers knew their animals personally and often developed some affection for them, even if in the end they butchered them. But during the twentieth century, particularly in North America, competitive economic pressures and agricultural policies transformed farming from a traditional way of life to an impersonal profit-seeking endeavor. In order to produce huge quantities of meat at competitive prices, animals, especially poultry and hogs, were removed from the land and crowded into large facilities, in which feeding, temperature, lighting and manure removal were mechanized—or, in the case of cattle, placed in crowded feedlots. Today, especially in the U.S., most meat and eggs are produced in these facilities, which are known as *Concentrated Animal Feeding Operations (CAFOs)* or, more colloquially, *factory farms*.

In the U.S., for example, egg-laying hens are as of this writing still confined in small cages called battery cages, with several other hens. Since the cages have wire bottoms the chickens are incapable of engaging in their instinctive dust-bathing behavior. The crowding may be so tight that they cannot stretch their wings. The tips of their beaks, which are sensitive to pain, are often chopped off to prevent their pecking each other under these conditions. Crowding also makes the establishment of a natural pecking order impossible. About half the chicks hatched for egg-laying establishments are, of course, male. These are useless for laying eggs, so they are killed by breaking their necks, asphyxiating them or tossing them into a mechanical grinder. All of this is done indoors. The animals never see the sun.

Conditions are likewise dismal for broiler chickens, turkeys, veal calves and pigs in factory farm operations, cattle on feedlots, and all of these animals in the various transportation and slaughterhouse regimes they must endure.

Factory farms often degrade the environment and may affect human health. They produce significant quantities of methane, a greenhouse gas. Crowding promotes infectious disease, and so antibiotics are often included in the animals' feed. This facilitates the evolution of antibiotic-resistant strains of bacteria, which can then infect the human population. Massive slurries of feces and urine are kept in holding ponds, which may leak, polluting surface water or ground water. Using grain to feed animals for meat production requires, moreover, more water, energy, and land than does direct human consumption of vegetable crops.

Factory farming came to dominate meat and egg production in several of the developed nations, but especially the U.S., in the second half of the twentieth century. Long before that, however, contrary forces were in motion. Around the time of the Enlightenment moral reformers in Europe began to raise objections to the treatment of certain animals, most prominently horses, which were at that time the main source of power for transportation.

By the end of the nineteenth century, the humane movement, as it came to be called, had in many places stimulated the enactment of anti-cruelty statues. These laws applied, however, primarily to horses, to companion animals (such as dogs and cats), and sometimes to captive wild animals. They explicitly excluded agricultural or laboratory animals; animals that were hunted, fished or trapped; and animals that were regarded as pests, such as rats and mice. Animals regarded differently by humans have thus received vastly different degrees of legal protection, though the intrinsic differences among them may be small.

Only in recent years, and only in certain places, have there been legal restraints on routine cruelty in factory farms. Progress is especially noteworthy in the European Union. In addition to strict laws protecting companion animals (which provide stringent penalties for neglect or abandonment of an animal in one's care), the EU has placed many specific requirements on the treatment of agricultural animals, has banned battery cages and is phasing out crates for sows and veal calves.

Opponents of factory farming argue that it causes great suffering to large numbers of animals. But do these animals really suffer? This leads us into one of the deepest mysteries of philosophy: the problem of consciousness.

• 5.2 WHAT WE KNOW OF ANIMAL CONSCIOUSNESS

Consciousness—or, more precisely, what philosophers call phenomenal consciousness—is difficult to define. It can perhaps be characterized negatively as the sort of experience we lack under total anesthesia or in perfectly dreamless sleep. In such unconscious states, information-processing activity still occurs, but we experience nothing. We breathe and sometimes even move. Conscious awareness is wholly lacking. We are phenomenally conscious only to the extent that we experience thoughts, desires, perceptions, feelings, or the like.

All instances of consciousness for which we have solid evidence are products of functioning central nervous systems. But not all functioning nervous systems produce consciousness. In dreamless sleep, for example, our nervous systems, though suppressed, are still functioning. Some animals, such as insects, probably never achieve consciousness, even though they have active nervous systems. A housefly, for instance, has eyes that detect movement and produce quick evasive action, which is why swatting it is so tricky. But that doesn't show that it is phenomenally conscious. It seems more likely that flies are like robots, which, though not phenomenally conscious, can nevertheless be quite active and responsive.

Humans, too, though generally conscious, have unconscious behavioral responses. Our eyelids close automatically, for example, when a small object hurls toward them, even before we have a chance to become conscious of it.

Though cognitive science has lately made great strides in understanding how minds work, the exact nature and mechanisms of consciousness are still unknown. This section sketches what we know at present—or, at least, what the best evidence suggests—about consciousness in non-human animals.

One form of phenomenal consciousness that has figured much in animal ethics and axiology is sentience. **Sentience**, as the term is used in the animal ethics literature (and as it is used here), is the ability to enjoy or suffer—to have experiences that are not only conscious but pleasant or unpleasant. These experiences may be sensory, as is the case with localized bodily pleasure or pain, or they may be more diffuse and emotional—as with contentment, fear or depression.

Nearly all living humans are sentient—though individuals who are brain dead, and probably also fetuses at early stages of gestation, are not. Some people are afflicted by a very rare genetic anomaly called congenital analgesia that prevents them from feeling bodily pain. This condition is dangerous, since it makes it easy for these people to injure themselves without knowing it. But they have other forms of sentience.

Many non-human animals are sentient as well. While Descartes and others have doubted this, the evidence for sentience in many non-human animals is quite strong. It can be classified into three main types: behavioral, evolutionary and neurophysiological.

Much of the behavioral evidence is, and has always been, commonplace. A dog with a leg injury whimpers and limps. When it is lonely it whines. When it is happy or excited, it moves rapidly and wags its tail. Cats hiss in fear or anger and purr with contentment. When sick, many animals become unresponsive and withdrawn, just as we do. Many also learn from their positive and negative experiences, to avoid what has hurt them and return to what has given them pleasure. Many form emotional bonds. But not all animals do. Insects and spiders, for example, lack most of the behaviors typically associated with sentience in vertebrates.

The second line of evidence for animal sentience is evolutionary. In humans it is obvious that sentience facilitates learning based on past experience. Our nervous systems generate pleasure in eating, drinking, rest and sex (all of which are crucial for survival or reproduction), and they generate suffering when we injure, poison or sicken ourselves (actions that threaten survival). Positive experiences reinforce behavior and negative experiences discourage it. Thus sentience enables us to learn from past experience to behave in ways that promote survival and reproduction. We observe the same behavioral ability in other animals. An animal may, for example, avoid a particular plant because it was once injured by its thorns. Since animals evolved from the same ancestors that we did, the explanation of this ability in them is most likely the same as in us: they learn from pleasure and pain. It would be bizarre, for example, if their avoidance of harmful stimuli was not the result of pain but of something else entirely. The best explanation is that they feel pain, as we do, and for the same evolutionary reasons.

Evolutionary theory also sheds some light on the question of which organisms are sentient. If the survival value of sentience lies in its facilitation of associative learning, then it should occur only in organisms that can learn in that way. Nearly all vertebrates—including fishes, amphibians, reptiles, birds and mammals—can. Whether any non-vertebrates do is controversial, though some non-vertebrate animals exhibit simpler forms of learning. Many kinds of organisms, however, including plants, fungi, and microorganisms, exhibit no sign of learning in this way; so presumably they are not sentient. This expectation is corroborated by the fact that they have none of the neural hardware associated with sentience.

For such reasons, many cognitive scientists think that sentience arose with the centralization of the nervous system early in vertebrate evolution. But there is also some evidence for sentience in certain crustaceans, octopi and squid (Varner 2012: ch. 5; Broom 2007; DeGrazia 1996).

The third line of evidence for animal sentience is neurophysiological. We know a good bit about the mechanisms of pleasure and pain in humans. Anesthesiologists, for example, are familiar enough with the neural circuitry of pain to be adept at controlling it. Our nervous systems are equipped with specialized receptors, called ***nociceptors***, which respond to pressure, heat, or tissue damage. When nociceptors send signals through the neural fibers that connect them with the brain, we feel pressure or heat or pain. Some anesthetics work by blocking these signals. Others work by affecting the way the brain processes them. Similar neural structures occur in other vertebrates, evidently with the same functions. Veterinary anesthesiologists thus successfully use the same anesthetics and analgesics that control pain in humans to control pain in many vertebrate animals.

It is a mistake, however, to suppose that the mere presence of nociceptors proves that an organism can feel pain. Whether the animal can feel pain depends in part on whether the nociceptors are wired up in the right way to the appropriate circuitry of the brain. Some nociceptors in humans are wired into reflex arcs that send signals only to the spinal cord. When we touch a hot stove, for example, nerves send a fast signal to the spinal cord that automatically triggers a withdrawal reflex in the hand. This all happens unconsciously. We feel no pain until separate and slower neural fibers transmit signals from other nociceptors to the pain processing areas of the brain. The responses of some animals to tissue damage may be of this purely unconscious sort. Many non-vertebrates—crustaceans, for example—have nociceptors, but their nervous systems are generally much simpler than those of vertebrates. So the firing of their nociceptors may not produce conscious pain.

Bodily pain is one sort of negative experience, but there are negative emotions too, such as depression. These also occur in many vertebrates, often via the same brain structures as in humans. Activity in the amygdala, for example, a structure central to the vertebrate brain, plays a significant role in the arousal of fear and anger in both human and non-human vertebrates.

The evidence for vertebrate sentience is thus quite strong. One can, of course, doubt that animals are conscious. But one can likewise doubt that one's best (human) friend is conscious. This unnerving thought, known to philosophers as "the problem of other minds," is worthy of philosophical rumination. But to act on it would be mad. Yet the evidence for consciousness in animals is nearly as strong as the evidence for consciousness in other humans. Humans, of course, can describe their feelings in ways that animals can't, so the evidence is stronger for other humans than it is for non-human animals. But many animals can vocalize too, in ways that we can understand.

We should not, however, assume that animals' experiences are the same as ours. Sentience undoubtedly varies greatly in quality and degree among species. In the case of our nearest relatives, the great apes, there are, no doubt, many similarities. But for fish or frogs the differences are probably vast. Beware the seductions of anthropomorphism!

Beyond the vertebrates, evidence for any sort of consciousness is thin. But little scientific work has been done on the question. Our ignorance is vast. We should not jump to any conclusion prematurely.

There are other capacities besides sentience that play important roles in ethics and axiology. The most important of these is **_moral agency_**, the ability to act for moral reasons. Clearly, the reasoning abilities of some humans surpass those of any non-human on this planet. Yet precursors, or prototypical forms, of certain kinds of both reasoning and moral behavior are apparent in many animals. Animals also vary widely in intelligence, self-awareness and the ability to plan and anticipate their own futures. The extent to which various animals are capable of any of these forms of consciousness is still under investigation.

• 5.3 THE MORAL STATUS OF SENTIENT ANIMALS

Moralists, both religious and secular, have always denounced wanton cruelty to animals. But often they have done so out of concern not for the animals, but for humans. Kant, for example, wrote:

if a man has his dog shot, because it can no longer earn a living for him, he is by no means in breach of any duty to the dog, since the latter is incapable of judgment, but he thereby damages the kindly and humane qualities, which he ought to exercise in virtue of his duties to mankind. Lest he extinguish such qualities, he must already practise a similar kindliness towards animals; for a person who already displays such cruelty to animals is also no less hardened towards men.

(Kant 1997: 27:459)

Kant's reasoning here is both virtue theoretic (cruelty to animals demeans human character) and consequentialist (those who are cruel to non-human animals become thereby cruel to humans, which is bad for their human victims). But it denies that animals themselves are morally considerable. It is therefore anthropocentric.

Anthropocentrism has, in fact, generally been taken for granted. This is true not only of those ethics which, like Kant's, are explicitly anthropocentric (given the assumption that only humans are rational agents), but even of some that make room for the moral considerability of animals. John Stuart Mill, for example, in the second chapter of his book *Utilitarianism*, writes that the goal of ethics "is an existence exempt as far as possible from pain, and as rich as possible in enjoyments . . . secured to all mankind; and not to them only, but, so far as the nature of things admits, to the whole sentient creation." But he does not develop the implications of this thought, and throughout most of the twentieth century successive generations of utilitarians largely ignored animals.

Anthropocentrism, both ethical and axiological, was taken for granted, not only by the heirs of the Enlightenment, but also by many who reacted against it. Influential figures among the existentialists, for example, beginning with Friedrich Nietzsche in the late nineteenth century, held that apart from the human creation of values, the world is valueless, meaningless, or absurd. Thus they completely overlooked the significance of events for sentient non-humans.

Section Outline: Section 5.3 initiates a discussion of non-anthropocentric axiologies and ethics. It is divided into three subsections. Section 5.3.1 explains three conceptions of animal welfare and their relation to conceptions of human welfare; section 5.3.2 surveys and criticizes a number of reasons for excluding non-human animals from moral considerability; and section 5.3.3 considers an important argument for the moral considerability of some animals: the argument from marginal cases.

5.3.1 Animal Welfare

Axiological non-anthropocentrism is the view that conditions may be good or bad for non-humans in many of the same ways that they are good or bad for humans—that, in other words, human values are not the only values. This assumption is empirically grounded in the evidence for animal sentience that was summarized in section 5.2. What happens to animals that can enjoy and suffer matters, not just from a human standpoint, but to the animals themselves. In other words, things can be good or bad for sentient animals independently of human valuing.

Good or bad how? Section 2.3.2.2 laid out the three main axiologies used by utilitarian moral theories. These are applicable not only to humans, but to sentient non-humans.

Hedonistic views take goodness to be pleasure and badness to be pain. Thus they assess an animal's level of welfare by the extent to which the pleasures it experiences outweigh the pains.

Preference-satisfaction views take goodness to be preference satisfaction and badness to be preference frustration. Like humans, sentient animals have preferences. Still, as in the case of humans, preferences may sometimes conflict with the directives of pleasure and pain. Some animals that are kept in apparently comfortable captivity seem, for example, to prefer freedom, even at the price of pain.

One objection to preference-satisfaction axiologies in the human case, as was noted in section 3.2.5, is that satisfying our preferences is often not good for us. This is clearly the case with our appetites for many fats and sugars, which we inherited from our ancestors, who developed them in environments where access to fats and sugars was difficult. The same sort of thing can happen with animals. For the most part, evolution has equipped wild animals with genetically based preferences that keep them healthy and reproductively fit. But these preferences function well only in environments similar to those in which the animals evolved. Wolves, for example, happen to like the taste of ethylene glycol, an ingredient in automotive antifreeze. Evolution failed to select against this preference, because there was no antifreeze in the environments in which they evolved. Today, however, they may come upon puddles of the stuff in parking lots. If they lap it up, satisfying their natural preference, they die an agonizing death. Thus satisfying preferences is not always beneficial, even for non-human animals.

Health, however, is good for any animal that has it. Thus, as in the human case, many theorists advocate for animals an **objective welfare** view, which defines goodness for an animal largely in terms of health. But sometimes, as in the human case, they also incorporate enjoyment and the absence of suffering into their criterion, thus subsuming hedonistic welfare within objective welfare.

In sum, conceptions of animal welfare vary in much the same way that conceptions of human welfare do. But there is near universal agreement on this fundamental fact: events can go better or worse for sentient animals. It follows that value did not first arise with the appearance of *Homo sapiens*.

5.3.2 Reasons for Excluding Non-Humans from Moral Considerability

The fact that things can go better or worse for sentient animals does not by itself logically imply that they are morally considerable. A being is morally considerable (i.e., is a moral patient) only if we ought to have moral concern for it. But to reason from the premise that things can go better or worse for sentient animals to the conclusion that we ought to be morally concerned about them is to make a move from "is" to "ought," from a descriptive statement to a prescriptive one. There is, as we saw in section 2.2.1, no valid way to deduce a non-trivial prescriptive statement from non-prescriptive premises.

In this instance the descriptive statement (that events can go better or worse for sentient animals) is also evaluative, since it concerns what is *good* for them. But that makes no essential difference, for it is not prescriptive. We can, in other words, coherently suppose that threats to animal welfare engender no responsibilities on our part. But it is also conceivable that we do have responsibilities to animals. To show either that we do or that we do not (i.e., that non-human animals either are or are not morally considerable) requires further argument.

One way to argue that non-human animals are *not* morally considerable is to maintain that only humans satisfy some criterion necessary for moral considerability. But what criterion? Obviously not sentience, since both human and non-human animals are sentient.

According to some religious views, what makes humans alone morally considerable is that we alone have immortal souls or, perhaps, some special relation to God. But how could we verify that humans alone have these things? If we do, when in our evolutionary history did we acquire them? Various faiths have various answers (or non-answers) to such questions, but we have no empirical way of assessing them. More fundamentally, why should possession of an immortal soul or being in a special relation to God be necessary for moral considerability? Couldn't we have moral responsibilities to animals even if they lack these things?

Philosophers' traditional reason for asserting that only humans are moral patients is that only humans are rational. It is true, on this planet at least, that only humans are capable of certain kinds of rationality, such as the reasoning needed to understand this book. But not all humans have such capacities. Infants and small children, the congenitally mentally disabled, and people afflicted by Alzheimer's disease, among others, may be no better at reasoning than some non-human animals. Yet we still have ethical responsibilities to these people. Moral agents, of course, must be rational, but moral patients needn't be. Rationality is not, therefore, a requirement for moral considerability.

There are other ways in which humans are unique. Nothing else on Earth has a language or technology that matches ours in complexity. Probably nothing else has the degree of self-awareness that some of us attain. Certainly no other creature commands the power that we do. But none of these unique capacities is a requirement for being morally considerable.

Perhaps, then, we should say that the criterion for moral considerability is just . . . being a member of the species *Homo sapiens*. But in the absence of further justification, this criterion is arbitrary, like drawing the line of moral considerability at the border of one's nation, class or race. Moreover, it leaves too many questions unanswered. Why, for example, couldn't pre-human hominids have had moral responsibilities to one another? And why wouldn't we have moral duties to extraterrestrial visitors? In either case there would be moral patients not of our species.

In short, there seems to be no requirement of moral considerability that is fulfilled only by humans. Whenever we try to limit moral consideration just to humans by using a narrow criterion such as rationality, we find that it leaves out humans that we ought to consider. But, if we broaden the criterion enough to include all human moral patients, then, unless we arbitrarily stipulate that the criterion is just *being human*, we find that it applies to some non-humans as well.

5.3.3 The Argument from Marginal Cases

Our inability to find an informative and rationally defensible criterion that confines moral consideration just to humans is the basis for perhaps the best known argument for the moral considerability of animals: the **argument from marginal cases**:

> Any reasonable (and hence non-arbitrary) criterion of moral considerability sufficiently wide to include "marginal" humans (e.g., infants, the mentally disabled) also includes some non-humans.
> Any correct criterion of moral considerability must include these marginal humans.
> ∴ Any correct and reasonable criterion of moral considerability includes some non-humans.

The argument is valid. The second premise is almost universally accepted. Hence the only real point of controversy is the first premise. This first premise is supported by our failure to find a non-arbitrary criterion of moral considerability that excludes non-humans. But that failure, while suggestive, does not prove the premise. It is at least conceivable that there is a non-arbitrary criterion that includes the appropriate "marginal" humans and excludes all non-humans but that that criterion has simply been overlooked. Hence the argument's soundness may still be questioned.

Yet its conclusion is plainly right: we do have moral responsibilities to *some* non-human animals. It is morally wrong, for example, to neglect or abuse a dog or cat—not merely because such behavior violates social expectations, tends to make us more violent, or besmirches our character but, more fundamentally, because it harms the animal. We owe it to the animal, in other words, not just to ourselves or to our fellow humans, not to inflict such harm. It follows that at least some sentient animals are morally considerable.

How far should this consideration extend? Perhaps the most startling fact about contemporary human treatment of animals is its inconsistency. Even those who love dogs or cats are often indifferent to the misery of similarly sensitive and intelligent pigs which are routinely made to endure great misery *en masse* in factory farms. Confusion and disagreement regarding the proper treatment of animals is rife within global culture.

The remainder of this chapter considers attempts to resolve these inconsistencies and develop more coherent and compassionate ethical views. To make consistent sense of our responsibilities to animals, we need a comprehensive, carefully articulated and convincing animal ethic. In 1975 Peter Singer published an attempt to provide it.

5.4 SINGER'S *ANIMAL LIBERATION*

Singer's *Animal Liberation* is the most influential book ever written on animal ethics. Many rightly regard it as a major stimulus for the contemporary animal rights movement—though, as a utilitarian, Singer himself had, as we shall see, little use for the notion of rights.

Almost from the start, Singer provides a very simple criterion of moral considerability, which he borrows from Jeremy Bentham. It is worth quoting in full the relevant passage from Bentham's *Introduction to the Principles of Morals and Legislation*, written at the apex of the Enlightenment:

> The day *may* come when the rest of the animal creation may acquire those rights which never could have been withholden from them but by the hand of tyranny. The French have already discovered that the blackness of the skin is no reason why a human being should be abandoned without redress to the caprice of a tormentor. It may one day come to be recognized that the number of the legs, the villosity of the skin, or the termination of the *os sacrum*[1] are reasons equally insufficient for abandoning a sensitive being to the same fate. What else is it that should trace the insuperable line? Is it the faculty of reason, or perhaps the faculty of discourse? But a full-grown horse or dog is beyond comparison a more rational, as well as a more conversable animal, than an infant of a day or a week or even a month, old. But suppose they were otherwise, what would it avail? The question is not, Can they *reason*? or Can they *talk*? but, Can they *suffer*?
>
> (Bentham 1789: ch. XVII, §1 IV, n.)

Singer agrees: an appropriate criterion of moral considerability, he thinks, is the capacity to suffer. (Note, incidentally, Bentham's use of the argument from marginal cases on the way to this conclusion.)

Many people, of course, recognize that animal suffering is ethically significant, but many think it is less significant than the suffering of humans. Singer thinks that this opinion is just as arbitrary and indefensible as racism or sexism, which belittle the importance of the interests of people of other races or genders than oneself. Thus he dubs it "speciesism." He defines **speciesism** as "a prejudice or attitude of bias in favor of the interests of members of one's own species and against those of members of other species." To develop a comprehensive, consistent and objective animal ethic, he thinks, we must overcome speciesist prejudice.

Section Outline: Section 5.4 is divided into four subsections. Section 5.4.1 explains Singer's central argument for the conclusion that factory farming is morally wrong (he uses similar arguments against several other contemporary uses of animals). Section 5.4.2 considers the moral significance of killing animals in relation to Singer's view. Section 5.4.3 explains Singer's advocacy of vegetarianism. And section 5.4.4 critiques Singer's view.

5.4.1 Singer's Central Argument

In opposition to speciesism, Singer advocates what he calls a ***principle of equality***. This is an ethical principle, not an assertion of any sort of empirical equality. It is, indeed, the major prescriptive premise from which Singer derives his moral conclusions. The idea is that when we decide how to act "the interests of every being affected . . . are to be taken into account and given the same weight as like interests of any other being" (Singer 1990: 5). We may condense this into the slogan: *equal consideration for equal interests.*

Interests, as Singer understands them, are conscious preferences. Every sentient being, Singer quite reasonably assumes, has an interest in not suffering. Moreover, the strength of that interest depends only on the intensity of the suffering itself, not on the species of the sufferer. If your toe is crushed, the resulting agony is bad, and this is against your interest. If a dog's toe is crushed, causing it the same degree of agony, then that is equally against the dog's interest. Singer's equality principle thus implies that it is just as wrong to crush the dog's toe as to crush yours. More generally, how wrong it is to cause a given amount of suffering does not depend on the species of the sufferer.

Implicit in the equality principle is the idea that greater suffering deserves greater consideration. If crushing the dog's leg instead of its toe would cause it still greater suffering, then crushing its leg would be worse than crushing either its toe or your toe. It doesn't matter that you are human and the dog is just a dog. To give special consideration to the interests of one's own species is, according to Singer, speciesism, just as giving greater consideration to the interests of one's own racial group is racism. Both are arbitrary and unjustified.

While Singer's equality principle implies equal *consideration* for equal suffering, it does not imply equal *treatment*, because different animals may suffer differently given the same treatment. Thus, for example, it is unacceptable to slap a baby with the same force that one might slap a horse. Slapping the horse may not hurt it at all and be necessary to get its attention, while a similar slap to a baby may be child abuse.

The emotional effect, too, of similar treatment may be very different in different species. Caging a wolf that normally ranges over great distances may distress it greatly, but caging moles that normally live in burrows may not distress them at all, if they have places to burrow. Hence the same sort of treatment may cause emotional suffering in one case but not in another.

It is, of course, difficult to compare interests in not suffering among different species, and the difficulty is compounded if interests in not suffering are compared with other sorts of interests—such as interests in pleasure. Precise comparison may not be possible at all. But Singer thinks that precise comparison is not always needed. It is obvious, for example, that torturing an animal causes greater suffering to the animal than depriving a human of some small pleasure causes to the human.

Animal Liberation is an extended argument against many commonly accepted ways of causing animal suffering, including hunting, fishing, rodeos, bullfights, and most animal research. In terms of the numbers of animals affected, however, the most important argument is the one against factory farms. Some of the methods of factory farms were alluded to in section 5.1.3. "[U]nder these methods," says Singer, "animals lead miserable lives from birth to slaughter" (Singer 1990: 97). But factory farms, he argues, are unnecessary. Meat is not nutritionally essential for most humans. Most people eat it out of custom or because they like the taste. Moreover, the intermittent pleasure people get from eating meat pales in comparison with the continual suffering of animals confined under factory farm conditions. It would plainly be morally wrong to force humans to suffer in this way for the sake of someone else's pleasure. Hence, given the principle of equality, it is equally wrong to force this suffering upon animals. More explicitly, Singer's argument is as follows:

> Factory farming causes many animals severe suffering for the sake of modest benefits that could be achieved without such suffering.
> Any action that causes many humans severe suffering for the sake of modest benefits that could be achieved without such suffering is morally wrong.
> To evaluate the moral worth of an activity, the suffering of every sentient being affected by it must be taken into account and given the same weight as like suffering of any other sentient being.
> ∴ Factory farming is morally wrong.

Properly understood, this argument is valid.

The first premise is an empirical claim about the experiences of animals in factory farms and the ease of supplying our nutritional needs and culinary desires by other means. The benefits that Singer is referring to are those of meat-eating: taste and nutrition. To say that these could easily be achieved in other ways is not to say that we could produce the same amount of meat for the same price in humane ways. Singer thinks we could not. His point, rather, is that there are tasty and nutritious substitutes for meat. That there are nutritious substitutes is an empirical fact. But taste is more subjective. The crux of the premise, then, is its implicit claim that the specific pleasure that people get from the taste of meat is not great enough to outweigh the great and prolonged suffering of animals in factory farms.

The second and third premises are both prescriptive. They are the premises by which Singer moves from "is" to "ought"—that is, transforms his axiology into an ethic. Singer takes the second premise to be an obvious ethical truth; it is, in fact, implicit in any of the standard utilitarian choice principles (see section 2.3.2.3), even those that are wholly anthropocentric. Singer doesn't specify exactly which choice principle he is using, but since this premise follows from any of them, it doesn't matter.

The third premise is the principle of equality. Its function is to extend the coverage of the choice principle to include sentient animals. We can deny it, Singer thinks, only by arbitrarily espousing speciesism.

In sum, the argument is this: factory farming causes severe suffering for the sake of benefits the like of which could easily be obtained otherwise; this suffering is so great that to impose it on humans for the sake of such benefits would obviously be wrong; hence by the principle of equality, to impose it on animals for the sake of such benefits is equally wrong.

5.4.2 The Question of Killing

Singer's argument in *Animal Liberation* is based entirely on the wrongness of the suffering endured by animals, not on the wrongness of their deaths. This is not because Singer thinks that killing is unobjectionable, but rather because he thinks that it involves considerations that would unnecessarily complicate the argument. The suffering that factory farms cause is quite enough, in his view, to condemn them.

But what of killing itself? The obvious utilitarian objection to killing is that it deprives the animal of the experiences it would have had if it had lived, thus diminishing the amount of welfare in the world. If, however, a new animal is born to replace it, bringing new experiences into the world, as happens in ongoing agricultural operations, total welfare need not be diminished. Thus this obvious utilitarian objection does not apply to sustained agricultural operations that raise animals humanely, slaughter them painlessly, and replace them with new animals. (Even if welfare is not diminished, however, a weaker utilitarian objection might apply: namely that welfare is not *maximized* in such operations—in other words, that there are agricultural arrangements that produce greater total utility and hence should be adopted instead. This, however, would be more difficult to prove, and Singer does not attempt it.)

Singer wants to reject even humane animal agriculture, but the utilitarian theory of *Animal Liberation* provides no straightforward argument against it. A deontologist, whose concern is for the individual rather than the aggregate, could argue that slaughter is wrong merely because it harms or disrespects the individual animal, but this argument is not available to Singer the utilitarian.

What does Singer do? In *Animal Liberation* he argues, somewhat like Kant (see section 5.3), that condoning slaughter causes us think of animals as mere objects, which contributes to bad character in humans and mistreatment of animals generally. (The irony is delicious: Singer, the consequentialist, argues like Kant, the deontologist, who, as was noted in section 5.3, used consequentialist and virtue-theoretic arguments!) Few were convinced by Singer's reasoning regarding humane animal agriculture.

Perhaps, in the end, even Singer himself wasn't, for he later developed another argument against painless killing and replacement. According to this new argument, killing an animal that is self-aware, has a sense of its own future, and prefers to live harms it by leaving its future-oriented preferences unsatisfied. Such harm, Singer thinks, cannot be offset by replacing it with a new animal (Singer 2011: ch. 5). But the assumptions of this new argument, too, are controversial. And it applies only to animals that are self-aware, have a sense of their own future and prefer to live. It is doubtful that chickens, for example, have these capacities.

5.4.3 Vegetarianism

Singer reminds us, however, that the vast majority of agricultural animals, whether they have a sense of their own future or not, are raised inhumanely and so suffer significantly while alive whether or not they are harmed by being painlessly slaughtered. So his central argument against factory farming, which depends only on the unjustifiability of causing such suffering, still holds. If painless slaughter itself is wrong, then that would strengthen and broaden Singer's case against animal agriculture, but it is not crucial to his case against factory farms. Singer argues, furthermore, that any form of animal agriculture on a scale large enough to feed today's populations will probably cause considerable suffering. Hence, he concludes, we should refrain from eating the meat of any sentient animals.

Singer does not object to the consumption of eggs, provided these are obtained from humanely treated birds. But this is not true of eggs from factory farms, where hens are subject to inhumane conditions and male chicks are routinely destroyed *en masse*.

There are issues, too, with dairy products. Milk producers separate lactating mothers (chiefly cows, but sometimes also goats, sheep or buffalo) from their young, causing emotional distress to both. Large dairy operations feed lactating animals very rich diets, which are not good for them, and breed them for ever-greater production. Cows are often given bovine growth hormone to increase production even further. Frequently under these conditions they suffer from mastitis. So milk production—especially large-scale mechanized milk production—is not harmless.

We should also refrain from eating fish, Singer thinks, because common fishing techniques cause them to suffer—though the pain of a fish on a hook, in a net, or on a boat is of relatively short duration, compared with the misery of animals confined in factory farms. Death, moreover, deprives fish of further experience without compensatory creation of new fish, thus, other things being equal, reduces total welfare. (Considered environmentally, this is the problem of overfishing and declining fish stocks.)

With respect to animals of questionable sentience, such as shrimp, snails, lobsters or shellfish, Singer concedes that they may not feel pain, but thinks nevertheless that they "should receive the benefit of the doubt" (Singer 1990: 174).

In sum, Singer's reasoning points to an almost exclusively vegetarian diet. There are, of course, degrees of vegetarianism, and Singer does not suppose that many people will accept all of these conclusions. Changing one's diet is, in any case, challenging; and those who make the transition successfully generally do so in stages. The most important step, Singer thinks, is to refuse the products of factory farms.

One might wonder what good this would do, since factory farms will continue to exploit animals regardless of what any individual does. But even one person refraining from meat decreases demand slightly and may ultimately affect how many animals are killed. Moreover that person's example may inspire others to do the same. Thus, says Singer, individual efforts can prevent some suffering. Moreover, it is not merely a matter of a few individuals. The number of vegetarians is large and growing—though still small as a percentage of the population—and the food industry is, for economic if not ethical reasons, adapting to their choices.

5.4.4 Objections to Singer's Theory

Singer's vegetarianism strikes many people as unnatural. That, however, is not an effective objection against it. It is true that humans evolved as omnivores, whose diets contained meat. But most people can be quite healthy on a balanced vegetarian diet—often healthier than on the meat-rich diets of developed nations.

Moreover, the fact that something has been natural to humans is not by itself a reason to favor or continue it. Humans are also naturally territorial and sometimes naturally aggressive; but such behavior is often maladaptive in civilized society. Indeed, given the facts of human history, it is at least arguable that slavery, rape, theft and murder are natural to humans. But that is no argument in their favor.

A more interesting objection to Singer's theory is this: the animals in factory farms exist only because we breed them for food; thus without factory farms they would never exist at all. Their lives in factory farms are short, but at least they get to live. So, since it is better to live than not to live, it is better for them that factory farms exist.

To this objection, Singer replies that an utterly miserable life is not worth living and that animals in factory farms are so miserable that it would in fact be better for them never to have been born (or hatched). Singer's claim that the value of living can be outweighed by the disvalue of suffering is fairly uncontroversial, at least in the case of non-humans. Veterinarians, for example, often "put animals to sleep" to end their suffering. But whether the suffering of animals in factory farms is so great that it would be better for them never to live is difficult to determine.

Though Singer intends his theory to apply to all sentient animals, he is in fact concerned primarily with domesticated animals. Some of his opponents have objected, however, that in application to wild animals his theory yields absurd results. Since, for example, predation causes suffering to untold numbers of wild animals, the theory seems to imply that we should try to prevent it. But Singer denies this:

> Judging by our past record, any attempt to change ecological systems on a large scale is going to do more harm than good. For that reason, if for no other, it is true to say that, except in a few very limited cases, *we* cannot and should not try to police all of nature.

(Singer 1990: 226)

Imagine, for example, that we try to save Alaskan caribou from wolves by scattering tofu burgers about for the wolves, and suppose they come to prefer tofu burgers to caribou. The caribou population would increase; the old, weak or sick would not be culled; and the tundra might become overbrowsed. The wolves might grow fat and lazy. The mice, on which the wolves also feed, would multiply. We cannot predict where the cascade of effects would end, but chances are that in the long run there would not be less suffering.

Singer's reply may be adequate for the present. Yet it is difficult to escape the conclusion that if we somehow ever do get smart and powerful enough to re-engineer nature (or numb animals pharmacologically) so as to remove their suffering, we ought on Singer's view to do so. Many environmental ethicists find this implication abhorrent.

5.5 A DEONTOLOGICAL ANIMAL ETHIC: TOM REGAN'S *THE CASE FOR ANIMAL RIGHTS*

In *The Case for Animal Rights*, first published in 1983, Tom Regan articulates a deontological animal ethic that contrasts sharply and instructively with Singer's utilitarianism. As his title suggests, Regan's theory, unlike Singer's, posits animal *rights*.

Against Singer's utilitarianism, Regan raises the familiar charge that in its preoccupation with total goodness it may ignore individual rights or distribute burdens and benefits unfairly. Thus, for example, Singer's theory seems not to rule out the use of animals as research subjects, so long as the good produced by the research outweighs the suffering of the animals. But according to Regan, to treat animals in these ways (merely as means to our ends) is to disrespect them and violate their rights.

Singer disagrees. Like Bentham, who described talk of natural rights as nonsense, while conceding that this "nonsense" had political uses, Singer does not rely on rights. He regards rights talk as "a convenient political shorthand . . . even more valuable in the era of thirty-second TV news clips than it was in Bentham's day." But, he adds, "in the argument for a radical change in our attitude toward animals it is in no way necessary" (Singer 1990: 8).

Yet without a concept of individual rights, Singer has no clear argument against the exploitation of animals when (as in the case of successful medical research) the good consequences of that exploitation outweigh the bad. Regan sees this as a weakness of his view.

In the same vein, Regan criticizes Singer for valuing only animals' interests, not the animals themselves. On Singer's view, he notes, animals themselves have no *inherent value*. The value associated with them lies entirely in the fulfillment of their interests. They are in a sense mere "receptacles" of utility. It is as if Singer were valuing only the contents of a cup, and not the cup itself:

> On the receptacle view of value, it is *what goes into the cup* (the pleasures or preference satisfactions, for example) that has value; what does not have value is the cup itself (i.e., the individual himself or herself). The postulate of inherent value offers an alternative. The cup (that is, the individual) has value. . . . [It] does "contain" (experience) things that are valuable (e.g., pleasures), but the value of the cup (individual) is not the same as any one or any sum of the valuable things the cup contains.
>
> (Regan 2004: 236)

Since Singer's utilitarianism values only fulfillment of interests, not individuals as such, it implies that utility remains constant if, for example, we raise animals humanely, kill them suddenly and painlessly for meat, and breed new ones to replace them; for in that process the totality of satisfied interests remains unchanged. Of course the animals that are killed are deprived of further experiences, and Singer, as we saw in section 5.4.2, objects to this. But, as Regan notes, new animals are bred and their experiences replace the experiences of the old ones. We destroy old cups and create new ones, but the new cups are kept as full as the old. There is no loss of value, because the value is in the contents, not in the cups—that is, in the experiences, not in the animals.

Regan thinks that it is a mistake to focus on the totality of experiences. On his view, slaughter is a wrong done to the animal itself. It cannot be made right by creating a different animal.

Section Outline: The following account of Regan's ethic is divided into five sections. Section 5.5.1 explains his concept of inherent value. Section 5.5.2 explains and critiques his view that certain kinds of individuals, whom he calls subjects of a life, have inherent value equally. Sections 5.5.3 and 5.5.4 describe his respect and conflict-resolution principles. And section 5.5.5 draws out further implications of his view and provides further critique.

5.5.1 Regan's Axiology: Inherent Value

Slaughter is wrong on Regan's view because it violates the individual's right to respectful treatment. Here his view can be seen as a modification of Kant's view of persons. Kant held that persons (autonomous, rational beings) possess a superlative value that he called "dignity" (section 2.3.1.1). Because of this dignity they are worthy of respect (that is, of being treated as ends, not merely as means). He apparently took it for granted that all humans are persons in this sense. Regan points out that some humans (infants, children and the mentally disabled) are neither autonomous nor rational, yet are still worthy of respect. That respect cannot be based on the Kantian notion of dignity, which requires autonomy and rationality. Rather, Regan argues, it is based on something analogous that is found also in animals. He calls this something *inherent value*.

An individual has inherent value, according to Regan, if it is a ***subject of a life***. By this he means, roughly, that it cares about and can remember and anticipate how it is treated and what happens to it. More specifically, says Regan, a subject of a life has:

- beliefs and desires
- perception
- memory
- a sense of the future
- emotional life
- sentience
- ability to initiate goal-directed action
- psychophysical identity over time
- individual welfare (experiences are better or worse for it).

Both non-human and human animals may be subjects of a life. But not all of them are. Subjects of a life must not only be sentient; they must have an emotional investment in their futures and desires that they aim to satisfy. They do not live just for the moment.

All but the most severely cognitively impaired humans are subjects of a life in this sense. But Regan thinks that all adult mammals are too—and perhaps some birds—though he doubts that other vertebrates (reptiles, amphibians, fish, etc.) are. Regan thinks it is possible that things other than subjects of a life may have some other kind of inherent value, but he does not develop this thought (Regan 2004: 245). The only sort of inherent value that he clearly posits is the inherent value of subjects of a life.

Inherent value is the moral worth of the individual as such. It does not, according to Regan, depend on the quality of the individual's experience. A person or animal with a happy life has no more inherent value than one with a miserable life. The happy life is preferable experientially, of course, but the moral value of the individual is the same in each case. Both moral agents and moral patients have inherent value merely because they are subjects of a life; being an agent does not give you more of it. Inherent value is, furthermore, not a status that we earn by our actions, nor does it depend on our usefulness to others.

5.5.2 The Principle of Equality of Individuals

In fact, according to Regan, all subjects of a life, both human and non-human, have *equal* inherent value. This equality is not an empirical matter; subjects of a life differ greatly in nearly every empirical respect: intellectual abilities, emotional makeup, capacities for experience, and so on. We must assume equality, Regan thinks, because if we don't then we are committed to the idea that some individuals, being of lesser moral worth, deserve less consideration than others. This idea, says Regan is "morally pernicious." Historically, it has resulted in such objectionable forms of discrimination as "chattel slavery, rigid caste systems, and gross disparities in the quality of life available to citizens of the same state." Moreover, it is unjust, since no individual is responsible for the nature, gifts and talents that she or he was born with (Regan 2004: 234).

Thus Regan denies that some individual subjects of a life have greater inherent value than others. But then he commits a logical fallacy; for he goes on to conclude that all subjects of a life have *equal* inherent value. That does not follow. Here are two counterexamples: assume that no subjects of a life have more inherent value than others; still, there might be either no such thing as inherent value at all, or the inherent values of some subjects of a life may be **incomparable with** (that is, neither greater than nor less than nor equal to) the inherent values of others.

The first counterexample questions Regan's assumption that inherent value exists. There is such a thing as animal welfare, as was explained in section 5.3.1, but inherent value is allegedly something quite different. It has nothing to do with the animal's health or the qualities of its experiences. It is a kind of absolute moral status that Regan posits for subjects of a life, apparently to counteract patterns of human thought that produce injustice. The empirically inclined may dismiss it as a moral fiction.

The second counterexample points to the possibility of value incomparability—a possibility all too frequently overlooked in axiology and in ethics. Incomparability is inequality without superiority. That is, if two individuals are incomparable in moral value, they are not equal, yet neither has greater value than the other. They are just too different for comparison. To say that two values are incomparable is not merely to say that we have no idea how to compare them. Rather, it is to say that no ranking of greater than, less than or equal to between them is correct. (For a more detailed discussion of incomparability, see section 7.3.2.)

What these counterexamples show is that even if no individual has greater inherent value than any other, it does not follow that all subjects of a life have equal inherent value. They show, in other words, that the idea that all subjects of a life have equal inherent value, which Regan calls the principle of **equality of individuals**, rests on shaky non-empirical ground. Even if we reject this principle, however, there is something to be said for the remainder of Regan's ethic.

5.5.3 The Respect Principle

The claim that all subjects of a life have inherent value—indeed, have it equally—does not by itself imply anything about what we ought to do (Regan 2004: 248). To derive ethical responsibilities from this claim, Regan must invoke a prescriptive principle, the **respect principle**, according to which we ought to treat those who have inherent value in ways that respect their inherent value—unless we have overriding ethical reasons to the contrary. To treat something with respect means, in Regan's thinking, as in Kant's, to treat it as an end and not merely as a means or mere object. What Regan calls the respect principle is thus a generalization of Kant's categorical imperative—specifically, of the formula of humanity (see section 2.3.1.1). Regan's respect principle widens the scope of the formula of humanity from humanity to all subjects of a life. It is the fundamental prescriptive premise in his moral reasoning.

Kant thought that the categorical imperative was uniquely justified by reason alone—that anyone who thought carefully, impartially, and clearly enough could see its truth. But many reasonable people have demurred. So Regan does not claim such a justification for his respect principle. Rather, he offers it as part of an ethical theory that, as he tries to show, is superior to all extant rivals. That doesn't mean that his theory is ultimately true. It merely means, if he is right, that this is the best theory we have for now. (Consequentialists and others would, of course, disagree.)

From the respect principle, Regan derives a principle of non-harm. The argument is straightforward and valid:

1 We ought to treat those who have inherent value in ways that respect their inherent value unless we have overriding moral reasons to the contrary. (Respect principle)
2 To harm something that is inherently valuable without overriding moral reasons to do so is to fail to treat it with respect.
∴ 3 We ought not to harm those with inherent value, unless we have overriding moral reasons to do so. (Principle of non-harm)

The principle of non-harm asserts, as Regan understands it, a *right* not to be harmed. Regan derives other rights (e.g., the right to life, the right to be treated justly) by similar reasoning.

Rights, on Regan's view, are not absolute. They can be overridden by other moral considerations. They are, to use the legal and philosophical jargon, **prima facie** rights. Thus, for example, even though an animal has a right not to be harmed, we may harm it in self-defense, since we have an overriding right to protect ourselves. But such overriding considerations must be *moral*. It is a clear violation of rights, for example, to harm an animal just for our amusement.

From the respect principle and the rights that follow from it, a great many specific ethical implications follow. Subjects of a life may not be owned as property, since to regard them as property is to treat them merely as means. Regan likens it to slavery. Subjects of a life may, however, be adopted as household companions. Subjects of a life may not be killed for any unnecessary benefit. This includes the benefit of meat-eating, since nearly all meat-eating is unnecessary. Regan's principles therefore clearly imply, as Singer's do not, that even animals raised humanely on family farms should not be slaughtered and eaten. Nor, on Regan's principles, should subjects of a life be hunted, kept in zoos, or exploited in circuses or rodeos, since these activities, too, treat them merely as means. These implications follow from Regan's respect principle independently of his claim that all subjects of a life have equal inherent value.

Regan's theory has equally radical implications for animal research. Although a good bit of animal research (e.g., the testing of cosmetics on animals) is clearly not morally necessary, there may be strong ethical justification for research on animals that could lead, for example, to the cure of life-threatening diseases. In such cases, given Regan's principles, the rights of animals conflict with vital human needs. What overrides what? The postulate of equal inherent value functions here to give animals *equal* rights. Just as we would not do research on unconsenting humans even to cure life-threatening diseases, so too, thinks Regan, should we not do research on animals, which cannot give consent. Thus Regan favors a total ban on animal research.

5.5.4 Conflict-Resolution Principles

On any theory of rights, there are cases in which the rights of some individuals conflict with the rights of others. Additional rules are therefore needed to resolve these conflicts. Regan provides two such conflict-resolution principles. The first is the

> *Minimize overriding (miniride) principle*—special considerations aside, it is better to override the rights of the innocent few than the rights of the innocent many—if the harms to all are comparable.

This is just common sense. If faced with a choice between violating many similar rights or violating few, we should, other things being equal, violate the few. Regan's second principle, however, is quite controversial. This is the

> *Worse-off principle*—special considerations aside, if we must choose between harm to the few and harm to the many, and the harm to the few would make them worse off than any of the many would be if harm to the many were chosen, we should choose harm to the many.

The idea here is that when faced with a choice of two harms, one smaller and one greater, one should always choose the smaller harm, even if it occurs to many more people. Suppose the smaller harm is a broken arm and the larger harm is having both arms broken. Then we should choose the smaller harm, even if it occurs to more individuals. If the choice is between breaking one arm on each of a thousand individuals or both arms on just one individual, we should choose to break the arms of the thousand.

Utilitarians, of course, reject this principle, since breaking the arms of the thousand would result in a greater total loss of utility. But Regan is not concerned with totals. He is only concerned with individuals. The worse-off principle is justified, he thinks, by its all-things-considered fit with our intuitions. This, however, is widely disputed.

We won't pursue Regan any further into this thicket. The deeper you look the more complicated, and often controversial, deontological rules become. It is not surprising, then, that the details of Regan's ethical theory have never won wide acceptance. Nor has any other very complete system of deontological rules for animal ethics.

5.5.5 Implications and Objections

The contours of Regan's notion of obligation differ significantly from those of Singer. Like Singer, Regan condemns factory farms and advocates vegetarianism, but he goes further in absolutely rejecting the use of animals for research, the use of animal products, including milk and eggs, and even ownership of animals, which he regards as a form of slavery. However, the class of animals to which Regan's ethic applies (subjects of a life; that is, adult mammals and possibly birds) is smaller than the class of animals to which Singer's ethic applies (sentient animals, including all, or nearly all, vertebrates, and possibly some non-vertebrates as well). Thus, for example, while Singer regards fish as moral patients, and rejects fishing for that reason; Regan does not.

Regan does think that we should refrain from fishing, but not out of ethical consideration for the fish. His reason, rather, is that fishing encourages "formation of habits and practices that lead to the violation of the rights of animals who are subjects-of-a-life" (Regan 2004: 417). Thus Regan uses the same strategy to oppose cruelty to fish and yet deny them moral consideration that Kant once used for animals in general (see section 5.3).

Predation appears to be a problem for Regan, as it is for Singer. For if subjects of a life have a right not to be harmed, then doesn't that give them rights to protection against predators? Regan thinks not, because he regards rights as violable only by moral agents. Lightning, for example, may kill someone, but it cannot violate her rights, because it is not a moral agent. Her death is tragic but not morally wrong. Likewise, if a fox kills a grouse, it does not violate the grouse's rights, because the fox is not a moral agent. But if a hunter, who is a moral agent, kills the grouse, that does violate the grouse's rights and is morally wrong.

As moral agents we have no duty, according to Regan, to maximize goodness, but we do have a duty not to violate rights. Thus we may not hunt, but we have no obligation to protect animals from non-human predators.

But what about predators of human moral patients? Consider a helpless child being stalked by a mountain lion. Surely we should intervene, even though the lion is not a moral agent. But now consider a helpless fawn being stalked by the same lion. Both the child and the fawn are mere moral patients. Both are, or will be, subjects of a life. They are, according to Regan, of equal inherent value. It would seem, on Regan's view, that we ought to treat the two cases alike. But suppose we do. Then if we save the child, we should also save the fawn. But Regan denies that we should interfere with predation by animals upon animals. On the other hand, if we let the mountain lion kill the fawn, then, it seems, we should also let it kill the child. This is plainly wrong. It's not clear how Regan would resolve this dilemma. Hence predation still seems to present at least a theoretical problem for Regan's theory.

Here's another problem: suppose we must choose between killing an innocent animal—say, a dog—and killing an innocent human. (Maybe a bomb-wielding terrorist is using both as living shields and we must shoot at least one in order to shoot the terrorist and prevent him from detonating the bomb, which would kill thousands.) Both the dog and the human are subjects of a life. They have, according to Regan, equal inherent value. So it would seem that there's no criterion for choosing. Should we simply toss a coin? Regan gives the common sense answer: we should shoot the dog. But why? Its inherent value is supposedly the same as that of the human. Yet there is, says Regan, a difference. There is more richness and opportunity, hence more value in the life of a human than in the life of a dog. Thus it is worse to deprive a human of life than to deprive a dog of life.

This reverses the cup metaphor. The cups (the dog and the human) are equally valuable, but their contents (lives or experiences) are not, and so in such cases we must decide on the basis of the value of the contents, not the value of the cups. This answer makes sense as far as it goes, but it raises worries about the appropriateness of the distinction between the individual and the life (the cup and the contents). We will not pursue these worries further here.

Given that Regan ascribes rights to all subjects of a life, both wild and domesticated, his theory has significant environmental implications. Nearly all large-scale human activities (agriculture, surface mining, the construction and use of roads, building projects, etc.) displace, injure or kill many subjects of a life—especially rodents, such as mice and voles, which are often numerous in the soil. Hence the rights Regan ascribes to non-humans conflict with the plans of humans. While it is not always clear what should override what, it is clear that adoption of Regan's theory would impede such projects and thus slow environmental damage. This may be seen either as an objection to or an advantage of Regan's theory, depending on your perspective.

Given these strong environmental implications, one might suppose that Regan would be sympathetic to those environmentalists who ascribe inherent value not only to individual animals, but to species or ecosystems. Yet he has no such sympathies and steadfastly maintains an individualistic axiology. With respect to endangered species he says:

> The rights view does not recognize the moral rights of species to anything, including survival. . . . That an individual animal is among the last remaining members of a species confers no further right on that animal, and its right not to be harmed must be weighed equitably with the rights of any others who have this right.
>
> (2004: 359)

The rights view supports saving an endangered species, then, only insofar as it happens to support saving members of that species. Species themselves have no moral status. But organisms of most species are not even sentient, much less sub-jects of a life, so presumably they have no rights at all. These species, then, would receive no moral protection via the rights of their members, and hence no moral protection at all—unless we value them for anthropocentric (e.g., scientific or aes-thetic) reasons.

One important thinker who argued that ecosystems have moral status was the great conservationist and nature writer, Aldo Leopold. Leopold had advocated hunting and fishing, sustainably practiced, so as not to damage the ecosystem. But Regan thinks that it is morally wrong for human moral agents to act as predators. He attacks Leopold's ethic in this polemical passage:

> The implications of this view include the clear prospect that the individual may be sacrificed for the greater biotic good, in the name of "the integrity, stability and beauty of the biotic community." It is difficult to see how the notion of the rights of the individual could find a home within a view that, emotive connotations to one side, might be fairly dubbed "ecological fascism"
>
> (Regan 2004: 361–62)

Regan's point is that just as fascism values a nation, a people, or a culture above the individual, and thus subverts individual human rights, so does Leopold's land ethic, by valuing the ecosystem above individual animals, subvert individual animal (perhaps also human) rights. We'll consider Leopold's side of this dispute in section 6.7.1.

• 5.6 VARNER'S RULE UTILITARIANISM

Some animal ethicists have constructed theories that attempt to unite the best features of Singer's and Regan's views. Gary Varner, for example, has developed a rule-utilitarian ethic that employs rule-based reasoning much as Regan's ethic does, but justifies the rules themselves consequentially.

Varner posits two different sets of rules for two distinct categories of sentient animals: the merely sentient and near-persons. (Persons, who are moral agents, comprise a third category.) The *merely sentient* are animals that can enjoy and suffer, but "live entirely in the present" (Varner 2012: 22) and so do not experience themselves as having more than just an immediate past or future. *Near-persons* are more like Regan's subjects of a life, having "a robust, conscious sense of their own past, present, and future" (Varner 2012: 21). Such animals include great apes (chimpanzees, gorillas, orangutans), cetaceans (whales and dolphins), and elephants. There is also evidence, Varner argues, for thinking that monkeys, parrots, corvids (crows, ravens, magpies, jays and nutcrackers), and even rats, have a sense of themselves as enduring over considerable stretches of time. For many other animals, the jury is still out (Varner 2012: ch. 8, esp. § 8.5).

There is an obvious affinity between Varner's two-level classification and the two categories of animals that Singer mentions in his later argument against killing and replacement (section 5.4.2). Like the later Singer, Varner thinks it is morally wrong to inflict unnecessary suffering on merely sentient animals but offers no argument against killing them painlessly and replacing them.

His rules for near-persons, however, are more akin to Regan's rules for subjects of a life. Near-persons' awareness of their own pasts and futures entitles them, he argues, to *prima facie* rights, presumably including rights to life and non-harm (Varner 2012: 286). Yet unlike Regan, Varner draws no sharp line between those who have rights and those who do not. He admits that the distinction between near-persons and the merely sentient is a matter of degree, and he avoids the mistake of supposing that all near-persons are morally equal. In these respects Varner's view is a compromise between Singer's and Regan's—and hence between utilitarianism and deontology.

• 5.7 CARRUTHERS' CONTRACTUALISM

There are, of course, thinkers who reject the whole idea of extending moral consideration to animals. Contractualists, for example, who see ethics as an idealized contract among rational moral agents, have, by and large, been skeptical of animal ethics. The reason is obvious: it makes little sense to think even of idealized contract negotiations with animals, who are not rational and cannot articulate their demands. Peter Carruthers, a contractualist inspired by John Rawls, writes:

> As Rawls has it, morality is, in fact, a human construction . . . Morality is viewed as constructed *by* human beings, in order to facilitate interactions *between* human beings, and to make possible a life of co-operative community. . . . To suggest, now, that contractualism should be so construed as to accord equal moral standing to animals would be to lose our grip on where moral notions are supposed to come from, or why we should care about them when they arrive.
>
> (Carruthers 1992: 101–2)

Not all animal ethicists, of course, think that animals' standing should be *equal* to that of humans, and those who do qualify that claim in various ways. But, putting that objection aside, does Carruthers give us any reason to think that animals should have no moral standing at all?

Carruthers suggests that by admitting the moral considerability of animals we would lose our grip on where our moral notions come from and why we should care about them. But this is not in general true. Many people have adopted animal ethics without any such ill effects. Advocates of animal ethics do, of course, disagree with Carruthers regarding the purpose of morality. (They may see its purpose, for example, as the flourishing, not merely of the human community, but of all sentient life.) And typically they are not contractualists. But moral thinking is not limited to contractualism.

• 5.8 CARE ETHICS

Other authors have developed care ethics for animals (Gaard 1993; Adams and Donovan 1995; Donovan and Adams 1996; Warren 2000; Engster 2006). Because care ethics emphasize the value of relationship, and often also the importance of emotional bonds, it tends to have more application to domesticated animals, especially companion animals, than to wild animals. Since according to animal care ethics, the strength of an agent's responsibilities to an animal varies with the agent's relationship to the animal, care ethics tends to support very strong obligations to companion animals and weak or nonexistent ones to wild animals. Critics argue, therefore, that just as anthropocentric care ethics doesn't fully account for our responsibilities to human strangers (see section 3.5.2), so animal care ethics fails to account adequately for our responsibilities to animal "strangers." Indeed, if the strengths of our responsibilities to animals depend on the strength of our emotional bonds to them, then it seems to follow that people who have no emotional bond to animals would have no responsibilities to them.

• 5.9 ROLSTON ON ANIMALS

Environmental ethicists, in contrast to animal ethicists, have generally been more interested in wild than domesticated animals. Among the first environmental ethicists to articulate an animal ethic was Holmes Rolston III. Rolston is a naturalist and lover of the outdoors who derives his ethic from a positive evaluation of nature itself. On his view, not only sentient animals, but non-sentient organisms, species, ecosystems and nature itself are morally considerable. This section concerns only his ethic for sentient animals. But we will consider other aspects of his ethic in section 6.6.1.

Rolston knows well that nature is violent, but he finds it in no need of improvement. Predation, death and even pain, he thinks, are in their natural context good:

> predation does not all that obviously increase suffering. Slow death by starvation or disease is not more pleasant than nearly instantaneous death by tooth and claw. Predation prevents overpopulation from the surplus of young and culls the aged and the diseased. We may judge, in fact, that bighorns, coyotes, caribou, ducks, squirrels, bluebirds in their wild places selected over evolutionary time as adapted fits in their niches, already have something approaching the richest psychological and biological lives available to them within the constraints of their ecosystems. Suffering, though present, has been trimmed to a level that is functional, bearable, even productive.
>
> (Rolston 1988: 57)

Thus Rolston's ethic is based not merely on the interests or capacities of animals themselves but on standards set by nature as a whole. We ought, he says, to "follow nature," by ensuring that our actions are biologically satisfactory. Animal ethics should therefore *not* be based primarily on respect for rights or protection of welfare, but rather on "the appropriateness or fitness of the animal's place in the ecosystem" (Rolston 1988: 58).

Because he sees natural predation as good, Rolston has no objection to human predation—that is, to hunting or fishing *per se*. Hunters and fishers are, of course, moral agents and so differ from their non-human counterparts, but so long as their predation follows natural patterns—that is, is practiced for sustenance, not merely for sport—there is nothing wrong with it. Rolston, however, condemns trapping, trophy hunting, sport fishing, and any method of taking animals that is unsustainable.

Rolston regards the concern of animal welfare theorists with the suffering of animals, especially wild animals, as excessive:

> The obligation to universal benevolence is too strong. It fails to incorporate any moral tolerance of processes of wild nature—letting a strayed albatross die, or a beached whale or dolphin, or a turtle attacked by sharks.
>
> (Rolston 1988: 54)

Yet he agrees with animal welfare theorists that when humans are responsible for harming wild animals, as for example when a deer is hit by a speeding car, there may be a duty to relieve their suffering.

Rolston's animal ethic is embodied in two principles, both of which apply to any animals, wild or domesticated, that we interfere with:

> **Non-addition principle:** Culturally imposed animal suffering is permissible only insofar as it does not exceed ecologically functional suffering.
>
> **Subtraction principle:** It is good but not obligatory to reduce pointless suffering in non-human animals.
>
> (Rolston 1988: 61)

We have, according to Rolston, no duties at all to individual wild animals unless we have interfered with them. Thus, in particular, we have no duties to aid wild animals that are suffering from non-human causes.

The non-addition principle follows from Rolston's conception of nature as morally satisfactory. It allows us to cause suffering in fulfilling our vital needs, but only to the extent that such suffering typically occurs in nature. It clearly permits, for example, meat production in farms where the animals are allowed to live in a setting that is reasonably natural to them and so do not suffer more than they would in nature. But as regards factory farms Rolston defers judgment: "Whether modern industrial farming introduces suffering in excess of ecological norms will have to be investigated elsewhere" (Rolston 1988: 79).

The subtraction principle is a weak animal welfare ethic—permitting but not requiring the reduction of pointless suffering. It allows us, for example, but does not require us, to rescue a beached dolphin.

The most fundamental objection to Rolston's theory is that it overestimates the appropriateness of nature as a guide for human moral agents. Just which aspects of nature are we to imitate and which to ignore? An asteroid impact is a natural phenomenon, more destructive than a nuclear war. Does that license equivalent destruction on our part? Of course, Rolston is not thinking in these terms or on this scale.

Still, nature is not an explicit guide, and one could as easily read horrific principles of action into it as paradigmatically moral ones. Moreover, even if we restricted ourselves to following nature only in the ways Rolston recommends, it may not be best to rest content with that. "Nature," concedes Rolston, "is not a moral agent; we do not imitate nature for interhuman conduct." "But," he adds, "nature is a place of satisfactory fitness, and we take that as a criterion for some moral judgments. We endorse a painful good" (Rolston 1988: 58–59). Maybe, but why not hold supposedly rational human moral agents to criteria higher than those set by non-rational nature, even when dealing with animals and nature itself?

5.10 PALMER'S RELATIONAL ETHIC

Clare Palmer, who works in both animal ethics and environmental ethics, has developed an animal ethic which, like Rolston's, is concerned primarily with non-domesticated animals. Central for Palmer is the assumption that the best way to treat wild animals, provided that we have not harmed them so badly that they need our assistance, is to leave them alone. She calls this assumption the *laissez-faire* intuition.

Many animal ethicists would agree. But some, like Singer, think that the reason to leave wild animals alone is that any other policy (giving tofu burgers to wolves, for example) would cause so much ecological disruption that it would do more harm than good. Palmer doesn't dispute this, but for her it is not reason enough. She thinks that even if we could improve the welfare of wild animals with no bad side effects, we should still leave them alone (Palmer 2010: 78). Unless we have already interfered with them, they have nothing to do with us; hence, on Palmer's view, there is no relationship on which moral duties could be founded. For Palmer, in other words, our ethical responsibilities depend upon our relationships. Her ethic is thus relational in the manner described in section 3.5.2. Palmer, however, does not regard her theory as a care ethic, primarily because she rejects the idea that responsibilities depend on emotional bonds (Palmer 2010: 51–53).

The *laissez-faire* intuition contrasts sharply with the proposition—which Palmer also accepts, and with which nearly all animal ethicists agree—that we have duties to care for and assist domesticated animals. This may seem odd, given that wild and domesticated animals are similarly sentient. A pig, for example, kept as a household companion, has virtually the same ethically relevant capacities as a wild boar living in a forest far from humans. Biologically, the two are so similar that they can inter-breed. The human who keeps the pig clearly has responsibilities to provide for its needs. Yet according to the *laissez-faire* intuition no one has such duties toward the boar. Why the difference?

Animal ethics typically assume that our duties to animals are determined by their capacities—their abilities, for example, to suffer, to have interests or desires, to be benefited and harmed, or to have a sense of the past and future. But if our responsibilities depend on their capacities, and the capacities of wild and domesticated animals are similar, why aren't our responsibilities toward wild and domesticated animals similar?

Palmer's answer is that our responsibilities to animals are determined not just by their capacities, but also by our interactions with them. Of course animals must, she thinks, have certain capacities, such as sentience, to qualify as moral patients. And there are minimal moral standards that govern our behavior toward all sentient animals, wild or domesticated. We may not, for example, cause them gratuitous suffering. But beyond that it is mainly our relationships with animals that determine our responsibilities toward them.

More specifically, she says, our responsibilities to both human and non-human animals are proportional to the degree to which our activities affect them. With respect to humans, Palmer assumes that our duties to assist other people are weak or nonexistent when their lives are independent of ours. If, however, we have done them an injustice (by, for example, conquest, colonization, slavery, or resource exploitation), and especially if that injustice has benefited us or our group, then even if we do not ordinarily interact with them and even if they are very different from us, we have a responsibility to help or compensate them. It is no different, she argues, with animals. Our duties to assist them are weak or nonexistent when their lives are independent of ours—as are the lives of animals in the wild. But if we humans have, for example, made them dependent on us by domesticating or breeding them, then we have clear duties to provide for their needs. And if we have harmed them or made them more vulnerable, as is the case for many animals whose habitat we have degraded, then even if we do not ordinarily interact with them, we have responsibilities to them to compensate for the damage we have done—by, for example, restoring the habitat or providing new habitat elsewhere.

One of the most novel features of her book is Palmer's observation that there is a large class of animals that are neither wild nor domesticated, which ethicists usually ignore. This class includes feral animals, captive animals, and (most importantly) animals not bred by humans that inhabit what Palmer calls a "contact zone." Contact zones are places in which humans and animals live in close proximity and sometimes interact. Virtually all non-domesticated animals living in cities or suburbs and many living in rural areas belong to this class. Because our lives are not independent of these animals, she thinks, we have some responsibilities to assist those that we have harmed (e.g., birds that crash into windows, animals wounded by traffic, etc.) or made vulnerable, but we have no responsibility to assist fully wild animals, even when they are suffering.

Palmer's theory is subject to the standard objection against relational ethics generally: that it gives a poor account of responsibilities to strangers—in this case, animal strangers. Capacity-based animal ethics generally imply that we do have moral obligations to help wild animals in distress (beached dolphins, for example), even if we have done nothing to cause the distress. Palmer thinks that that may be a fine thing to do. She might even concede that allowing a beached dolphin to die when you could help it would be hard-hearted. But she thinks that we have no moral responsibility to rescue it. At issue here is a special instance (for the case of animals) of an ancient and quite general ethical question: must we be Good Samaritans? Contemporary moral theories are divided on this question. Relational theories are pushed by their own logic toward answering it in the negative.

5.11 THE LESSONS OF ANIMAL ETHICS

Animal ethicists disagree about whether value lies in animals themselves or their experiences (or both), which animals are morally considerable, which among them (if any) have rights, whether and how some are morally equal (with one another or with humans), and what justifies human responsibilities to them. Nevertheless there are many points on which most animal ethicists agree:

- Sentient animals can in an objective sense be benefited or harmed.
- Sentient animals are morally considerable.
- To cause unjustified suffering to animals is morally wrong.
- Suffering can outweigh the value of an animal's life; that is, it can be so great as to make the animal's life not worth living.
- It is morally wrong to take the life of an animal that has a sense of its own future (or is a subject of a life or a near-person) without special justification.
- We have special ethical responsibilities to provide for animals that are directly under our care.
- We should not attempt to modify wild nature (by, for example, reducing predation) in order to increase animal welfare—at least not in our present state of knowledge.
- Hunting or fishing for mere sport or entertainment—rather than for sustenance, population management, or some other weighty reason—is morally wrong.
- Factory farms cause unjustifiable levels of suffering (and serious environmental problems as well); we should withdraw support from them by excluding their products from our diets.

Some of these principles remain quite controversial, of course, among the public. But animal ethics, though young by philosophical standards, is already making significant inroads into law and global culture. We may expect additional conclusions from animal ethics and subsequent changes in public opinion as cognitive science advances and moral sensibilities evolve.

5.12 ANIMAL ETHICS FOR THE LONG TERM

We have so far traversed a broadening path from near-term to long-term anthropocentrism and then beyond the human species into animal ethics. Are there broader ethics still? Certainly there is room for a long-term version of animal ethics, just as there is a long-term anthropocentric ethics, but so far the literature on this topic is thin. The general outlines of a theory are, however, not difficult to discern.

First and foremost, the reasons given in section 4.1 and its subsections to show that future people are no less important morally than present people apply as well to non-human animals. For animals, too, objective value does not diminish with distance in time from us.

But because we know nothing about specific individuals in the distant future, long-term animal ethics must focus on larger and coarser phenomena—e.g., populations and the conditions necessary for their flourishing. (Non-identity considerations of the sort mentioned at the end of section 4.5 yield the same conclusion.) Because any large-scale policy will inevitably harm many individuals in endeavoring to help others, long-term decisions can't be made on individualistic deontological principles. We must consider individuals in aggregate, and so our reasoning must generally be consequentialist.

As with long term anthropocentric ethics, long-term animal ethics faces population issues. One novel twist occurs with respect to Parfit's repugnant conclusion. In anthropocentric ethics, that conclusion arises because (as was noted in section 4.6.2) there are two ways to increase welfare or happiness: making people happier or making more happy people. The repugnant conclusion is the realization that making more happy people can increase total happiness even while the happiness of existing people *decreases*—so long as the decrease is less than the happiness of the additional people. The worry, then, is that maximizing happiness might require us to produce a huge number of barely happy people—and, probably as a result, a depleted planet.

But if we expand moral consideration to include sentient non-humans, this worry diminishes. We can increase total happiness by increasing the numbers of any sort of creature that will be happy—and Earth can support many more non-humans than humans. We might, then, increase happiness by restoring rich habitats replete with sentient life—both human and non-human. This life should be diverse, for too many animals of one kind—human or not—would likely disrupt ecological processes, making life harder for all, and hence decreasing total happiness. It seems likely, then, that to increase happiness we need to limit, or even reduce, human population—while preventing losses of other sentient beings, and perhaps even increasing their numbers.

Yet we are doing just the opposite. Indeed, while we are increasing our own numbers, we are driving other sentient beings to extinction. Conservation biologists warn that these extinctions are accelerating. Among our nearest relatives, the primates, for example, almost half of the 634 remaining species are listed by the International Union for Conservation of Nature as "in danger of becoming extinct" (IUCN 2010). These are richly conscious animals. They are capable of happiness. Their progressive disappearance suggests, along with many other lines of evidence, that we are not creating a happier world.

● SUGGESTIONS FOR FURTHER READING

The two classics of animal ethics are Peter Singer's *Animal Liberation* (Avon, 1990, originally published in 1975) and Tom Regan's *The Case for Animal Rights* (University of California Press, 2004; originally published in 1983). Singer's book is quite accessible. Regan's is more philosophical and more challenging.

A more comprehensive treatment than either of these classics is David DeGrazia's *Taking Animals Seriously: Mental Life and Moral Status* (Cambridge, 1996).

For a provocative feminist approach to animal ethics, see Carol J. Adams, *The Sexual Politics of Meat* (Continuum, 1995).

Two important recent additions to the philosophical literature are Clare Palmer's *Animal Ethics in Context* (Columbia, 2010) and Gary Varner's *Personhood, Ethics, and Animal Cognition: Situating Animals in Hare's Two-Level Utilitarianism* (Oxford, 2012). The latter contains a fine discussion of animal consciousness. Both are well worth reading.

The Animal Ethics Reader, edited by Susan J. Armstrong and Richard G. Botzler (Routledge, 2003) is a good collection of work in the field.

6

ethics of life

Chapter 5 considered the extension of moral consideration to sentient animals. *Sentientism* is the view that moral consideration should extend no further. This chapter questions that view. Sentience (the ability to enjoy and suffer) evolved as a means for enhancing survival and reproduction—and therefore, arguably, presupposes deeper purposes. Even non-sentient organisms have, in an intelligible sense, goods of their own. Some theorists, valuing their good, want to extend moral consideration to all living beings. Ethics that take this step are called *biocentric*.

Biocentric means "life-centered." *Ethical biocentrism* is the view that all living things are morally considerable. Sometimes the term "living things" is taken to denote only individual organisms, in which case the biocentrism is *individualistic*. Individualistic biocentrists thus hold that only individual organisms are morally considerable and that groups of organisms are morally considerable only insofar as the members of those groups are. But, largely under the influence of ecological thinking, some biocentrists include among living things such aggregate entities as colonies or populations of organisms, species, ecosystems, or even the entire biosphere. These forms of biocentrism are said to be *holistic*. Holistic biocentrists hold that some biological aggregates, such as species or ecosystems, have moral considerability beyond the total moral considerability of their members. Holistic views that emphasize protection of ecosystems are called *ecocentric*.

Chapter Outline: Chapter 6 begins with individualistic views (sections 6.1–6.4) and then moves on to holistic approaches (sections 6.5–6.7). Section 6.8 critiques both. Section 6.9 considers biocentric ethics for the long term.

6.1 GOODS OF THEIR OWN

A fundamental assumption shared by all forms of individualistic ethical biocentrism is that all living organisms, not just sentient ones, have *goods of their own*. In other words, they themselves can be benefited and harmed; and harm or benefit to them is an objective fact, independent of human valuing and cognition. This is hardly controversial. Sunlight, soil nutrients, and water in proper proportion are, for example, good for photosynthetic plants. More generally, any living organism may be harmed by wounds, excessive heat or cold, desiccation, disease, lack of nutrients, etc. Unlike sentient animals, of course, non-sentient organisms do not consciously experience things as good or bad. But they can be harmed or benefited nevertheless.

Organisms have goods of their own because they have their own biological purposes. These include maturation, self-maintenance (e.g., obtaining nutrients, excreting wastes, respiring, etc.) and also, typically, reproduction. Such purposes are defined and initiated under appropriate environmental conditions by the genetic programs encoded in their DNA and RNA. Thus what is good for a non-sentient organism is, to a first approximation, what enables it to carry out the functions defined by its genetic programs—in other words, what makes it healthy. What is bad for it is what interferes with these functions—in other words, what makes it unhealthy. (This is true, however, only to a first approximation. I will add an important qualification in section 6.4.2.)

Humans, of course, differ from non-sentient organisms, not only in that we are sentient, but also in that we can choose or intelligently alter some of our purposes. Still, we share some genetically determined purposes with other forms of life. We too must obtain nutrients, excrete waste, respire, and so on, and whatever impairs these functions harms us. In these respects we are not different from other living things.

There is, of course, also a sense in which things other than organisms can be harmed or benefited. Motor oil is good for automobile engines. We might even say that freezing weather is good for icicles. But automobiles and icicles differ from organisms in that they have no purposes of their own, and hence no goods of their own. The harm or benefit is not to them but to us.

With icicles, this is obvious. They are not, like organisms, genetically equipped with instructions that define and initiate their purposes and thus determine what is good or bad for them. There is nothing comparable to DNA or RNA in an icicle. We may delight in an icicle and so think that its formation and preservation are good. But that sort of good is good *for us*, not for the icicle. The same is true, so far as we know, for all non-living natural objects (e.g., rocks, atoms, stars): they have no purposes—and hence no goods—of their own.

Automobiles are different. Unlike icicles, they have fairly well-defined purposes: they are vehicles for transporting people and their stuff. As a result, some things (e.g., regular oil changes) are good for a car, in that they enable the car to fulfill these purposes, and some things (e.g., running the engine without oil) are bad for it in that they thwart these purposes. Still, a car's purposes are not its own. They are the purposes for which it is made or used by humans. To harm a car—say, by running its engine without oil—is not to interfere with what *it* aims to do, but merely to impair its utility for the purposes of its human users. The same is true of all, or nearly all, artifacts (e.g., forks, buildings, musical compositions): they have purposes, but not purposes of their own. Hence they have no goods of their own.

Some day, perhaps, humans will create self-generating, self-maintaining, self-directing robots that do have purposes of their own. If so, then these exceptional artifacts may have goods of their own. But that possibility need not concern us here.

The fact that non-living things lack goods of their own does not logically imply that they have no moral significance. Virtue ethicist Rosalind Hursthouse, for example, makes room in her ethic for moral attitudes toward some non-living things. She advocates, for instance, the virtue of wonder toward things sublime and magnificent even if they are not alive. Thus on her view we should experience wonder at the sight of the Grand Canyon, and this implies certain moral responsibilities—e.g., the responsibility not to rim it with Coke machines. But the reason to refrain from installing Coke machines there is not that they are bad for the canyon (which, as a geological feature has no good of its own), but that doing so would demean us—because, in other words, it would be vicious (Hursthouse 2007).

Conversely, the fact that non-sentient organisms have goods of their own does not logically imply that they do have moral significance; for, we cannot deduce an "ought" merely from an "is." The weeds in a garden or the bacteria infecting a cut in someone's finger have goods of their own. But, admitting this, we may still consistently, and in accord with common sense, deny that they are morally considerable. We ordinarily kill them without a qualm, taking for granted that they have no ethical significance.

Advocates of sentience as a criterion of moral considerability agree with this common- sense approach. They emphasize that even though non-sentient individuals can be harmed or benefited, they have no conscious experience of this. Since they have no feelings, nothing can matter to them. Assuming, then, that ethics needs consider only those individuals for whom things matter, it follows that non-sentient individuals are not morally considerable.

But must we assume this? Biocentrists favor a more inclusive view, maintaining that non-conscious living things either are worthy of respect, or contribute to the world's morally relevant goodness. The former idea is deontological, the latter consequentialist. These two ideas are considered in sections 6.3 and 6.4, respectively. Each posits an "ought" principle from which an ethic can be deduced. Before considering them, however, I want to turn to an extraordinary view which, while in a sense individualistic and having some affinities with deontology, is better regarded as eluding these Western categories.

6.2 GANDHI, NAESS AND DEEP ECOLOGY

One of the most remarkable biocentrists of the last (or any) century was Mohandas Gandhi (1869–1948). Known by the spiritual title "Mahatma," Gandhi achieved world fame for his leadership of the non-violent civil disobedience campaign that freed India from British domination and has inspired non-violent political movements ever since.

Both Gandhi's biocentrism and his political life were byproducts of a quest for what he called Truth—or God. (He regarded these as the same thing.) Just as scientific truth is unattainable by biased observers, so, Gandhi thought, spiritual truth is unattainable by those attached to selfish interests and desires. Selfish desire was, he held, an inward form of violence (*himsa*) and the root of outward and more palpable forms. The nonviolence (*ahimsa*) by which he conducted the struggle for Indian independence was, accordingly, not so much a political strategy as a spiritual path, designed to bring both sides closer to a realization of Truth. A "perfect vision of Truth," he held, "can only follow a complete realization of Ahimsa" (Gandhi 1948: 615–16).

To realize *ahimsa* completely, as Gandhi understood it, is to practice it not just toward humans but toward all living beings: "In its negative form, it means not injuring any living being, whether by body or mind. . . . In its positive form *Ahimsa* means the largest love, the greatest charity" (Gandhi 1916). Consequently, "[t]o see the universal and all-pervading spirit of Truth face to face one must be able to love the meanest of creation as oneself." This requires, he said, "identification with everything that lives" (Gandhi 1948: 615–16).

Underlying these ideas was a metaphysical belief in the absolute oneness of life. Every living being, whether sentient or not, is, Gandhi believed, a manifestation of this one Truth. The more violent we are, the more we separate ourselves from it and fall into illusion. Conversely, the more we identify with other living beings, seeing ourselves in them, the better we know Truth.

Gandhi saw his own life as a series of "experiments with Truth," which involved limiting desires and living as simply as possible. He took great care not to harm living beings unnecessarily, subsisting largely on fruit, nuts, and sometimes goat's milk—a diet that required the killing of neither animals nor plants.

Many environmentalists have been inspired by Gandhi's life and thought. Perhaps the most prominent was the Norwegian philosopher and mountain climber Arne Naess (1912–2009). Naess began his career in the 1950s as a philosopher of language; but, aroused by reading Rachel Carson's *Silent Spring* during the 1960s, he became an ardent activist. In 1970 he and others halted the building of a dam at Mardalsfossen, a waterfall in a Norwegian fjord, by chaining themselves to rocks. At about the same time, he embarked on an academic study of Gandhi's ideas and developed his own environmental philosophy, which incorporated Gandhi's idea that moral maturation amounts to increasing identification with all that lives.

Naess called the process of increasing identification Self-realization. (He capitalizes the term "Self" to indicate that it denotes an expanded version of what we ordinarily think of as the self.) In alienated, self-involved people, he thought, the self (uncapitalized) is just the familiar ego. But the more we care about others, including non-human others, the more our identity is shaped by our relations to them. Their goods become our goods. The boundaries of our concern expand to create a larger Self:

> There is a process of ever-widening identification and ever-narrowing alienation which widens the self. The self is as comprehensive as the totality of our identifications. Or, more succinctly: Our Self is that with which we identify.
> (Naess 1984: 261; see also 1987: 35–36 and 1990: 188n)

Identification, as Naess understands it, is "a spontaneous, non-rational, yet not irrational, process through which *the interest or interests of another are reacted to as our own interest or interests.*" The process is iterative and expansive:

> from identifying with "one's nearest," higher unities are created: through circles of friends, local communities, tribes, compatriots, races, humanity, life and, ultimately, as articulated by religious and philosophic leaders, unity with the supreme whole, the "world" in a broader and deeper sense than usual.
> (Naess 1984: 263)

The connection of Self-realization to environmentalism lies in that it sees moral significance in all living beings. Naess' own efforts to identify with all living beings led him to advocate "biospherical egalitarianism—in principle": the idea that all living beings have an "equal right to live and blossom." The "in principle" clause is a reminder that "any realistic praxis necessitates some killing, exploitation and suppression" (Naess 1973: 103).

Naess coined the term "deep ecology" to describe a global movement that embodies this egalitarian biocentric view, together with various associated principles and practices. To his particular form of deep ecology, which also incorporates the ideal of Self-realization, he gave the odd name Ecosophy T. ("T" is an arbitrary label indicating that his is one of many ecosophies—that is, deep ecological philosophies.) Today, however, the term "deep ecology" often simply means what Naess called Ecosophy T. That is how I use the term here.

Deep ecology motivates concern for other living beings by assimilating it to concern for ourselves. We naturally care for ourselves. But if you identify, say, with the creatures of a local forest, then they become a part of your "Self"—at least to the extent that you regard a threat to them as a threat to you. Hence you are motivated to protect them—from pollution, say—just as you would protect yourself. Self-realization transmutes care for the environment into personal hygiene.

But why identify with the forest creatures in the first place? For Naess, as for Gandhi, at least part of the answer lies in a metaphysical belief in the oneness of life. Given the unity of life, progressive identification (Self-realization) enables us, they think, to achieve deeper understanding of it than we could attain otherwise. Both Naess and Gandhi maintain that we therefore ought to seek Self-realization as a form of wisdom. The ethical principle that we ought to treat the interests of other living beings as our own—a much intensified version of the Golden Rule—is their fundamental "ought" premise.

Naess' biocentric egalitarianism follows an assumption that few would question. The assumption is this: as a being with interests (goods of my own), *I* have a right to live and flourish—where "I" refers to the person who is considering Naess' ideas. Combining this with the principle that I ought to treat the interests of others as my own, it follows that I ought to grant other living beings this same right to live and flourish.

But there are problems with this ethic, both in theory and in practice. On the theoretical side, the doctrine of oneness of life that underlies it is murky (some would say unintelligible).

On the practical side, Self-realization, especially when combined with Naess' egalitarianism, seems to mire us in inconsistency. Consider, for example, the problem of tending a garden. Some plants there thrive at the expense of others; their leaves shade other leaves beneath, their roots monopolize the soil, preventing or stunting the growth of competing plants. We may vaguely value all the plants in the garden, including even the weeds, but we cannot treat the interests of very many of them, nor of the insects that eagerly gobble them up, as our own, if we hope to enjoy a harvest. Promotion of some interests comes always at the expense of others. There are always trade-offs.

Naess' notion of equal rights to blossom and flourish is of little use for actions that involve trade-offs between harming some things and harming (or failing to protect) others. Regardless of what we do, it seems, we are condemned to violate the rights of hosts of living beings. Even if we do nothing, our immune systems are constantly engaged in a war to the death against microorganisms. To his credit, Naess doesn't take his talk of rights very seriously. They are only rights "in principle" after all. But that's a problem too, because it makes his ethic imprecise and ambivalent.

Gandhi didn't think in terms of rights. Instead he talked of progressive reduction of violence against living beings. That, at least, is a consistent aspiration—though, as Gandhi conceded, its final achievement is an impossible ideal—in this life, at least. But it doesn't help with the practical problem of making trade-offs.

Self-realization carries the risk, moreover, of leading us not to deeper truths, but into a web of anthropomorphic illusions. Even if all life is somehow one, there is no guarantee that a person's efforts to identify with other living beings will provide a reliable understanding of that unity. One's "insights" might be mere reflections of one's own interests. Ecofeminist Val Plumwood puts an interesting twist on this idea. Noting that many deep ecologists are concerned mainly with wilderness preservation, she writes:

> For deep ecologists who view the route to ecological selfhood in terms of the concept of self-realisation advanced by Arne Naess, in which the self is identified with as much of the world as possible, wilderness must be seen as part of the self. There certainly seems to be something problematic and even paradoxical in the notion of relating to uncolonised areas via their incorporation into or assimilation to self.
>
> (Plumwood 1993: 161–62)

Plumwood's worry is that deep ecological Self-realization can readily slip over into self-aggrandizement and neglect of nature's otherness. This could lead deep ecologists to impose their will on others, both non-human and human, while under the delusion of being deeply and sympathetically understanding of them.

Gandhi would have agreed. Self-realization, to the degree it is possible at all, can be achieved, he often said, only in the utmost humility.

• 6.3 DEONTOLOGICAL BIOCENTRISM

Though deep ecology was influential among radical environmentalists in the late twentieth century, it is far from the mainstream of Western ethics. We now turn to a number of biocentric theories whose connections with the Western tradition are stronger—though they too are still regarded as radical. This section and its subsections concern theories with roots in the Kantian deontological tradition. Section 6.4 and its subsections consider contrasting consequentialist forms of biocentrism.

Deontological theories, introduced in section 2.3.1, are ethical theories that evaluate actions as right according to their conformity with ethical rules. The rules are to be followed even when better overall consequences could be obtained by violating them. The emphasis is on doing what is right, rather than promoting goodness, and on the individual, rather than the aggregate.

Section Outline: Sections 6.3.1 and 6.3.2 explain the ethical thought of two influential biocentric deontologists: Albert Schweitzer and Paul Taylor. A general critique of deontological biocentrism follows in section 6.3.3.

6.3.1 Schweitzer's Reverence for Life

One of the most famous biocentrists in the modern Western world was Albert Schweitzer (1875–1965). Schweitzer, a German, was extraordinarily accomplished —a philosopher, theologian, concert organist, physician, medical missionary, and winner of the Nobel Peace Prize.

The idea of reverence for life that was to become the *leitmotif* of his thinking struck him in 1915 while he was travelling on a steamboat amidst the teeming life of an African river. "Reverence" is a translation of the German word *Ehrfurcht*, which connotes awe and humility in the face of a mysterious power. Schweitzer understands that power as **will-to-live**, an impulse toward life that, he assumes, is present in every living being, and the same in all, but consciously felt only in some. It is for him the starting point of ethics:

> True philosophy must commence with the most immediate and comprehensive facts of consciousness. And this may be formulated as follows: "I am life which wills to live, and I exist in the midst of life which wills to live." . . . . Ethics thus consists in this, that I experience the necessity of practicing the same reverence for life toward all will-to-live, as toward my own.
>
> (Schweitzer 1923: 66)

Schweitzer's reasoning runs something like this:

1　Ethics requires the same reverence toward the same characteristics in others as in myself.
2　I (rightly) have reverence for the will-to-live within me.
3　There is will-to-live in everything that lives.
∴　4　Ethics requires reverence for the will-to-live in everything that lives.

The argument is valid in form. Premise 1 is the "ought" premise. It asserts a principle of fairness or impartiality similar to the Golden Rule, but, like Naess' principle of Self-realization, it is exceptionally broad in scope; the "others" mentioned need not be human—or even sentient.

Premises 2 and 3 employ Schweitzer's concept of will-to-live. Whether they are true depends upon the exact meaning of "will-to-live." This is not easy to ascertain. Premise 2 is true enough, if what it says is that we care deeply about our own lives. But what we care about primarily are our *conscious* lives. Will-to-live cannot, however, require consciousness, for that would make premise 3 false.

Perhaps we could interpret will-to-live anachronistically as the functioning of the organism's genetic program. That would preserve the truth of 3, which would then mean: "There is a functioning genetic program in everything that lives." But 2 would then mean: "I (rightly) have reverence for the functioning genetic program within me." This is odd enough to be doubtful for most of us. Hence, it seems, we can understand will-to-live in a way that makes premise 3 true only by casting doubt upon 2. There is no obvious understanding of will-to-live that makes both premises clearly true simultaneously. Thus no unequivocal interpretation of the argument seems to be sound.

Still, our inability to find a sound interpretation of Schweitzer's argument does not settle the question of whether ethics requires reverence for life. For that, we need a clearly sound argument, pro or con. Perhaps we could make progress toward a solution by further clarifying the concept of reverence.

Reverence is a moral attitude akin to Kantian respect, though more theological in tone. Schweitzer was, in fact, influenced by Kant, primarily through the works of the nineteenth-century German philosopher Arthur Schopenhauer, who himself borrowed heavily from Kant. Schweitzer's ethic is therefore deontological. Consequences don't matter. Though the suffering and death throughout nature is horrific and the consequences of our moral efforts are puny in comparison, he insists that the ethical person must nevertheless, as a matter of principle, do what she can to revere and promote life. Schweitzer doesn't put it this way, but his fundamental ethical principle, like Regan's, is a generalization of Kant's formula of humanity. Echoing Kant, we might express it this way: always treat will-to-live, whether in yourself or another, as an end and never merely as a means.

That we should treat other living things as beings with purposes of their own seems appropriate, since that is what they are. But how, exactly, does one do so? Schweitzer, like nearly all deontologists, advocates a principle of non-harm, together with duties of assistance, both applying to individuals:

A man is really ethical only when he obeys the constraint laid on him to help all life which he is able to succour, and when he goes out of his way to avoid injuring any living thing. He does not ask how far this or that life deserves sympathy as valuable in itself, nor how far it is capable of feeling. To him life as such is sacred. He shatters no ice crystal that sparkles in the sun, tears no leaf from its tree, breaks off no flower, and is careful not to crush any insect as he walks. If he works by lamplight on a summer evening, he prefers to keep the window shut and to breathe stifling air, rather than see insect after insect fall on his table with singed and stinking wings.

(Schweitzer 1923: 66)

Schweitzer, according to those who knew him, walked his talk.

But *ice crystals?* Why mention things that are not alive and have no will of any kind? The answer, I think, is that Schweitzer has fallen under the spell of Schopenhauer's metaphysics. Schopenhauer held that will is the source of *all* action in the universe. It is therefore present not only in living, but also in non-living things. His metaphysics is appallingly speculative by today's standards, but it was popular among early twentieth-century intellectuals. Its apparent influence on Schweitzer reinforces worries about the clarity of Schweitzer's concept of will. If Schweitzer had taken this metaphysical conception of will seriously, it might have transformed his ethic of reverence for life into an ethic of reverence for cosmic process. But he didn't. The ice crystal example is an isolated anomaly. Elsewhere Schweitzer applies his principle of non-harm only to living things.

But even restricted to living things, Schweitzer's ethic of reverence for life, like Gandhi's ethic of nonviolence, is an ideal that cannot be fully realized. We cannot live without destroying life. Schweitzer exhorts us nevertheless to resist compromise:

Man does not make ethical progress by assimilating instruction with regard to accommodations between the ethical and the necessary, but only by hearing ever more clearly the voice of the ethical element, by being ever more under the control of his own yearning to maintain and enhance life, and by becoming ever more obstinate in his opposition to the necessity of destroying and injuring life. . . . No one else can determine for him where lies the utmost limit of the possibility of continuing to maintain and cherish life. He alone has to judge by allowing himself to be led by a sense of responsibility for other lives raised to the highest degree possible. We must never let this sense become dulled and blunted. . . . The good conscience is an invention of the devil.

(Schweitzer 1923: 69)

Many would reject this ethic as too demanding, but in Schweitzer's view they demand too little of themselves.

Schweitzer did not adequately justify his ethic, primarily because he relied too much on the dubious and equivocal notion of will-to-live. Yet by the fervor of his words and the example of his life he, like Gandhi, issued to the world a remarkable moral challenge.

6.3.2 Taylor's *Respect for Nature*

Paul Taylor provides a more scholarly approach to deontological biocentrism in his 1986 book *Respect for Nature: A Theory of Environmental Ethics*. The book's thesis is that we can be ethically justified in respecting the inherent worth of wild living things. By "living things" Taylor means "individual organisms, species-populations and biotic communities" (Taylor 1986: 46). But he focuses chiefly on individual organisms, and in this section I will do the same.

To respect a living thing is, according to Taylor, to promote or preserve its good as an end in itself, for the sake of that living thing—to treat it, in other words, as an end and not merely as a means or object (Taylor 1986: 46). Taylor thus advocates a respect principle which, like Regan's and Schweitzer's, generalizes Kant's humanity formulation of the categorical imperative. Instead of urging us, as Kant did, to "treat *humanity*, whether in yourself or another, as an end and never merely as a means," Taylor argues that we should treat *all living things* as ends and never merely as means. Each living entity, he writes,

> must not only be thought of as having a good of its own; it must also be regarded as having inherent worth. When so regarded, the entity is considered to be *worthy of respect* on the part of all moral agents. The attitude of respect is itself then seen to be the only suitable, appropriate, or fitting attitude to take toward the entity.
>
> (Taylor 1986: 73)

Inherent worth, as Taylor understands it, is the value of a living thing itself (as opposed to its value for other things and also to the value of its welfare) that makes it worthy of moral respect (Taylor 1986: 75). Taylor's concept of inherent worth generalizes Regan's notion of inherent value (section 5.5.1), which in turn generalizes Kant's conception of dignity (section 2.3.1.1). Taylor's reasoning may be summarized as follows:

> 1   All living things have both goods of their own and inherent worth.
> 2   We ought to respect whatever has inherent worth.
> ∴ 3   We ought to respect all living things.

It is, of course, true, as was explained in section 6.1, that all living things have goods of their own. But both premises also employ the notion of inherent worth. To understand them, we need to replace the term "inherent worth" in each by the definition given above. For premise 2, this replacement yields the statement, "we ought to respect whatever has the sort of value that makes it worthy of moral respect." This statement is an empty tautology—true but wholly uninformative.

However, when we perform this replacement for premise 1, we obtain a much more substantial and hence more controversial claim: "All living things have both goods of their own and the sort of value that makes them worthy of moral respect." This is far from obviously true. We may doubt that *all* living things—even, for example, bacteria, parasites and weeds—have the sort of value that makes them worthy of moral respect. Premise 1, therefore, needs further support. We'll see how Taylor supports it shortly, but first let's consider what the argument establishes if it is sound.

The argument's conclusion, statement 3, follows validly from its premises. It is Taylor's respect principle, his generalization of Kant's categorical imperative, asserting in effect that we ought to treat all living things as ends and not merely as means.

From his respect principle, Taylor derives, as Regan did from his, a principle of non-harm (he calls it non-malevolence) together with many other deontological principles. And, again like Regan, he formulates rules that determine priorities in cases when these principles come into conflict. He also provides an account of bio-centric moral virtues. The resulting ethical machinery is complex, cumbersome and controversial. We need not consider the details here.

Instead, let's return to the crux of Taylor's argument for his respect principle: premise 1, the statement that all living things have both goods of their own and inherent worth. Taylor says that to grasp the justification for this premise we must adopt what he calls the "biocentric outlook." This involves several things: appreciating the fact that all living things have goods of their own, understanding humanity's ecological relation to the community of life, and (most crucially) acknowledging that we have no greater inherent worth than members of other species, even those that are not sentient.

Traditionally, as Taylor notes, ethical theory has taken the superior ethical value of humans for granted, rooting it in capacities such as "rationality, aesthetic creativity, individual autonomy, and free will" that we alone are assumed to possess. Everyone agrees that these capacities are valuable. But, asks Taylor, valuable to whom and for what?

> The human characteristics mentioned are all valuable to humans. . . . Clearly it is from the human standpoint that they are being judged as desirable and good . . . that is, a point of view in which the good of humans is taken as the standard of judgment. All we need to do is to look at the capacities of animals and plants from the standpoint of *their* good to find a contrary judgment of superiority. The speed of the cheetah, for example, is a sign of its superiority to humans when considered from the standpoint of a cheetah's good. If it were as slow a runner as a human it would not be able to catch its prey. And so for all the other abilities of animals and plants that further their good but are lacking in humans. In each case the judgment of human superiority would be rejected from a nonhuman standpoint.
>
> (Taylor 1986: 130)

We are superior in many ways, Taylor thinks, but only relative to our human interests, not in any absolute sense. Thus, he concludes, our inherent worth is no greater than that of any other living thing.

Taylor is right about this much at least: capacities like ours would be less valuable to creatures whose goods are very different from ours. But that doesn't show that our inherent worth is no greater. Differences in inherent worth, if they exist, could not adequately be assessed either from their point of view or from ours, since both are biased, but only from an impartial standpoint. Taylor thinks that the biocentric standpoint is just that. If we can attain it, he thinks, we will see that humans are not superior in inherent worth to other living things. Many a lifelong naturalist would agree.

From this claim that humans have no more inherent worth than other living things, Taylor draws his most astonishing conclusion: non-humans are *equal* in inherent worth to humans:

> Rejecting the notion of human superiority entails its positive counterpart: the doctrine of species impartiality. One who accepts that doctrine regards all living things as possessing inherent worth—the same inherent worth, since no species has been shown to be either "higher" or "lower" than any other.
>
> (Taylor 1981: 83)

This inference, however, is fallacious. Equality of inherent worth does not follow, even if we add the obviously implicit and uncontroversial assumption that non-humans have no greater inherent worth than humans. Taylor, like Regan when he argued for the equality of inherent value (section 5.5.2), has overlooked the possibility of value incomparability. Two individuals, each with inherent worth, might be so unlike that neither one's worth is greater than or equal to that of the other. Indeed, if all living things have inherent worth, then in view of the vast differences among them, it would be rather miraculous if the inherent worth of each were always in fact greater than, equal to, or less than that of every other.

Fortunately for Taylor, this doctrine of **species impartiality**—that all living things have the same inherent worth—is not crucial to his case for premise 1. All he really needs to show is that living things have some inherent worth, perhaps not the same in each case. But is there evidence even for that? It is empirically evident that all living things have goods of their own. But these are goods *for* the individual. They constitute its welfare. Inherent worth is supposed to be, by contrast, the moral value *of* the individual itself, in virtue of which it is respect-worthy. But how does one detect moral value in virtue of which an individual is respect-worthy? There seems to be nothing empirical about it. The very fact that Taylor regards inherent worth as equal in all living things, while others find this absurd, suggests—as does the similar dispute over Regan's concept of inherent worth—that we are here not dealing with a matter of determinable fact. Clearly, Taylor's deontological biocentric ethic is not adequately justified.

6.3.3 Critique of Deontological Biocentrism

A pervasive difficulty for deontological theories, as we have seen repeatedly (sections 2.3.1.3, 4.4.3, and 5.5.3–5.5.4), is that conflicts arise in attempts to follow their rules. Usually deontologies begin with high-level principles—a respect principle, a principle of non-harm, or various rights principles—and derive more specific rules from them.

But then we see that it is impossible to avoid disrespecting or harming or violating the rights of some individuals without disrespecting or harming or violating the rights of others. So we need rankings of rules or conflict-resolution principles to tell us when we can make exceptions to the main rules, and these themselves may turn out to have exceptions which in turn require new rules. Rules proliferate *ad nauseam*. Rules sufficient to decide actual cases may be as labyrinthine, and nearly as arbitrary, as statutory laws—and still in application they require judgment and interpretation.

Biocentrism, which increases the numbers and kinds of entities that must be considered, exacerbates this problem exponentially. Schweitzer ignores the issue by sticking to simple rules of reverence and non-harm and exhorting us to "be led by a sense of responsibility for other lives raised to the highest degree possible." But that decides little and leaves nearly everything to our interpretation. Taylor makes a grand effort, providing well over 100 pages of rules and their justifications. But why precisely *these* rules? Taylor's justifications are not wholly convincing, and there are obvious alternatives, some of which may strike us as better. Readers close the book bewildered.

Deontological biocentrism is, in essence, the project of respecting each living thing as an individual—of treating it as an end and not as a mere object or means. But this, as we have seen, is impossible. There are too many living beings, with too many conflicting aims. We must treat some living things as mere means—those that we eat, for example—unless, like Gandhi, we refuse to eat even living plants. Even so, we may have to protect our fig trees from monkeys, birds or insects. It is impossible in practice not to treat some living beings as mere objects.

Yet the fact that we cannot respect all living things does not imply that we cannot respect many. Schweitzer did so when he closed his windows while working by lamplight in the summer, to prevent the deaths of insects. Few would be willing to go that far, but we might reasonably and practically adopt a qualified biocentric respect rule—something like this:

> We ought to respect a wide range of living beings, including even some that are non-sentient.[2]

Could such a modified rule be justified? I'll attempt an answer that question in section 7.3.1.1.

There is another route that biocentrism might take. Rather than seeking to respect each living being, or as many individual living beings as is practical, we might take a more global view, aiming to promote goodness overall. That way lies consequentialism.

● 6.4 CONSEQUENTIALIST BIOCENTRISM

The aim of a consequentialist biocentric ethic is, roughly, to produce as much good with as little harm for as many living beings as practical. Several philosophers—most notably Robin Attfield (1991) and Nicholas Agar (2001)—have advocated such ethics. A consequentialist ethic has (as was explained in section 2.3.2 and its subsections) two components:

1. An axiology, which defines goodness and badness, determines the class of individuals for whom situations can count as good or bad, and explains how to compare goodness or badness of an action for both individuals and groups of individuals; and
2. A choice principle, which determines how the rightness or wrongness of actions depends upon their good and bad consequences for these individuals.

Biocentric consequentialists of the individualistic persuasion agree that the class of individuals for whom situations can be good or bad is the class of all living organisms, but on other deep and difficult issues they disagree. I think that many of these difficulties can be overcome, but we are far from overcoming all of them.

Section Outline: Section 6.4's discussion of individualistic consequentialist biocentrism is divided into five parts. Section 6.4.1 sharpens the concept of biocentric consequentialism by contrasting it with the most familiar form of consequentialism: utilitarianism. Then, in sections 6.4.2–6.4.4, I lay out what I regard as the best version of biocentric consequentialism. Section 6.4.5 critiques that view.

6.4.1 Biocentric Consequentialism vs. Utilitarianism

All biocentric forms of consequentialism buck tradition. Traditional consequentialists are sentientists, believing that moral consideration should extend only to sentient animals. They are, either hedonistic or preference utilitarians, who think that all value comes down to pleasure and pain, or preference satisfaction and frustration. They typically assume that pleasure and pain and preferences are conscious mental states, and from this they infer that all value originates in conscious mental states and hence that only sentient beings can be moral patients.

The idea that conscious states are the only source of value is often explained by invoking the philosophical distinction between intrinsic and extrinsic value. Many good things have no value in themselves but derive their value from some other source. A dollar bill, for example, is in itself a worthless piece of paper. It derives its value from an economic system within which it can be exchanged for things of more immediate value. Good things whose goodness is derivative in some such way are said to be *extrinsically valuable*. Other good things are allegedly valuable in themselves; they are said to be *intrinsically valuable*.

To determine what is intrinsically valuable, we ask repeatedly for any good thing why it is good. Take, for example, good food. Why is it good? Let's answer as a hedonist might. There are two obvious reasons: it is good because (1) it is nutritious, and (2) it tastes good—that is, gives us pleasure. Food is not, in other words, *intrinsically* good. Its goodness is derived from the nutrition or pleasure we can obtain from it. Now we continue the questioning. Why is nutrition good? Well, because it contributes to health. Why is health good? Again, there are two obvious answers: because it feels good to be healthy, and also because it facilitates doing the things we want to do. Why is it good to do the things we want to do? Because that gives us pleasure.

The series of answers has in each case led ultimately to pleasure. Why, then, is pleasure good? The hedonist's answer is something like this: "it just *feels* good; the goodness is inherent in the experience." And that is as far as the answers go. Pleasure, say the hedonists, is just intrinsically good. Furthermore, since such why-questioning always seems to lead to pleasure or the absence of pain, pleasure is the only thing that is good intrinsically, and pain is the only thing that is bad intrinsically. Each thing is good or bad, moreover, precisely in proportion to the pleasure or pain that it produces. Hence, according to hedonism, all value resides ultimately in the conscious mental states of pleasure and pain.

Preference utilitarians tell a similar story; but instead of pleasure and pain, they think that such why-questioning leads always to preference satisfaction or frustration. Good things are good because they are preferred, even if sometimes they are painful. Bad things are bad because they frustrate preferences, even if sometimes they are pleasurable. But preferences, too, are conscious mental states. Hence, according to both hedonistic and preference utilitarians, the ultimate sources of value are conscious mental states. On these views, either non-conscious beings have no goods of their own or, if they have them, their goodness is ethically irrelevant. The implication is that non-conscious beings are not morally considerable.

But consciousness is a tricky business. For one thing, it comes in degrees. Not all of our preferences or desires—perhaps not even all of our sufferings and enjoyments—are fully conscious. Do our preferences, for example, matter morally in proportion to our consciousness of them? Do preferences that are present but inaccessible to phenomenal consciousness count for nothing? Here we find ourselves on uncertain ground. It is not clear, even in the human case, that only conscious states should count as determiners of morally relevant value. But if unconscious preferences might determine morally relevant value for humans, why not for non-humans as well—perhaps even for non-sentient non-humans? Perhaps conscious states are not the origin of all value after all.

There is, as was first noted in sections 2.3.2.1 and 3.3.2, a third kind of axiology that gauges value, not (or not exclusively) by conscious mental states but by objective criteria of welfare, such as health. This is objective welfare axiology. It can readily be generalized to non-sentient organisms, since each organism's genome defines for it a reasonably objective conception of health. Most contemporary objective welfare theorists resist this generalization, but nothing about objective welfare axiology *per se* forces them to do so.

Traditional utilitarians, however, reject objective welfare theories as short-sighted and shallow. They think, for example, as was noted a few paragraphs back, that the welfare value of health is merely extrinsic—derived entirely from the pleasure or preference satisfaction it gives.

Yet from a Darwinian perspective, it is this traditional view that is short-sighted and shallow. Why-is-it-good questions need not stop at pleasure or preference satisfaction. The questions "Why is pleasure good?" or "Why is preference satisfaction good?" have illuminating evolutionary answers. Pleasure is good, of course, in that it feels good. But evolution has arranged things so that what feels good tends in the animal's natural habitat to promote health, survival or reproduction (section 5.2). Hence pleasure was originally—and still is, under favorable conditions—*extrinsically* valuable in facilitating realization of these biological values. Likewise, preference satisfaction tends—again in the animal's natural habitat—to be good, not merely in itself, but for the sake of the same basic biological values. The animal's most fundamental preferences are implicit in its genome.

Thus both pleasure and preference satisfaction evolved as means to the continuation of life and health. There is no reason in principle why an ethic could not regard these more fundamental and original biological values as morally significant.

6.4.2 The Welfare of Living Beings

Goodness for a sentient being cannot, however, be entirely explained by biological evolution or genetics. It may be shaped by learning as well. The pleasures, pains, preferences and purposes of sentient animals, and especially of humans, are deeply dependent on their individual experiences. In humans, values are also sculpted by education, training and propaganda, and sometimes by our personal efforts at character development. As a result, many things that we value have little to do with health, survival or reproduction. Still, what is good or bad for any living being—humans included—is determined to some extent by the biological values implicit in its genome.

What, then, to begin with the simplest case, is objective welfare for a non-sentient organism? Taylor suggests that it amounts to achievement of the normal lifecycle stages for its species:

> A butterfly that develops through the egg, larva, and pupa stages of its life in a normal manner, and then emerges as a healthy adult that carries on its existence under favorable environmental conditions, might well be said to thrive and prosper. It fares well, successfully adapting to its physical surroundings and maintaining the normal biological functions of its species throughout its entire span of life. When all these things are true of it, we are warranted in concluding that the good of this particular insect has been fully realized. . . . All the foregoing considerations hold true of plants as well as animals.
>
> (Taylor 1986: 66–67)

But this is not quite right. At least one of the normal lifecycle stages, reproduction, generally does not contribute to the organism's "faring well." This is true especially for non-sentient organisms, most of which never interact with their offspring. It is especially true in those species of insects and spiders in which the female devours her mate after mating. Reproduction can hardly be good for him. But reproduction weakens females too. In many species, females die after laying their eggs. In some species (salmon are perhaps the best known example), reproduction destroys both parents.

Thus although reproduction is the beginning of all goodness for offspring, it cannot be assumed to be good for parents. We need to distinguish, then, between those actions that benefit the organism itself and those that benefit organisms to which it is related. Those that benefit the organism itself (that is, tend to establish, maintain or enhance its survivability or health) are known as *autopoietic* functions. Examples include capturing sunlight, water or nutrients, resisting disease, respiring, healing injuries, growing, eliminating wastes, and so on.

I call those actions that benefit related entities *exopoietic* (Nolt 2009). Reproduction is one example. Nurturance is another—although it does not occur in all species. Many social functions are exopoietic as well. The stings of hornets, bees and wasps, for example, have the exopoietic function of defending the hive or nest against intruders. Stinging typically does not benefit the individual and in some cases destroys it.

We may define the welfare of non-sentient individuals simply as the degree of their autopoietic functioning—roughly, their survivability. Let's call this their *biotic welfare*. We may also think of biotic welfare as health, excluding exopoietic functions. Exopoietic functions contribute to biotic welfare too, but to the biotic welfare of other individuals—not, in general, to the biotic welfare of the individuals that perform them.

Biotic welfare is most naturally conceived on a non-negative scale. Zero, the lowest value, represents complete absence of autopoietic functioning—that is, death. It seems most reasonable to assume that sophisticated organisms, which are capable of many forms of autopoietic functioning, can achieve higher levels of biotic welfare than those that are capable of only a few. It follows that the capacity for biotic welfare is not equal among species. The resulting biocentric axiology is not egalitarian.

In sentient animals there is an additional dimension of welfare: *hedonic welfare*—the sum of the values of their enjoyments, which count positively, and of their sufferings, which count negatively. A sentient animal's *total welfare* at a given moment is a kind of "sum" of its biotic and hedonic welfares at that moment. The total welfare of a fox at a given time, for example, is roughly the extent to which it is at that time physically fit and feeling fine.

At death hedonic welfare vanishes—that is, reverts to zero. If the total welfare of a sentient animal from now until its death will be continually negative, so that it exists in a kind of living hell, then it would be, as the saying goes, "better off dead." Veterinarians euthanize suffering and moribund animals for this reason. Some jurisdictions also permit voluntary euthanasia for humans on similar grounds. But there is no such thing as being "better off dead" for non-sentient individuals. Since they do not suffer, their welfare can never drop below zero. We can imagine a sentient being in hell, but not a hell for trees.

For sentient animals in their natural habitat, hedonic and biotic welfare are closely correlated. The healthy animal feels well; the sick or injured or malnourished animal suffers. Under these conditions sentience tends to augment high biotic welfare and to subtract from low biotic welfare.

For sentient animals outside their natural habitats, however, biotic and hedonic welfare often diverge. Emotionally sensitive animals in zoos, factory farms, or research facilities, for example, may suffer considerably from their confinement, even if their keepers ensure their biotic welfare (physical health). Humans and other sentient animals on morphine may experience intense euphoria even if seriously injured. Thus in such "unnatural" circumstances, hedonic welfare may become largely independent of biotic welfare.

Total welfare for humans exhibits still greater complexity. It includes their biotic welfare, their hedonic welfare, and whatever additional goods are unique to them. (See the discussions of such goods in sections 2.3.2.2, 3.3.1 and 4.6.1.) Thus humans are capable of more kinds of welfare—and hence, presumably, of greater welfare—than anything else.

The **total welfare** for a *population* (set) of individuals at a given moment is the sum of the total welfares of its members at that moment. If, for example, an organism has a given level of welfare at a certain time, two such organisms in the same condition at that time or another have total welfare twice as large, three have total welfare three times as large, and so on.

The welfare of an individual varies with time. It is less when the individual is injured, ill, or suffering, greater when the individual is happy and healthy. An individual's **lifetime welfare** can be thought of, roughly, as its average total welfare over its lifetime, multiplied by the length of its life.[3] Lifetime welfare thus varies with the length of the lifetime. Given two organisms with the same constant positive level of welfare, for example, if one lives longer than the other, then it has the greater lifetime welfare. Conversely given two organisms with equal lifetimes, if one has greater average welfare, it has the higher lifetime welfare. It is possible for the lifetime welfare of a sentient animal to be negative, in which case, presumably, it would have been better for the animal never to have been born (or hatched).

I have so far been treating welfare as an objective quality, or set of objective qualities. My account generalizes those objective welfare axiologies described in sections 2.3.2.2, 3.3.1, 4.6.1 and 5.3.1. But some biocentric consequentialists begin with a preference axiology and generalize that. Gary Varner, for example, once defended a form of biocentric consequentialism that grouped preferences, considered preferences and biologically based needs all together under the heading of "interests" (Varner 1998: 62). Though Varner later repudiated this view (2003), Nicholas Agar has defended a similar generalization of preference axiology. Agar sees an organism's genetically based goals, even if unconscious, as analogous to desires, projects, or preferences. He calls them "biopreferences." What is good for a non-sentient organism, on his view, is what satisfies its biopreferences; what is bad for it is what frustrates them.

The main problem with this view, as with all preference-based axiologies (see section 3.2.5) is that preference satisfaction is not always good. One reason for this is habitat change. Many nocturnal insects, for example, have a biopreference to fly toward light, presumably as a means of orientation. This worked well in their ancient habitat, whose only common, bright and steady nocturnal light source was the moon. But it harms them now that humans have filled the night with electric lights. Today, driven by this biopreference, they exhaust themselves by futilely orbiting light sources that their genetically based neural program assumes to be forever out of reach.

Another reason why satisfaction of an individual's biopreferences is not always good for that individual is that many biopreferences are exopoietic—or, as Agar (2001: 97–100) puts it, other-directed. Among these he includes the "biopreference of many organisms to find an appropriate mate or mates, reproduce and nurture off-spring, etc." (Agar 2001: 124). But, as we saw above, an individual's exopoietic functions, while tending to increase the welfare of its group, need not contribute to its welfare, and often weaken or even destroy it.

Exopoiesis is not, of course, a bad thing overall. It may be the ultimate source of altruism, and hence even of ethics. The point, rather, is that we should not count satisfaction of preferences (or biopreferences) as good for the organism when it does the organism no good and perhaps even harm. This, in essence, is the reason given in sections 2.3.2.2 and 3.2.5 for rejecting preference axiology and moving to an objective welfare axiology in the human case. It is also the reason for defining welfare for non-sentient organisms as the degree of their autopoietic functioning, and not as achievement of their normal lifecycle stages or fulfillment of their biopreferences.

It might be objected that even when an individual's preference is not exopoietic and satisfaction of that preference is not good for that individual, still that satisfaction is somehow good in itself. The value of the satisfaction of the moth's biopreference to fly toward the streetlight, for example, would on such a view be intrinsic. In other words, the satisfaction of that desire would just be good—period. (Hedonists, as was noted in section 6.4.1, often say something similar about pleasure.) But we may justly be skeptical of the existence of forms of goodness that are not good *for* anything (Nolt 2009). For these reasons I prefer the objective welfare view described earlier in this section.

6.4.3 Comparing and Aggregating the Welfare of Living Beings

But on what scale can we measure the objective welfare of living beings? There are at least three things to measure, not just one: biotic welfare, hedonic welfare and those forms of welfare that are unique to human persons or near-persons. Is there any way to rank all these values on the same scale?

I doubt it. In fact, I doubt that there can be a wholly non-arbitrary ranking even for a single form of welfare—hedonic welfare, for example—between members of widely differing species (Nolt 2013b). Degrees of welfare for living beings or populations of them cannot, in other words, be linearly ordered, like a scale of temperature. They can only be partially ordered, like a network. Partially ordered values cannot be represented on a numerical scale—and hence, in particular, not on a monetary scale.

If we think of welfare values as arrayed in a kind of network, we must imagine some as connected to others by threads of comparability (being greater than, less than or equal to one another) and some as not so connected. These others are incomparable (neither greater than, less than nor equal to one another). The welfare of a healthy tree, for example, is clearly greater than the welfare of a diseased tree of the same age and kind. The welfares of identical organisms in identical conditions are equal. In other instances, however, welfares are incomparable. The welfare of a healthy tulip poplar tree is, for example, probably neither greater than nor less than nor equal to the welfare of a healthy (but presumably also non-sentient) tarantula. Tarantulas and trees are so different that their welfares are incomparable. But not always; presumably, a healthy tree has greater welfare than a nearly dead tarantula, whose welfare level is approaching zero.

There are many other cases in which the welfares of very different organisms are comparable. Any organism, for example, whose welfare is positive (greater than zero) has higher welfare than any sentient animal whose welfare is negative (less than zero). Healthy complex organisms with many autopoietic functions usually have greater welfares than healthy but less complex organisms with fewer autopoietic functions. The welfare of sentient non-humans with both high autopoietic welfare and high hedonic welfare exceeds the welfare of most other non-human organisms.

The fact that different kinds of welfare are sometimes comparable is one of the sources of my optimism (mentioned at the outset of section 6.4) that many of the problems of biocentric consequentialism can be solved.

Another is the fact that for both biotic and hedonic welfare, there is a natural zero value. This provides a touchstone for comparison of the welfares of sentient and non-sentient individuals. If, for example, a sentient animal suffers so much that its lifetime welfare is negative (that is, it would have been better never to have been born), then its lifetime welfare is less than zero. But since the welfares of living non-sentient organisms are invariably positive (greater than zero) the animal's welfare is less than that of any non-sentient organism.

Finally—and perhaps most importantly—lifetime welfare differences among living beings cannot be infinite. In other words, no individual can have a lifetime welfare so high as to be greater than the lifetime welfares of infinitely many other individuals, even of the lowest kind (say, bacteria), assuming their welfares are even in the slightest degree positive. The argument is as follows:

Consider any happy, healthy person. She descended by an enormously long series of reproductive steps from one-celled organisms, whose lifetime welfare, though positive, was among the lowest. Because at each step in this series, the offspring resembled the parent (or parents) fairly closely, at no step could there have been an infinite difference between the lifetime welfare of the offspring and that of the parent(s). But a finite series of non-infinite differences cannot add up to an infinite total difference. Hence the difference in welfare between the simplest archaea or bacteria and a happy, healthy person cannot be infinite.

This conclusion is likely to offend human pride, but, remarkably, and somewhat reassuringly, it does not imply that there is some finite number of bacteria whose lifetime welfare is greater than that of a happy, healthy person. I will explain that, along with further reasons for optimism that some of the problems of biocentric welfare aggregation and comparison can be solved, in section 7.3.2.

What it does suggest, however, is that it is sometimes right to sacrifice some amount of human welfare to prevent loss of welfare to non-human, and even non-sentient, beings. There might, for example, be an endangered species of plant that can grow only in one place that humans want to develop. The plant may be ugly and have no possible use or value for humans, and failure to develop the land may result in loss of human welfare. Still, because the welfare of any living being has some finite value, and the extinction of the plant would (let us suppose) eliminate a vast number of future individuals of that species over the coming millennia, the potential welfare loss of the extinction is great. And because there are no infinite differences between human welfare and the biotic welfare even of non-sentient beings, it is possible that the sacrifice to humans of not developing the land is not that great. If so, then bio-centric consequentialism implies that we should forego the development. No non-biocentric ethic would yield such a conclusion.

If, in this way, some rough but objective and intelligible comparisons can be made among the welfares of entire populations of living beings, then objective biocentric consequentialist decision-making is possible.

6.4.4 Biocentric Consequentialist Decision-Making

In consequentialist ethics generally, it is the choice principle that bridges the gap between description and prescription—that takes us, in other words, from "is" to "ought." More precisely, the choice principle specifies how the rightness of action (the "ought") depends upon the good and bad consequences of the various options (the "is"). The classical consequentialist choice principle is: do what maximizes total welfare for the entire population affected by the choice. Total welfare is the sum of positive and negative welfare for the whole population. Biocentric consequentialists have usually assumed this sort of maximizing choice principle.

But there is little chance that it could be used in practice. Part of the problem is lack of knowledge: often we do not *know* what will maximize welfare. This is espe-cially true for decisions involving large-scale or long-term consequences. But the more fundamental and less familiar reason why we often cannot maximize welfare is that the total welfares for the various options may be incomparable. Knowing more would not solve this problem.

Incomparability may seem fatal to consequentialist decision-making. But that is too pessimistic a view. The choices before us often include some options that yield lower welfare than others. At least we can rule these lower values out. The only troubling incomparabilities are those among the better options. When faced with relatively good options that are incomparable with one another, we cannot always choose the best, because there may be no best. We cannot, therefore, always maximize welfare. But if there are no better options than these, and we have no other information to go on, then it is rational to choose any one of them (Hsieh 2007; see also section 7.3.2).

A broad biocentric choice imperative that avoids this problem (assuming that objective and intelligible comparisons can sometimes be made among the aggregate welfares of groups of living beings) is:

Avoid actions that are, on the whole, objectively worse for life.

More precisely: avoid doing what would produce less aggregate objective welfare for living beings than other possible actions would. This principle straightforwardly generalizes the classical choice principle. For if among the available options there is a best (that is one that produces the greatest welfare), and we always avoid the worse, then in comparing all available options, we will choose the best. In other words, we will do what maximizes total welfare for living beings. If there isn't a best, then the principle leaves us free to choose among any of those options for which there are none better.

Still, this sort of decision procedure is merely a theoretical ideal. For large-scale biocentric decisions (those that consider big populations or broad expanses of time) detailed welfare comparisons are, of course, wholly impractical. Decisions, furthermore, require revision as time passes. Thus there is a recurring process of decision, action, and assessment, followed by revised decision, which begins a new cycle. For the biocentric consequentialist, this process is analogous to the task of keeping to high ground (high total welfare) while negotiating a route through a rugged landscape. This landscape, however, has the disconcerting property that some of its heights (which represent high welfare totals) are neither greater than nor equal to nor less than some others. We have to keep looking ahead, because a route that runs over high ground now may lead down into a deep valley later. Thus we can't apply our choice principle just to the next moment—to what lies immediately ahead. We need far-sighted strategy. Sometimes it may be necessary to choose a lower path now to reach greater heights later. The choice principle should therefore be applied, not just to the next moment, but to entire routes that lie ahead. But we can't see all the features along a given route, especially those that are more distant. We can't, then, simply survey all available routes and pick one that is no worse than any other.

There are, no doubt, better or worse decision strategies. But, given the incompleteness of our knowledge and the incomparability of many welfare values, the complexities are daunting. Despite my optimism that some of the technical theoretical problems of biocentric consequentialist decision-making can be solved, rigorous application may remain impractical. If so, then biocentric consequentialist policy and practice might simply amount to maintaining or restoring environmental conditions that, to the best of our knowledge, are sustainably better, rather than worse, for life in general.

6.4.5 Critique of Consequentialist Biocentrism

The standard objection to consequentialist theories in general is that in benefiting the whole, they can fail to respect individuals (section 2.3.3). But that objection has little force when the individuals in question are non-sentient non-humans. We cannot in practice treat every living being as an end; and, since justice is primarily a matter of social arrangements, there seems to be little point in speaking of justice for June bugs or juniper trees.

More forceful is the objection that in worrying about the welfare of June bugs and juniper trees, we may commit injustices against humans. There is some danger of that. But biocentric consequentialism values humans too. Indeed (as was explained in section 6.4.2), because humans are capable not only of biotic but also hedonic and culturally created forms of welfare, we typically count more than anything else. And we must also beware of the opposite danger of counting human welfare too highly. The best biocentric consequentialist theories aim for a mean between these extremes.

Animal rights deontologists object to consequentialism because it apparently permits the painless killing of animals, provided that those animals are replaced by others (sections 5.4.2, 5.5). Conceivably someone might object that biocentric consequentialism likewise permits the (necessarily painless) killing of non-sentient organisms for the greater good. But this objection, too, lacks force. The killing of some non-sentient organisms is unavoidable no matter what we do, and it is better that it should contribute to the greater good than otherwise.

A much more significant objection, already mentioned, is that because biocentric welfare values are often incomparable, biocentric consequentialism cannot lead us to a single right course of action. I have conceded that this is true (section 6.4.4), but it is doubtful that *any* ethical theory can provide unique choice over so broad a domain. The notion that an ethic can always prescribe single correct choice of action may simply be naïve.

We might worry too that biocentric consequentialism requires too much expertise. Assessing the aggregate welfare for living beings resulting from various actions requires not only a deep knowledge of environmental science, but also a firm grasp of consequentialist reasoning and of heretofore largely undeveloped techniques of value aggregation. Even Taylor's complex deontological rules are easy to use by comparison. To this objection there are two responses.

The first is that the technologies we use are so powerful and destructive that using them ethically must inevitably make great demands on our understanding. But that response, however true (and appropriate for policy-makers), is of little help to ordinary people, who simply haven't the time or energy to deal with such technicalities.

The second response is that it is possible to formulate some fairly simple rules that encapsulate much of what ordinary people need to know: "live simply," "minimize use of fossil fuels," "eat low on the food chain," "buy organic," "favor local producers," "reduce, reuse, recycle," and the like. Such rules are justified consequentially, in that when we follow them the results tend to be better for life than when we don't. Thus, for everyday use, biocentric consequentialism can take the form of rule consequentialism, rather than act consequentialism (section 2.3.2.4).

But who formulates these rules? The best answer is that ideally many people do—both independently and collaboratively. Ethics based not on authority but on reason should be so transparent that anyone who learns the relevant science, accepts fundamental ethical principles, avoids prejudice, and can evaluate prescriptive reasoning will have a good sense of what the rules should be.

The fundamental ethical principle articulated in section 6.4.4 is: avoid actions that are, on the whole, objectively worse for life. One can still ask: why? We are nearing the point at which philosophical answers, if they are honest, run out or start circling back on themselves. Yet I will venture an answer in section 7.3.1.2.

• 6.5 WHY STOP AT ORGANISMS?

Welfare for a non-sentient organism was defined in section 6.4.2 as the degree of its autopoietic functioning. But we noted there that the genetic program of an organism also gives it exopoietic functions. These enhance the health and survivability of related entities: their species, their colony, their offspring, etc. Offspring certainly have their own autopoietic functions, and their welfare can be considered in the same way as that of their parents. But some theorists hold that such higher level aggregate entities as beehives, populations of algae, or even whole species have independent goods of their own. A worker bee that gathers honey for the hive or wards off intruders acts exopoietically, enhancing the health and survivability of the hive, but the hive itself seems to function as an autopoietic unit, enhancing its own health and survivability through the functioning of its bees. It may even function exopoietically, reproducing by sending out a swarm to create a new hive. Do beehives then—or even populations or species—also have goods of their own?

At lower levels of the hierarchy of biotic organization, too, certain functional components of organisms—for example, organs, organ systems, cells, or organelles—have both autopoietic and exopoietic functions. Each functions to maintain itself, but it also functions exopoietically to contribute to the health and survivability of the organism as a whole, and often of its other components. These functional components of organisms can also be healthy or not. Do they too have goods of their own?

Once we accept that organisms as simple as bacteria have goods of their own, it is difficult to deny this. Take organelles, for example. Two kinds of organelles found within the cells of many organisms—mitochondria and plastids—are thought to have originated as bacteria that developed symbiotic relationships with their hosts. Though their functions were much modified in the process and they now depend on the cellular environment for survival, this is no reason to think that they no longer have goods of their own. Cells also have autopoietic functions. Moreover, there seems to have been a continuous evolution from colonies of one-celled organisms (which had goods of their own) into multi-cellular organisms. Again there is no reason to think that the cells making up multi-cellular organisms no longer have goods of their own. Organs and organ systems did not originate as separate organisms, but they are systems of cells that have unified functions and might also be thought of as having goods of their own, for they too can be harmed or benefited.

This superfluity of goods is bewildering. But perhaps the fact that the welfare of an organism (its autopoietic functioning) encompasses the welfares of its components can help us to find order in it. What is good for a cell or organ in your body is (assuming that it is functioning correctly) good for you. Thus instead of counting the welfare of each organelle or cell separately, we may regard them as included in the organism's overall welfare. By this sort of reckoning, presumably, more complex organisms with greater numbers of intricately integrated autopoietic components must, other things being equal, be capable of higher levels of biotic welfare. Thus, for example, welfare of a healthy anteater would be much higher than the welfare of an ant, which has fewer autopoietic components. This scheme has the further advantage of establishing a good bit of comparability among the biotic welfares of disparate organisms. The structure of non-anthropocentric value so conceived reflects the exquisite complexity of life itself.

We may still encounter trouble, however, if we continue on to lower levels of biotic organization, attributing goods of their own to such molecular-scale structures as genes—or continue upward to higher levels, attributing goods of their own to entire species or ecosystems.

Let's begin with genes. Richard Dawkins popularized a controversial gene-centered view of life in his 1976 book *The Selfish Gene*. Genes, on this view, have the function of perpetuating themselves, and organisms are merely the "survival machines" they build for the job. This makes it appear not only that genes are ultimate biological value-determiners, but that what they prescribe is not organismic welfare, but their own perpetuation. A gene, as Dawkins understands it, is not a specific strand of DNA within a particular cell, but the totality of all the strands of DNA that are replicas of it in the cells of any individual of any species in which it occurs (Dawkins 2006: 88). It thus exists at various points in space, over a long period of time (sometimes hundreds of millions of years). Can such a strange collective entity really have a good of its own?

Perhaps—but with two qualifications. First, even if genes do have goods of their own, this doesn't mean that their "survival machines" don't. The fact that organisms have goods of their own is well established. Second, we seem already to have accounted for the goods of genes in considering the welfare of organisms. The gene-centered view is just a different way of cutting the same pie. Since the functioning and survival of genes is inseparable from the biotic welfare of the totality of organisms that contain them, the aggregate welfare of the totality of genes is apparently identical with the aggregate biotic welfare of organisms generally. We have here, it seems, not two distinct kinds of value, but one kind of value parceled out in two different ways. In any case, there are, so far as I know, no serious proposals for gene-centered ethics, and so we need not pursue the idea further.

A second, and more important, challenge to biocentric individualism comes from holistic theories—theories according to which such entities as species, ecosystems or

perhaps even the entire biosphere have goods of their own distinct from the aggregate goods of the individuals that comprise them. Sections 6.6 and 6.7 and their
subsections consider these.

• 6.6 SPECIES ETHICS

The European wild boar (*Sus scrofa*) is a sensitive and intelligent animal. It is omniv-
orous, feeding on roots, tubers, bulbs, nuts, worms, insects and small animals, which
it unearths by digging furrows in the ground. In a forest, the resulting damage to
the understory ecology is extensive. Around 1950 a few of these boars escaped
from a North Carolina hunting preserve and found their way into the Great Smoky
Mountains National Park. There they multiplied rapidly. By the late 1970s, the
loss—especially to rare native species of plants, but also some salamanders and invertebrates—had become so worrisome that the National Park Service began sending
rangers into the back country to trap or shoot the boars. Since then, many thousands
have been killed. But, although the ecological damage has been reduced, wild boars
still root up the park's forest floor (NPS 2003).

In this instance the Park Service has prioritized the protection of certain species
(including non-sentient plants and invertebrates) over the interests of thousands of
highly sentient wild boars. Their reasons are complex, involving political, aesthetic
and public health considerations, as well as (for some Park Service employees, at
least) biocentric ones. But, to simplify, let's consider just biocentric reasons involving the boars and the rare and endemic species of plants. The Park Service assumes
that the plant species are of greater ethical importance than thousands of individual
sentient boars. This is not to say that an individual plant is more significant than a
boar—only that the plant *species* is. Let's call any view according to which species
are morally considerable a ***species ethic***.

A species, according to the traditional textbook definition, is a group of individuals
that can interbreed to produce fertile offspring. But this definition is quite limited.
It does not apply to organisms such as fungi that reproduce asexually or to those,
such as bacteria, that promiscuously exchange genetic material across species lines.
Moreover, in plants especially, what are generally regarded as separate species often
interbreed to produce fertile offspring. This textbook definition is also largely inapplicable to long-extinct species whose ability to interbreed can no longer be ascer-
tained. In practice, species boundaries for both fossil and living species are often
defined by ***morphological*** criteria—that is, by the physical shape and structure of
the organisms. But often they are also defined wholly or in part by ***phylogenetic***
criteria, which group organisms together not by their current forms but by their evolutionary histories. These three definitions all produce somewhat different species
classifications. All three are to a certain degree vague. None is uniquely correct.

Our understanding of species value depends to some degree on which definition we
choose. On the textbook and phylogenetic definitions, a species is, like a family or
dynasty, a group of individuals united by kinship. But this makes species value hard

to explain. It is at least controversial that families have a special kind of value beyond the values of the individuals that comprise them. Families are valuable, of course, but their value is generally explained by the benefits they provide for their members.

On the morphological definition, a species is a group of individuals sharing a common form. Interestingly, when species are defined this way, extinction need not be the end of them. New organisms having that form could later, in theory at least, evolve or (more plausibly) be reconstructed by genetic engineers. They would not be members of the same species on the phylogenetic definition, but they would be on the morphological definition.

Section Outline: The discussion of species ethics is divided into five sections. Section 6.6.1 explains Holmes Rolston's account of the objective intrinsic value of species. Section 6.6.2 questions the viability of Rolston's conception, suggesting instead that, although humans can value things intrinsically, there is little reason to believe in objective intrinsic value in Rolston's sense. Section 6.6.3 explores the notion of species welfare. Section 6.6.4 considers the value of biodiversity. And section 6.6.5 takes a brief glance at the practice and politics of species protection.

6.6.1 Rolston and the Intrinsic Value of Species

One of the foremost proponents of species value is Holmes Rolston III, whom we met in section 5.9. Rolston thinks of a species as "a coherent, ongoing form of life expressed in organisms, encoded in gene flow, and shaped by the environment" (Rolston 1988: 136). This definition combines phylogenetic and morphological elements. Rolston approaches the idea of species value by tracing analogies between species and individuals. Like individuals, species are born and die, though for species birth is a speciation event and death is extinction. *Speciation* occurs when a species evolves into one or more new species. It is thus a kind of species-level reproduction, though the new species are not duplicates of the old. Species extinction occurs either when all members of the species die or when the species evolves into one or more new species. Like individuals, species have a genome, which, however, is distributed among and operates at the level of individuals and is not entirely the same in each. Rolston notes, moreover, that like many individual animals a species "learns" new adaptations, as natural selection gradually modifies its gene pool in response to environmental changes. The "knowledge" thus acquired is preserved through time by replication of the surviving genes, which provide the species with a kind of "memory."

Rolston argues that species have goods that are distinct from the aggregate goods (that is the sum of the individual goods) of their current members. Moderate predation by Arctic wolves upon caribou, for example, is bad for the individual caribou killed but good for the caribou species. Wolves tend to cull the sick and the weak (though also, sometimes, healthy young), reducing disease in the species, keeping it from overpopulating and overusing its range, and enhancing its genetic fitness. For similar reasons, it is good for species that regularly produce many offspring that a large portion of those offspring die before reproducing. This is not good, of course, for the individuals that die prematurely. But it helps to keep population in balance and enhance the fitness of the species.

We might expect then, that Rolston would define species value as species welfare— that is, as value *for* the species, how well it is doing for itself. But instead he thinks of it as intrinsic value—the value *of* the species. The ***intrinsic value*** of species for Rolston—like dignity for Kant (section 2.3.1.1), inherent value for Regan (section 5.5.1) and inherent worth for Taylor (6.3.2)—is a kind of moral status that entails both objective value and respect-worthiness. It is greater, according to Rolston, than the totality of the intrinsic values of its members. Thus to reduce a species to extinction is a kind of "superkilling" (Rolston 1988: 144). It kills not only the remaining members of the species, but also the species itself, a life form that began long before those members did. Two sorts of value are lost, the value of the members and the value of the species, and the latter is by far the greater. Indeed, the value of a non-sentient species may outweigh the values of many members of a sentient species. Thus Rolston's theory would support the Park Service in saving a few species of rare native plants by killing thousands of individual wild boars.

But Rolston's ethic leaves many unanswered questions. Are all species of equal intrinsic value, or do their intrinsic values differ? If they differ, are the differences comparable or not? How are they to be assessed? . . . and so on.

Rolston emphasizes that the intrinsic value of a species can be maintained only so long as its habitat is preserved with it:

> It is not preservation of *species* that we wish but the preservation of *species in the system*. It is not merely *what* they are but *where* they are that we must value correctly. . . . species can only be preserved *in situ*. . . . The species–environment complex ought to be preserved because it is the generative context of value. *Ex situ* preservation, while it may save resources and souvenirs, does not preserve the generative process intact. Besides missing half the beauty of what is taking place, it misses the burden of human duties.
>
> (Rolston 1988: 153–54)

That, however, still doesn't tell us what the intrinsic value of species is, or how to assess it. We may wonder, moreover, what the intrinsic value of a species has to do with what "we wish," with beauty, and with "the burden of human duties." "Intrinsic value" that is characterized by human wishes or duties appears to be a product of human concerns, rather than something non-anthropocentric that exists objectively.

6.6.2 Hargrove and Intrinsic Valuing

Eugene Hargrove is one of many environmental ethicists who doubt the objective existence of what Rolston calls intrinsic value. The fact that it is supposed to be not only a kind of value but also a moral status (so that it embodies both "is" and "ought") suggests to Hargrove that it is not discovered in nature but projected there by ethical theorists. Still, whether or not species have intrinsic value objectively, it is possible, Hargrove maintains, for us to *value* them intrinsically—that is, non-instrumentally—not for how they might benefit us but just for what they are. An entity is intrinsically valued, according to Hargrove,

> insofar as some person cherishes it, holds it dear or precious, loves, admires, or appreciates it for what it is in itself, or so places intrinsic value on its existence. This value is independent of whatever instrumental or commercial value it might have. When something is intrinsically valued by someone, it is deemed by that person to be worthy of being preserved and protected because it is the particular thing that it is.
>
> (Hargrove 1992)

Nature lovers the world over value species intrinsically. But that does not mean that what they value in them is the sort of objective intrinsic value that Rolston posits. The Endangered Species Act of 1973 (U.S.) states that species "are of esthetic, ecological, educational, historical, recreational, and scientific value to the Nation and its people" (section 2(a)(3)). These various "values" pick out particular aspects of species for which many people value them intrinsically: beauty, complex ecological relationships, historical significance, and so on. These aspects are valuable *for us*, but not in any obvious way for the species themselves, for the universe, or for anything apart from us. They are, as Hargrove puts it, *anthropocentric* intrinsic values. (Recall that by "intrinsic" Hargrove merely means "non-instrumental.") Such anthropocentric values contribute to human welfare and must therefore be accounted for in any consequentialist ethics, anthropocentric or not—as well as in environmental law and policy.

Hargrove thus demonstrates that we can ascribe intrinsic (that is, non-instrumental) value to species as a matter of human interests, even if there is no such thing as objective intrinsic value. On Hargrove's view, the intrinsic value of species is a form of value that they have *for us*.

Objective intrinsic value of the sort Rolston advocates seems, by contrast, not to be value *for* anyone or anything. It's just objective value, period. But the existence of such a thing may be doubted—especially since Rolston characterizes it in terms of human wishes and duties, and provides no objective criteria for assessing it.

6.6.3 Species Welfare

There is, however, another conception of species value that clearly is objective and non-anthropocentric: the degree to which things are going well *for* a species—that is, the degree of its welfare or survivability. This sort of value is regularly and objectively assessed by conservation biologists. A species is doing well if, among other things, its members are healthy, sustainably numerous, widely distributed geographically (which protects the species from localized threats), and genetically diverse. More generally, it is doing well to the extent that its prospects for survival are good.

Is the welfare of a species just the aggregate welfare of its members (that is the sum of their individual welfares), or is it a new level of value, in addition to that aggregate welfare? Robin Attfield, who thinks of welfare as fulfillment of interests, takes the former view, at least if we regard the species as its current population. So understood, "a species has no interests over and above those of its members"; its interests "reduce to those of the current members without remainder" (Attfield 1991: 150).

That, however, is not the best way to define species, as Attfield himself acknowledges; for how well a species is doing depends not only on the welfare of its present members, but also on its future prospects, at least in the near term. A species is not doing well, regardless of how its current members are doing, if those members differ little from one another genetically or are located only in a small geographic area; for low genetic diversity and narrow distribution reduce species survivability. Therefore species welfare, properly understood, is not reducible without remainder to the aggregate welfare of its *current* members.

The main thing that is missing here, I think, is consideration of the welfare of future members. A species, after all, is a group that lasts longer than any of its members. Its welfare at a given time consists not only of the welfare of its present members but also of the prospects for continued generation of future members whose lives may go well. (This is what the conservation biologists' criteria for species welfare are assessing.) If we think of the **lifetime welfare** of a species as the total amount of welfare for the species from the time it comes into existence until its extinction, then I see no reason not to assume that its total lifetime welfare is the aggregate lifetime welfares of its individual members over the same time span.

On this conception, when human action drives a species to extinction, the loss to that species is the difference between what the lifetime welfare of that species would have been had that extinction not occurred and what it is, given the extinction. Because the extinction of a species not only kills its present members, but eliminates future ones, this difference, which measures the total loss to that species, can be very great, vastly greater than the lifetime welfare of any single member of the species. The extinction of a species generally also harms other species that depended on it, adding to the total loss. In this sense species extinction is, as Rolston observes, a kind of "superkilling," of much greater significance than the deaths of individuals.

The extinction of a species can, no doubt, be compensated by the creation of new species. This is how nature herself keeps non-anthropocentric value high. But in times during which species are lost without such compensation, non-anthropocentric value declines steeply. This is what seems to be happening today.

6.6.4 The Value of Biodiversity

To get a synoptic picture of how well species are doing generally, biologists often speak of biodiversity. On the simplest conception of biodiversity, species richness (see section 1.2.5) the more species there are per unit area (or volume) the more biodiverse a habitat is.

It is sometimes held that species diversity, or some other form of biodiversity, has its own special kind of objective non-anthropocentric value, distinct from the welfare of individuals or of species. This notion has certain affinities with an older and more general idea, dating at least from the Neoplatonic philosophers of the early Christian era, that being itself is good, and hence that the more kinds of things there are in the world, the better. Theologians sometimes inferred that God, being infinitely good, must create as much good as possible, and hence must eventually bring all possible kinds of things into being—an idea that philosopher Arthur O. Lovejoy (1961) dubbed the principle of plentitude. But because this principle applies to non-living as well as living things, and because it is bound up with ancient metaphysical doctrines that have been widely abandoned, it has had little direct influence in environmental ethics.

More familiar is the fact that many of us value biodiversity simply because we enjoy variety. But that is an anthropocentric value, of the sort discussed in Chapter 3. This chapter concerns non-anthropocentric thought.

Among non-anthropocentric reasons for preserving biodiversity, perhaps the most compelling is that biodiversity fortifies life itself against extinction. The greater the diversity of species and the greater the genetic diversity within species, the higher are the chances that life will endure whatever catastrophes befall. But the long-term preservation of life need not be regarded as a separate value, beyond the welfare of individuals, present and future. Many environmental philosophers (e.g., Maier 2012) doubt that biodiversity has any special kind of non-anthropocentric value of its own.

Even if it has no special value of its own, however, biodiversity is crucial to life's welfare and survival. We can imagine high biotic welfare without biodiversity. Think, for example, of a planet with huge numbers of healthy individuals, all of a single species. That might be possible for a time, provided that these organisms were simple and self-sufficient. But without other organisms there to create ecological cycles, sooner or later they would probably exhaust their resources. And unless they diversified and evolved, they would face extinction as environmental conditions changed. Thus without biodiversity, life would not be likely to survive for long. Therefore, although biodiversity may have no special inherent value, its value for the continuation of life is extraordinary.

6.6.5 Endangered Species: Law, Ethics and Policy

Practice is always less clear-cut than theory, and so it is with species ethics. This section illustrates the peculiar melange of ethics, law and political strategy that emerges in the practice of species ethics, under the jurisdiction of the Endangered Species Act.

The Act itself is an intricate set of rules whose aim is to conserve species and the habitats on which they depend. The ethical theory that justifies the Act is anthropocentric. Some of the Act's proponents made non-anthropocentric pronouncements, such as, for example, that species have an inherent right to exist. But most, regardless of their personal beliefs, stuck to anthropocentric arguments, largely for pragmatic reasons (cf. Nash 1989: 174–77; and sections 3.1 and 3.6 above).

The Act has two main ethical justifications. The first is rule-based and ultimately deontological: that species protection is required by obligations incurred by the U.S. under previous international conservation agreements. The ethical rule invoked here is simple: keep your promises—including promises to other nations.

The Act's primary ethical justification, though, is that it is in the interests of citizens and the nation to preserve the "esthetic, ecological, educational, historical, recreational, and scientific value" of species. The reasoning here is utilitarian: species preservation adds to human good. But law is rigid, in a non-consequentialist fashion. Species were protected regardless of how much or how little they contributed to human well-being. As a result, the Act quickly came into conflict with both government projects (e.g., the Tellico Dam in Tennessee) and private economic development. A 1978 amendment created an interagency federal committee (popularly called the "God committee") that could grant exceptions to the Act in some such cases. This provision for consideration of competing anthropocentric values made the law more clearly utilitarian, but also weakened it considerably.

The law had, of course, and continues to have, vocal opponents. Some question even the need for species preservation, arguing that extinction is a natural phenomenon and therefore nothing to worry about. But this is misleading. The natural or "background" extinction rate is low enough that speciation can replace the lost species with new ones, and then some. Thus, throughout most of life's history, biodiversity has steadily increased. But if extinctions greatly exceed background rates, biodiversity drops, sometimes catastrophically.

Other opponents argue merely that we need not preserve all species—especially those of such "primitive" groups as insects, fungi, or microorganisms. (Congress evidently agrees; the Endangered Species Act does not in fact protect certain insects that pose risks to humans—or any fungi or microorganisms.) Given such a selective policy, we might save certain representative species from each family, order or genus of "lower" organisms, and not worry about the rest.

Yet many, including Rolston, hold that all species should be protected. The policy of saving only representative families, orders or genera is mistaken, he argues, because it treats these abstract classes as valuable, though they have no value of their own, and regards the "real historical entities," the species, as mere means of preserving them. Value, however, is lost with each species that is lost. Furthermore, he notes, such a policy would inhibit speciation, since two species that have just emerged from a parent species are quite similar, and under this policy at most one would be protected. Moreover, the losses allowed by such a selective policy would ripple through ecosystems unpredictably (Rolston 1988: 136–37).

To Rolston's objections we might add the following pragmatic argument: many species have already been lost, and losses will accelerate into the foreseeable future. To save what we can, we must resist as many losses as is practically possible.

In fact, species protection today is already spotty. Not every species that is eligible for protection under the Endangered Species Act, for example, is actually being protected, for Congress has not provided the U.S. Fish and Wildlife Service (USFWS), which administers the Act, with the necessary funds. I know this from personal experience. In 2003 I filed a citizen petition with the USFWS to list the Berry cave salamander (*Gyrinophilus gulolineatus*) as an endangered species. This rare and unobtrusive amphibian occurs only in a few caves, several of them threatened by development, all of them near my home in Knoxville, Tennessee. I was told that in order to list the salamander, the USFWS would first have to conduct a study to determine whether listing was justified and then create and implement a habitat protection plan; that these processes cost both money and staff time; and that, given budgetary realities, they would likely be postponed indefinitely. Some years later, the Center for Biological Diversity bundled my petition together with many others and successfully sued the USFWS, demanding action on all of them. Responding to the suit, the USFWS ruled in 2011 that the Berry cave salamander "warrants addition to the federal list of threatened and endangered species." Actual listing, however, still awaits availability of funds.

This example illustrates not only the disconnect between law and species protection, but also a disconnect between ethical thinking and species protection. With respect to the law, while all endangered species are supposed to be protected, which ones actually receive protection depends on economic and political contingencies. With respect to ethics, the reasons for which they receive protection are not always those stated in the law. Though I, for example, have over the years developed a good bit of interest in and affection for *Gyrinophilus gulolineatus*, my original motive for filing the petition was largely to prevent construction of a road, the James White Parkway extension, that would have degraded existing neighborhoods, encouraging suburban sprawl and burgeoning traffic. The Endangered Species Act has often been used for such purposes, which are tangential to and yet consistent with species protection. Practice is always less clear-cut than theory. In any case, the result increased the salamander's chances of survival. Legal obstacles, including those involving the salamander, delayed construction of the road for many years, and in 2013, as a result of continued local opposition, the project was cancelled.

The Endangered Species Act recognizes, as does Rolston, that species protection is in practice bound up with habitat protection. First among the purposes listed in the Act is "to provide a means whereby the ecosystems upon which endangered species and threatened species depend may be conserved" (§ 2(b)). The Act thus protects ecosystems as a means of protecting species. But some have argued that ecosystems should be regarded as more than mere means.

6.7 ECOCENTRISM

Ecocentrism is a form of holistic biocentrism according to which ecosystems are morally considerable. It is consistent with, and may be held in conjunction with species ethics or individualistic forms of biocentrism, but it may also be held independently.

An *ecosystem* is an assemblage of organisms of different species living in some degree of interdependence in the same habitat, together with the non-living components of that habitat (soil, water, air, sunlight, etc.). This definition, though standard, is admittedly rather vague. Various analogies or models are used to give it more structure and substance.

Ecosystems are sometimes described as super-organisms whose parts have functions in much the same way that the organs of ordinary organisms do. The trees of a forest ecosystem, for example, are its "lungs," whose primary function is gas exchange. They don't look like lungs, of course, unless you compare their branching structure with that of the lung's bronchi. In both cases, branching provides a very large surface area for gas exchange. Trees, however, are a kind of "negative" lung, in that their branches are solid structures, whereas the branches of ordinary lungs are cavities. Trees are negative lungs in another way, too, for while lungs absorb oxygen and emit carbon dioxide, trees absorb carbon dioxide and emit oxygen. The oxygen that lungs provide to the body is distributed throughout the body where it is used in various metabolic processes. The carbon dioxide absorbed by trees is used in photosynthesis, and carbon extracted from it is incorporated into their tissue. When trees die and decay or parts of them are eaten, this carbon is distributed and used throughout the ecosystem, just as oxygen is distributed and used throughout the body. Streams form the circulatory system of a forest ecosystem, transporting nutrients and carrying away wastes, just as blood does in an animal body. Wetlands are its kidneys, filtering impurities out of this circulatory system. Such analogies can be extensively elaborated. Together they comprise the *organismic model* of ecosystems. The organismic model suggests that just as organisms have goods of their own, so must ecosystems.

Another model that suggests the same thing is the *community model*. On the community model, an ecosystem is like a community whose members are the individual organisms. These individuals generally pursue their own interests, but as in a human community, each has a role to play in the community and each makes use of others, so that complex interdependencies develop. Damage to the community and its members ensues if these interdependencies are disrupted. The community is strong and healthy if they are robust and abundant.

Still other ways of looking at ecosystems provide different understandings. The *thermodynamic model*, for example, sees an ecosystem as a complex of material and energy flows. Material flows include the oxygen–carbon dioxide cycle between animals and plants, the nitrogen cycle, the carbon cycle, and so on. The primary source of energy, sunlight, is converted into chemical energy by photosynthetic plants and distributed throughout the ecosystem via food chains. It is not so easy to think of an ecosystem as having a good of its own when we conceive it thermodynamically.

None of the three models gives a complete account of what an ecosystem is. The organismic and community models are, moreover, at least partly metaphorical. Ecosystems are in some ways *like* organisms or communities, but it does not follow that whatever is true of organisms or human communities is true of ecosystems. In particular, we cannot legitimately infer from the fact that organisms or human communities have goods of their own that ecosystems have goods of their own.

It was noted in section 6.6 that species may be defined in several ways. Though each of the definitions is itself fairly clear, the fact that there are at least three of them makes the species concept ambiguous and complicates conceptions of species value. With ecosystems, the problem is more or less the reverse. There is essentially just one definition—the one given at the beginning of this section. But this definition is so vague that it tells us virtually nothing about how big an ecosystem is or where and when it begins and ends. It seems, moreover, that ecosystems may be nested, one inside the other. The ecosystem of a mountain stream may be part of a larger ecosystem, or of several, that occupy the mountain from which it flows; and these may in turn be components of a still larger ecosystem that covers the entire mountain range. Perhaps Earth's biosphere is the grandest ecosystem of all. And, by some accounts at least, ecosystems can be very small as well. There is much medical interest today in the particularized microfloral and microfaunal ecosystem that inhabits the gut of a human person. Moreover, even if we consider only ecosystems of roughly the same size, the location of the boundary between any two adjacent ones is to a considerable degree arbitrary. In sum, ecosystems are remarkably poorly defined entities. Still, they have received much attention from environmental ethicists.

Section Outline: Section 6.7.1 explains the most famous and influential ecocentric ethic of all time: Aldo Leopold's land ethic. Section 6.7.2 considers the much disputed issue of the non-anthropocentric value of ecosystems.

6.7.1 Leopold's Land Ethic

The most influential ecocentric ethic was, and still is, that of Aldo Leopold. He called it the land ethic. In part because Leopold was a superb nature writer, his best known work, *A Sand County Almanac*, first published in 1949, reached a wide audience. Leopold began his career as a forest ranger, stationed in the Apache and Carson national forests in New Mexico and Arizona. His job was to travel into the back country with a pack horse and rifle and shoot wolves and mountain lions. The aim was to benefit ranchers and deer hunters, who saw these predators as pests. The folly of this plan began to dawn on him after he and a companion shot a wolf and watched her die:

> We reached the old wolf in time to watch a fierce green fire dying in her eyes. I realized then, and have known ever since, that there was something new to me in those eyes—something known only to her and the mountain. I was young, then, and full of trigger-itch; I thought that because fewer wolves meant more deer, that no wolves would mean a hunters' paradise. But after seeing the green fire die, I sensed that neither the wolf nor the mountain agreed with such a view. . . .
>
> (Leopold 1970: 138–39).

During the ensuing years Leopold witnessed the gradual unfolding of a tragedy:

Since then I have lived to see state after state extirpate its wolves. I have watched the face of many a newly wolfless mountain, and seen the south-facing slopes wrinkle with a maze of new deer trails. I have seen every edible bush and seedling browsed, first to anaemic desuetude, and then to death. I have seen every edible tree defoliated to the height of a saddle-horn. . . . In the end the starved bones of the hoped-for deer herd, dead of its own too-much, bleach with the bones of the dead sage, or molder under the high-lined junipers.

(Leopold 1970: 139–40)

The predators had an unappreciated ecological function: to maintain a balance between the deer herd and their forage. With their elimination the deer population exploded, exhausted its food supply, and collapsed.

The title of the essay containing this reminiscence is "Thinking Like a Mountain." This, of course, is metaphorical. Leopold did not believe that mountains think. It signifies long-term ecological thinking—which Leopold was among the first to achieve.

What today we call an ecosystem, Leopold describes as "the land." When he is think-ing scientifically, Leopold uses a thermodynamic model to describe the land, pic-turing it as a biotic pyramid, with the bottom layer, the soil, supplying nutrients to plants, plants feeding herbivores, herbivores feeding carnivores, and smaller carni-vores feeding larger ones. The land, he writes,

is not merely soil; it is a fountain of energy flowing through a circuit of soils, plants and animals. Food chains are the living channels which conduct energy upward; death and decay return it to the soil. The circuit is not closed; some energy is dissipated in decay, some is added by absorption from the air, some is stored in soils, peats, and long-lived forests; but it is a sustained circuit, like a slowly augmented revolving fund of life.

(Leopold 1970: 253)

In thinking ethically, Leopold employs the community model of ecosystems, which gives his ethic a communitarian flavor. But, ever the naturalist, he thinks also in evolutionary terms. Communities evolve, he asserts, because of "the tendency of interdependent individuals or groups to evolve modes of co-operation"—that is, symbioses (1970: 238). In human communities, which evolve culturally, these sym-bioses are called "ethics."

All ethics so far evolved rest upon a single premise: that the individual is a member of a community of interdependent parts. His instincts prompt him to compete for his place in the community, but his ethics prompt him also to co-operate (perhaps in order that there may be a place to compete for).

The land ethic simply enlarges the boundaries of the community to include soils, waters, plants, and animals, or collectively: the land.

(Leopold 1970: 239)

Viewed ecologically, expansion of the human community to include the land is the cultural evolution of a new symbiosis. Viewed ethically, it is moral progress.

Though it sometimes sounds communitarian, Leopold's ethical thinking is eclectic and difficult to categorize. He has deontological and consequentialist tendencies too. This passage sounds both communitarian and deontological:

> a land ethic changes the role of *Homo sapiens* from conqueror of the land community to plain member and citizen of it. It implies respect for his fellow members, and also respect for the community as such.
>
> (Leopold 1970: 240)

We are to respect (treat as ends and not merely as means?) the land community and our fellow members within it.

But Leopold also characterizes right and wrong behavior with respect to the moral community in terms of its consequences:

> A thing is right when it tends to preserve the integrity, stability, and beauty of the biotic community. It is wrong when it tends otherwise.
>
> (Leopold 1970: 262)

Here the aim is to preserve goodness—in the forms of integrity, stability, and beauty.

It was this consequentialist dictum that aroused the ire of deontologist Tom Regan. Since (as Leopold would admit) preserving the integrity, stability, and beauty of the biotic community sometimes involves killing sentient animals (the invasive wild boars in the Great Smoky Mountains National Park, for example), Regan saw this dictum as a prescription for violating animal rights. He thus charged Leopold with "ecological fascism" (section 5.5.5).

But Leopold was no fascist of any kind. His brief dictum is not a general definition of right and wrong, but a limited principle intended to govern human behavior with respect to the land. He meant it, moreover, as an addition to, rather than a replacement for, existing ethical principles. We are to respect not only the biotic community, but also our fellow members. Human rights, at least, are to remain secure.

Even economies are to remain secure. Immediately after defining right and wrong treatment of the land, Leopold adds—as if to reassure those whose first instinct is to shield their wallets—"Of course it goes without saying that economic feasibility limits the tether of what can or cannot be done for the land. It always has and it always will" (1970: 262).

Still, Leopold's land ethic was radically innovative. It was the first ethic, so far as I know, to propose a respect principle for ecosystems. (Indeed, such a principle would have been unthinkable much earlier. The concept of an ecosystem emerged only during Leopold's lifetime, and the term "ecosystem" was not coined until 1935 (Nash 1989: 57).) Leopold's ethic is innovative as well in its non-anthropocentrism.

But perhaps its most daring innovation is that—in opposition to much of the post-Enlightenment tradition—it is non-individualistic. We are to respect the biotic community as a whole, not just individuals.

Individuals—non-human individuals, at least—are in fact expendable on Leopold's view. He hunted and fished his whole life, evidently regarding killing an animal as consistent with respecting it, so long as the kill was skillful and clean, good use was made of the flesh, and the take was sustainable. His ethic requires the eradication of invasive non-native animals, even if these are subjects of a life. And if ecosystems are damaged by extirpation of predators, the land ethic supports restoration of the predators, even if this means that they will kill more subjects of a life. To animal rights advocates like Regan these conclusions are abhorrent.

Though Leopold's ethic has affinities with both deontology and communitarianism, its broadest justification is distinctly consequentialist. Why should we respect the biotic community and its members? Because in this way a symbiosis—a co-operative relation that benefits both us and the community—will evolve. Leopold thus justifies his ethic as a whole by its consequences.

To evaluate the claim that adopting the land ethic would produce a mutually beneficial symbiosis, we need to know what it would mean to benefit an ecosystem. Here Leopold's account hits turbulence. What is good for an ecosystem, he seems to say, is the preservation of its integrity, stability, and beauty. But none of that seems exactly right.

Integrity has to do with the system of interdependencies—symbioses—that characterize an ecosystem. These provide mutual benefits for the system's inhabitants, but it's not clear that they benefit the ecosystem itself—unless it is just the aggregate of its inhabitants.

Stability was thought in Leopold's time to be a normal characteristic of mature ecosystems, but contemporary ecology emphasizes the pervasiveness of change. Since change is apparently the norm, it is not clear why stability *per se* should be good for ecosystems, except perhaps insofar as it entails their survival. But even that wouldn't much clarify things, since the very notion of ecosystem survival is poorly defined. We lack clear criteria for determining when one ecosystem is replaced by another, as opposed to merely changing.

Finally, why beauty should be correlated with ecosystem welfare is not at all clear. Beauty is a notoriously subjective phenomenon. Many people find a well manicured lawn more beautiful than an old growth forest. In sum, none of these three concepts is a very helpful or accurate criterion of value for ecosystems.

6.7.2 Ecosystem Value

What, then, is ecosystem value? Ecosystems have, of course, various values *for humans*, just as species do. They provide us, for example, with ecosystem services. But these are anthropocentric values of a sort that we have already considered (section 3.3.1).

It is sometimes held that ecosystems have objective non-anthropocentric *intrinsic* value. We have met such an idea before. In sections 6.6.1–6.6.2 we considered the idea that species have such a value. But there seem to be no objective criteria for applying it, and the possibility of intrinsic valu*ing* (section 6.6.2) suggests that it is theoretically dispensable. The same objections apply to the concept of intrinsic value for ecosystems.

The American philosopher Eric Katz has argued that the value of ecosystems (and of natural individuals as well) lies at least in part in their autonomy—that is, in their wildness and freedom from human domination. Katz's use of Kant's term "autonomy" is deliberate, for he thinks that, like human autonomy, the autonomy of ecosystems is worthy of respect (Katz 1993). That analogy, however, is apt to be misleading. For Kant autonomy is conscious free choice unfettered by external control. But ecosystems are neither conscious nor capable of choice, so the only thing that Katz's notion seems to have in common with Kant's is freedom from external control. Why should freedom from external control—or perhaps the systems that have such freedom—be worthy of moral respect?

There is, of course, a long tradition, stemming from Romanticism and deeply rooted in American culture, of valuing wildness. Thoreau wrote, "I love the wild no less than the good" (1962: 260). But such love is the product of a particular human sensibility. It may be true that we ought to preserve wilderness because its mere existence ennobles the human spirit. But the good here is anthropocentric. There is no plainly intelligible way in which wildness *per se* is good for ecosystems themselves.

This issue comes to a head in the debate over the ethics of ecosystem restoration. Katz argues that once we disrupt an ecosystem, we cannot, even by the most careful restoration or redesign, completely re-create either it or its value, for the wildness is gone, and all that we can construct is a human artifact:

> Once we dominate nature, once we restore and redesign nature for our own purposes, then we have destroyed nature—we have created an artificial reality, in a sense, a false reality, which provides us the pleasant illusory appearance of the natural environment.
>
> (Katz 1992: 396)

Yet life goes on in a restored ecosystem, and that life, though perhaps degraded, is quite real. The mere fact that we once restored a system may reduce its significance for us, but it makes no difference that we know of to the system or its non-human inhabitants. To the extent that the restoration duplicates the original, it is just as good so far as they are concerned. It follows that wildness, or autonomy in Katz's sense, are anthropocentric values. We may thus leave them aside, for this chapter concerns values that are non-anthropocentric.

Probably the most widely discussed non-anthropocentric form of ecosystem value is **ecosystem health**. This concept has its roots in the organismic model of ecosystems. Health for an organism is functional integrity. It implies that the organism's components are functioning well individually and in concert. Since their functions are scripted by the organism's genome, it is a fairly well-defined concept. But ecosystems have no such central "script" or plan. Hence what counts as a healthy ecosystem is much less clear. Is an ecosystem that is undergoing transition to a new ecosystem healthy or unhealthy? In a sense it is dying, but in another sense it is giving birth.

There are some clear cases. Obviously a coastal mangrove ecosystem besmirched by a massive oil spill is not healthy. But the general unclarity of the concept of ecosystem health is unsettling.

As a practical measure, environmental and governmental agencies sometimes construct what are called "ecosystem health indicators." These may include measures of water purity, species diversity, invasive species, human land use alterations, and so on. While such indicators are measurable and often provide important information to policy-makers, they do not add up to a complete conception of ecosystem health.

Perhaps an analytic approach would be more fruitful. Instead of trying to define goodness or welfare for ecosystems holistically, we might ask first how value is distributed among the organisms within the system and then whether ecosystem welfare can be understood as some aggregate of value for those individuals. (This is similar to the approach taken with species in section 6.6.3.)

Value relations among individuals within an ecosystem are complex. The welfare of an individual non-sentient organism is, of course, just the degree of its autopoietic functioning (section 6.4.2). But organisms also have exopoietic functions that either make possible or add to the welfare of others. Reproduction is an exopoietic function that creates new organisms, thus providing them with genetic instructions and making their welfare possible. Nurturance, social behavior, symbiosis and the like are exopoietic functions that enhance the welfare of others.

Let's call an organism's total contribution by exopoiesis to the welfare of other organisms its **exopoietic benefit**. The exopoietic benefit of an organism is perpetuated for as long as it has descendents. Goods that we enjoy today—vision, for example— are among the exopoietic benefits that we inherit from ancient organisms (fishes, amphibians, reptiles) that passed on to us genetic instructions for making eyes and the sort of brain needed to use them. Of course, no specific ancestor is responsible for our vision. Untold numbers of our ancestors passed along the basic genes governing sight. Some contributed modifications. Hence each made a necessary contribution to our current welfare. But each was also ancestor to many other individuals, perhaps individuals of other species, to whom it also contributed genes.

Exopoietic benefits are benefits that an organism acts to provide to related organisms. But organisms benefit other organisms in other ways as well. Some organisms are exploited by others for such purposes as food or shelter. Think, for example, of the great number and variety of organisms (birds, squirrels, insects, fungi, etc.) that make use of a single tree.

Both exopoiesis and exploitation are among the interdependencies that are constitutive of an ecosystem. Presumably both contribute to ecosystem welfare. Yet the primary beneficiaries of both are organisms themselves. Is ecosystem welfare, then, just the aggregate welfare of the ecosystem's present inhabitants? I don't think so. As with species, an ecosystem's welfare at a given time depends not only on the aggregate welfare of its population at that time, but also on its future prospects. Its welfare at a given time is, roughly, the aggregate welfare of its inhabitants then, together with the likelihood that the aggregate welfare of its later inhabitants will be high. That likelihood will depend, among other things, on the genetic diversity of the ecosystem's inhabitants (since diversity fosters resilience) and also on such things as climate stability and freedom from pollution or other destructive interferences.

We might define the lifetime welfare of an ecosystem as the aggregate lifetime welfares of all of its inhabitants over the time that it exists. Since the welfare of each inhabitant includes all the benefits it acquires by autopoiesis, by its exploitative actions, and by the exopoiesis of other members of that system, this definition accounts for goods generated by the ecosystem's interdependencies. It has the further advantage of yielding a fairly definite concept of total ecosystem welfare no matter where we draw the boundaries of the ecosystem in space and time—provided that we draw them somewhere. That is, it does not presume that ecosystems are naturally defined entities.

The notions of ecosystem welfare at a given time and of lifetime ecosystem welfare are not holistic, for they analyze the welfare of an ecosystem into the welfares of its individual inhabitants over time. They do not, in other words, ascribe to the ecosystem any special value independent of the welfares of these individuals. Thus while valuing the welfare of ecosystems more highly than that any of their component individuals, these notions are nevertheless consistent with biocentric individualism.

In such an ethic, the welfare of each living being counts toward the welfare of the whole and hence (by the consequentialist choice principle) matters morally. Complex organisms typically have greater welfare than simpler organisms, which generally have a lesser capacity for welfare. The welfare of each species is greater than that of any of its members, for its value includes all of theirs—though it need not be greater than the totality of the members' welfare over its lifetime. The lifetime for each ecosystem is likewise greater than that of any of its inhabitants. Ecosystem processes are, of course, of great value as well, but their value lies in the contribution they make to the welfare of multitudes of individuals. Even the welfare of autopoietic components of an organism adds to the total welfare, though their welfare is subsumed into the welfare of the organism whose components they are. Organisms have value, moreover, not for the present alone, but by the exopoietic processes of reproduction and nurture, for an open and indefinitely long future. This conception of value is bewilderingly intricate. But so is life.

● 6.8 A PRAGMATIC CRITIQUE OF BIOCENTRISM

Biocentric ethics, whether holistic or not, is eminently controversial. Among its most astute critics are John O'Neill, Alan Holland and Andrew Light. In the jointly authored book *Environmental Values* they launch a broadside against non-anthropocentric theories in general and biocentric ethics in particular.

Arguing from an anthropocentric, pluralistic, and pragmatic view, they maintain that biocentric ethics are superfluous, for conservation initiatives that succeed in the policy arena nearly always rely on anthropocentric arguments. (The Endangered Species Act is one instance, as we saw in section 6.6.5.)

O'Neill, Holland and Light are, moreover, skeptical, as am I, of such notions as inherent worth (Taylor) or intrinsic value (Rolston and others), noting (as section 6.6.2 did) that we may value natural individuals, species or ecosystems intrinsically (that is, non-instrumentally) even if there are no such properties (O'Neill *et al.* 2008: 116–19).

They also reject objective welfare consequentialism, which they characterize as an "itemising approach," in view of the plurality of welfare types or kinds of individuals that it recognizes as morally considerable. The incomparability of some welfare values (section 6.4.3) is, they contend, fatal to consequentialist decision-making—at least insofar as it appeals to a maximizing choice principle (O'Neill *et al.* 2008: ch. 5). (I agree, but, as was noted in section 6.4.4, biocentric consequentialism can do without a maximizing choice principle; see also section 7.3.2.)

More fundamentally, they hold that conservation is not a matter of "itemization," of keeping as many species or ecosystems going in as good a condition as possible, for it is the local and particular that we value, not biodiversity in the abstract:

> We value an ancient woodland in virtue of the history of human and natural processes that together went into making it: it embodies the work of prior human generations and the chance colonization of species, and has value because of the processes that made it what it is. No reproduction could have the same value, because its history is wrong. In deliberation about environmental value, history and process matter and constrain our decisions as to what kind of future is appropriate.
>
> (O'Neill et al. 2008: 175–76)

(I agree, too, that biodiversity in the abstract is not what we primarily do or should value; the non-anthropocentric value of biodiversity is at bottom the value of individual living beings.) History and process matter, they say, because their stories add significance to our lives:

> We make sense of our lives by placing them in a larger narrative context, of what happens before us and what comes after. Environments matter because they embody that larger context. . . . Particular places matter to both individuals and communities in virtue of embodying their history and cultural identities. Similar points apply to the specifically natural world.
>
> (O'Neill et al. 2008: 163)

What we value in the environment is not, then, according to O'Neill *et al.*, what is good for non-human beings, but rather what is significant *for us*.

It is true, of course, that we often rightly value environments for the historical and cultural significance they hold for us. And doubtless this significance helps to motivate both individuals and policy-makers to protect them as the unique entities that they are. No biocentrist would deny that. There are many other anthropocentric reasons to protect them as well. But biocentrists contend that there are also non-anthropocentric reasons.

O'Neill *et al.* doubt that biocentric reasons can matter much to policy-makers or ordinary people. They think that biocentric ethics stretches such concepts as health, welfare or intrinsic value so far that they begin to lose their human meaning. It makes too many things morally considerable, straining human sensibilities and depriving morality of salience and motivating power. It employs an abstract vocabulary that is insensitive to our attachments to the local and particular. People will make great sacrifices to protect their homes and lands, but not to protect "biodiversity." Thus biocentrism is pragmatically ineffective; it "does not produce some special set of moral trumps that overrides considerations of human justice and human interests" (O'Neill *et al.* 2008: 180–81).

These are important criticisms. Biocentrism does face profound practical and motivational difficulties. It is, after all, a reformist ethic, designed to expand our moral thinking, cultivate new sensibilities, and perhaps even reshape our identities. Moral reform is a hard sell. But, given humanity's relentlessly growing domination of all other life, human rights and interests need a counterweight. And one can still hope (and work) for moral progress, even though the pace of that progress remains, as always, tragically slow.

Admittedly, biocentrism offers no trumps. But neither, ultimately, does any other ethic. What it does provide is a broader and more impartial perspective from which we can value and defend, not just what is easy or politically expedient to value and defend, but something much deeper, older and more encompassing: the objective good of life.

• 6.9 BIOCENTRISM FOR THE LONG TERM

Section 4.1 and its subsections explained why future people are morally no less important than we are. More generally, there is no reason at all to think any objective value (e.g., biotic welfare) diminishes with distance into the future from where we stand at present. Future value matters, and since there is potentially a lot more of it than there is of present value, its moral importance is vast.

If the arguments of sections 6.6 and 6.7 and their subsections are correct, then the non-anthropocentric values of species and ecosystems are determined not only by the aggregate welfares of their present members or inhabitants, but also by the prospective aggregate lifetime welfares of their future members or inhabitants. Since both species and ecosystems last longer than their component individuals, species ethics and ecosystem ethics are concerned primarily with future value. They are ethics for the long term.

ethics of life

Moreover, again because objective value does not diminish with distance from us in time, individualistic biocentric ethics, too, should be long term. But the further we look into the future, the less we can knowingly affect particular individuals and the more we must concern ourselves with the welfare of aggregates, such as species. Non-identity considerations (section 4.5) point to the same conclusion. Thus long-term biocentric ethics, even if individualistic in theory, must be holistic in practice.

Unfortunately, given the realities of climate change, ecosystem preservation may no longer be a realistic objective. As was noted in section 1.2.5.3, as the Earth heats up and species move at differential rates to higher altitudes or toward the poles, ecosystems are being pulled apart. Moreover, habitat destruction and biological invasions continue apace. We can expect many ecosystems to lose their identities. Since there is no clear answer to the question "When does an ecosystem change so much that it becomes another?" it is impossible to say exactly when in this process an ecosystem vanishes.

But perhaps this is not the right question to ask. If non-anthropocentric value resides fundamentally in individuals, rather than in the ecosystem, it does not depend directly on whether the ecosystem itself is preserved. What matters is what is happening, on the whole, to individual organisms and to future prospects for individual organisms. The transformation of one ecosystem into another is not like the death of an organism, which reduces its welfare to zero, but rather like the transformation of one community into another. Some relationships are destroyed, but new ones emerge.

The problem is that today such transformation, more often than not, amounts to degradation. Climate change and worldwide habitat destruction are disrupting long-established interdependencies in ways that lower survival prospects for most non-human life. The global aggregate welfare of non-human life is declining.

We cannot stem these losses by restoring lost or degraded ecosystems to something like their pre-human or pre-industrial conditions. We can't even maintain ecosystems as they are today. We are changing the planet too rapidly for that. Yet future prospects for species clearly depend on the availability of habitat to which they can at least adapt and in which they can form new ecosystems. They depend too on a rich and deep gene pool, for that is what enables a species to adapt. Preserving these things through a tidal wave of change is the challenge that conservation biologists now face. Even with our best efforts it is certain, given existing habitat destruction and greenhouse gas emissions (not to mention anticipated increases in human population and consumption), that many species and ecosystems will be lost. Non-anthropocentric good will continue to decline.

Geologist James Kirchner and biologist Anne Weil, writing in the journal *Nature*, assert that "today's anthropogenic extinctions will diminish biodiversity for millions of years to come" (Kirchner and Weil 2000: 177–80). "Our results," they say,

> suggest that there are intrinsic "speed limits" that regulate recovery from small extinctions as well as large ones. Thus, today's anthropogenic extinctions are

likely to have long-lasting effects, whether or not they are comparable in scope to the major mass extinctions. Even if *Homo sapiens* survives several million more years, it is unlikely that any of our species will see biodiversity recover from today's extinctions.

(Kirchner and Weil 2000: 179)

If the harm we are doing outlasts our species, that can hardly be ethically insignificant. Yet regarding the time beyond human extinction, when there are no longer human rights to respect or human interests to consider, anthropocentric ethics has nothing to say. Any theory capable of explaining its ethical significance must therefore be non-anthropocentric.

• SUGGESTIONS FOR FURTHER READING

There is no book more influential or more beautifully written in environmental ethics than Aldo Leopold's *Sand County Almanac* (first published in 1949). This is a must-read.

Also of great importance is *Environmental Ethics: Duties to and Values in the Natural World* by Holmes Rolston III (Temple University, 1988). Rolston advocates a holistic biocentrism from the viewpoint of a keen observer of the natural world.

The best collection is *Environmental Ethics: An Anthology*, edited by Andrew Light and Holmes Rolston III (Blackwell, 2003).

A recent and important, but difficult, work, critical of moral uses of the concept of biodiversity, is Don Maier's *What's So Good About Biodiversity? A Call for Better Reasoning About Nature's Value* (Springer, 2012).

Finally, for those interested in applications of environmental ethics to policy, I recommend the forthcoming *Routledge Companion to Environmental Ethics*, edited by Benjamin Hale and Andrew Light.

7

applications and speculations

A central theme of this book has been the progressive expansion of the scope of ethics, in response to humanity's ever-increasing power. But with each step in that expansion, conceptions of ethics have become more complex. Worse, we have not just one environmental ethic but many, and attempts to resolve differences among them trail off into philosophical thickets. Given these difficulties, how can we manage to act ethically?

Chapter Outline: There are two ways to answer: practically and theoretically. Accordingly, this chapter is divided into two parts: applications (sections 7.1 and 7.2), which deal with practice, and speculations (sections 7.3 and 7.4), which deal with selected aspects of theory.

Fortunately, there are some questions to which all, or nearly all, ethical theories give similar answers. In these cases the right action is clear. Section 7.1 discusses five such questions. In other cases, there is less agreement among the theories or the right action depends on empirical matters that are uncertain. Yet some answers can reasonably be ruled out, and much can be learned by assessing the arguments for and against those that are not. Two examples of questions of this sort are considered in section 7.2.

Sections 7.3 and 7.4, which advance some speculations, are the most philosophical and tentative parts of this book. Both attempt to look beyond the plurality and complexity of the theories discussed so far toward some simpler and deeper theoretical unity. Section 7.3 considers three theoretical issues left unresolved in earlier chapters and speculates on solutions. Section 7.4 ventures a general diagnosis of the environmental crisis and proposes two general strategies for solving its problems.

The chapter and book close with a brief postscript (section 7.5).

7.1 SOME CLEAR MORAL IMPERATIVES

There are many conclusions on which most or all theories of environmental ethics agree—so many that it is impossible to discuss them all here. This section presents, by way of illustration, cases for each of five broad conclusions on which most or all environmental ethical theories agree. None of the five arguments is novel, though all are (among the general public at least) controversial. Each implies further, more specific conclusions that some readers may regard as radical.

There is much to be learned by examining the arguments for both the conclusions and sub-conclusions carefully. The issues are convoluted, and it is possible that some of the conclusions are erroneous. If so, there are flaws in the arguments. Readers who dismiss a conclusion without locating the flaw may happen to be right, but they will miss much. Readers who locate the flaw and then dismiss the conclusion will learn part of what those other readers are missing—but not all; for the conclusion of a flawed argument might still be true and hence should not be dismissed without a solid argument to the contrary. Some of these arguments, however, may be sound. Those arguments would be particularly instructive.

Section Outline: Section 7.1 consists of five subsections, each of which supports a broad ethical conclusion, together (in some cases) with arguments for subsidiary conclusions. The five main conclusions are that: eliminate the use of fossil fuels (section 7.1.1), protect species and habitat (section 7.1.2), eat ethically (section 7.1.3), build a sustainable economy (section 7.1.4), and reduce human population (section 7.1.5).

Little is said in these sections about how to implement the imperatives. Implementation depends on a plethora of empirical matters that are well beyond the scope of environmental ethics. Any responsible discussion of implementation would, moreover, require a great many more pages than are available here.

7.1.1 Eliminate the Use of Fossil Fuels

This section concerns energy policy, both personal and political. Its conclusions should be news to no one. They are strongly supported by nearly all ethical theories, in conjunction with the best contemporary science. Yet, in large part because they threaten entrenched power interests, they are widely denied.

Section Outline: Section 7.1.1.1 provides a rule-based argument for the conclusion that we ought quickly to eliminate all unnecessary uses of fossil fuels. Section 7.1.1.2 examines an objection to this argument from a consequentialist standpoint. Section 7.1.1.3 draws a further conclusion: that we must transition completely to non-fossil energy sources well before burning all the fossil fuels that remain—in other words, that we must leave fossil fuels in the ground.

7.1.1.1 Don't Use Fossil Fuels Unnecessarily

Perhaps the single most urgent moral imperative for humanity today is: eliminate all unnecessary uses of fossil fuels. This section examines the following rule-based argument for that imperative:

1   Harms caused by carbon dioxide emissions (suffering, disability and death in both humans and non-humans) are so great in total and so prolonged that nearly any emission, even a small one, contributes significantly to those harms.

2   We have no practical way to use fossil fuels without carbon dioxide emissions.

3   We should not contribute significantly and unnecessarily to suffering, disability, and death.

∴ 4   We should not use fossil fuels unnecessarily.

(For a more detailed treatment of this argument, see Nolt forthcoming.) Premises 1 and 2 are empirical claims. Premise 3 is a moral rule. I'll discuss each in turn.

Premise 1 asserts, first, that the burning of fossil fuels causes great and prolonged harm. As was noted in section 1.2.6.2, fossil fuel consumption is:

- The largest contributor to anthropogenic climate change—whose effects include: higher temperatures, severe weather events, flooding, droughts, increased melting of glaciers and polar ice, rising sea levels, etc.;
- Largely responsible for ocean acidification;
- A major source of atmospheric particulate matter;
- The chief source of anthropogenic sulfur dioxide (mainly from coal);
- The largest contributor to anthropogenic nitrogen oxide pollution and hence to ozone pollution;
- A main contributor to acid deposition;
- A source of nitrous oxide which increases stratospheric ozone depletion;
- A significant contributor to a global decline in human physical activity, which is a chief cause of several of the world's worst health problems;
- One of the most important forms of natural resource depletion;
- Directly responsible for habitat destruction in the form of strip mining, mountaintop removal, shale oil extraction, road building, etc.; and
- One of the main causes of biodiversity loss, chiefly through climate change. The ocean acidification and elevated temperatures (with their cascade of further harmful consequences) are likely to persist for thousands of years.

Among the consequences will be the suffering, disability or death of vast numbers of people—probably hundreds of millions, even before the end of this century, and the tally will continue long after that (section 1.2.3.2). The loss to non-human life may amount to a mass extinction, reducing biodiversity for millions of years (section 1.2.5.3). These are harms unprecedented in human history.

Premise 1 also asserts that even small emissions can contribute significantly to the harms of climate change. The case for this claim was made in section 1.2.3.3, and need not be repeated in detail here.

No specific emission, of course, causes any particular climatological event. It would be wrong to think, for example, that your driving an automobile will cause a drought that makes people thirstier hundreds of years from now. All CO_2 emissions mix together in the atmosphere, and all together contribute to all of the subsequent harms. Hence each emission is responsible for subsequent harm in proportion to its share of the total global emissions. But the total harm over centuries will be so great that even a tiny fraction of it may be substantial. Therefore the harm attributable even to a tiny fraction of the total global emissions may likewise be substantial. If, for example, global CO_2 emissions ultimately cause a hundred million deaths, and some corporation or region produces a ten-thousandth of the total emissions, then its share of the total harms is 1/10,000 of that hundred million—that is, 10,000 deaths.

Premise 2 plays only a minor role in the argument. It serves as a reminder that almost no use of fossil fuels is "innocent." There are some experimental technologies for capturing carbon dioxide emissions and storing them underground, but such technologies are expensive and not widely available. You can buy carbon offsets, which typically compensate for emissions by financing the reduction of emissions elsewhere, or by removing carbon dioxide from the atmosphere—often by planting trees which take in carbon dioxide and emit oxygen. Such offsets can, if scrupulously administered, compensate for emissions, but they do not eliminate them.

Premise 3 asserts that we should not contribute significantly and unnecessarily to suffering, disability and death. The conclusion is intended broadly, so that "we" means all of us, individually and collectively—including corporations, governments, you and me. The crux of this premise is its concept of necessity. This is intended in a moral sense. An action is **necessary** in this sense only if there are no morally acceptable and practically available alternatives.

Premise 3 is a moral rule. Moral rules are often justified by deontological theories, but they can also be justified by rule consequentialist theories or by virtue theories. I'll briefly sketch all three sorts of justification.

Premise 3 is fairly easy to justify deontologically. It is a non-harm principle, akin to the non-harm principles considered in sections 2.3.1.2, 4.4.1, 5.5.3, 6.3.1, and 6.3.2. Non-harm principles follow straightforwardly from such more fundamental principles as the Golden Rule, the categorical imperative, and broader non-anthropocentric respect principles. They are just about as basic as ethics gets. The non-harm principle stated in premise 3 is implicitly long-term, so that it cannot be derived from a near-term anthropocentric ethic. But near-term anthropocentric ethics discriminate unjustly against future people and so are unsuitable for decisions that affect them. Every other deontological theory discussed in this book supports premise 3. Deontological animal ethics or biocentric ethics broaden the premise, and hence strengthen the overall reasoning, since they require us to consider not only harms to humans, but also harms, respectively, to animals and to all living beings, and thus vastly increase the quantity of harm that we must consider.

Rule consequentialists use the same sorts of rules that deontologists do, but rather than deriving them from more fundamental rules, such as the Golden Rule or the categorical imperative, they justify them by their likely consequences. The rules they choose are those which would, if widely followed, lead to the best consequences. A rule prohibiting actions that contribute significantly and unnecessarily to suffering, disability and death would, if widely followed, pretty clearly lead to overall good consequences. Hence, without looking too much into the details, it seems likely that plausible versions of rule consequentialism would support premise 3.

Virtue theories support rules that are constitutive of good character. Refusing to contribute significantly and unnecessarily to suffering, disability and death is certainly constitutive of good character. Therefore, virtue theories too support premise 3.

In sum, long-term deontological, rule-consequentialist and virtue theories all support premise 3. The only ethical point of view from which a serious objection to premise 3 is likely to arise is act consequentialism. We'll consider an act consequentialist objection in section 7.1.1.2.

All three of the argument's premises thus have strong support. What follows from these premises, is that we should not use fossil fuels unnecessarily in ways that produce even small emissions. There is a question about how small an emission counts as "small." We don't at present have a useful answer to that question. So I have stated the conclusion more loosely: we should not use fossil fuels unnecessarily. That seems true enough for practical purposes.

What does this conclusion mean in practice? A use of fossil fuels is necessary, according to the definition given above, only if there are no morally acceptable and practically available alternatives. It is easy to find examples of fossil fuel use that are—for now, at least—clearly necessary in this sense. The fossil-fuel-powered tractors needed to cultivate and harvest crops, for example, and the trucks needed to transport them to population centers are morally necessary, because people must be fed, and in many places no workable alternatives to these tractors and trucks are yet available.

It is also easy to find examples of fossil fuel use that are clearly *unnecessary*. Overpowered or oversized cars, decorative electric lighting, recreational motor boats, hot tubs, big screen TVs, leaf-blowers, and other luxury items are not to any degree morally necessary. (Electrically powered examples are included here, since in most nations electricity is still produced primarily by the burning of fossil fuels.)

In other cases, the technologies in question are necessary, while the particular uses are clearly not. The morally acceptable alternative is simply not to use them. The heating and cooling of buildings is still today accomplished largely by the burning of fossil fuels. These functions are necessary in some climates (people cannot live or work in conditions that are too cold or too hot, so there are no morally acceptable alternatives), but both heating and air conditioning are often used excessively and hence unnecessarily. In those cases there is a morally acceptable alternative: turn them down, or off.

Still other uses of fossil fuels are neither clearly necessary nor clearly unnecessary. To these, the argument still applies, but perhaps with less force. Is it necessary, for example, for Jack Jones to drive a car to work? Work, I assume, is morally necessary for most adults, and so if driving is the only way to get to Jack's workplace, it *may* be necessary. But maybe Jack is athletic enough to ride a bike (which would also provide him with exercise), maybe he could use public transportation or a car pool, or maybe he could live close enough to his workplace to walk. In some cases, maybe he could telecommute. Or maybe he has an opportunity for another job that doesn't require driving. Thus whether Jack's driving to work is necessary is not so clear.

It is not possible to say in abstract generality which uses of fossil fuels are necessary and which are not. Moral responsibilities vary from individual to individual. The responsibilities of parents, for example, often differ widely from those of non-parents. Hence what is morally necessary also varies from individual to individual. But for almost all of us, except for the most poor, there are unnecessary uses of fossil fuels that we ought to eliminate immediately and borderline uses that we ought to work toward eliminating.

Collectively, through governments and businesses, we need to develop new technologies and infrastructure that make now-necessary fossil fuel uses obsolete.

7.1.1.2 An Act-consequentialist Objection

An important objection to the argument of the previous section is that it ignores the immense benefits of fossil fuel use. Fossil fuels power most of the world's economy. They heat us and cool us, provide for the cultivation and transportation of our food, and fuel our cars. If we eliminated all their unnecessary uses, we would lose wealth. If we replaced them with alternative energy sources, practically everything would be more expensive and less available.

This is an act-consequentialist objection. For the strict deontologist, these benefits don't matter; the fact that fossil fuel use is killing and injuring large numbers of morally considerable beings is enough to make any morally unnecessary use of them wrong—period. Of course even a deontologist would typically hold that some beneficial uses of fossil fuels should be maintained for now—namely those that are morally necessary to meet basic human needs. That is why the argument of the previous section permits fossil fuel uses where there are no morally acceptable and practically available alternatives. There is no disagreement regarding necessary uses of fossil fuels.

The real debate, then, is whether the wealth or welfare that we gain from unnecessary fossil fuel use is benefit enough to outweigh the costs. Anyone who holds that it is probably assumes an anthropocentric point of view, since the benefits are almost exclusively to humans, and the losses to non-humans are profound. Let's grant that anthropocentric perspective through the remainder of this section.

We should not, however, grant any attempt to weigh the costs and benefits by the methods of neoclassical economics; for neoclassical economics reduces all value to subjective preferences, and these, as we have seen, are poor indicators of actual human welfare. As was explained in section 3.2.5:

- Preferences, when manipulated by propaganda and advertising, as they often are, have more to do with the aims of the manipulators than with the welfare of humanity.
- Some preferences (e.g., for fatty food) are biological in origin and dysfunctional in contemporary societies, so that satisfying them is objectively harmful.
- Some preferences are the result of addictions; again satisfying them is objectively harmful.
- People are often benefited by events for which they had no preferences.
- Sometimes people are benefited more by eliminating than by satisfying certain preferences.

Actual human preferences are therefore not accurate guides to human welfare. If we want to do what's best for humanity, we need a more objective approach.

Besides, *our* preferences—that is, the preferences of currently living humans—are more or less irrelevant to the welfare of future people. Yet they are the ones who will suffer the worst effects of our fossil fuel use; and over the coming decades, centuries and millennia there will likely be far more of them than there are of us. Using our preferences to decide whether to burn fossil fuels is no more morally defensible than one person using her preferences to decide the fate of many. Just as there is no moral reason for her to ignore the welfare of her contemporaries, so there is no moral reason for us to ignore the welfare of future people.

Thus, as was explained in section 4.6.1, the appropriate notion of goodness for long-term consequentialist ethics is not preference satisfaction but objective welfare. What anthropocentric consequentialists should be concerned about is the difference our fossil fuel use makes to the objective welfare of present and future humans.

Welfare loss due to climate change is already great. The damages of climate change and ocean acidification will likely continue over thousands of years. Each fossil fuel use contributes to these damages (section 1.2.3.3). It is therefore fairly obvious that in the long run no unnecessary use of fossil fuels produces more good than harm. Accordingly, even purely anthropocentric act-consequentialist reasoning—if it is long-term and based on objective human welfare—implies that all unnecessary uses of fossil fuels are wrong.

That conclusion is strengthened if we adopt a broader non-anthropocentric ethic. Thus the objection raised at the outset of this section makes no difference. On any reasonable ethical theory we ought to eliminate all unnecessary uses of fossil fuels.

7.1.1.3 Leave Fossil Fuels in the Ground

But there is more. In addition to eliminating currently unnecessary uses of fossil fuels, the world must transition to non-fossil sources of energy as soon as possible, so that even our now-necessary fossil fuel uses become unnecessary. The chief non-fossil options available today are hydroelectric, solar, wind, biofuel, geothermal, and nuclear energy sources. Among these the most controversial is nuclear power. It receives special treatment in section 7.2.1.

The transition away from fossil fuels is morally urgent because of the extremely long-term dangers of climate change and ocean acidification. But it is necessary in any case, because we will run out of fossil fuels in the foreseeable future. We must, however, stop burning fossil fuels long before we run out; for if we don't, then we will raise the land surface temperature as much as 20°C (36°F). This would virtually eliminate grain production and render most of the planet too hot for humans to survive unprotected outdoors (Hansen *et al.* 2013). It would also, beyond any doubt, ensure a mass extinction. Burning all fossil fuels may be the most destructive thing humanity is capable of doing.

The danger of this error is great. Fossil fuels are highly concentrated, and hence extremely valuable, energy sources. Once industries have invested great trouble and expense in extracting them, their use is virtually inevitable. Continued extraction therefore negates long-run conservation efforts. If some of us stop using fossil fuels and others consume what we didn't, at best we will have achieved only a short delay in an epic tragedy. The only sure way to mitigate this tragedy is to leave some large portion of the remaining coal, oil and natural gas in the ground.

This might be achieved in an orderly way by global extraction taxes or global carbon emission taxes. Ideally taxes would be heaviest on the most carbon-intensive fuel, coal, so that its extraction and use would be phased out first. Such taxes would raise overall energy prices, providing greater incentives for conservation and efficiency, making alternative energy sources more competitive, and sparking innovation. But they might also slow economies painfully. Pain, however, is inevitable. We can postpone some of it by continuing to burn fossil fuels while they last. But then, as they run out, and for millennia to come, things will be much worse.

The transition away from fossil fuels is, however, unlikely to be orderly. Any scheme for reducing and ultimately eliminating fossil fuel use threatens the immediate security and wealth of individuals, corporations and governments worldwide. There will be fearful, angry, and sometimes violent opposition. If we succeed in leaving some fossil fuels in the ground, it will only be by the hard work and painful sacrifice of many.

7.1.2 Protect Species and Habitat

On any reasonable ethic, whether anthropocentric or not, there are excellent reasons for protecting species and their habitats. The Endangered Species Act summarizes some of the near- and long-term anthropocentric reasons, proclaiming the need to preserve species and habitat for their "esthetic, ecological, educational, historical, recreational, and scientific value." This list, however, omits the values, both economic and non-economic, of ecosystem services (section 1.2.5.2). We might also add the value of wildness, or natural autonomy in Katz's sense (section 6.7.2), if it is not already covered under "aesthetic value." Non-anthropocentric ethics augment all these reasons by promoting awareness of the goods of living nature. Whether consideration is given to animals, individual organisms, or biotic systems, the need for habitat is obvious; and no life continues without the continuation of species.

Thus regarding the general need to protect species and habitat, all the theories considered in this book agree.

There was until recently a robust consensus on protecting ecosystems as well. Given the rapidity of climate change, however, that goal may no longer be realistic. Ecosystems, as was explained in section 1.2.5.3, are disintegrating as species migrate at differential rates to higher elevations and latitudes, and as other stressors take their toll. Many existing ecosystems are therefore probably already doomed—though, as was noted in section 6.7, exactly when an ecosystem comes to an end is far from clear. To survive, species will have to adapt and reassemble themselves into novel ecosystems.

Given the magnitude of these changes, nature conservation can no longer be what it once was. We can no longer hope to preserve large natural areas as living natural history museums in which the past is retained for present human edification and enjoyment. It will no longer be possible to preserve living systems as they were in the past.

Another likely consequence is that the distinction between *native* and non-native species, so important to traditional conservation biology, may lose significance. A species is native to a place if it has been there a very long time—typically thousands of years, at least—having either evolved there or arrived without human interference. Some robust species will, no doubt, remain in places to which they are native; but those places will change around them so much that their being native may be reduced to a mere curiosity. It will not imply, as it once did, integration into old and well established patterns of life.

Conservation biologists will, however, have to wrestle increasingly with the problem of invasive species. The nature of the threat varies widely. Some invasives—for example, the many fungi that blight plants—are disease organisms. Others, such as kudzu, a fast-growing vine, overgrow or outcompete native plants. Still others, such as domestic cats, prey on local animals. Feral cats on islands, for example, are reportedly responsible for at least 14 percent of global bird, mammal, and reptile extinctions (Medina *et al.* 2011).

Despite such growing threats, preservation of habitat continues to make sense, even as some inhabitants move out and new organisms move in. Often incoming organisms are not invasive. Some fit neatly into ecological niches that have been vacated by other species and so are generally beneficial.

Some habitats, however, cannot be saved. Over the next few centuries shorelines will move inland as oceans rise, and shoreline habitats will be inundated. Glaciers and the summer Arctic ice cap (possibly both ice caps) will melt, and the species that now rely on them will have no habitat left. Still, most geographical habitats (mountain ranges, rivers, oceans, lowlands, etc.) will stay put and might be protected against degradation and human encroachment, providing nurseries for new ecosystems to form.

Beyond the consensus on trying to preserve species and habitat there is deep disagreement. Anthropocentrists see no ethical reason to protect the welfare of individual non-humans, except as it affects human welfare. Sentientists see no ethical reason to protect the welfare of individual non-sentient creatures, except as it affects the welfare of the sentient. Strict biocentric holists see no ethical reason to protect the welfare of any non-human individuals, except as it affects biotic systems. We'll return to such disagreements in section 7.2.2.

7.1.3 Eat Ethically

Nothing is more personal than eating—taking in nutrients from the environment and making them part of us. Hunger is one of our most fundamental drives. The pleasure of sharing food enlivens and unites cultures and families. We celebrate with food and use it to show our love. Eating, understandably, is therefore a touchy subject. Thinking clearly and ethically about food is difficult. Yet doubtless eating is subject to ethical constraints. We all, for example, condemn cannibalism.

The chief problem in eating ethically is that there are so many complications to consider. These include:

- *Health consequences:* As was noted in section 1.2.2, five of the world's top six causes of death are related to lack of exercise or dietary excess. Excessive consumption of sugars, saturated fats and salt are among the main culprits.
- *Energy use:* Food that is processed, transported long distances, or refrigerated requires more energy than food that is fresh, transported short distances, and consumed before refrigeration is needed. The shorter the distance from farm to plate, and the less that happens in the meantime, the better—not only for conserving energy, but for health.
- *Water use:* Food that is grown on irrigated lands requires more water than food that is not. Meat requires more water than plant foods. (See section 1.2.4.2.)
- *Pollution:* Food that is produced organically results in less pollution than food that is produced using artificial pesticides, herbicides or petroleum-based fertilizers.
- *Soil loss:* Clearing of forests—especially rainforests—for agricultural land degrades soils; so does much conventional agriculture. Organic agriculture is better for conserving rich soils. Avoiding meat (especially beef) from tropical areas helps to conserve rainforest soils.
- *Waste:* Heavily packaged food wastes materials and energy, as does failing to eat what you buy.
- *Animal suffering and animal rights:* Factory farms are sources of misery to great numbers of animals—and often to their workers. There are better ways for humans to feed themselves and create employment. Some of the animals that we treat this way are near-persons or subjects of a life.
- *Biodiversity loss:* Excessive taking of wild animals or plants threatens many species. Particularly worrisome are overfishing of the world's oceans and (in poor areas) the hunting of threatened and endangered species for bush meat.

The number and variety of these considerations is bewildering. No one can take them all into account all of the time. But everyone can take some of them into account some of the time. Simple rules may help: "eat local," "eat low on the food chain," "eat compassionately"—or, my personal favorite, author Michael Pollan's elegant imperative: "Eat food. Not too much. Mostly plants" (Pollan 2007). (By "food" Pollan means something that is recognizable as having once been alive, as opposed to what he calls "edible food-like substances"—that is, highly processed industrial concoctions.)

A general ethical principle that is applicable to almost all personal food choices is: if one action causes more harm than another, and it costs you little (in time, money or gustatory pleasure) to choose the less harmful, then do so. This principle, or something like it, is a matter of common sense; and it can be readily derived from deontological, consequentialist and virtue theories alike. It makes little difference, then, what ethical theory we appeal to—though the broader the scope of the theory (that is, the wider it makes the moral community) the stronger are the principle's implications.

Animal ethicists, most notably Singer (section 5.4.1), have built a strong non-anthropocentric case for rejecting the products of factory farms. Factory farms also cause environmental problems (sections 1.2.6.2 and 5.1.4). And human health considerations, too (section 1.2.2), weigh heavily in favor of low meat consumption. The overall case against consuming factory farm products is conclusive. I know of no ethical theorist who defends factory farms as they exist today.

Yet none of the theories considered in this book provides a conclusive argument for strict vegetarianism or veganism. Singer's view applies only to sentient animals. If crustaceans, for example, are non-sentient, then his argument provides no reason not to eat them. Reagan's theory applies to an even smaller range of animals—subjects of a life. Gandhi advocated a strict form of vegetarianism—though, because he drank goat's milk, he was not vegan. But he did not offer much of an argument for this. It was embedded in his spiritual practice. It should be kept in mind, however, that the absence of a conclusive argument for strict vegetarianism does not amount to an argument in favor of eating meat.

The most effective way to eat more ethically is usually to start with small, readily achievable changes and to practice them until they become habits—ideally, habits that enhance the joy and conviviality of eating. To avoid wasting time and energy in constantly thinking about consequences, many people take a rule-consequentialist approach; deciding in advance which categories of food they will eat and which they will not, and sticking to that. Much can be accomplished, too, simply by getting food from the right places. Among the right places—for many of the reasons listed above—are local farmers' markets. They are also pleasant and neighborly places to shop. Even greater, for many, are the pleasures of the garden.

7.1.4 Build a Sustainable Economy

Economies are social arrangements for the efficient production and distribution of goods, services, and employment. Humans institute and maintain them by fallible government and imperfect laws, in order to satisfy human desires. There is a widespread, though mostly unspoken, impression that the current economic system is an inevitable product of human nature and cannot be changed. Perhaps this idea comes in part from the assumption, explicit in neoclassical economics, that human beings must always maximize satisfaction of their own preferences. Naturally, we often do what we prefer. But to some extent, such behavior is instilled or reinforced in people by the current economic system, in self-fulfilling prophecy. To some extent, too, the current economy stimulates and manipulates our preferences.

To be ethical, however, is to act from higher, broader and more circumspect reasons. People working ethically together have sometimes achieved historic changes that self-interested preference-satisfaction maximizers could never have accomplished. Consider, for example, the abolition of slavery and the partially successful world-wide struggles for human rights. These historic achievements, far from maximizing the reformers' preference satisfaction, cost many of them their lives. Organized ethical action could likewise transform, though only with considerable work and sacrifice, the global economy.

The economy as now constituted is designed to respond only to relatively short-term human preferences, and to the constraints of current law. In the long run it is blind. Left to its own devices, it will plow mechanically on into whatever tragedies lie ahead. It therefore needs intelligent redesign and intelligent guidance. The number of possible economies that have never yet been tried is infinite. There have to be better arrangements.

Given that the purpose of an economy is to produce and distribute goods, services, and employment efficiently, at the very least, we need an economy that can do that sustainably. Recall the definition of sustainability given in section 4.7: we are acting sustainably with respect to a particular value if:

1. We adequately realize that value for our generation; and
2. Our actions do not compromise the ability of future generations to maintain its adequacy.

A **sustainable economy**, then, is an economy that:

1. Efficiently provides adequate goods, services, and employment for our generation; and
2. Does not compromise the ability of future generations to efficiently maintain an adequate supply of goods, services, and employment.

Since economies are created to serve humans, their ethical justifications are anthropocentric. The claim that economies should be sustainable can be justified either by deontological or consequentialist arguments of the sorts considered near the end of section 4.7. On the need for sustainable economies, all reasonable ethical theories concur.

But what counts as "adequate goods, services, and employment"? Pretty clearly a minimum requirement is that they suffice to fulfill basic needs, maintain human rights, and provide opportunities for meaningful human lives. This is a high standard. We are far from achieving it globally. We have, therefore, failed to meet even the first condition of sustainability.

We have also failed to meet the second. The current global economy is unsustainable in that it is compromising the ability of future generations, both near and distant, to efficiently maintain an adequate supply of goods, services and employment. It is doing so by:

- Polluting the air with greenhouse gases, which produce climate change that will impair future life generally, and hence future economic activity (section 1.2.3);
- Depleting the fossil fuels that currently power most of our economic activity (section 1.2.4.1);
- Acidifying the oceans, which will make them less productive of food (section 1.2.1.3);
- Depleting sources of fresh water that are needed not only for domestic and industrial use, but also for food production (section 1.2.4.2);
- Depleting non-renewable metals that are needed by many sectors of the economy (section 1.2.4);
- Continually increasing land usage, much of it to feed growing appetites for meat (section 1.2.6.2);
- Depleting natural systems, whose ecosystem services are needed by economies, and by all living beings (section 1.2.5 and its subsections).

Ours is not a sustainable economy. We need to construct a sustainable economy quickly.

Generalizing, we may say that the global economy is unsustainable because it has failed to keep its activities within ecological limits. Everything on Earth is finite. (It has been said that solar energy is an exception. But, while it is true that the sun will keep shining practically forever by human standards, the amount of sunlight the Earth receives each day is finite. There are, therefore, limits on the amount of solar power we can produce.) Earth is limited, too, in its capacity to sequester carbon dioxide; to neutralize ocean acidity; to supply fossil fuels, metals, and fresh water; and to maintain ecosystem services, especially while ecosystems are disintegrating.

A primary design principle for sustainable economies, then, is: stay within ecological limits. This is the central idea of **ecological economics**, a discipline that arose in the 1980s as the integration of two older and sometimes antagonistic disciplines: ecology and economics. Ecological economics sees economies as subsystems of ecological systems and hence as subject to their limits. Ecological economists may adopt some of the methods of neoclassical environmental economics—seeking, for example, to internalize externalities (see section 3.2.3 and its subsections)—but their fundamental ethic is different. Rather than basing all decisions ultimately on human preferences, as neoclassical economists do, they see ecological limits as boundaries that may not be crossed, regardless of anyone's preferences. This is because crossing them would undermine fundamental processes upon which the whole economy depends. Their reasoning, like that of all economists, is anthropocentric. What they fear in crossing the limits is harm to humans. Still, their thinking is circumspect and long-term in ways that neoclassical economics is not.

To be sustainable, an economy must work within ecological limits and so must be guided by some form of ecological economics. It must, accordingly, be powered by renewable energy sources and must not deplete the environmental materials and services (so-called **natural capital**) on which it necessarily depends. Ecosystem services must be kept intact. Critical materials—e.g., metals, soils and fresh water—must be recycled or renewed. Wastes must also be recycled, either artificially, or by being released into the environment so slowly that they do not overwhelm natural recycling processes. These requirements are obvious and widely recognized.

But all of this is easier said than done. Even with the great and destructive power of fossil fuels, we have not managed to supply adequate goods, services, and employment to many people today. And now we must quickly relinquish that power. It will take decades to develop a new infrastructure based on non-fossil energy that recycles and renews materials effectively. In the meantime, we will have to rely heavily on conservation and efficiency. This has definite and quite stringent implications.

To use goods and services efficiently is to use them where they will do the most good. A sustainable economy does not waste materials and energy on things that are not good for people, or that in the long run do more harm than good. It provides food, but not junk food; reliable transportation, but not personal SUVs; affordable housing, but not mansions. It is, therefore, an economy that distributes goods, services, and employment more equitably than at present. It does not, like neoclassical economics, favor the preferences of the rich (see sections 3.2.4 and 3.2.5).

More generally, an ecological economics should not, like neoclassical economics, regard goodness as preference satisfaction. Ecological economic theory, being long-term and (again, like most economic thinking) consequentialist, should, for reasons explained in section 4.6.1, regard goodness as objective welfare. It is unfortunate, therefore, that some ecological economists still cling to the neoclassical economic conception of welfare as a "psychic state"—that is, as preference satisfaction (Daly and Farley 2004: 17). Instead it should be designed to promote aims that are clearly objectively good—among them, health, adequate (but not luxurious) wealth, education, security, meaningful relationships, and the like.

In theory, the transition to a sustainable economy could be accomplished largely by taxing heavily anything that is harmful to both the present and future, and reducing or eliminating taxes on objective human goods. In practice, any such changes would be, and are, stiffly resisted. Sustainability, like other great historic ethical goals, will not be achieved without conflict.

To achieve sustainability globally, rich nations must provide financing, technology, and expertise to developing nations to divert them from their current path of burning ever more fossil fuels (Caney 2005; Shue 1999). This would serve the common good, both present and future, and it would be just; for developed nations have so far been responsible for most of the world's carbon emissions. In theory, it could be accomplished by international agreement. No nation, however, parts with its riches easily. Here, too, we can expect conflict.

But what better option do we have? Our current path clearly leads to worse ends.

The transition must happen quickly by historical standards. As ecological economists Herman Daly and Joshua Farley note:

> In the past, numerous civilizations have crumbled as they have surpassed ecological barriers. Examples are the civilization on Easter Island, the Mayan empire, and the early civilizations of the Fertile Crescent. Fortunately, these were isolated incidents in which only the local carrying capacity was overwhelmed . . . However, as trade expands, local limits to scale become less relevant and global limits more so. While trade may decrease the chances of surpassing sustainable scale in any one area, it also means that if we do surpass it, we are more likely to do so for the planet as a whole. Consequently, it becomes more difficult to learn from our mistakes as we go. Thus, globalization requires us to get it right the first time.
>
> (Daly and Farley 2004: 331–32)

The first time is upon us.

The reasoning of this entire section has been strictly anthropocentric. But the same conclusions follow with greater force under any of the non-anthropocentric theories discussed in this book.

7.1.5 Reduce Human Population

Nearly all of the projections surveyed in Chapter 1 suggest that we will not deviate much from our destructive and unsustainable path for some decades yet. History, like a great ship, has great inertia. This implies a further imperative: we should—at least while our economy remains predominantly destructive over the long term—reduce human population.

This is not a misanthropic thought. It follows simply from rational consideration of long-term human welfare. A strictly anthropocentric argument suffices. Here is such an argument, in consequentialist form:

1 We have three options as regards population in the coming decades: to let it increase, keep it the same, or reduce it somewhat. (Reducing it greatly is not a morally acceptable option.)
2 Reducing population somewhat over the coming decades would be more difficult and would result in fewer people living in the short term than the other two options, but would cause less environmental damage in the long term, than letting the population stay the same or grow.
3 The long-term environmental damage from high population over the next few decades would reduce long-term total welfare more than would the

difficulties and smaller population associated with reducing population over the coming decades.
4   We should choose the option that yields the greatest total welfare.
∴ 5   We should reduce population over the coming decades.

The premises, of course, require further explanation.

With regard to premise 1, it is obvious for any time period that, comparing population at the beginning of that period with population at the end, it will either increase, stay the same, or decrease. Population, as was noted in section 1.2.6.3, depends on life expectancy and fertility. Shortening people's lives is not morally acceptable—except perhaps, for certain exceptional cases, as when people are in severe, incurable and intractable pain. But such exceptions can have virtually no effect on population totals. Population decrease can, however, be accomplished over decades by morally acceptable decreases in fertility. In particular, there is strong evidence that the following strategies are generally effective in reducing the birth rate:

• Provide education and meaningful employment for women;
• Provide free or low-cost access to birth control;
• Publicize the fact that contraception is safer than early or frequent child-bearing; and
• Ensure care for the elderly (since one reason people in developing nations have many children is to ensure that someone will care for them in their old age) (Ryerson 2012).

Population decrease, as contemplated in premise 1, would be accomplished by strategies such as these.

Premise 2 lists the morally significant consequences of the three options. Reducing population over a matter of decades is, as this premise acknowledges, no easy matter. It would require expensive social policies and would likely be met with much resistance. There would, moreover, likely be a loss of welfare due to the fact that in the near term there would be fewer people to enjoy life. Yet failing to reduce population, especially during decades when fossil fuels are still being used, will certainly result in greater environmental damage. As was noted in section 1.2.6,

total environmental damage = damage per capita × population.

That is (assuming non-decreasing damage per capita), the greater the population over the next few decades, the greater the environmental damage, particularly from climate change (Cafaro 2012). The damage of climate change is, moreover, very long-lasting: thousands or tens of thousands of years in the cases of temperature elevation and ocean acidification, possibly millions in the case of biodiversity loss (see sections 1.2.1.3, 1.2.3.2 and 1.2.5.3).

Premise 3 provides an overall evaluation of these consequences, in terms of objective human welfare. It asserts that the long-term environmental damage of a higher population over the coming decades would reduce total welfare more than reducing population would. There are two reasons for this. First, the long-term environmental damage, especially from climate change, will likely cause great suffering and large numbers of deaths while it persists, and it will persist for far more than decades. Second, that damage is likely to reduce the total number of people that the Earth can sustain. Hence by reducing population now we are likely to enable greater numbers of people to live sustainably in the future—assuming that we eventually do develop sustainable economies. This would be most likely to keep overall human welfare high in the long run. Of course premise 3 also assumes that in the long run (centuries or millennia) there will still be people. But that is likely (section 1.3).

Premise 4 is a standard consequentialist choice principle. From these four premises—assuming that premise 2 has listed the main consequences of moral significance—the conclusion follows.

Once again, this argument is entirely anthropocentric. But, again, if we bring in non-anthropocentric considerations (as in section 5.12) the reasoning becomes stronger still.

We need be in no rush, then, to "be fruitful and multiply." Making more people today, while our economy is unsustainable, only diminishes human welfare, and the welfare of all life, in the long run.

• 7.2 TWO OPEN ETHICAL QUESTIONS

On some important ethical questions, the prominent theories of environmental ethics do not all agree. This can be either because there is disagreement regarding empirical questions that have little to do with the theories themselves or because the theories themselves yield conflicting conclusions, even assuming that answers to the empirical questions are known. There are many examples of both kinds. The following two sections consider just one of each.

Section Outline: Section 7.2.1 takes up the question "Should we generate more nuclear power?" Though the ethical principles needed for an answer are fairly clear, they depend on empirical estimates and projections that are much disputed. Section 7.2.2 asks "whither conservation?"—that is, what form can biological conservation take on a planet that is losing life so rapidly and changing so quickly? Here the empirical facts limit what we can do, but our goals depend on our ethics, and regarding the appropriate ethics there is much disagreement.

7.2.1 Should We Generate More Nuclear Power?

There is an urgent need to eliminate the use of fossil energy sources. One of the most potent alternatives is nuclear power. This section therefore considers the question: Should we generate more nuclear power?

Section Outline: Section 7.2.1.1 examines the parameters of the question, introducing some basic facts, and considers various ethical approaches. Section 7.2.1.2 takes up an artificially simplified version of the problem, where our choices are limited to nuclear power and fossil fuels. Section 7.2.1.3 looks at a more realistic array of options.

7.2.1.1 *The Basics of the Problem*

Nuclear power is energy generated by nuclear reactors. This energy, initially in the form of heat from nuclear fission, is converted by steam turbines into electricity, which is the usable output. All existing nuclear power plants are fission-based. Though researchers have been trying to develop practical fusion power plants for over half a century, none yet exist, and the technical obstacles are so great that their advent is at best still decades away. This section is therefore concerned only with fission reactors.

Nuclear reactors produced about 5 percent of the world's energy and 12 percent of the world's electricity in 2011. Fossil fuels produced, by comparison, about 82 percent of the world's energy and 68 percent of its electricity (IEA 2013: 6 and 24). Our question, then, is: given that we must phase out fossil fuels, should we increase nuclear power as we do so?

Some opponents of nuclear power argue deontologically that we should *not*, because nuclear power generation is so dangerous that it is likely to cause unacceptable harms or rights violations. Dangers include: release of large amounts of radioactive material (either by accident or deliberate attack), the use of nuclear power facilities to produce nuclear weapons, and the creation of highly radioactive waste that remains deadly for tens or hundreds of thousands of years.

But this deontological answer is, on its own, too simple. We know we must stop burning fossil fuels soon. Yet the world economy runs chiefly on fossil fuels. To phase out fossil fuels and not replace them with other workable forms of power generation is also likely to cause unacceptable harms or rights violations. The dangers include global economic depression, widespread famine, and resultant violence.

Nuclear power is not, of course, our only option. We can conserve energy and replace the fossil fuels with renewable sources—wind, the sun, biofuels, geothermal heating and cooling, and so on. But will these be enough? Might we not still need nuclear power to prevent global economic collapse? More generally, which of the various possible global energy strategies is best?

These questions suggest the need for painstaking consequentialist reasoning. When there are dangers in every action and anything we can do is likely to violate human rights, then (as was explained in section 4.4.3) deontological rules are not likely to yield a solution. We must reason consequentially instead.

The most appropriate form of consequentialism will, furthermore (for reasons explained in sections 2.3.2.2, 3.3, 4.6.1, and 6.4.2) be based on objective welfare—objective human welfare if it is anthropocentric, and objective human, animal and perhaps biotic welfare if it is not. Finally, since the dangers of both nuclear and fossil fuel energy are long-term, this ethic must be long-term as well. The right sort of theory for the problem is, therefore, some version of long-term objective welfare consequentialism.

7.2.1.2 Nuclear Power vs. Fossil Fuels

Before we address the complexities of the question, "should we generate more nuclear power?" it may help to consider a simpler problem: if forced to choose between nuclear power and fossil fuels as the main source of the world's power for, say, the next 50 years, which should we pick? This simpler problem artificially narrows down the range of options to two and so is much easier to solve.

Our method for solving it is a decision table. But we won't have exact numbers or probabilities, so I won't actually construct a table, but will proceed informally, following the five steps for constructing decision tables (section 2.2.3.2):

1. List the possible options for action. These must be mutually exclusive; that is, it must be impossible for more than one to occur.
2. List all the possible outcomes (i.e., sets of consequences) for each option.
3. Determine the probability of each possible outcome for each option.
4. Assign a value (positive, negative or zero) to each possible outcome of each option.
5. Select the option (or, in case of a tie, any one of the options) with the greatest expected value.

To do all of this in full detail would take a large report, so what follows is merely a quick summary of the reasoning.

We have artificially narrowed down the problem to two options: generating most of the world's energy for the next 50 years with nuclear power or with fossil fuels. These are mutually exclusive, so that takes care of step 1. On to step 2 . . .

What happens if we choose fossil fuels is pretty well known, so we need list only one possible outcome. There will be benefit: the world will have power—at least for the 50-year period specified above. But there will be many long-term harms. These were described in section 7.1.1.1.

To complete step 2, we must consider the potential effects of nuclear power. It too is probably capable of supplying most of the world's power for the specified 50-year period. But consideration of harmful effects yields a variety of possible outcomes. One is simply that everything goes well: we get the power we need, and nothing terrible happens. The others involve greater or lesser harms. I will ignore a host of details and focus only on the three major dangers mentioned earlier: release of large amounts of radioactive material from the reactors, proliferation of nuclear weapons, and the problem of nuclear waste. (Also I will not be more careful than is necessary in classifying these potential outcomes.)

The most immediate danger is the potential for catastrophic release of radioactive material. There have been two such catastrophic accidents and many lesser ones.

The first was a meltdown of a single reactor at Chernobyl in Ukraine in 1986. The cause was operator error. The second event, triggered by an earthquake and tsunami on March 11, 2011, destroyed four nuclear reactors at the Fukushima Daiichi plant in Japan. Three of the four melted down. Radioactive cooling water continues to leak from the plant at the time of this writing (September 2013). Estimates of deaths from the Chernobyl event range from 50 to 475,000 (Shrader-Frechette 2011: 65). (The lower figures are from proponents of nuclear power, the higher from opponents, who include estimates of eventual deaths from cancer due to radiation exposure for people far from the plant.) The long-term effects of the Fukushima disaster have not yet, so far as I know, been thoroughly assessed. Even on the most conservative estimates, such releases of radioactive materials pose significant dangers. They may result, moreover, not only from accidents, as these two did, but also from terrorist or military attacks.

The second danger is proliferation of nuclear weapons; for the technologies that produce nuclear power can be modified to create nuclear weapons. Nuclear weapons and nuclear war vary considerably in deadliness. The worst potential outcome, a full-scale thermonuclear war, could kill billions of people and plunge the planet into a **nuclear winter**—a substantial period of cold and darkness caused by soot lifted into the atmosphere from the nuclear explosions and resulting fires. The resultant suffering and death are unimaginable. There are also many more limited and less deadly, but still horrific, possibilities (Robock and Toon 2012; Toon *et al.* 2007).

Finally, there is the problem of nuclear waste. Nuclear power plants produce high-level radioactive waste consisting mainly of spent fuel or materials from its reprocessing. If untreated, this waste remains more radioactive than the ore from which the fuel was created for about 10,000 years (NEA 1989). Currently much of it is stored in casks onsite at nuclear plants, where it must constantly be monitored and guarded against terrorist attack. There are hundreds of such plants worldwide. Most experts think that the waste would be safer if collected, stored, monitored, and guarded in deep underground repositories, but efforts to create such repositories have become mired in controversy. There are, however, various ways in which the waste can be treated to reduce (though not eliminate) the hazards.

We have now considered the major possible outcomes for nuclear power generation. This completes step 2. I'll do step 3, estimating the probabilities of the various outcomes and step 4, evaluating those outcomes, simultaneously.

Let's assume that we can keep the world economy going for another 50 years using either mostly fossil fuels or mostly nuclear energy and that these two strategies are roughly equal as regards their benefits (the chief benefit being to supply the world with power). The probabilities and values that will differentiate the two technologies, then, are those of their potential harms. So to complete steps 3 and 4, we need to estimate the probabilities and values (or, better, disvalues) of the harmful outcomes. We'll express losses primarily in terms of fatalities—which provide a rough measure of lost objective human welfare.

Given the past history of nuclear accidents—two catastrophic ones and a number of lesser ones—the probability of further catastrophic releases of radioactive substances if generation of nuclear power is increased is not negligible. Each such event would cost many lives—in the worst cases, perhaps hundreds of thousands of them.

With nuclear proliferation leading to nuclear war, mortality could be much greater—from hundreds of thousands to billions. But, except in the case of a large thermonuclear war, most of the harm would be relatively short-lived by historical standards. Hiroshima and Nagasaki, the only places on Earth that have experienced nuclear attack, are teeming cities today.

It should, moreover, be kept in mind that nuclear war could occur whether or not we increase the use of nuclear power. So what matters, insofar as our analysis of nuclear power is concerned, is not probability of nuclear war *per se*, but how much more probable nuclear war becomes if we increase production of nuclear power. I know of no estimates of this quantity in the literature. Here is a guess: increasing nuclear power generation does not significantly raise the probability of large-scale thermonuclear war, but it does significantly, though not enormously, raise the probability of smaller scale nuclear conflict, which could be expected to kill, perhaps, millions of people.

Nuclear waste is a long-term issue. Given that high-level nuclear waste is stored at power plants around the world, the probability of fatal incidents is substantial. But these incidents are likely be local and to cause relatively small numbers of casualties. As time passes the industry may establish safer repositories or find ways to make the waste itself safer. Incidents may still occur, but though the waste lasts a very long time, even over that time very large numbers of casualties are improbable.

In sum, increasing nuclear power generation might not have any catastrophic effects; but, on the other hand, it might produce significant numbers of fatalities—perhaps hundreds of thousands or millions, by major accident or proliferation-induced limited nuclear war. It could also lead to a large thermonuclear war, though that seems less likely. Air pollution from the burning of fossil fuels is, by contrast, already killing over a million people each year (section 1.2.2); and climate change, largely from the burning of fossil fuels, is likely to kill tens of millions in this century. Moreover, climate change persists for thousands of years and, with continued use of fossil fuels for 50 more years, it is likely to precipitate a mass extinction. The burning of fossil fuels has many other detrimental effects as well. Thus fossil fuels are more likely to do more long-term damage than is nuclear power. This completes steps 3 and 4.

Step 5 is now obvious: if the choice were between nuclear power and fossil fuels as the main source of the world's power for the next 50 years, we should choose nuclear power. The expected value of burning fossil fuels is lower, because its harmful outcomes are generally more certain and (except for nuclear war, which is not certain) more lethal to humans. The probability of mass extinction is also greater with continued use of fossil fuels. Adopting a non-anthropocentric ethic thus only strengthens the case for nuclear power over fossil fuels.

7.2.1.3 Nuclear Power vs. Conservation and Renewables

Fortunately, we need not choose between nuclear power and fossil fuels. Various non-fossil energy sources are available, though the most prominent of them are intermittent. Windmills stop when the wind is calm; photovoltaic panels generate little power at night. Hence both need to be supplemented either by energy storage systems or steadier energy sources. Nuclear power plants, by contrast, are steady sources—at least when operating normally.

So we come back to our original question: as we eliminate fossil fuels, should the world generate more nuclear power? The basic outlines of a consequentialist answer are clear: yes, if we can't generate enough power with other non-fossil energy sources to meet human needs, so that overall harm is likely to be greater than if we didn't add nuclear power; no, otherwise.

But ethics alone can't tell us whether we can create a non-fossil economy that will meet human needs well enough so that nuclear power is not necessary. That is an empirical question, and its answer depends on a host of other empirical matters: How much capacity for renewable energy is there? How deeply can we cut our energy use by eliminating unnecessary power consumption? How much renewable energy infrastructure can we afford? How much of the transition to renewables is politically feasible? Answers to all these questions are hotly disputed, and they change as new technologies are developed and political winds shift.

We therefore can't answer the question "Should the world generate more nuclear power?" without further information. Perhaps if we looked hard enough, we could find the necessary answers in existing studies. Perhaps more studies need to be done. But, in any case, that is as far as we can go in this book. We know how to answer the question if we can get the relevant information.

7.2.2 Whither Conservation?

Regarding the issues discussed in sections 7.1.1–7.1.5, all, or nearly all, of the ethical theories are in agreement, and non-anthropocentric arguments merely add strength to anthropocentric ones. In the previous section (7.2.1), the form of the ethical reasoning was clear and again non-anthropocentric considerations only strengthened the anthropocentric ones. These sections might therefore seem to suggest, as pragmatists sometimes argue, that non-anthropocentric theories do not fundamentally change our ethical conclusions and that anthropocentric reasoning is all we need.

Obviously that's not quite true, because non-anthropocentric considerations do often strengthen environmental reasoning. There are, however, cases in which non-anthropocentric theories introduce novelties so great that they conflict with anthropocentric theories. Different kinds of non-anthropocentric theories may also conflict with one another.

The convergence between anthropocentric and non-anthropocentric theories that we have encountered so far is largely an artifact of my selection of material. The intent of section 7.1 and its subsections is to present conclusions on which all, or nearly all, of the ethical theories agree.

One discipline in which the theories tend to differ widely is conservation biology. This young and rapidly changing field is therefore fruitful ground in which to explore theoretical differences.

Section Outline: The following sections consider three ethical problems in conservation biology: whether we ought to help species affected by climate change move to more suitable habitats (section 7.2.2.1); whether we ought to restore old ecosystems, create new ones—or, more drastically, resurrect extinct forms of life or invent artificial ones to replace those that have been lost (section 7.2.2.2); and whether our responsibilities to life extend to times beyond human extinction (section 7.2.2.3).

7.2.2.1 Assisted Colonization

We have noted that as the Earth heats up, species need to move to higher latitudes or altitudes in order to stay within tolerable temperature ranges (sections 1.2.5.3 and 7.1.2). This is relatively easy for flying animals, but more difficult for most other forms of life. Landscapes are fragmented by roads and cities. Rivers have been dammed. Forests (which provide cover and shade) have in many places been eliminated. For species that already inhabit mountain peaks, the only option is to move toward the nearest pole, but impassable lowlands may lie in the way. Contemporary landscapes, in sum, present a multitude of barriers to species movement. Many conservation biologists have therefore begun to advocate programs of *assisted colonization*—that is, moving species, often across natural or artificial barriers, to a new habitat that is now more suitable for them than the old, in order to prevent extinctions.

The proposed benefit, of course, is to the species (and hence to its present and future members). The main worry is that the ecosystems to which the species are moved will be compromised by the colonization (Sandler 2010). Assisted colonization therefore pits species conservation against ecosystem conservation.

There is, as was noted in sections 6.6.3–6.6.5, a strong biocentric argument for preserving as many species as possible: loss of a species entails loss of all of its future members and of any further species that might have evolved from it; hence it eliminates great non-anthropocentric value from the world. Given that humans have already eradicated many species and will eradicate many more, this gives us reason to resist further loss. This argument works whether or not we assume that the welfare of a species is something more than the aggregate welfare of its members. That is, it is compatible both with biocentric individualism and with a more robust species ethic. It now appears, moreover, that in many cases assisted colonization may be the only way to save species. Thus the case for assisted colonization is strong.

Yet ecocentrists and those who, like Rolston, value species only within their native habitat (see section 6.6.1), resist assisted colonization. Ecocentrists may fear disruption of ecosystems more than loss of species. Their worries are, however, open to the objection (voiced in section 7.1.2) that ecosystem preservation is a lost cause anyway and we had better focus on preserving species and habitat. A similar objection can be raised against Rolstonians: better to preserve species in new habitats where they can form new ecosystems than not to preserve them at all.

Rolstonians and ecocentrists may reply it is too soon to give up altogether on the preservation of ecosystems. It may still be possible to hold the world's total temperature increase to something like 2°C, in which case some ecosystems might yet be preserved.

Anthropocentric arguments regarding assisted colonization tend to reflect the same division between preserving species and preserving ecosystems. They are, if anything, more various than non-anthropocentric arguments, since anthropocentric reasons for preserving species or ecosystems or both are many and diverse. Some of these reasons were listed at the beginning of section 7.1.2. Those that emphasize species preservation are likely to support assisted colonization; those that emphasize ecosystem preservation are likely to oppose it. Those that emphasize both are likely to be conflicted.

It would, of course, be foolish on any view to move a species to a place where it was likely to threaten an ecosystem by way of threatening other species of equal or greater value. Conservation biologists engaged in assisted colonization thus have to predict how species are likely to interact with novel habitats and assess how valuable various species are. Mistakes are inevitable in such endeavors. Assisted colonization is therefore risky and should not be undertaken casually.

7.2.2.2 Restoration, Rewilding, Resurrection and Artificial Life

After we have degraded or destroyed an ecosystem or a habitat, should we attempt to restore it? Conservation biologists have generally answered yes. **Restoration ecology**, which attempts to repair or restore ecosystems (by, for example, reforesting, removing invasive and non-native organisms, controlling erosion, and the like) has therefore become an important subfield of conservation biology.

Traditionally, the goal was to restore the ecosystem to its pre-disturbance state and preserve it in that state. But, given climate change, restoration may give way to something more like rewilding. **Rewilding** is the restoration of large-scale ecosystems unencumbered by human development, interlinked by corridors that facilitate migration, and sufficiently biodiverse to support large predators. Rewilding does not aim to restore past conditions precisely. It may instead introduce non-native species to fill particular ecological niches (Donlan *et al.* 2006).

The discovery of well-preserved tissue from some prehistoric animals (e.g., woolly mammoths frozen in ice) has even led to suggestions that some species of extinct organisms might be **resurrected**—that is, brought back to life through the use of biotechnology, and possibly reintroduced into nature. Whether this could actually be accomplished is still unclear, but the idea has been floated (Gill 2013).

Another possibility, which is almost certainly technologically feasible, is **artificial life**—genetically engineered organisms of kinds that had not existed before. Organisms might be genetically engineered, for example, to withstand the rigors of an over-heated planet.

These possibilities lie on a continuum of increasing human interference with nature. Which are ethically acceptable? Where should we draw the line? That depends, of course, on the consequences of each. Let's consider all of them first under the assumption that each can be implemented successfully with no very harmful unintended consequences. Later we'll consider the possibility that something might go seriously wrong.

Even assuming that these techniques can all be applied successfully, there is disagreement among anthropocentrists regarding whether they should be. Those who, like Eric Katz, value nature primarily for its wildness, autonomy and freedom from human interference, may oppose even assisted colonization and restoration (see section 6.7.2). Those who value nature largely for its historical and cultural significance (e.g., O'Neill *et al.*—see section 6.8) are likely to favor restoration but may balk at rewilding, resurrection and artificial life. Those interested primarily in other anthropocentric values—e.g., ecosystem services, economic value, aesthetics, recreation, or scientific value—may take other positions.

What about non-anthropocentrists? Again, still assuming that the techniques can be applied successfully, there is, perhaps surprisingly, no obvious sentientist or biocentric consequentialist objection to any of them. The idea in all cases is to increase biodiversity or biotic welfare—though, with the more extreme techniques, by highly artificial means. But artificiality is an anthropocentric concern. A resurrected mammoth doesn't care how it got here. If the experiment succeeds and the mammoth's welfare is high, then it is on its own terms doing just fine. Hence there is no special sentientist or biocentric consequentialist objection to any of these techniques—provided that they are successful in increasing biodiversity and objective welfare without significant negative unintended consequences.

There lies the rub. Once we drop the ridiculously unrealistic assumption that there will be no unintended bad consequences, things change.

The least risky strategy is restoration. It is unlikely to produce significant harm (though it could) and thus is ethically acceptable, if applied with caution, on pretty much any ethical view that is not heavily dependent on the value of human non-interference. Assisted colonization and rewilding are more risky; but, again, if done slowly and cautiously, especially in places where restoration is no longer feasible, they would be ethically acceptable on many theories.

The ethics of resurrection and artificial life are less clear, because the risks of unintended consequences are much higher. The ostensible motive for all of these techniques is to rectify biodiversity or welfare loss. That honorable motive could, however—especially in the cases of resurrection and artificial life—morph into "just to see if it can be done"—or something more insidious. The metaphor that comes to almost everyone's mind in contemplating such scenarios is Frankenstein's monster. The danger is not literally a monster, of course, but a cascade of harmful, unpredictable and uncontrollable events. The introduction of resurrected or novel life forms is risky, and it is difficult to gauge the risks. It is safer, easier, cheaper, and more respectful to preserve the astonishing life forms that are already here.

7.2.2.3 Post-Human Ethics

Individuals, in contemplating their own deaths, often have some moral concern for their successors. We know that the human species will not survive forever and that life will probably go on after we are gone. Should we as a species have analogous moral concerns for our non-human successors?

This idea was broached at the end of section 6.9, where it was noted that the bio-diversity losses that we are triggering may last for millions of years and that none of our species is likely ever again to see the Earth as rich as it is today. It is as if we are squandering a vast inherited fortune that we might have passed on to our heirs—only the heirs in this case will be non-human.

Value anthropocentrists may scoff at this idea. When all humans are gone, then on their view there is no more value, so there is nothing for ethics to be concerned about. Just so, an egoist, who values nothing but his own welfare, would see no value in passing anything on after his death. That opinion exposes the selfish shallowness of egoism. Likewise the thought that what happens to other creatures after human extinction is ethically irrelevant exposes the species-centered shallowness of anthropocentrism (Nolt 2013c).

Here the difference between anthropocentric and non-anthropocentric ethics emerges starkly: the non-anthropocentrist thinks that leaving a depleted world to our non-human heirs is morally wrong. The anthropocentrist does not.

7.3 PHILOSOPHICAL FUNDAMENTALS

This book is only an introduction. There are loose ends everywhere. The big ideas discussed here can all be pursued to greater depth. This section gives a taste of how, pursuing to somewhat deeper levels three disparate ideas that have played significant roles in this book.

Section Outline: Section 7.3.1 attempts to construct justifications for two fundamental, far-reaching, and controversial biocentric "ought" premises. Section 7.3.2 explores the notion of value incomparability, which has played a couple of important roles in this book. Section 7.3.3 considers whether we are stuck with an irreducible plurality of theories in environmental ethics, or whether it may be possible to merge the various theories considered here, perhaps with modifications, into one "grand unified theory" of ethics.

7.3.1 Justification of Basic Moral Principles

Ethical theories provide justification for the "ought" premises used in moral reasoning. But the theories themselves employ prescriptive statements. How, then, can those statements be justified? Part of the work of an ethical theory is to explain this. Thus, for example, Kant held that the categorical imperative is evident to those who can rise above their personal inclinations and impartially comprehend the value of autonomous rationality. Unlike Kant, religious versions of the Golden Rule do not tout human rationality. (The religions are in that respect wiser than Kant, for human nature is far from rational.) But both agree that we ought to treat others not only with impartiality, but also with compassion. Jesus' parable of the Good Samaritan (who, shunning prejudice, cares for a stranger) illustrates this combination of impartiality and compassion. Consequentialists likewise advocate impartiality, aiming to make the world a better place, not just for themselves, but for all. Still, in each case, one can ask: Why do that? Attempts to answer push our moral thinking deeper.

Section Outline: Section 7.3.1 ventures tentative answers for two moral principles discussed in this book, a biocentric deontological respect principle (section 7.3.1.1) and a biocentric consequentialist choice principle (section 7.3.1.2).

I have chosen to argue for biocentric principles, because biocentrism is the most comprehensive form of ethics, and hence the most challenging to justify. If it is possible to show why we ought to follow biocentric ethical principles, then arguments for the more restricted fundamental principles of anthropocentric or animal ethics ought to be straightforward.

Of course, you may conclude that I am overreaching and that my attempts to justify these biocentric principles fail. If so, keep in mind that similar justifications may nevertheless succeed for narrower, but still controversial, forms of ethics—in particular, for animal ethics or long-term anthropocentrism—or that justifications other than those given here might succeed instead.

7.3.1.1 A Biocentric Respect Principle

Paul Taylor (Section 6.3.2) advocated a very strong deontological respect principle:

> We ought to respect all living things.

To respect, in an ethical sense, is to treat as an end (that is, a thing with its own goods and purposes) and not as a mere object or means. Yet, as was noted in section 6.3.3, it is not practically possible to treat all living things as ends. So near the end of that section, I proposed a weakened version of Taylor's respect principle:

> We ought to respect a wide range of living beings, including even some that are non-sentient.

This principle is more likely to be practicable, but what would living it mean? Answers range from the radical non-violence of Gandhi or the theologically tinged reverence of Schweitzer to more modest and commonsensical efforts to avoid harming living beings wherever possible. What all these ideas have in common is a sense that ours are not the only purposes or goods on this planet, that Earth is not just for us, and that we should, insofar as possible, allow our fellow beings—the members of our extended family—to live and flourish. In short, they all counsel a broad and beneficent humility.

But why accept that? More precisely, why should we treat at least some living things as beings with goods of their own, rather than as mere objects—that is, respect them—even if they are non-sentient?

One obvious answer is: because that is what they are—beings with goods of their own, not mere objects. But another question follows: Why treat them as what they are? Why not exploit them, appropriating their purposes to ours? Predators do. The owl does not treat the mouse as a being with a good of its own. It swoops from the twilight sky, grabs the mouse in its talons, flies to a nearby branch, and devours it without mercy. For the owl the mouse is a mere means—mouse meat. The owl respects nothing—except perhaps its mate and its young.

So it is not enough to say that we should respect beings with goods of their own simply because they are ends and not mere objects. It wouldn't make sense for us to respect mice if we were owls. If there is a reason for *us* to respect living beings like mice that have goods of their own, it must involve something special about us—some way in which we differ from owls.

One crucial difference is that each of us can to some degree transcend our own perspective. In virtue of our complex brains and cultural heritage, we can shed prejudices, broaden our point of view, and on occasion even modify our fundamental goals. Owls can't do any of that. More generally, we—many of us, at least—have a voluntary capacity for **self-transcendence**—that is, for valuing the welfare of others as an end, even if those others are strangers who are very different from us (Nolt 2010a; Partridge 1981).

Of course, the fact that we *can* value the goods of others as ends doesn't by itself imply that we *ought* to. To get an "ought" conclusion, we need an "ought" premise. It is not easy to find any "ought" premise broad enough to yield biocentrism that non-biocentrists will accept.

One might become convinced of biocentrism by close, open, prolonged acquaintance with nature. Many naturalists become biocentrists in this way. But that doesn't *prove* anything. People who seldom encounter nature simply won't get it.

There is, however, a less direct but more promising approach. The core idea is that we ought, for self-interested reasons, to value as widely as possible—that is, to become self-transcendent toward—many different living beings, including many that are not sentient. Thus, ironically, a line of anthropocentric thinking leads to the conclusion that we ought to become value biocentrists. If we do, then considerations of integrity ought to lead us further to *ethical* biocentrism. I have developed this argument in detail elsewhere (Nolt 2010a). What follows is a sketch.

Self-transcendence brings with it a remarkable power: the power to sustain realistic earthly hope in even the most dire of circumstances—even in the face of death. To see how, consider what we lack in its absence. Imagine a person who is not self-transcendent at all. He is an egoist, valuing only what is good for him. His life is therefore ultimately hopeless; for sooner or later he will die, and when he does every earthly good that matters to him will come to an end. As he grows older and his death approaches, then, he must either deceive himself about the approach of his death, take refuge in otherworldly hopes, or face the increasing threat, if not the actual fact, of hopeless despair.[4]

Self-deception is burdensome and risky. It requires vigilant closed-mindedness. Even then, one can never entirely suppress the truth. Therefore, without otherworldly hopes (to which we will return shortly), our hypothetical egoist will have to struggle not to see the vacuum of value that lies ahead, and still he may ultimately fail and fall (as many people do toward the end of their lives) into despair.

But this is true only if, as we have assumed, he is not self-transcendent. Suppose instead that he loves just one other person—genuinely loves, so that he values what is good for that other person as an end. Then even if he knows that he is going to die soon, he can still have realistic hope for the one he loves. Not everything that matters to him need come to an end with his death.

Of course the one he loves could die first, and then he would be back in the same hopeless situation as before. He can, however, make his hopes less vulnerable by loving more—that is, by broadening his self-transcendence. Imagine, for example, that he loves many friends and family members. Then he can hope for the well-being of them all, and he can maintain stronger and surer hopes for others as his death approaches. The wider his self-transcendence, the greater are his possibilities of hope.

Of course, all those that he loves will eventually die too. So his hope cannot extend very far into the future—a few decades at most. But there is no reason why his self-transcendence should be limited to other humans. He could love the birds that visit his bird-feeder, the water grasses that grow by the river, or the fireflies that light warm June nights, and hope, realistically, that they will fare well. They will die too, of course, but they will give rise to others, in practically endless succession. He need not know or love them as individuals, anyway, but only with a kind of indifference to their identities.

Such hope for a broad range of life need not be anthropomorphic. One need not believe that the grasses or the fireflies are conscious in any way. It requires only a belief in the possibility of their objective well-being—and we know that is possible.

To the extent that this person broadens self-transcendence, his death will be to him a small loss relative to the goodness of all that he loves. He therefore has the possibility of maintaining high hopes until the end. Self-transcendence enables us to hope realistically even when we are powerless and action is futile. It does so by displacing our hopes for ourselves to others, who may flourish after we are gone.

Of course there is a down side. The more we love, the more loss we are likely to suffer; for those whom we love die too—or drift away. Among many hopes, many will fail. But if we continue to love, other hopes replace them. We mourn, but do not wallow in despair. There is an ecological analogy here: diversity in hope increases hope's resilience—its sustainability. Specific hopes come and go, but a sufficiency of hope remains. Hope for a broad range of life, including even non-sentient beings, is the most diverse, and hence the most resilient and sustainable kind of earthly hope that we can attain.

One might object that at the rate we are degrading non-human life there is not much to hope for. But that is short-sighted. As was noted in section 1.3, life itself is incredibly resilient. It has persisted for billions of years and may well persist for billions more. In human terms, that is practically forever.

Wide self-transcendence, then, does make realistic earthly hope possible, even for the very long term, and even under adverse conditions. That is good, because hope is a human need. The absence of hope is despair, and despair is a malady and a misery. Judging by the current popularity of antidepressants, it is an epidemic.

But do we really need *earthly* hope? Some people—those who cannot believe in an afterlife—certainly do. For them there is no other option. Many people, however, do believe in an afterlife, and for them that belief may suffice to keep their hopes up. We might wonder, however, whether their hopes are *realistic*. Some peoples' beliefs about the afterlife contradict those of others; so some of these beliefs must be wrong. Many who believe in an afterlife suspect that they could be mistaken. Their hopes are therefore precarious and may dissolve before the end. The more precarious are their otherworldly hopes, the more they need earthly hopes.

Suppose, however, that there is an afterlife, and that some people have sustainable true beliefs about it. Still, those hopes may be earthly hopes—as they are in certain doctrines of bodily resurrection or reincarnation. But suppose there is an afterlife entirely beyond Earth and that people can truly and sustainably hope for it. Still, it seems likely that the more realistic hopes those people can sustain, the better. While anticipating their own welfare in the afterworld, it is probably still good, too, for them to hope for the welfare of those who will remain on Earth.

To summarize, sustainable realistic *earthly* hope is a need for many and probably a good for all. If we had more of it, there would be less despair. Despair is pervasive in contemporary culture. Therefore we (both individually and collectively) ought to cultivate and sustain the most robust, realistic earthly hopes that we can. But the most sustainable earthly hope requires self-transcendence toward a wide range of living beings, including even non-sentient beings.

Now the argument requires just one further step. To be self-transcendent toward something is to value its welfare, and our actions ought to reflect what we value.

To value the welfare of something and nevertheless treat it as a mere means or object would in an obvious, though non-logical, sense be inconsistent, perhaps even hypocritical. A person who acted that way would lack integrity. We therefore ought to respect the beings whose welfare we value—those toward which we are self-transcendent. In sum, the reasoning is as follows:

1   We (individually and collectively) ought to do our best to sustain realistic earthly hope throughout our lives.
2   We can best do so only by self-transcendence toward a wide range of living beings, including some that are non-sentient.
3   We ought to be self-transcendent toward a wide range of living beings, including some that are non-sentient. (1,2)
4   We ought to respect that toward which we ought to be self-transcendent.
∴ 5   We ought to respect a wide range of living beings, including some that are non-sentient. (3,4)

Conclusion 5 is the respect principle whose justification is the purpose of this section.

This argument grounds a biocentric respect principle in a moral need to sustain human hope (premise 1). This premise is an anthropocentric ethical principle. And yet its conclusion is non-anthropocentric. It might, then, seem that I have contradicted myself, for if our reason to value the welfare of non-human beings as ends is that it will help to sustain human hope, then apparently we are *not* respecting those living beings as ends, but merely as means to the human end of sustaining hope.

It is important, however, to distinguish between the objective welfare of living beings and our valuing of that welfare (self-transcendence), which is a subjective state of the human being. The means to sustainable earthly hope, according to the argument, is self-transcendence. We can aim for self-transcendence merely for our own benefit, but to achieve it is to transform our values and reasons for action—to value as ends goods that are *not* ours. Hence if we achieve it, we value as ends *both* our own welfare and that of a wide range of other living beings. There is nothing inconsistent in that.

Still, an ethic that merely counsels us to respect some unspecific range of living beings is unsatisfyingly vague and partial. It might serve as a guide for a hopeful personal life, but it would never do for conservation biology or public policy.

7.3.1.2 A Biocentric Choice Principle

The previous section argued for a biocentric respect principle. This section aims to justify the biocentric consequentialist choice principle that was introduced in section 6.4.4:

Avoid actions that are, on the whole, objectively worse for life.

More precisely, this means: avoid doing what would produce less aggregate objective welfare for living beings than other possible actions would. The question to be answered in this section is: Why should we?

Some biocentrists might hope to answer by appeal to the momentum of history. Good people, they might observe, have always believed in not harming members of their own group (family, community, nation, race, faith, etc.). But over time the moral community has grown. Most educated people now acknowledge that, ideally at least, "our group" includes all humans. With the development of animal and environmental ethics, "our group" may widen still further, even to all life.

Mere historical momentum, however, is not a good argument. Historical trends can be wrong.

To deduce the biocentric choice principle, which is an "ought" statement, we need at least one "ought" premise. I'll use three in the argument below, but the one with which I will begin is the biocentric *respect* principle that was the conclusion of section 7.3.1.1:

> We ought to respect a wide range of living beings, including some that are non-sentient.

One shortcoming of this respect principle is that it is unsatisfyingly partial. My strategy will be to transform it by a principle of fairness into a more impartial imperative. But that impartial imperative will turn out to be excessively idealistic. So I'll need to temper it with a dose of realism. Here goes . . .

I assume, in accord with the conclusion of section 7.3.1.1, that we ought to respect a wide range of living beings. But to stop there is unsatisfying, because for many of the living things within that range, there are similar living things not within it for which the principle requires no respect. This is because the range itself is specified more or less arbitrarily by the self-transcendent person. Someone might, for example, achieve self-transcendence primarily by being a lover of musicians, birds, and forest trees. She should then, by the argument of section 7.3.1.1, respect these things. Suppose she does. Then even if she respects nothing else, she satisfies the biocentric respect principle. Yet from an impartial point of view her respect is excessively narrow. There are many people other than musicians, many animals other than birds, and many plants other than the forest trees that she respects but whose moral significance is not much different from that of musicians, birds, or forest trees.

Ideally, it seems, she ought to be more impartial. She should not respect only those things that she loves. She should treat similar cases similarly. But if she did that with strict consistency, then she would wind up respecting all living beings.

This she cannot do. As was noted in section 6.3.3, we cannot consistently respect all living things (that is, treat them as ends, not as mere objects), if only because we must kill to live. So even though ideally she ought to respect all living beings, practically she can't.

What should she do? Here we need yet another prescriptive assumption, one that I think accords with moral common sense: if we can't do what is ideal, then we ought to do what we can that best approximates that ideal. She can't avoid harming or destroying some life; at best, she can only see to it that what she does is not worse for living things in general than other things she might do. She ought, therefore, to avoid doing what is, on the whole, objectively worse for life. In summary:

1   We ought to respect a wide range of living beings, including some that are non-sentient.
2   Ideally, we ought treat similar cases similarly.
∴   3   Ideally, we ought to respect all living beings. (1,2)
4   We can't respect all living beings.
5   If we can't do what is ideal, then we ought to do what we can that best approximates that ideal.
6   We can best approximate respect for all living things by avoiding doing what is, on the whole, objectively worse for life.
∴   7   We ought to avoid doing what is, on the whole, objectively worse for life. (3,4,5,6).

Conclusion 7 is the biocentric choice principle.

While the respect principle of section 7.3.1.1 was inadequate as a guide for conservation biology or public policy, this choice principle is quite in line with the aims of conservation and impartial enough for public policy. Of course its implications need to be made more precise. But that is what this book has been up to ever since that choice principle was introduced in section 6.4.4.

Nothing in this argument or its conclusion implies that the welfare of humans and that of non-humans must count equally in figuring up what is better or worse for life. Treating similar cases similarly means that the welfare of each living being counts in proportion to its degree; and, as was explained in section 6.4.2, capacity for welfare differs greatly among species, ranging from next to nothing, in the case of the simplest forms of life, to very considerable, in the case of humans.

Much about the argument of this section could be questioned. Certainly it is not the final word. But I'll leave the questioning to you. My purpose in constructing it was to provide, not some ultimate proof (in ethics, that is rarely, if ever, possible), but rather a reasonable answer to the question "Why should we avoid doing what is, on the whole, objectively worse for life?"—and so to illustrate how a biocentric choice principle might be justified.

7.3.2 Value Incomparability

This section is somewhat more technical than the rest of the book. Still, I include it here because its implications for ethics and axiology are surprising and illuminating.

Recall that a pair of values is incomparable if neither is greater than nor less than nor equal to the other. Incomparable values are just different—period. Incomparability became an issue in two different contexts in this book. First, in the case of consequentialist theories that deal with a variety of values (e.g., health, pleasure and learning), values of different types may be incomparable. This difficulty arises most notably with objective welfare theories and is most acute for non-anthropocentric objective welfare theories, which include non-human as well as human values (see sections 3.3.1, 6.4.3, 6.4.4, 6.4.6, and 6.8). Second, incomparability provided counterexamples to two deontological arguments for equality—Regan's argument for the equal inherent value of subjects of a life (section 5.5.2) and Taylor's argument for the equal inherent worth of all living things (section 6.3.2).

These counterexamples definitively refute the arguments of Regan and Taylor. But in section 6.4.3 I expressed guarded optimism that the problems of aggregating sometimes incomparable values could be successfully handled. I noted, for one thing, that even if some pairs of values are incomparable, others are not. We usually think of values as being arrayed on a single linear scale, so that each is either greater than, less than or equal to any other. This is called a *linear ordering*. But when some pairs of values are incomparable, we have what mathematicians call a **partial ordering**. The difference is illustrated in the following diagrams (which mathematicians call Hasse diagrams) (Figure 3):

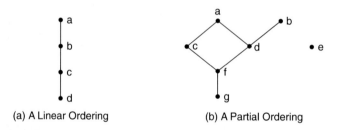

(a) A Linear Ordering   (b) A Partial Ordering

Figure 3 Examples of Linear and Partial Orderings

While linear orderings always form a line, partial orderings can take many forms. The one illustrated here is only an example. In these diagrams, dots represent values. One value is greater than another if (and only if) you can follow a series of connecting lines from it consistently downward to the other. As in algebra, we may abbreviate 'is greater than' by '>'. Thus in Figure 3(a) we have:

$a > b > c > d$.

This is the usual sort of linear ordering. But in Figure 3(b), we have:

$a > c > f > g$,

$a > d > f > g$, and

$b > d > f > g$.

Figure 3(b) portrays **a** and **b** as incomparable—and likewise **c** and **d**. Value **e** is incomparable with everything but itself (it is, of course, equal to itself, as is every other value). This figure therefore illustrates how, even when some values are incomparable, others may still be comparable. That is one of the reasons that I gave in section 6.4.3 for thinking that biocentric consequentialist theories might be able to handle the problems of aggregating sometimes incomparable values.

A second reason was that biocentric welfare values have a natural common zero point, to which most, if not all, welfare values can be compared. (No zero point is specified, however, in either diagram of Figure 3).

A third reason for optimism noted in section 6.4.3 was that there are no infinite differences among lifetime welfares. To these reasons, I will here add three more.

The fourth is that in partial orderings, some incomparable pairs of values are *bounded*—that is, there are values greater than or equal to both members of the pair and values less than or equal to both. Thus, in Figure 3(b) the incomparable values **c** and **d** are bounded above by **a** and below by **f**. Bounds limit the "width" of the incomparability. Any value greater than or equal to the upper bound or less than or equal to the lower is automatically comparable to the two mutually incomparable values. Thus **g**, being less than **f**, is automatically less than both **c** and **d**. By judicious use of bounds, approximate comparison among incomparable values is possible.

A fifth reason for optimism is the phenomenon of **emergent comparability**, in which adding together values that are incomparable with one another (or with a third value) yields a new value that is comparable with (greater than, less than, or equal to) them all. To illustrate, consider apples and oranges, whose values are often used as a metaphor for incomparable values (as in the saying "That's like comparing apples and oranges."). Suppose, for example, that an apple and an orange are incomparable in, say, nutritional value. Each is nutritionally better than the other in some respects and worse in others, so that there is no non-arbitrary way of ranking them on a single scale. Still, the sum of their values (that is, the value of an apple *and* an orange) is plainly greater than (and so comparable with) the value of each.

A sixth reason for optimism is that there are formal rules for aggregating (adding) sometimes incomparable values, though published treatments of these (e.g., Carlson 2008) are quite technical.

Finally, as I noted at the end of section 6.4.3, even though there are no infinite differences among the lifetime welfares of living beings, this does not imply the discomforting conclusion that there is some finite number of bacteria whose lifetime welfare is greater than that of a happy, healthy person. I'll now explain that remark.

Two things could happen when we start adding up the lifetime welfares of identical bacteria of a given type. The first is that as we reach some very large number *n* (perhaps larger even than the astronomical number of bacteria on Earth), the total lifetime welfare for *n* bacteria exceeds the lifetime welfare of a happy, healthy person. Many people find this alarming. (What? My lifetime welfare is worth less than the welfare of a mess of bacteria?)

The second, and less readily noticed, possibility is, in view of the enormous qualitative differences between human and bacterial welfare, more plausible than the first. It is that for very large n, the total lifetime welfare for n bacteria becomes incomparable with the lifetime welfare of a happy, healthy person; but, no matter how much larger we make n, it never becomes greater.

Either way there is some colossal number of bacteria whose total lifetime welfare is not less than the lifetime welfare of a happy, healthy person—though in the second case, it is also neither greater than nor equal to the person's welfare. Some may find this second, and more plausible, possibility less discomforting.

For all of these reasons, I conjecture that the conceptual barriers to aggregating and making rough comparisons among sometimes incomparable values are not wholly insuperable.

Given that we can aggregate sometimes incomparable values, we can also use them to make rational consequentialist decisions. Section 6.4.4 introduced this choice principle: avoid actions that are, on the whole, objectively worse for life. To illustrate, suppose the values in Figure 3 represent the aggregate welfare totals for seven potential options **a** – **g** that we might choose. The choice principle implies that we ought to reject **c**, **d**, **f** and **g**, since for each of these there are better options. This leaves three options—namely **a**, **b** and **e**—for which there are no better options. None of these is maximal, since all are incomparable with one another. The choice principle therefore does not decide among these three. If we have nothing further to go on, then we may choose any of them. That is not maximization, but it is still rational choice.

If we are lucky, however, other considerations may narrow our choice still further. Note that **e** is sort of a "wild card" option. It's not comparable to any of the other options. This may make us uneasy enough to rule it out if **a** and **b** are recognizably good options.

Moreover, considerations of boundedness may be useful in decision-making. If the values of two incomparable options are closely bounded, then, despite their incomparability, they are not very different, and it may be reasonable to choose arbitrarily between them. If, for example, **d** in Figure 3(b) is not much worse than either **a** or **b**, then that's a reason to think that the choice between **a** and **b** can be made more or less arbitrarily, since, though **a** and **b** are incomparable, the difference between them cannot be great. However, if **d** is much worse than both, then they may differ greatly, and that may be reason to seek further information relevant to the decision—though in the end we may still have to make an arbitrary choice.

7.3.3 A Grand Unified Ethic?

Pragmatists maintain that our greatest need is not better ethical theories but better and more responsible action. Surely they are right. Yet action without clear goals is apt to go awry. Ethical theories are humanity's best efforts at thinking clearly about ultimate goals. Moreover, we need a way to transmit accumulated ethical thought to new generations, and ethical theories serve that purpose as well.

Unfortunately, we have inherited a multiplicity of sometimes conflicting ethical theories. Deontology, consequentialism and virtue theory are the three most prominent forms. This multiplicity makes ethics difficult to learn, confusing to apply and intellectually disappointing. One of my reasons for focusing this book on moral reasoning as well as moral theories is that often a line of moral reasoning is more plausible than the theory that supplies its prescriptive premises. This is especially true when several theories support those premises. But that procedure is not ideal. A single theory that deftly handled all our ethical reasoning would be much more satisfying.

The situation in ethics is in some ways reminiscent of that in physics, where general relativity theory explains phenomena on large scales, quantum mechanics explains phenomena on small scales, and none of the many attempts to merge the two into a single "theory of everything" has succeeded. Even within the realm of quantum phenomena we lack what is called a "grand unified theory" that would smoothly unite theories of weak, strong and electromagnetic interactions.

In ethics, as in physics, we need different theories for different applications. But, like the physicists, few ethicists are entirely comfortable with this. A grand unified *ethic* might yield greater elegance and understanding—provided that it would work.

There are efforts to create such an ethic. Most are efforts to unite deontology and consequentialism, sometimes in the expectation that the result will then also yield a virtue theory. One of the best and most recent attempts is Derek Parfit's monumental treatise, *On What Matters*, published in 2011. There Parfit argues that Kantians, contractualists and consequentialists are all "climbing the same mountain on different sides"—in other words, that their theories, properly understood, merge into a single theory. Although there is much more to the book than this, Parfit's central idea, in paraphrase, is that acts are wrong just in case they are disallowed by some principle that:

1. Would make everything go best if it were a universal law;
2. Every rational person could will to be a universal law; and
3. No one could reasonably reject.

(Parfit 2011: 412–13)

Clause 1 is rule consequentialist in that it characterizes right action as action that follows the rules that make things "go best." Clause 2 is straight from Kant's universal law formulation of the categorical imperative. Clause 3 expresses a common feature of contemporary contractualist deontologies. Thus Parfit's principle unites all three.

Parfit's theory is a contender for the title of "grand unified ethic," but already many objections have been raised against it. Who knows whether in the end something like it will prevail? And even if so, it is unlikely to serve as the "ethic of everything," because it is anthropocentric.

• 7.4 ATTUNING POWER AND CARE

Environmental ethics enlarges the scope of morality, urging us to think globally, for the long term, and beyond the human species. It is demanding in ways that traditional ethics never were. That is as it should be, for we know more and are more powerful than we ever were.

It may not seem that way. We often feel overwhelmed by the complexities of contemporary life. Some people, of course, really do lack power; they are blown about by the winds of poverty or war. But we who are not destitute—the majority of readers of this book—rely every day upon powers that previous ages could only have described as magic.

You flip on a light. Power flows from the grid and illuminates the room. Magic. Probably that power was produced at least in part by the burning of coal. If so, the light energy that floods your room began as sunlight that was slowly captured by many generations of plants hundreds of millions of years ago. Over eons those plants were transformed into coal. The coal was blasted from the earth and transported to a power plant by truck or rail. The plant burned the coal, the heat made steam, the steam turned great turbines, the turbines turned a generator, and the generator forced electrons to race in long circuits that pass through your light. Meanwhile from the stack of the power plant came a plume of CO_2 that will make the atmosphere just a little warmer for a very long time. Such power we command at the flip of a switch.

Of course most of that would still occur if you didn't flip the switch. But turning on your light adds to the demand for power, and the machinery of the economy more or less automatically fits supply to demand. Where more electricity is demanded, more will be produced. The power company will prosper. You and many others will receive the bill.

Likewise, almost everything we do has effects that reach out across space and reverberate through time. You pull an item off a store shelf. The store's inventory drops by one, signaling demand. Supply follows. You drive a car, flush a toilet, take out garbage. Other large-scale processes and systems respond.

Call the ensemble of events that you can affect, to the degree that you can affect them, your **field of power**. Your field of power is strongest where you live and work, for there your effects on life around you are most direct and intense. But it reaches anywhere that supplies the things you consume and to any place affected by your wastes. It extends, too, though extremely weakly and diffusely, via your greenhouse gas emissions through the global atmosphere and oceans. But it does not extend everywhere. You have no morally significant effect on the moon.

Just as your field of power tends to fade with distance, so it tends to fade into future time. If you have (or will have) children, your effect on them is (or will be) profound. But your actions will also affect many things hundreds or thousands of years from now, though your portion of each of the effects will be miniscule.

Picture your field of power as red shading on the landscape, perhaps superimposed on a Google map. There's a lot of bright red where you live and work, some not-so-bright red along the routes you travel and the places you visit, a little red in the places that supply the things you consume. Probably there is no perceptible red in Antarctica. There is some red in the atmosphere and oceans. It may be so faint that you can't see it, but it is there.

Now move forward in time. Maybe the red darkens in places as you acquire power and influence, or maybe not, but at a certain moment the darkest red suddenly vanishes. That is the time of your death. Yet some red persists, slowly fading over time, eventually becoming imperceptible. That is your posthumous influence on the world. It persists minutely for thousands of years in the atmosphere and oceans and still longer, though still minutely, in the diminishment of life on Earth.

Environmental ethics is the theory of how a person or an institution ought to care for the living beings within his or her or its field of power. By "care for" I mean not just worry about, but deliberately do things that make a difference, even a minute one.

Call the ensemble of events that you care for, to the degree that you care for them, your **field of care**. Like your field of power, your field of care is strongest where you live and work. You care for family, friends and co-workers—some close by, some far away. Maybe you care for companion animals. Probably you also care for your future and for the futures of those close to you—though, of course, care diminishes into the future.

Picture your field of care as the green shading superimposed upon the landscape. Since your care is probably focused on a small number of people (including yourself), and perhaps some companion animals, the places where you interact with those people and animals are bright green. For many people, there is little green anywhere else. People seldom care much for the environmental effects of the factories and farms that supply what they buy, the vehicles that transport them, the manufacture of their packaging, and the effects the remaining waste will have. These processes are within our fields of power, since we influence them, at least slightly, by choosing what to buy or not to buy, but they are mostly outside our fields of care. In general, then, our fields of care are small compared to our fields of power.

It was not always so. The fields of power of tribal humans extended about as far as they could walk. Their ability to harm things at any moment extended as far as they could shoot an arrow, throw a rock, or toss a spear. Our fields of power have exploded with the growth of technology and the global economy, but our fields of care have not.

Ideally field of power and field of care should match; for where care exceeds power, it is squandered impotently, and where power exceeds care, we act carelessly. The optimal attunement is a perfect coincidence of power and care—red and green superimposed on the same areas with the same intensities. This avoids both the error of squandering power and the danger of using it carelessly.

The environmental crisis springs from this disparity between power and care. We have too much power, not enough care. Hence we act carelessly. Virtually every environmental problem exhibits this pattern. Thus there are two general solutions: enhance care or reduce power. (We can, of course, do both.)

Fortunately, advances in technology help to expand the range of our care. We have satellites in the sky and observers on the ground across the planet. The internet enables us to find out what is happening almost anywhere in the world. Computer models that forecast the future are growing increasingly accurate. We know much of what we need to know to act with care. We have ingenious technologies that can solve or at least ameliorate many of the problems. And some of us have money or time or talents that can help if we choose to care. This book, too—and environmental ethics in general—indeed, environmental thought in general—are aimed at expanding care.

But our capacity for caring, though expandable, is not infinitely so. We can't care for everything—not even everything within our fields of power. We can't even come close. We are too powerful and our effects on the world are too many and too complex. When faced with such complexity, human creatures whose cognitive and emotional capacities evolved to wield power on a tribal scale quickly reach the limit of their caring.

At that limit, if we still want to avoid careless destruction, there remains only the opposite solution: to draw back our power toward the bounds of our care; to live more carefully, deliberately, and simply—with less power, but perhaps more hope.

• 7.5 POSTSCRIPT

The twenty-first and succeeding centuries will bring a series of great tragedies for life on Earth. Some of these could have been avoided but are now unavoidable. Yet not everything will be lost. The inevitability of great tragedies is not a reason to acquiesce to still greater ones. Everywhere there are people working to save what still can be saved and to restore some of what has been lost. They need help.

This book has presented ethical arguments and theories. Both are useful for clear thinking about goals. But ethics is not the study of arguments or theories. It's not about what you think or believe. It's about what you do and what you are.

• SUGGESTIONS FOR FURTHER READING

The fossil fuel problem and the climate problem are inextricably linked. A fine work on climate ethics is John Broome's *Climate Matters: Ethics in a Warming World* (Norton, 2012).

Barbara Kingsolver's *Animal, Vegetable, Miracle: A Year of Food Life* (Harper, 2007) is a superb book on eating joyfully and ethically.

The standard text in ecological economics is Herman E. Daly and Joshua Farley's *Ecological Economics: Principles and Applications* (Island Press, 2004).

A recent collection on the population issue is *Life on the Brink: Environmentalists Confront Overpopulation*, edited by Philip Cafaro and Eileen Crist (University of Georgia, 2012).

For those interested in looking more deeply into the nuclear issue, I recommend two books: *Nuclear Energy in the 21st Century*, 3rd ed., by Ian Hore-Lacy (World Nuclear University Press, 2012); and *What Will Work: Fighting Climate Change with Renewable Energy, Not Nuclear Power* by Kristin Shrader-Frechette (Oxford, 2011). The first states the nuclear industry's case for nuclear power; the second argues against it.

Finally, on the ethical ramifications of incomparability, a good source is *Incommensurability, Incomparability and Practical Reason*, edited by Ruth Chang (Harvard, 1997).

notes

1. The large triangular bone at the base of the spine. In many animals, it terminates in a tail. In humans, it terminates in the coccyx, a series of vestigial tailbones.
2. I use the term "living beings" in formulating this rule, rather than Taylor's term "living things" because, although the two, as I understand them, have the same denotation and hence are interchangeable, "thing" has the connotation, inappropriate in this context, of a mere object, whereas "being" more readily connotes a living thing that might be worthy of respect.
3. The mathematically inclined may prefer to think of it as the definite integral over time, from the beginning to the end of an organism's life, of its momentary total welfare.
4. I owe this idea to philosopher John Hardwig.

glossary

acid deposition	acid rain, acid snow, or acid fog or dry acidic particles that settle directly out of the air; acid deposition results chiefly from air pollution by nitrogen oxides and sulfur dioxide.
act consequentialism	a form of consequentialism according to which the rightness or wrongness of each action is determined individually by its consequences—as opposed to rule consequentialism
agent-centered prerogative	the controversial principle that individuals may appropriate to themselves what they need for a fulfilling life before worrying about spatially or temporally distant others
anthropocentrism	human-centeredness
anthropocentric ethic	any ethic according to which only human beings are morally considerable
anthropogenic	created by humans
anthropogenic global climate change	a process by which humanity's emissions of greenhouse gases are altering the world's weather patterns and climate by increasing the global average temperature
anthropomorphism	in animal ethics, the tendency to attribute human thoughts and feelings to non-human animals
argument	a set of declarative statements, one of which is intended as a conclusion and the rest of which, the premises, provide intended evidence for the conclusion
argument from ignorance	the argument that, based on the assumption that we can know little or nothing about the preferences of future people, concludes that we have no responsibilities to them
argument from marginal cases	the argument that some non-humans are morally considerable because any reasonable criterion of moral considerability sufficiently wide to include "marginal" humans (e.g., infants, the mentally disabled) also includes some non-humans, and any correct criterion must include these "marginal" humans
artificial life	genetically engineered organisms of kinds that do not occur in nature

assisted colonization	the movement of species to new habitat that has become more suitable for them than the old, in order to prevent extinctions
autonomy	conscious free choice and self-control
autopoiesis	those actions of an organism that tend to establish, maintain or enhance its survivability or health
axiological anthropocentrism	the idea that things have value only for humans and insofar as humans grant them that value
axiological non-anthropocentrism	the idea that things can have value for (i.e., can be good or bad for) some non-humans
axiology	a theory of what is morally valuable and why; axiologies of consequentialist ethical theories determine the class of moral patients, define what counts as good or bad for them, and explain how to aggregate (that is, add up) and compare degrees of goodness or badness for groups of them.
behaviorism	a tendency of thought that flourished in the twentieth century, which rejected talk of mental phenomena as "unscientific" and focused on outward behavior instead
biocentric ethic (biocentrism)	any ethic according to which all living things are morally considerable; however, different versions of biocentrism interpret the notion of a "living thing" differently.
biodiversity	variation among living organisms, species and ecosystems
biodiversity loss	loss of any form of biodiversity, but most especially global species diversity
biotic welfare	the degree of a biological entity's autopoietic functioning—roughly, its survivability
bounded pair of values	two values for which there exists at least one value greater than or equal to both and at least one less than or equal to both; it is noteworthy that some incomparable pairs of values are nevertheless bounded.
cap-and-trade	a scheme for reducing pollution by setting a limit (the cap) on total pollution and establishing a market in allowances to pollute, the total of which does not exceed that limit
capital	in neoclassical economics, wealth in all of its forms; the means of human preference satisfaction
care ethic	a kind of ethic, often associated with feminine thought, whose aim is to foster good relationships; care ethics emphasize interdependence rather than autonomy, nurturance rather than justice, and action based on sympathetic hearing of the stories of all involved rather than application of abstract ethical rules.
carrying capacity	the number of individuals that a certain kind of habitat can support indefinitely without degradation

categorical imperative	Immanuel Kant's fundamental ethical principle; there are several versions of it, two of which are discussed in this book: the formula of humanity and the formula of universal law.
chlorofluorocarbons	various compounds of carbon with fluorine and/or chlorine, often called CFCs; they are largely responsible for the thinning of the stratospheric ozone layer, and some are potent greenhouse gases.
choice principle	in consequentialist ethical theories, a principle that stipulates how the rightness or wrongness of actions depends upon their good and bad consequences.
classical utilitarianism	the sort of utilitarianism developed by Jeremy Bentham and John Stuart Mill; it defines the utility of an action as the degree to which the resulting happiness exceeds the resulting unhappiness, and assumes a maximizing choice principle.
climate change	see **anthropogenic global climate change**
collective action problem	in situations where individuals have a reason to act only if others do, the problem that no one may act because each is waiting for others to act first
communitarian ethic	a kind of relational ethic according to which our responsibilities are constituted by membership in the various communities to which we belong and are often owed to those communities as wholes
community model	in ecology, the idea that the organization of an ecosystem is in many ways analogous to that of a community
concentrated animal feeding operation (CAFO)	see **factory farm**
conclusion	in an argument, the declarative statement for which the premises are alleged to provide evidence
consequentialist ethic	a form of ethical theory according to which rightness or wrongness of an action is a function of its good or bad consequences for all affected moral patients
consequentialist reasoning	a form of argument according to which the rightness of an action is determined, not by its conformity with ethical law, but by the goodness of its known or probable results
considered preferences	preferences that a fully informed person has carefully examined and rationally endorsed
contingent valuation	in environmental economics, a stated-preference method of shadow pricing that surveys people regarding their willingness to pay for non-market goods in order to establish prices for those goods
contractualism	a kind of ethical theory that regards morality as an idealized social contract to which all reasonable people can rationally assent

cost–benefit analysis	an economic form of consequentialist prescriptive reasoning that uses a decision table to determine a choice of action
counterexample	for an argument, a possible situation in which its premises are true and its conclusion is untrue
cyanobacteria	certain bacteria that obtain their energy through photosynthesis; often misleadingly called blue-green algae, they are especially important in ocean ecosystems, where they constitute an important part of the food chain and produce much of the world's free oxygen.
decision table	a computational method used in consequentialist reasoning to determine which option for action is most likely to produce the best result
demandingness objection	the objection, often raised against broad act consequentialist theories, that they leave us too little time, resources and energy for our own projects or interests
deontology	a kind of ethical theory that provides procedures for determining what the ethical rules are and that evaluates actions as right if they conform to these rules and wrong if they violate them
descriptive statement	an assertion about how things are or were or will be, as opposed to how they should or should not be
dignity	an unconditional and superlative moral value that Kant ascribes to autonomous rational agents
distant future	the time after, perhaps long after, our deaths
ecocentrism	a form of biocentrism according to which ecosystems are morally considerable
ecofeminism	a synthesis of feminism and environmentalism based on the idea that the domination of women reflects the same patterns of thought and behavior as the domination of nature
ecological economics	a discipline that arose in the 1980s which integrated two older and sometimes antagonistic disciplines: ecology and economics; it treats economies as subsystems of ecological systems and hence as subject to their limits.
ecological footprint	an estimate of the area of biologically productive land and water needed to provide resources we use and to absorb our waste
ecosystem	an assemblage of organisms of different species living in some degree of interdependence in the same habitat, together with the nonliving components of that habitat
ecosystem health	the much-contested analog for an ecosystem of health for an organism
ecosystem services	ecosystem processes that benefit humanity

emergent comparability	addition of values incomparable with one another (or with a third value) that yields a new value that is comparable with (greater than, less than, or equal to) them all
end	an individual with purposes that are legitimately its own; also, a goal or aim, as opposed to a means
environmental economics	a form of neoclassical economics that has developed ways of assigning prices to non-market goods in the service of environmental policy; *see also* **ecological economics**
environmental ethics	the attempt to expand moral thinking and action in two directions:beyond the human species and into the distant future.
equality of individuals, principle of	Regan's idea that all subjects of a life have equal inherent value
equality, principle of	Singer's idea that we ought to give equal consideration to equal interests of every being affected by our actions
ethical anthropocentrism	the idea that *only* humans are morally considerable
ethical pluralism	the acceptance or use of more than one ethical theory
ethical theory	a broad philosophical account of what moral action is and how it is justified; also called a *moral* theory
eutrophication	a process in which high concentrations of nutrients introduced into a body of water increase the growth of algae, which then die and decompose, reducing dissolved oxygen levels, often to the detriment of other aquatic organisms
exhaustiveness	with regard to a set of options for action, the inclusion in that set of all options possible under the given circumstances
exopoiesis	those actions of an organism that tend to establish, maintain or enhance the survivability or health of related organisms—e.g., reproduction, defense of the group, nurturance, etc.
exopoietic benefit	an organism's total contribution by exopoiesis to the welfare of other organisms
expected value	for an option in a decision table, the sum of the probabilities times the values for each possible outcome of that option
externality	in neoclassical economics, a cost or benefit that is not accounted for by the market and is therefore not reflected in market price
extrinsically valuable	having a derivative form of goodness; valuable but not intrinsically valuable
factory farm	the sort of large, industrialized facility, designed for economic efficiency, in which most animals used

	for meat and eggs, particularly in the U.S., are kept and fed
feminism	the idea that women are systematically subject to certain forms of oppression and that this is wrong
fertility	with respect to population statistics, the average number of children per woman for a given population
field of care	for a given person, the ensemble of events that she cares for, to the degree that she cares for them
field of power	for a given person, the ensemble of events that she can affect, to the degree that she can affect them
formula of humanity	the version of Kant's categorical imperative according to which we should always treat people as ends and never merely as means
formula of universal law	the version of Kant's categorical imperative according to which we should act only according to maxims that we could will to be universal laws
fossil fuel	a combustible fuel found in the earth that was produced by geological processes from the remains of ancient plants; the main forms are coal, oil, natural gas, and peat.
fungibility	for economic goods, the property of being equivalently exchangeable with other economic goods
future people	people who will live but have not yet been born, as opposed to people who might live but in fact will not
genetic diversity	variation among genomes, often within the same species—a form of biodiversity
geoengineering	any of a variety of hypothetical global-scale engineering techniques, often suggested as means for transforming the earth's climate
global species diversity	a conception of biodiversity that includes not only the number of species worldwide (global species richness) but also considerations regarding the abundance of each species, noting especially those populations that are declining, threatened, or endangered
global species richness	the number of species of a given type that exist worldwide
good of its own	an ability to be benefited or harmed objectively—that is, independently of human valuing or cognition
greenhouse gases	any of various gases that trap heat from the earth's surface that would otherwise be radiated out into space, and thus increase global average temperature
habitat disruption	the degradation or destruction of species habitats by such means as clearing of forests, draining of wetlands, growth of cities, etc.

hedonic welfare	for a sentient animal, the sum of the values of its enjoyments, which count positively, and of its sufferings, which count negatively
hedonism (or hedonistic axiology)	the idea that goodness is pleasure and badness is pain
hedonistic utilitarianism	a form of utilitarianism based on a hedonistic axiology; it defines the utility of an action as the degree to which the resulting pleasure exceeds the resulting pain.
holistic biocentrism	a form of biocentrism according to which some biological aggregates, such as species or ecosystems, have moral considerability beyond the total moral considerability of their members
imperative	a suggestion or command to do or not do something
incomparable pair of values	two values, neither of which is greater than, equal to, or less than the other
individualistic biocentrism	a form of biocentrism according to which only individual organisms are morally considerable and groups of organisms are morally considerable only insofar as the members of those groups are
inherent value	in Regan's animal ethic, a kind of moral value possessed by every subject of a life
inherent worth	in Taylor's philosophy, the value of a living thing itself (as opposed to its value for other things and also to the value of its welfare) that makes it worthy of moral respect
internalization	in neoclassical economics, the process of accounting for non-market costs or benefits by assigning them a price
intrinsic value	in the philosophy of Rolston and others, a kind of moral status that involves both objective value and respect-worthiness
intrinsic valuing	valuing something for its own sake, not as a means to anything else
intrinsically valuable	valuable in itself; valuable in a non-derivative way.
invalid argument	an argument for which a situation is possible in which its premises are all true and its conclusion is untrue; an argument for which there is a counterexample
invasive species	species that are not native to and adversely affect an ecosystem or human habitat
just savings principle	in Rawlsian philosophy, a principle that requires each generation to pass on to its immediate successors, insofar as is within its power, means sufficient for a just society
liberalism	in political philosophy, the view that people should within reasonable limits be free to conduct their lives in accord with values and goals that they choose

life expectancy	the average age of death for a given population
lifetime welfare	for an individual, its average total welfare over its lifetime, multiplied by the length of its life; for a species, the total welfare for the species from the time it comes into existence until its extinction (in my individualistic view, this is just the total lifetime welfare of all the individuals—past, present and future—that comprise it; on holistic views it is something more than that).
linear ordering	in value theory, a scale of values in which each is greater than, less than, or equal to any other
logic	the study and practice of rational thought
long-term anthropocentric ethic	a theory of our responsibilities to distant future people
long-term ethic	an ethic concerned not only with contemporaries but also with moral patients who will be born after we have died
mass extinction	an episode in which Earth loses some large proportion (60 or 75 percent, depending on which author you consult) of its species in a geologically short interval
maxim	a prescriptive rule; in Kantian philosophy, a moral rule
means	something used by an agent for that agent's purposes
mere patient	a moral patient that is not a moral agent
merely sentient	sentient but without a robust, conscious sense of one's own past, present, and future
minimize overriding (miniride) principle	Regan's principle according to which, special considerations aside, it is better to override the rights of the innocent few than the rights of the innocent many—if the harms to all are comparable
monotheism	belief in one supreme God
moral agency	the ability to act for moral reasons
moral agent	one who is competent to perform ethical actions and whose actions ought to be governed by ethics
moral community	the set of morally considerable beings; the set of moral patients
moral considerability	the status of being one who matters ethically, or whose welfare or interests matter ethically and for whom ethical action can be taken
moral patient	one who is morally considerable
moral theory	*see* **ethical theory**
morphological	in biology, having to do with an organism's physical structure
mutual exclusivity	a condition that obtains among a set of options for action if each rules out the others
native species	with respect to a particular habitat, a species that has been there a long time—typically thousands of years—

	having either evolved there or arrived without human interference
natural capital	means of satisfying human preferences that are supplied by nature—e.g., ecosystem services
natural resource	a supply of something found in the natural environment that can be used to satisfy human preferences
natural selection	the process by which a varied population of organisms that produce offspring similar to but not always exactly like themselves can, over time, develop into one or more populations of organisms with dissimilar traits; this process requires an environment hazardous enough to kill many of the offspring before they reproduce, but not so hazardous as to eliminate the population.
near-person	an animal that is not capable of the same level of rationality or moral agency as a normal human but nevertheless has a robust, conscious sense of its past, present, and future
near-term ethic	an ethic concerned almost entirely with moral patients whose life spans overlap ours
neoclassical economics	the currently most widely held theory of how supply, demand and various constraints shape markets, determining prices, production, labor costs and so on; it arose in the late nineteenth century, replacing the classical economic conception of value as cost of production with a more sophisticated preference utilitarian conception.
neutrality	refusal to take sides or make ethical judgments, refraining from action, and avoiding commitment; to be neutral is tacitly to accept the *status quo*.
nitrogen oxides	any of various gaseous chemical compounds of oxygen and nitrogen that are common air pollutants; they are released chiefly by the combustion of fossil fuels and use of nitrogen fertilizers and are frequently referred to as NO_x.
nociceptors	in the nervous system, specialized receptors that respond to pressure, heat, or tissue damage
non-addition principle	Rolston's idea that culturally imposed animal suffering is permissible only insofar as it does not exceed ecologically functional suffering
non-anthropocentric ethics	ethics that include some non-humans, as well as humans, in the moral community
non-identity problem	a philosophical puzzle resulting from the fact that different intergenerational choices may create different people, or even wholly distinct populations, so that efforts to prevent harm to certain future individuals may cause them never to exist

nuclear winter	a period of cold and darkness that could be caused by a nuclear war as a result of soot from nuclear explosions and fires being lifted into the atmosphere
objective	not determined by what humans think or desire; in nature, what exists objectively or is good objectively might have existed or been good even if humans had never evolved
objective welfare axiology	the idea that goodness for an individual is definable as a set of objective properties—e.g., health
objective welfare utilitarianism	a form of utilitarianism based on an objective welfare axiology; it defines the utility of an action as the degree of overall welfare that results from it.
objectivity	a collection of virtues that aim to transcend self-centered perspectives toward wider and truer understanding; to be objective is, among other things, to: seek to understand and compensate for your own prejudices, accept the findings of adequately conducted scientific research, strive for consistency, suspend judgment on factual issues when the evidence is inconclusive, cultivate awareness of your own fallibility, and seriously consider the well-informed opinions of others.
ocean acidification	the dissolution of carbon dioxide in the oceans, making them more acidic and threatening ocean life
organismic model	in ecology, the idea that the organization of an ecosystem is in many ways analogous to that of an organism
overexploitation	(in the biological sense) unsustainable taking of wild species
ozone	a highly reactive, gaseous form of oxygen that has three atoms per molecule instead of the usual two
partial ordering	an array of values, some of which are less than, equal to, or greater than others, but some pairs of which may be incomparable
particulate matter	a complex mixture of particles and droplets suspended in air, better known as smoke, haze, dust or smog
phylogenetic	having to do with evolutionary history
pollution	matter or energy that has been introduced into the environment in amounts sufficient to harm humans or other life forms
pragmatism	a characteristically American philosophy that advocates empiricism, experimentalism and democratic process and is concerned less with theory than with results
preference-satisfaction axiology	the view that goodness is preference satisfaction and badness is preference frustration
preference utilitarianism	a form of utilitarianism based on a preference-satisfaction axiology; it defines the utility of an action as the degree to which the resulting preference

	satisfaction exceeds the resulting preference frustration. Some versions equate utility so defined with degree of welfare or happiness.
premise	in an argument, a declarative statement alleged to provide evidence for the conclusion
prescriptive reasoning	reasoning whose conclusion is a prescriptive statement
prescriptive statement	an assertion that an action is right or wrong, that we ought or ought not (or may or may not) do it, or the like
prima facie principles	principles that hold unless overridden by other principles
pure intergenerational problem	Stephen Gardiner's intergenerational analog of the tragedy of the commons; it is more difficult than the tragedy of the commons, because mutual coercion (Hardin's solution to the tragedy) is impossible between widely separated generations.
pure time discount rate	a rate of reduction in value based on how far in the future that value occurs
relational conception of self	a conception of the self not as an autonomous ego but at least partly constituted by its relationships with others
relational ethics	any of various ethical theories according to which our moral responsibilities are engendered by our relationships with others.
renewable resource	a natural resource capable of being supplied continuously for an indefinitely long time by environmental processes.
repugnant conclusion	in the work of Derek Parfit, the conclusion that there are conditions under which we ought to increase population even though this reduces the welfare of already existing individuals; it is inferred from classical utilitarianism together with the observation that one way to increase total happiness is to add more happy people.
respect	(in the moral sense) treat as an end and not merely as an object or means
respect principle	a principle according to which we ought to treat a certain class of individuals with respect; in Regan's animal ethic, for example, it is the principle according to which we ought to treat those who have inherent value with respect.
restoration ecology	a sub-discipline of conservation biology whose aim is to repair or restore ecosystems
resurrection	in conservation biology, the idea of bringing extinct species back to life through the use of biotechnology

revealed preference	in environmental economics, a method of shadow pricing that uses market data to infer prices for non-market goods
rewilding	the restoration of large-scale ecosystems unencumbered by human development, interlinked by corridors that facilitate migration, and sufficiently biodiverse to support large predators
rule-based reasoning	an argument whose premises include one or more rules that state what is to be done under certain specific conditions, usually together with some additional statements asserting that those conditions hold, and whose conclusion is also prescriptive
rule consequentialism	a form of consequentialism according to which the rightness or wrongness of an action is at least usually determined by that action's accord with moral rules, but the rules themselves are justified by their ability to yield good consequences
satisficing	a choice principle, according to which we may choose any option whose consequences are "good enough" in the relevant context
self-transcendence	valuing of the welfare of others as an end
sentience	the capacity for suffering and enjoyment
sentientism	the idea that all and only sentient beings are morally considerable
shadow pricing	in environmental economics, the assignment of monetary values to non-market goods for regulatory purposes; the aim is to internalize externalities.
social contract theory	a form of ethical theory according to which the moral rules are those that would be agreed to by rational agents under certain idealized conditions
social discount rate	an annual percentage rate by which future outcomes, regardless of whether they are gains or losses, are counted less than present ones.
sound argument	an argument which is valid and whose premises are all true
speciation	the evolution of a species into one or more new species
species	according to the traditional textbook definition, a group of individuals that can interbreed to produce fertile offspring; according to morphological definitions, it is a group of individuals similar in structure; according phylogenetic definitions, a group of individuals with the same evolutionary history.
species diversity	a conception of biodiversity that includes not only the number of species in a given habitat (species richness) but also considerations regarding the abundance of

	each species, noting especially those populations that are declining, threatened, or endangered
species ethic	any ethic according to which species are morally considerable
species impartiality, principle of	Taylor's idea that all living things have the same inherent worth
species richness	number of species per unit area or volume—a kind of biodiversity
speciesism	a prejudice or attitude of bias in favor of the interests of members of one's own species and against those of members of other species
stated preference	in environmental economics, a method of shadow pricing that uses preference surveys to infer prices for non-market goods
subject of a life	in Regan's animal ethic, an individual that cares about and can remember and anticipate how it is treated and what happens to it
subtraction principle	Rolston's idea that it is good but not obligatory to reduce pointless suffering in non-human animals
sulfur dioxide	a gaseous pollutant with the chemical formula SO_2 that is emitted mainly by the burning of sulfur-bearing coal
sustainability	with respect to a particular value, the condition that we adequately realize that value for our generation, and that our actions do not compromise the ability of future generations to realize it adequately
sustainable economy	an economy that efficiently provides adequate goods, services, and employment for our generation, and does not compromise the ability of future generations to efficiently maintain an adequate supply of goods, services, and employment
thermodynamic model	in ecology, the representation of an ecosystem as a complex of material and energy flows
total welfare	for an individual at a given moment, a kind of "sum" of the values at that moment of the various kinds of welfare of which it is capable; for a population at a given moment, it is the sum of the welfares at that moment of the individuals that comprise it. *See also* **lifetime welfare**.
tragedy of the commons	Garrett Hardin's idea that with increasing wealth or population it is in each individual's interest to act in ways that deplete resources that are held in common, to the ultimate detriment of all
unsound argument	an argument that is either invalid or has at least one untrue premise
utilitarianism	a type of consequentialist ethical theory that regards the rightness of an action as a function of its utility.

                        *See also **utility, classical utilitarianism, hedonistic utilitarianism, objective welfare utilitarianism, preference utilitarianism, act consequentialism, rule consequentialism***.

utility   for a given action, the degree (positive, negative or zero) to which its good results exceed its bad ones, for all the moral patients whom it affects

valid argument   an argument whose conclusion is true in every possible situation in which its premises are all true; an argument for which there is no counterexample

value dualisms   opposed pairs of concepts, one of which is traditionally valued as superior and the other as inferior

veil of ignorance   in Rawlsian philosophy, an imaginary state in which people become unaware of their identities in order to ensure rigorous impartiality in negotiating rules for a just society

virtue ethic   an ethic whose aim is excellence of character

will-to-live   in Schweitzer's philosophy, an impulse toward life that is assumed to be present in every living being, and the same in all, but consciously felt only in some

worse-off principle   Regan's controversial claim that, special considerations aside, if we must choose between harm to the few and harm to the many, and the harm to the few would make them worse off than any of the many would be if harm to the many were chosen, we should choose harm to the many

references

Adams, Carol J. and Josephine Donovan (eds.) 1995. *Animals and Women: Feminist Theoretical Explorations*, Durham, NC: Duke University Press.

Agar, Nicholas 2001. *Life's Intrinsic Value: Science, Ethics and Nature*, New York: Columbia University Press.

Allen, Myles R., D. J. Frame, C. Huntingford, C. D. Jones, J. A. Lowe, M. Meinshausen, and N. Meinshausen 2009. "Warming caused by cumulative carbon emissions towards the trillionth tonne," *Nature* 458: 1163–66.

Archer, David, M. Eby, V. Brovkin, A. Ridgwell, C. Long, U. Mikolajewicz, K. Caldeira, K Matsumoto, G. Munhoven, A. Montenegro, and K. Tokos 2009. "Atmospheric lifetime of fossil fuel carbon dioxide," *Annual Review of Earth and Planetary Sciences* 37: 117–34.

Attfield, Robin 1991. *The Ethics of Environmental Concern* (2nd ed.) Athens, GA: University of Georgia Press.

Barnosky, Anthony D., Nicholas Matzke, Susumu Tomiya, Guinevere O. U. Wogan, Brian Swartz, Tiago B. Quental, Charles Marshall, Jenny L. McGuire, Emily L. Lindsey, Kaitlin C. Maguire, Ben Mersey, and Elizabeth A. Ferrer 2011. "Has the earth's sixth mass extinction already arrived?" *Nature* 471: 51–57.

Bentham, Jeremy 1789. *Introduction to the Principles of Morals and Legislation*, London: T. Payne and Son.

BP 2013. "Statistical review of world energy, 2013," www.bp.com/en/global/corporate/about-bp/statistical-review-of-world-energy-2013.html, accessed 25 January 2014.

Broom, D. M. 2007. "Cognitive ability and sentience: Which aquatic animals should be protected?" *Diseases of Aquatic Organisms* 75: 99–108.

Broome, John 2012. *Climate Matters: Ethics in a Warming World*, New York: Norton.

Cafaro, Phil 2012. "Climate ethics and population policy," *WIRES Climate Change* 3: 45–61.

Caney, Simon 2005. "Cosmopolitan justice, responsibility, and global climate change," *Leiden Journal of International Law* 18: 747–75; reprinted in Stephen M. Gardiner, Simon Caney, Dale Jamieson and Henry Shue (eds.) 2010. *Climate Ethics: Essential Readings*, pp. 122–45, Oxford: Oxford University Press.

Carlson, Erik 2008. "Extensive measurement with incomparability," *Journal of Mathematical Psychology* 52: 250–59.

Carruthers, Peter 1992. *The Animals Issue*, Cambridge: Cambridge University Press.

Convention on Biological Diversity (UN) 2010. *Global Biodiversity Outlook 3*, www.cbd.int/gbo3/, accessed 25 January 2014.

Daly, Herman E. and Joshua Farley 2004. *Ecological Economics: Principles and Applications*, Washington, DC: Island Press.

DARA (Development Assistance Research Associates) 2012. "Climate vulnerability monitor," 2nd ed., http://daraint.org/climate-vulnerability-monitor/climate-vulnerability-monitor-2012/report/, accessed 25 January 2014.

Dawkins, Richard 2006. *The Selfish Gene* (3rd ed.), Oxford: Oxford University Press.

DeGrazia, David 1996. *Taking Animals Seriously: Mental Life and Moral Status*, Cambridge: Cambridge University Press.

De-Shalit, Avner 1995. *Why Posterity Matters: Environmental Policies and Future Generations*, London: Routledge.

Desqueroux, H., J. C. Pujet, M. Prosper, F. Squinazi, and I. Momas 2002. "Short-term effects of low-level air pollution on respiratory health of adults suffering from moderate to severe asthma," *Environmental Research* 89, 1: 29–37.

Donlan, C. Josh, Joel Berger, Carl E. Bock, Jane H. Bock, David A. Burney, James A. Estes, Dave Foreman, Paul S. Martin, Gary W. Roemer, Felisa A. Smith, Michael E. Soulé, and Harry W. Greene 2006. "Pleistocene rewilding. An optimistic agenda for twenty-first century conservation," *The American Naturalist* 168, 5: 660–81.

Donovan, Josephine and Carol J. Adams (eds.) 1996. *Beyond Animal Rights: A Feminist Caring Ethic for the Treatment of Animals*, New York: Continuum.

EIA (U.S. Energy Information Administration, Office of Energy Analysis) 2013. "International Energy Outlook 2013," www.eia.gov/forecasts/ieo/, accessed 25 January 2014.

Engster, Daniel 2006. "Care ethics and animal welfare," *Joutnal of Social Philosophy* 37, 4: 521–36.

EPA (U.S. Environmental Protection Agency) 2013. "Environmental Justice," www.epa.gov/environmentaljustice/, accessed 31 January 2014.

Fox, Tim and Ceng Fimeche 2013. "Global food: Waste not, want not," Institution of Mechanical Engineeers, www.imeche.org/knowledge/themes/environment/global-food, accessed 25 January 2014.

Gaard, Greta (ed.) 1993. *Ecofeminism: Women, Animals, Nature*, Philadelphia, PA: Temple University Press.

Gandhi, M. K. 1916. "On *ahimsa*: reply to Lala Lajpat Rai," *Modern Review*, October 1916; reprinted in Raghavan Iyer (ed.) *The Moral and Political Writings of Mahatma Gandhi*, vol. II, p. 212, Oxford: Clarendon Press, 1986.

Gandhi, M. K. 1948. *Gandhi's Autobiography: The Story of My Experiments with Truth*, Washington, D.C.: Public Affairs Press.

Gardiner, Stephen M. 2003. "The pure intergenerational problem," *The Monist* 86, 3: 481–500.

Gardiner, Stephen M., Simon Caney, Dale Jamieson and Henry Shue (eds.) 2010. *Climate Ethics: Essential Readings*, Oxford: Oxford University Press.

Gill, Jacquelyn 2013. "Cloning woolly mammoths: It's the ecology, stupid," *Scientific American* blog, http://blogs.scientificamerican.com/guest-blog/2013/03/18/cloning-woolly-mammoths-its-the-ecology-stupid/, accessed 25 January 2014.

Global Humanitarian Forum 2009. *Climate Change: The Anatomy of a Silent Crisis*, www.ghf-ge.org/human-impact-report.pdf, accessed 25 January 2014.

Hale, Benjamin 2011. "Nonrenewable resources and the inevitability of outcomes," *The Monist* 94, 3: 369–90.

Hansen, James, Makiko Sato, Gary Russell and Pushker Kharecha 2013. "Climate sensitivity, sea level and atmospheric carbon dioxide," *Philosophical Transactions of the Royal Society, A* 371: 31.

Hardin, Garrett 1968. "The tragedy of the commons," *Science* 162, 3859: 1243–48.

Hargrove, Eugene C. 1992. "Weak anthropocentric intrinsic value," *The Monist* 75, 2: 183–207.

Hill, Thomas, Jr. 1983. "Ideals of human excellence and preserving natural environments," *Environmental Ethics* 5: 211–12; reprinted in Ronald Sandler and Philip Cafaro (eds.) 2005. *Environmental Virtue Ethics*, pp. 47–60, Lanham, MD: Rowman & Littlefield. (Page numbers cited are from the latter.)

Hong, Yun-Chul, Jong-Tae Lee, Ho Kim, Eun-Hee Ha, Joel Schwartz, and David C. Christiani 2002. "Effects of air pollutants on acute stroke mortality," *Environmental Health Perspectives* 110, 2: 187–91.

Hsieh, Nien-hê 2007. "Is incomparability a problem for anyone?" *Economics and Philosophy*, 23: 65–80.

Huemer, Michael 2008. "In defense of repugnance," *Mind* 117, 468: 899–933.

Hursthouse, Rosalind 2007. "Environmental virtue ethics," in Rebecca L. Walker and P. J. Ivanhoe (eds.) *Working Virtue: Virtue Ethics and Contemporary Moral Problems*, pp. 155–71, Oxford: Oxford University Press.

IAP (Interacademy Panel on International Issues) 2009. "IAP statement on ocean acidification," www.interacademies.net/File.aspx?id=9075, accessed 25 January 2014.

IEA (International Energy Agency) 2013. *Key World Energy Statistics 2013*, www.iea.org/publications/freepublications/publication/name,31287,en.html, accessed 31 January 2014.

IPCC (Intergovernmental Panel on Climate Change) 2007. *Climate Change 2007: Synthesis Report*, Cambridge: Cambridge University Press.

IUCN (International Union for Conservation of Nature) 2010. "World's most endangered primates revealed," www.iucn.org/?4753/Worlds-most-endangered-primates-revealed, accessed 31 January 2014.

Jamieson, Dale 2007. "When utilitarians should be virtue theorists," *Utilitas* 19, 2: 160–83; reprinted in Stephen M. Gardiner, Simon Caney, Dale Jamieson and Henry Shue (eds.) *Climate Ethics: Essential Readings*, pp. 315–31, Oxford: Oxford University Press, 2010. (Page numbers cited from the latter.)

Joslin Diabetes Center 2006. "High blood glucose: what it means and how to treat it," www.joslin.org/info/high_blood_glucose_what_it_means_and_how_to_treat_it.html, accessed 25 January 2014.

Kant, Immanuel 1785. *Groundwork of the Metaphysics of Morals*, in Immanuel Kant, *Practical Philosophy*, Mary J. McGregor (trans.), pp. 37–108, Cambridge: Cambridge University Press, 1996. (Page numbers refer to the standard German edition and are given in the margins of this book.).

Kant, Immanuel 1788. *Critique of Practical Reason*, in Immanuel Kant, *Practical Philosophy*, Mary J. McGregor (trans.), pp. 133–271, Cambridge: Cambridge

University Press, 1996. (Page numbers refer to the standard German edition and are given in the margins of this book.).

Kant, Immanuel 1795. *Toward Perpetual Peace*, in Immanuel Kant, *Practical Philosophy*, Mary J. McGregor (trans.), pp. 317–51, Cambridge: Cambridge University Press, 1996. (Page numbers refer to the standard German edition and are given in the margins of this book.)

Kant, Immanuel 1996. *Practical Philosophy*, Mary J. McGregor (trans.), Cambridge: Cambridge University Press. (Page numbers refer to the standard German edition and are given in the margins of this book.)

Kant, Immanuel 1997. *Lectures on Ethics*, Peter Heath and J. B. Schneewind (trans.), Cambridge: Cambridge University Press. (Page numbers refer to the standard German edition and are given in the margins of this book.)

Katz, Eric 1992. "The big lie: Human restoration of nature," *Research in Philosophy and Technology* 12; reprinted in Andrew Light and Holmes Rolston III 2003. *Environmental Ethics: An Anthology*, Oxford: Blackwell. (Page numbers cited are from the latter.)

Katz, Eric 1993. "Artefacts and functions: A note on the value of nature," *Environmental Values* 2, 3: 223–32.

Kirchner, James and Anne Weil 2000. "Delayed biological recovery from extinctions throughout the fossil record," *Nature* 404, 9: 177–80.

Kwon, H. J., S. H. Cho, F. Nyberg, and G. Pershagen 2001. "Effects of ambient air pollution on daily mortality in a cohort of patients with congestive heart failure," *Epidemiology* 12: 413–19.

Leopold, Aldo 1970. *A Sand County Almanac with Essays from Round River*, New York: Ballantine Books.

Light, Andrew and Holmes Rolston III 2003. *Environmental Ethics: An Anthology*, Oxford: Blackwell.

Lovejoy, Arthur O. 1961. *The Great Chain of Being*, Cambridge, MA: Harvard University Press.

Maier, Don 2012. *What's So Good About Biodiversity? A Call for Better Reasoning About Nature's Value*, Dordrecht, The Netherlands: Springer.

Matthews, H. Damon and Susan Solomon 2013. "Irreversible does not mean unavoidable," *Science* 340: 438–39.

Medina, Félix M., E. Bonnaud, E. Vidal, B. R. Tershy, E. S. Zavaleta, C. J. Donlan, B. S. Keitt, M. Le Corre, S. V. Horwath, and M. Nogales 2011. "A global review of the impacts of invasive cats on island endangered vertebrates," *Global Change Biology* 17, 11: 3503–10.

Mulgan, Tim 2008. *Future People: A Moderate Consequentialist Account of Our Obligations to Future Generations*, Oxford: Oxford University Press.

Naess, Arne 1973. "The shallow and the deep, long-range ecological movement," *Inquiry* 16; reprinted in Louis P. Pojman (ed.) *Environmental Ethics: Readings in Theory and Application*, pp. 102–5, Boston: Jones and Bartlett, 1994. (Page number cited refers to the latter.)

Naess, Arne, 1984. "Identification as a source of deep ecological attitudes," in Michael Tobias (ed.) *Deep Ecology*, San Marcos, CA: Avant Books.

Naess, Arne, 1987. "Self-realization: an ecological approach to being in the world," *The Trumpter* 4, 3: 35–42.

Naess, Arne, 1990. "'Man Apart' and deep ecology: A reply to Reed," *Environmental Ethics* 12, 2: 185–92.

Nash, Roderick Frasier 1989. *The Rights of Nature: A History of Environmental Ethics*, Madison, WI: University of Wisconsin Press.

NEA (Nuclear Energy Agency) 1989. "An analysis of principal nuclear issues," www.oecd-nea.org/brief/brief-03.html, accessed 7 February 2014.

Newton, Lisa H. 2003. *Ethics and Sustainability: Sustainable Development and the Moral Life*, Upper Saddle River, NJ: Prentice Hall.

Nickel, J. 1993. "The human right to a safe environment," *Yale Journal of International Law*, 18: 281–95.

NIH (National Institutes of Health) 2014a. "What causes high blood cholesterol?" www.nhlbi.nih.gov/health/health-topics/topics/hbc/causes.html, accessed 25 January 2014.

NIH (National Institutes of Health) 2014b. "Who is at risk for high blood pressure?" www.nhlbi.nih.gov/health/health-topics/topics/hbp/atrisk.html, accessed 25 January 2014.

NOAA (National Oceanic and Atmospheric Administration) 2009. "Study shows nitrous oxide now top ozone-depleting emission," www.noaanews.noaa.gov/stories2009/20090827_ozone.html, accessed 25 January 2014.

Nolt, John 2009. "The move from *is* to *good* in environmental ethics," *Environmental Ethics*, 31, 2: 135–54.

Nolt, John 2010a. "Hope, self-transcendence and environmental ethics," *Inquiry* 53, 2: 162–82.

Nolt, John 2010b. "Sustainability and hope," in Evan Selinger, Ryan Raffelle and Wade Robison (eds.) *Sustainability Ethics: 5 Questions*, pp. 143–70, Copenhagen, Denmark: Automatic/VIP Press.

Nolt, John 2011. "How harmful are the average American's greenhouse gas emissions?" *Ethics, Policy and Environment* 14, 1: 3–10.

Nolt, John 2013a. "Replies to critics of 'How harmful are the average American's greenhouse gas emissions?'" *Ethics, Policy and Environment* 16, 1: 111–19.

Nolt, John 2013b. "Comparing suffering across species," *Between the Species* 15, 2: 86–104.

Nolt, John 2013c. "Anthropocentrism and egoism," *Environmental Values* 22, 4: 441–59.

Nolt, John, forthcoming. "The individual's obligation to relinquish unnecessary greenhouse-gas-producing devices," *Philosophy and Public Issues* (new series).

NPS (U.S. National Park Service) 2003. "Non-native wild hog control," www.nps.gov/grsm/parkmgmt/upload/wildhog.pdf, accessed 31 January 2014.

O'Neill, John, Alan Holland, and Andrew Light 2008. *Environmental Values*, London: Routledge.

Palmer, Clare 2010. *Animal Ethics in Context*, New York: Columbia University Press.

Parfit, Derek 1984. *Reasons and Persons*, Oxford: Oxford University Press.

Parfit, Derek 2011. *On What Matters*, vol. I, Oxford: Oxford University Press.

Partridge, Ernest 1981. "Why care about the future?" in Ernest Partridge (ed.), *Responsibilities to Future Generations*, Buffalo, NY: Prometheus Books.

Peirce, Daniel S. 2000. *The Great Smokies: From Habitat to National Park*, Knoxville: University of Tennessee Press.

Plumwood, Val 1993. *Feminism and the Mastery of Nature*, London: Routledge.

Pojman, Louis P. (ed.) 1994. *Environmental Ethics: Readings in Theory and Application*, Boston: Jones and Bartlett.

Pollan, Michael 2007. "Unhappy meals," *New York Times Magazine*, 28 January 2007.

Primack, Richard B. 1993. *Essentials of Conservation Biology*, Sunderland, MA: Sinauer Associates.

Regan, Tom 2004. *The Case for Animal Rights*, Berkeley: University of California Press.

Robock, Alan and Owen Brian Toon 2102. "Self-assured destruction: The climate impacts of nuclear war," *Bulletin of the Atomic Scientists* 68: 66–74.

Rolston, Holmes III 1988. *Environmental Ethics: Duties to and Values in the Natural World*, Philadelphia, PA: Temple University Press.

Ryerson, William 2012. "How do we solve the population problem?" in Philip Cafaro and Eileen Crist (eds.) *Life on the Brink: Environmentalists Confront Overpopulation*, pp. 240–54, Athens, GA: University of Georgia Press.

SAF (Society of American Foresters) 2000. "SAF code of ethics," www.safnet.org/about/codeofethics.cfm, accessed 25 January 2014.

Sagoff, Mark 1988. *The Economy of the Earth: Philosophy, Law and the Environment*, Cambridge: Cambridge University Press.

Sandler, Ronald 2007. *Character and Environment: A Virtue-Oriented Approach to Environmental Ethics*. New York: Columbia University Press.

Sandler, Ronald 2010. "Ethical foundations of assisted colonization," *Conservation Biology* 24, 2: 424–31.

Sandler, Ronald and Philip Cafaro (eds.) 2005. *Environmental Virtue Ethics*, Lanham, MD: Rowman & Littlefield.

Schweitzer, Albert 1923. *Civilization and Ethics*, A. Naish (trans.), London: A&C Black. (Portions of ch. 26 are reprinted in Louis P. Pojman (ed.) 1994. *Environmental Ethics: Readings in Theory and Application*, pp. 65–71, Boston: Jones and Bartlett. (Page numbers cited refer to the latter.)

Shrader-Frechette, Kristin 2011. *What Will Work: Fighting Climate Change with Renewable Energy, Not Nuclear Power*, Oxford: Oxford University Press.

Shue, Henry 1999. "Global environment and intergenerational equity," *International Affairs* 75, 3: 531–45; reprinted in Stephen M. Gardiner, Simon Caney, Dale Jamieson and Henry Shue (eds.) 2010. *Climate Ethics: Essential Readings*, 101–11, Oxford: Oxford University Press.

Silva, Raquel A., Jason West, Yuqiang Zhang, Susuan C. Anenberg, Jean-François Lamarque, Drew T. Shindell, William J. Collins, Stig Dalsoren, Greg Faluvegi, and Gerd Folberth 2013. "Global premature mortality due to anthropogenic outdoor air pollution and the contribution of past climate change," *Environmental Research Letters* 8, 3: 1–11, http://iopscience.iop.org/1748-9326/8/3/034005/pdf/1748-9326_8_3_034005.pdf, accessed 25 January 2014.

Singer, Peter 1990. *Animal Liberation* (revised ed.), New York: Avon Books.

Singer, Peter 2011. *Practical Ethics* (3rd ed.), Cambridge: Cambridge University Press.

Solomon, Susan, Gian-Kasper Plattner, Reto Knutti, and Pierre Friedlingstein 2009. "Irreversible climate change due to carbon dioxide emissions," *Proceedings of the National Academy of Sciences*, 106, 6: 1704–09.

Solow, Robert 1993. "Sustainability: An economist's perspective," in Robert Dorfman and Nancy S. Dorfman (eds.) *Economics of the Environment: Selected Readings* (3rd ed.), New York: W. W. Norton.

Stocker, Thomas F. 2013. "The closing door of climate targets," *Science* 339: 280–82.

Taylor, Paul W. 1981. "The ethics of respect for nature," *Environmental Ethics* 3, reprinted in Andrew Light and Holmes Rolston III, 2003. *Environmental Ethics: An Anthology*, Oxford: Blackwell, 2003. (Page numbers cited from latter.)

Taylor, Paul W. 1986. *Respect for Nature: A Theory of Environmental Ethics*, Princeton, NJ: Princeton University Press.

Thoreau, Henry David 1962. *Walden and Other Writings*, Joseph Wood Krutch (ed.), New York: Bantam Books.

Toon, Owen B., Alan Robock, Richard P. Turco, Charles Bardeen, Luke Oman, and Georgiy L. Stenchikov 2007. "Consequences of regional-scale nuclear conflicts," *Science* 315: 1224–25.

UNESCO (United Nations Educational, Scientific and Cultural Organization) 2012. *Managing Water Under Uncertainty and Risk: United Nations World Water Development Report 4*, vol. 1. Paris: UNESCO.

United Nations 2013. *World Population Prospects: The 2012 Revision*, vol. I, New York: United Nations, http://esa.un.org/unpd/wpp/index.htm, accessed 25 January 2014.

Vanderheiden, Steve 2008. *Atmospheric Justice: A Political Theory of Climate Change*, Oxford: Oxford University Press.

Varner, Gary 1998. *In Nature's Interests? Interests, Animal Rights, and Environmental Ethics*, Oxford: Oxford University Press.

Varner, Gary 2003. "Review of Nicholas Agar's *Life's Intrinsic Value: Science, Ethics, and Nature*," *Environmental Ethics*, 25: 413–16.

Varner, Gary 2012. *Personhood, Ethics, and Animal Cognition: Situating Animals in Hare's Two-Level Utilitarianism*, Oxford: Oxford University Press.

Warren, Karen 1990. "The power and promise of ecological feminism," *Environmental Ethics* 12, 2: 121–46.

Warren, Karen 2000. *Ecofeminist Philosophy*, Lanham, MD: Rowman & Littlefield.

WHO (World Health Organization) 2009. "Global health risks: Mortality and burden of disease attributable to selected major risks," www.who.int/healthinfo/global_burden_disease/global_health_risks/en/index.html, accessed 25 January 2014.

WHO (World Health Organization) 2011. "Air quality and health fact sheet," WHO Media Centre, www.who.int/mediacentre/factsheets/fs313/en/index.html, accessed 25 January 2014.

World Bank 2012. "Turn down the heat: Why a 4°C warmer world must be avoided," http://climatechange.worldbank.org/sites/default/files/Turn_Down_the_heat_ Why_a_4_degree_centigrade_warmer_world_must_be_avoided.pdf, accessed 25 January 2014.

Zeebe, Richard E. 2013. "Time-dependent climate sensitivity and the legacy of anthropogenic greenhouse gas emissions," *Proceedings of the National Academy of Sciences*, 110. doi:10.1073/pnas.1222843110, August 2013.

INDEX

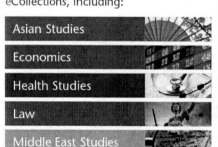